PEARL JAM
twenty

Simon & Schuster

New York   London   Toronto   Sydney   New Delhi

NOTES ON CONTRIBUTORS

Dave Abbruzzese, Pearl Jam drummer (1991–1994)

Jeff Ament, Pearl Jam bassist

Michele Anthony, President, Sony Music

Mark Arm, Green River/Mudhoney singer

Tim Bierman, manager of Pearl Jam's Ten Club fan organization

Ben Bridwell, Band of Horses singer/guitarist

Peter Buck, R.E.M. guitarist

Matt Cameron, Pearl Jam drummer (1998–present)

Jerry Cantrell, Alice in Chains guitarist/singer

Julian Casablancas, Strokes singer

Matt Chamberlain, Pearl Jam drummer (1991)

Chris Cornell, Soundgarden singer

Cameron Crowe, journalist and filmmaker

Kelly Curtis, Pearl Jam manager

Neil Finn, Split Enz/Crowded House singer/guitarist

Michael Goldstone, Mother Love Bone/Pearl Jam A&R representative

Stone Gossard, Pearl Jam guitarist

Dave Grohl, Foo Fighters singer/guitarist; former Nirvana drummer

Ben Harper, singer/guitarist

Jack Irons, Pearl Jam drummer (1994–1998)

Jim James, My Morning Jacket singer/guitarist

Eric Johnson, Pearl Jam tour manager (1991–1998)

Dave Krusen, Pearl Jam drummer (1990–1991)

Ian MacKaye, The Evens/Fugazi/Minor Threat singer/guitarist

Chan Marshall, Cat Power singer/guitarist

Mike McCready, Pearl Jam guitarist

Travis Morrison, Dismemberment Plan singer/guitarist

Brendan O'Brien, producer

Jim O'Rourke, Sonic Youth bassist/producer

Bruce Springsteen, singer/guitarist

Pete Townshend, The Who guitarist/singer

Corin Tucker, Sleater-Kinney vocalist/guitarist

Nicole Vandenberg, Pearl Jam publicist

Eddie Vedder, Pearl Jam singer/guitarist

Mike Watt, Minutemen/fIREHOSE bassist/singer

Nancy Wilson, Heart guitarist/singer

Neil Young, singer/guitarist

FOREWORD

I'll admit this to you right now. I'm a collector. I'll keep anything and everything. I'll keep a record, a receipt, a photo, a magazine, a card, a phone number long since disconnected. Everything. Any artifact that passes through my life is worthy of stuffing in a box and saving for appreciation on some distant later day. It's a bit of a burden, as any collector knows. At some point, the boxes own you. Moving is a horrific experience. And actually *finding* something you're looking for in these towers of boxes is always a futile endeavor. But there they sit, the boxes, and every once in a while, this pack-rat mentality can be a little bit profound.

Like today, randomly coming across two dusty containers. One of them is marked with a heavy black felt-tip pen: Pearl Jam—Stuff/'90s. And next to it is another box: PJ 2000s. All saved for a rainy day, and here it is. Raining.

The timing is interesting. We've been in the editing room for about a year, working on a film celebrating the band's first twenty years. I thought we'd searched every corner and crevice, called in every random news report and interview from every foreign market, transferred every essential piece of Super 8 from the band's visual archivists—and now I find more stuff. My own stuff, much of it too late to make the movie but just in time to make writing this introduction a little bit of a travelogue through the mementos and feelings from my own lucky first-row seat near the birth and amazing journey of this truly great American band.

They've grown from earnest young musicians, thrashing through their influences and emotions, hearts on their sleeves, to unjaded and barely prepared travelers through the portal of enormous international success, to unashamed participants in the politics of world events, to what they are now: musical survivors with passion unscathed. A Pearl Jam concert today is about much more than music. It's about the kind of clear-eyed spirit that comes from believing in people and music and its power to change a shitty day into a great one, or looking at an injustice and feeling less alone about facing it. If anything, that's the through-line in their twenty years. As bassist Jeff Ament told us, "There's not a single night I can remember when we were just going through the motions. Every night is just"—and here Jeff smiles with a touch of wonder—"pure stoke."

The boxes are filled with tapes and notes and bootlegs and music and notebooks. Digging deeper, there's a carefully adorned airplane vomit bag with these words on it, drawn in an inky sparkly pen. It reads: "From Eddie." And in it is an Ampex brand tape of early demos. I remember this tape. We were starting to make the movie *Singles,* in 1991, and we'd given the band jobs in and around the set. Jeff worked in the art department, and I'd borrowed much of his own stuff to decorate the apartments in the movie. Jeff had the greatest synthesis of art, sports, and film, all on his walls. From David Lynch, to obscure metal, to King's X, to players on the Supersonics, and more. (Sorry we lost some of your vinyl and that Joe Perry Project poster; I owe you an eBay replacement search, brother.) That Cuisinart mix of all that was important artistically and soulfully had a big effect on the ethic that would later spawn Pearl Jam. Art is everything, Jeff seemed to be saying with his life choices. (The creative wanderlust had drawn him from Big Sandy, Montana, to the comparative artistic mecca of Seattle.) Jeff's taste, and that of his musical cohort, guitarist Stone Gossard, was inspiring and genre bending, too. It was okay to like disco, hard rock, Kiss, Queen, and the blues. It all came out in their music, in the dark promise of their early band, Green River.

And look, here's a photo of the Seattle sky, late eighties. A dark blue horizon speckled with bright Northern stars—that's what the music sounded like then, indigo, flashy, melodramatic, and fun, too. With a sky like that, it's hard not to look up. And it's hard not to feel it, even locked away in a garage, slashing through chords and looking for the right mix of influences. It doesn't *always* rain in Seattle, but certainly music from the Northwest has its roots in players who stay indoors and play and listen and listen and play. A lot. Thus, the tradition of musicians who have the time to feel it and get it right.

Even from the beginning, there was a generosity about Pearl Jam. Jeff and Stone, guitarist Mike McCready, and, later, Eddie, all had an openness to music and the world, and an almost superstitious attention to the details of how this band would be different. The band itself sprung from a miracle. Stone and Jeff had been playing with a local luminary, Andrew Wood, a singer and writer of monumental charisma and talent. When Wood died from a heroin overdose on the eve of Mother Love Bone's first big tour, the loss was beyond seismic. Wood's garrulous spirit drew people to him, it was hard to forget him, but when a demo tape for Gossard and Ament's next musical project went forth into the world and found its way to a young San Diego surfer who connected immediately, no one could at first believe lightning could strike again, much less that fast. Before long, the shy surfer, Eddie Vedder, was sitting among us, staring down behind a sheet of wavy brown hair, barely speaking but trying to fit in. And every once in a while, Vedder would pull the hair out from in front of him, and look at us with those flashing, mischievous eyes and . . . you knew. This was a guy who shared the same high-stakes love of all that was possible.

One night, sitting cross-legged at a friend's house, listening to Neil Young tapes, Eddie told me the story of discovering that his biological dad was actually a family friend who'd passed away. It was a brief moment of somber reflection from Eddie, almost a confession about where some of the finely etched anger in his songs was actually coming from. But mostly we talked about Pete Townshend of the Who. Townshend is still a hero to both of us. Besides the Who, then unchallenged as the greatest band in rock, we both loved the *Rolling Stone* journalism of Townshend. Townshend still is rock's most articulate spokesman, surely the best rock journalist of them all, because he wrote from the inside out. Townshend wrote about a healing belief in the power of rock. There was nothing jaded and diseased about his relationship with music. His love of rock was almost religious, and so fervent that when the famous anarchist-politician Abbie Hoffman tried to grab a microphone and say a few words in the middle of the Who's performance at Woodstock, Townshend famously swatted him from the stage with his guitar. Hearing Eddie's recording on that first demo, I felt that same fervor. The music was a sanctuary, a place where something more than just rock might occur. Like the others, Vedder was a fan, and any fan knew that, handled correctly, music could take you rushing down the current to places you'd never imagined. That is, if you cared enough. And concentrated enough. This would be an experiment in alchemy. "I just want to play," I remember Eddie saying. "Just want to keep playing."

Message: No bullshit need interrupt.

Over time, Eddie's voice began to change. Those first few months, he'd carried himself with the demeanor of a guest at a dinner party he'd never expected to attend. Grateful, quiet, loving, and sweet. There's a moment in the film *Pearl Jam Twenty* when he speaks to band videographer Kevin Shuss after an early show. Flushed with the experience of what had just happened onstage, he alternately tells Kevin to fuck off, and then tells him he has three words for him: "I love you." That lopsided, sparkly smile, just before he exits frame—that was the Eddie Vedder who arrived in Seattle with a pocketful of dreams. He was immediately loved by strangers, and he also knew that he was carrying the hopes of all those Seattle players and friends and families who'd lived through the loss of Andy Wood and wanted badly for this group to succeed.

The audience for the band's first show at the Off Ramp was filled mostly with anxious and hopeful supporters. Eddie was nervous, swaying backward and forward, side to side, holding on to the mike stand like a young captain steering a pontoon ship. The songs are what stood out. Confident, honest, and memorable, there was one song that towered over the rest to me. "Release" was a song written from way down

deep, filled with openhearted emotion. It reached people instantly. That galvanizing moment, with audience and band coming together, set the stage for all that would follow. They changed their name to Pearl Jam. Soon the tornado of success would touch down, and all that followed was a lesson in learning on the job.

The songs guided them through the first album. The songs moved people, showed them a new style of commitment that had been increasingly absent in rock, and sure enough, in shockingly short order, the enormity of the group's popularity found them living under the white-hot heat of scrutiny. They proceeded in their own fashion, with ever-changing shows, and ever-changing rhythms, always staying close to their original instincts. Their original manager, Kelly Curtis, is still their manager. He, too, guides the band with a simple credo: Stay true to the music.

It's hard for a band to stay together. Success becomes its own built-in morphing machine. Friends and family change and shift, the bar for expectations changes, the financial issues sprout thorns and dissatisfaction. Cool heads grow hot with emotion. And then there are the distractions: side careers, drugs, lifestyle, bigger houses, and more. Soundgarden's Chris Cornell has a curious question, with no answer. "Why is it that American bands never stay together? It's the English bands, like the Rolling Stones or the Kinks—they stick around—but the American bands, they'll have one or two hits, and then one of them knocks over a grocery store and goes to jail, or gets on drugs, or decides he's the real leader and . . . it's over." Cornell shakes his head. "Early on, Pearl Jam had this positivity . . . and promise. A promise of integrity and faith that if you believe in us, we won't turn around and *shit* on you down the line." He laughs. "They made good on *that* promise, which is almost more important than just staying together."

I'm now opening the second box: PJ 2000s.

Here we see the second ten years, and the second act of a band that survived that first tidal wave of popularity. One of the surprises, picking through the artifacts, tour passes, press, and more, is that their stubbornness as artists sometimes had media detractors.

At times, even other bands found Pearl Jam's steadfast desire to keep playing, but grow *smaller,* absolutely confounding. The band would swear off videos and most interviews for years. That stubborn muscle was always there in them, though, all the way back to Vedder refusing to release "Black" as a single from *Ten,* even when all the record company bigwigs and radio station programmers were bombarding the band with demands for it. A note in the box, from the early 2000s, a conversation with Bono, and the subject of Pearl Jam comes up. "I don't understand it," Bono exclaims. "It's lonely being us, we want the competition, we want the music . . . I keep telling Eddie, 'Why don't you just make a fucking great rock record. Like the Rolling Stones used to! A great summer rock record filled with singles. Is it so hard? It's your responsibility.' They could be the greatest, biggest rock band in the world! Come on, Eddie!!!!" Bono paused. "I call him and tell him this. Why doesn't he listen?"

With the gift of clarity and ten years, it's now obvious that Pearl Jam did listen. They just didn't follow. Vedder, then guiding much of Pearl Jam's creative destiny, had his own course charted. It seems visionary now, but at the time, carefully pitching Pearl Jam away from a pursuit of global commercial domination seemed almost unfathomable. What band actively seeks . . . less? The answer lived in the group of fans that stayed with the band past the first explosive wave. The answer was onstage.

To anybody who lost track of Pearl Jam for a few years in the later nineties or the early 2000s, a surprise was awaiting them when they'd drop in on a live show. There was a passionate theater or arena filled with followers, keyed to nearly every lyric, and many of them had followed the band from show to show. It was not dissimilar from what Jeff Ament had seen in the nineties, checking out a series of Grateful Dead shows. He was blown away at the lack of distance between fan and band, and "the fact that they would get the greatest response from playing an obscure song they hadn't played in seventeen years. I remember looking at that and thinking, *That's* success."

"All that's sacred comes from youth," Vedder once wrote in "Not for You," but time has perhaps offered him a different perspective. He now charts the power of the lengthening career of Pearl Jam by watching the ongoing inspiration that is Neil Young's powerful body of work, or to the longtime surfers he sees in the water. They're the ones who are the wiliest, says Vedder, and they know how to seize the bigger waves better than the young ones, and with a minimum of wasted effort. A different kind of fervor also now fuels him. A father of two kids, blessedly too busy to ruminate much about his own complex childhood anymore, Vedder is writing with greater precision and depth with ease, and no less passion. While the others continually point to Eddie's growth and comfort in his own skin, and the inspiration that comes from working shoulder to shoulder with his committed love of their work together, Vedder himself points to the other members as the key: the graceful power of McCready's guitar, Stone Gossard's mercurial creative genius, Ament's soul and drive and artistic barometer, Matt Cameron's band-saving steadfastness, and even the well-fated arrival of Boom Gaspar on keyboards, allowing the group to perform anything from its entire history onstage.

This book is based on twenty years of interviews with the band, conducted from those early days, to our filming for *Pearl Jam Twenty*. They range from formative Seattle interviews to tour conversations done at soundchecks, or during recording, to chats recorded between takes on *Singles,* to recent conversations conducted by Jonathan Cohen based on his own meticulous research. I still don't know how Cohen found time to lash much of this together while still holding down his daily job of booking music for *Late Night with Jimmy Fallon*. But alas, such is the Herculean ability of a Pearl Jam fan on a mission.

Thanks also to the band members themselves, for opening up their homes, lives, and archives to us. They are friendly but private guys, as their fans know well. So the very act of releasing this bounty of information and souvenirs, clues and myths and facts, is all part of the group's ongoing sense of reinvention. Some might have never expected such an open-book approach. But then again, as we say in *Pearl Jam Twenty,* they have become over time the most dependably unpredictable band in rock.

Enjoy this map of a journey fueled by passion, music, instincts, humor, love, and the power of that moment in the dark when Pearl Jam takes the stage and everybody wonders, *Where will they take us now?* On that note, I will begin a new box, and dedicate it to a few of the indelible characters without whom I wouldn't have this rich treasure trove of memories and music from twenty years of loving the band. Thanks, Nancy, Buddy, Kelly, Eric, Jeff, Stone, Eddie, Mike, Dave, Jack, Matt, Chris, Kevin, George, Pete, and Neil. Happy birthday, guys.

Turn it up!

**Cameron Crowe
January 2011**

JEFF AMENT

Born: March 10, 1963, in Havre, Montana. His father, a barber, was the mayor of Big Sandy, Montana, for fifteen years. His mother played piano and introduced Ament to records, books, and drawing. Ament dropped out of the University of Montana after his sophomore year in 1983, and, with his bandmates in Deranged Diction, moved to Seattle, where he worked at the infamous Raison d'Etre coffee shop in the Seattle neighborhood of Belltown to save money for art school tuition. Before long, that band had collapsed and he'd joined Green River with Stone Gossard. When that group split in 1987, he and Gossard started fresh in Mother Love Bone. The band was preparing to release its first album when lead singer Andrew Wood died of a drug overdose in March 1990.

What was your first instrument? When/where did you start playing?

I took piano lessons from first to sixth grade in Big Sandy, Montana, from Mrs. Giebel. I mowed her lawn, raked leaves, and shoveled snow to help with the cost. From fifth grade through my sophomore year in high school, I played snare drum and percussion in the school band and also sang in the choir. I forgot all of this when I heard the Ramones and bought the same bass that Dee Dee played.

What was the inspiration behind why you wanted to play music?

Initially, it was Ted Nugent, Aerosmith, and Kiss, until I heard the Ramones, Devo, the Clash, and all the hardcore bands in California. Playing music was an occupation furthest away from what I thought was possible.

What are your earliest memories of a musical influence or hero?

My mom playing "Proud Mary" on the stereo, singing "The Sound of Silence" with my first grade classmates, and seeing the Jackson 5 on *American Bandstand.* My mom's brother, my Uncle

Pat, went to Germany with the Air Force and came back with all these rock records and a kick-ass stereo. He had long hair and he had tapestries up in his room. I remember he had this metal holder for his bottle of Spinata wine, which I would occasionally sneak a sip of. He would put headphones on me and play something like *Abraxas* by Santana, or Cream. It would just blow my mind. I was seven years old and found this other world.

What are some of the earliest/most influential concerts you attended?

My first show was Styx on their Equinox tour in 1975. They played Havre, Montana, at the NMC Armory. I didn't see another concert until I saw Van Halen in Great Falls in 1979. The most influential shows that I saw early on were X, the Clash, and the Who on my first visit to Seattle with some friends in 1982. I moved to Seattle the next year, and seeing Black Flag, the Ramones, Bad Brains, and a slew of hardcore bands at the Metropolis had the biggest influence on my musical life.

What are some of the best memories you have from playing early shows with your first bands?

Getting to play through a real PA was always a big thrill. Hüsker Dü giving us a joint and twenty dollars for opening up for them when the promoter screwed us. Mostly just trying to impress your friends. Hell, that's still how it is.

MATT CAMERON

Born: November 28, 1962, in San Diego. Cameron moved to Seattle in 1983 and quickly became immersed in the local music scene. In 1986 he took over the drum stool in Soundgarden, a position he held until the band broke up in 1997.

What was your first instrument? When and where did you start playing?

My first instrument was a secondhand drum set at the age of eleven. I had been banging on everything in the house since the age of three. Luckily, I had very supportive parents who were both big jazz fans.

What was the inspiration behind why you wanted to play?

Self-expression, trying to be like my heroes, girls, in that order.

What are your earliest memories of a musical influence or hero?

Buddy Rich, Count Basie, David Bowie. I saw all of these artists perform when I was eleven to thirteen years old.

What are some of the earliest and/or most influential concerts you attended?

In the mid to late seventies, I had the honor to see Queen, Kiss, Bowie, Cheap Trick, Thin Lizzy, Shelly Manne, Bobby Hutcherson, and Jaco Pastorius. I had my mind blown wide open at a very early age. I do not miss the M80s people used to bring to big rock concerts back then. It sounded like a war was breaking out between bands. I also remember a lot of kids partying way too hard the day of a big concert and ending up passed out in a pool of vomit during the show. I wanted to soak in every detail, so the idea of being too high to enjoy the concert experience made no sense to me. I guess I was an early straight-edger.

What are some of the best memories you have from playing early shows with your first bands?

Playing my high school graduation party in 1980 with the band Faultline at Fiesta Island in San Diego. We brought a generator, parked two vans in a V behind us, and started rocking. Our classmates (mostly from the smoking section) were rocking out and loving every moment. Two songs into our set, the cops showed up and asked for our permit. Oops. Not a great start to the summer of 1980.

Playing the Metropolis in 1983 with the band Bam Bam, my first year in Seattle, was a revelation because I found a music scene that fully accepted me.

My first Soundgarden show in 1986 at the Ditto Tavern was a baptism by fire. I had joined the group one week prior to the gig and I wanted to impress. The drummer I had replaced, Scott Sundquist, was in the front row critiquing my every move. I remember him saying from the front of the stage, "Kick drum too loud!" "Too fast!" et cetera. Opening for Love and Rockets in 1986 was a big Soundgarden moment for me. We had never played a show in a theater before, just local bars and such, so we were a little nervous. Our opening song, "Entering," sounded a lot like "Bela Lugosi's Dead" from their previous band Bauhaus. Both songs have a very similar drum intro, so when I got the cue, I laid into the beat, and I remember the first two rows looking at each other with mild confusion. Once Hiro Yamamoto and Kim Thayil hit the first gnarly guitar notes, there was no more confusion. It was the first big stage the band had played on—the Moore Theatre in Seattle—and after the show, I realized we had a sound that could fill any size venue, and we could hold our own with anyone.

Lastly, in 1998, one year after the breakup of Soundgarden, I got a call from Stone and Eddie asking me, "Hey, Matt, what are you doing this summer?"

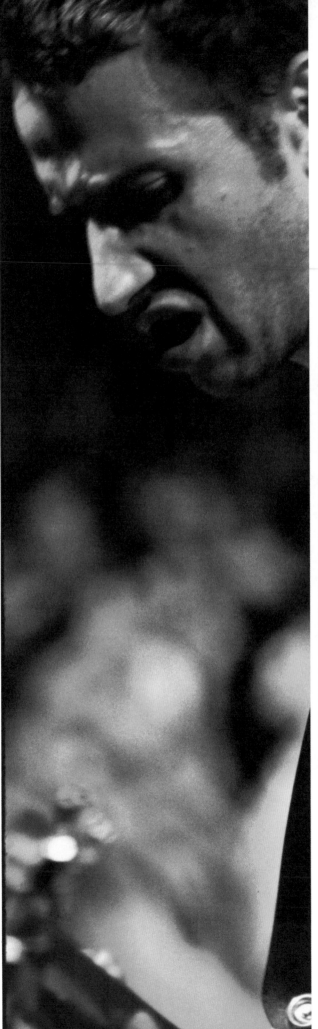

STONE GOSSARD

Born: July 20, 1966, in Seattle. His first band was March of Crimes, with future Soundgarden bassist Ben Shepherd, followed shortly thereafter by the Ducky Boys. Gossard and Jeff Ament met at a Seattle rock club in 1984 and spent three years playing together in Green River. As mentioned, after that band split, they formed Mother Love Bone.

What was your first instrument? When/where did you start playing?

Aside from a trumpet in third grade and some boys choir stuff in fourth (1975-ish), my first real instrument was the mandolin I got in 1980. There was a band called the Probes at my high school that were killing it and making everyone dance. They didn't have a mandolin, so I thought maybe if I learned some tricks I could get in. It was a lot harder than I thought. I was never asked to join.

What was the inspiration behind why you wanted to play music?

In 1981, at the urging of Steve Turner, I got a bass and then a guitar, and we formed Ducky Boys with Jeff Covell and Chris Peppard. Steve told me that garage rock was the way and that you can be crappy and still have cool songs and a band. It was a revelation. He liked the most underground, noisy punk, which I didn't really get. But he also loved Alice Cooper and even Black Sabbath. I never let go of that advice.

What are your earliest memories of a musical influence or hero?

Singing in kindergarten, maybe "Row, Row, Row Your Boat." Also, early-seventies AM radio and Simon & Garfunkel.

What are some of the earliest and/or most influential concerts you attended?

Randy Hansen's tribute to Jimi Hendrix in 1979, then UFO at Hec Edmundson Pavilion. My first punk show was Black Flag at Eagles Auditorium in 1982 or '83.

What are some of the best memories you have from playing early shows with your first bands?

It's fun now, but it used to scare me. I was nervous. But once we started getting drunk, it got better. More lose-your-mind rock 'n' roll!

MIKE MCCREADY

Born: April 5, 1966, in Pensacola, Florida, but moved to San Diego as a baby and then to Seattle at the age of four. His first band was called Warrior, followed by Shadow, with which he moved to Los Angeles in an unsuccessful bid at rock stardom. Thoroughly fed up with the music business, McCready was back in Seattle working at an Italian restaurant and attending community college classes when he began jamming with middle school acquaintance Stone Gossard on the material that eventually became the first Pearl Jam album.

What was your first instrument? When and where did you start playing?

My first guitar was a Matao Les Paul from my parents. It was black and cost a hundred dollars. They said I could get a guitar if I took lessons, which I did, from Mike Wilson. He was a fantastic teacher who taught me scales and Kiss songs and also made it fun, so I wanted to go back. My friend Danny Newcomb (Goodness, Rockfords) in 1978 would play Sweet's "Love Is Like Oxygen" for hours. I also joined his band Warrior with Chris and Rick Friel. We played a lot, but more on that later. I was eleven years old, and it changed my life forever. I remember throwing the guitar in the air at an Eckstein Junior High assembly, which I still have a picture of. Later I wanted to make it a gold top, so I chiseled—yes, chiseled—the top layer of the guitar off, then I spray-painted it gold. Ooops. It never was the same. I wish I knew where it was today.

What was the inspiration behind why you wanted to play music?

Well, I have to say Kiss. I was a Cub Scout, and then Kiss came along. I remember jumping around with a tennis racket pretending I was Paul Stanley or Ace Frehley. It also felt cool and was really fun to play in a band—probably to meet girls, too. I played my first "concert" at Jenny W.'s birthday party in 1978.

What are your earliest memories of a musical influence or hero?

My dad had the Jimi Hendrix *Band of Gypsys* record, and I remember being blown away by that. Certainly the local band TKO was a huge influence on me and Shadow. We loved their songs and to see Brad Sinsel live. It was the first tangible evidence to me of a great Seattle band. Kiss, again, were musical superheroes to me. Larger than life (no, I will not pay for that, Gene). I had a Kiss room with every wall covered. Alice Cooper, too. Heart put their stamp on Seattle music and influence me to this day. I love Nancy Wilson's guitar playing and Ann's singing. Later, Van Halen, Queen, Ted Nugent, Cheap Trick. (The reason I throw picks out to the audience.)

What are some of the earliest and/or most influential concerts you attended?

The Heats at Mural Amphitheatre; Van Halen on the Van Halen II tour at the Seattle Center Arena; Cheap Trick at Hec Ed Pavilion (waited all day and skipped school); TKO at Lake Hills, the Moore Theatre, or anywhere in the early eighties; Kiss in '79; Scorpions, Iron Maiden, Girlschool at Hec Ed Pavilion; Motörhead at the Paramount Theatre; the Girls in 1980 opening for the Ramones; and Silly Killers at Laurelhurst Club House. (Danny and I watched through the window.) Probably all the Warrior and Shadow concerts set in motion what I am today.

What are some of the best memories you have from playing early shows with your first bands?

Wow. Let's see.
Jenny W.'s birthday party in 1978. Warrior played a few originals: "The Wah Song," "Acid," "R.O.W."; also "One Way or Another" (Blondie), "Deuce" (Kiss), "Day Tripper" (the Beatles).
In 1979, Warrior at the Eckstein Junior High talent show. Big controversy over Danny Newcomb playing "The Star Spangled Banner" with his teeth. He did it when told he couldn't. Right on, Danny! In 1979, a Warrior concert for Symphony Fundathon under the Monorail. I had a completely homemade tie-dye outfit. I'm sure the symphony hated us.
In 1983, Shadow and Wild Dogs at Freemont Baptist Church; and Shadow, Overlord, and Culprit at Norway Center. In 1982, headlining at Port Orchard Armory. We signed autographs and took the ferry.
In 1983, the first Headbangers Ball at the Moore Theatre with Overlord and Culprit. Huge success! The second Headbangers Ball with Shadow, Metal Church, and TKO. We got booed off the stage. Also, Jeff Ament came over after our singer, Rob Webber, invited him to the show. Guess who was doing a guitar solo, finger tapping his Kramer Pacer as he walked in? I gave Jeff a picture of that last year. Who knew that we would later be rockin' side by side seven-hundred-plus shows later?
In 1985, Shadow (our last show as a five-piece) at Gorilla Gardens in the metal room and Green River in the punk room. Shadow's first three-piece show (Rick Friel, Chris Friel, and I) in a room in the Seattle Center for about one hundred people before we moved to L.A. December 1986, Shadow's first show at the Roxy in L.A. It only cost us seven hundred dollars to get on the bill! At least Tim Dijulio, Duff McKagan, Lauren, and about two other people were there at midnight on a Sunday. We played the Whisky about a month later. Green River played down the street at Club Lingerie, and we went by to say hi. Shadow played at Fender's, opening for Andy Taylor of Duran Duran in 1987. I met Rod Stewart there. Our final L.A. show was at Club Lingerie in 1987. I became a lead guitar player in those lean L.A. years—eating Top Ramen and payin' those dues.

EDDIE VEDDER

Born: December 23, 1964, in Evanston, Illinois, but grew up mostly in Southern California. In his twenties, he played in several San Diego bands, including Indian Style and Bad Radio. His friendship with former Red Hot Chili Peppers drummer Jack Irons led to his recruitment in the band that would become Pearl Jam.

What was your first instrument? When and where did you start playing?

A beat-up ukulele. To keep the strings taut, I had to wrap the headstock in masking tape. My first instrument, in a way, was one of those little green memo pad notebooks when I was really young. I'd write songs, putting arrows over the notes so I'd know which note was higher than the other. The ukulele thing probably happened when I was ten. My mom would go to garage sales or yard sales, clean up all the toys, and put them under the tree. I'd get a little racetrack, and a key piece of track was missing. I think it was probably a yard sale, and they just gave the ukulele to us as an act of pity.

What was the inspiration behind why you wanted to play music?

I just loved it. I was onto a record player early, early on; one of those plastic kids' record players that came with a single of "Puff the Magic Dragon." If we went to visit relatives, I'd take my little plastic record player, go find a room, and sit there with my records. I probably had three. Then I started raiding my uncle's singles collection and got into adult music fairly quickly. The crossover was "Yellow Submarine." I remember borrowing or perhaps stealing that single from him. He's ten years older, so if I was five, he was fifteen, and he had some pretty cool records. He wore an army jacket. He was just cool. This was probably 1969 or 1970. He'd give me records, but then he'd go off with his buddies, and I'd take a few more. I distinctly remember my mom on the phone saying, "Do you have *Hot Rocks*?" And I'd go [*sheepishly*], "Um, yeah," while I was cranking "Brown Sugar" or "Mother's Little Helper."

What are your earliest memories of a musical influence or hero?

When I was six, my parents started running a group home. My stepdad was going to law school, and my mom was waitressing. They found out they could get paid if they were foster parents and live in a house with ten or twelve other kids, ranging in age from ten to sixteen. There were super Irish kids and African American kids. It was in Evanston, Illinois, but right on the edge of where the city takes a turn for the worse. It was literally on the wrong side of the tracks. It was kind of gnarly when we first got there. My parents did a pretty good job turning it around. Down in the basement, there was a turntable, and all the kids were listening to Sly & the Family Stone and James Brown. So it went from me listening to the Jackson 5 to heavier stuff like Sly and James Brown and Otis Redding.

At one point, one of the kids, who was maybe fifteen, was given a huge record collection because he'd saved some guy's life, and that was another windfall of things to choose from. At that point, you didn't even know what to listen to first. You'd look at the record covers and be like, "Wow. What does Uriah Heep sound like?" [*Laughs*] After that, I started pulling out notebooks and writing little songs.

In high school, I was working at Long's Drugs in Encinitas, north of San Diego, and the assistant manager gave me two pieces of bootleg vinyl: *The Who Live at Long Beach* and *The Genius of Pete Townshend,* which is all the *Who's Next* demos. I was hearing Pete play all the instruments, and that unlocked a big door for me.

What are some of the earliest and/or most influential concerts you attended?

I saw Bruce Springsteen and the E Street Band with my uncle in 1977 at the Auditorium Theatre in Chicago. It was the first show of any kind I saw in person, I believe, unless there was one a year before. There was a little theater called La Paloma in Encinitas, California. It was the summer *The Last Waltz* came out. At this point, I'd had a few guitar lessons. My guitar teacher and I went to see Rick Danko play solo along with Jack Tempchin, who wrote "Peaceful Easy Feeling" and "Already Gone" for the Eagles. Rick Danko pretty much played acoustic, but he sang "Stage Fright" to a tape.

Then, all the bands I wanted to see weren't playing all-ages. So I had to get a fake ID to get into punk shows. I remember getting into an X show and it being a really big deal. I got right to the front, and Exene Cervenka handed me a Miller Lite to hold in between songs. I just had this feeling that it wasn't mine to drink; it was mine to hold while she played. I also saw the Pretenders at Golden Hall in San Diego. There was no barricade, and no monitor between me and Chrissie Hynde. People are pushing and shoving. I got pushed forward and my hand landed on Chrissie Hynde's left boot. She immediately flicked it off. I thought it was so fucking awesome. I saw Sonic Youth on the *Daydream Nation* tour. I didn't know if it was the greatest thing ever or if they were disrespecting us. [*Laughs*] By the next morning, I knew I had been changed.

What are some of the best memories you have from playing early shows with your first bands?

My sophomore year of high school, I played with a friend from class who knew so-and-so, who worked at the grocery store, who had a practice space in his garage and a nice amp. But he was really into the Eagles, and the keyboard player was into Styx, and the bass player was into the Cars, and himself. The drummer was in the school band. And then I'm into the Who, PiL, and Springsteen. It sounded like shit. Everybody would get their one or two songs to sing. You'd play at parties and pretty much just suck. As bad as the group was, the part of the night that the rest of the guys disliked most was when I got to sing. In the end, which shows how bad it was, they were like, "Uh, I think we're going to break up the band." And within a week, another guy with a better guitar and better amp had taken my place.

CHAPTER ONE

1962–1989

THE EARLY YEARS: 1962–1989

Years before their music helped define a generation, the members of Pearl Jam were just five kids playing air guitar in front of their bedroom mirrors, possibly while wearing Kiss face paint. Soon they were learning how to master instruments in attics, basements, and garages, scoring their first paying gigs, having their minds blown at their first arena shows, and falling in love with the magic and power of rock 'n' roll.

The ties that bind the band members are intricate, reaching from Chicago to Southern California to Seattle and back again. But the sturdiest building block of Pearl Jam is Green River, a band featuring guitarist Stone Gossard and bassist Jeff Ament that formed in Seattle in the summer of 1984.

After finishing his second year at the University of Montana, Ament dropped out and moved to Seattle to pursue music with his then band, Deranged Diction. But the group's progress stalled, and the following summer, Ament teamed with vocalist Mark Arm, whom he'd met while hanging around at the Seattle punk club Metropolis; guitarist Steve Turner; and drummer Alex Vincent to form Green River. The group's first show was at a Seattle keg party on July 1, 1984. By the fall, despite having made a terrible first impression on Ament, a fresh-out-of-high-school Gossard had joined on rhythm guitar.

"My first band had broken up, and Steve had joined them for our last six months," Arm says. "We were looking to start a new one, and we enjoyed Jeff's sound and antics in Deranged Diction, so we approached him. He played through a distortion box and jumped superhigh—you know, the important things. Originally it was the four of us, with Alex drumming. Stone got involved, but I don't remember exactly how that happened. He was just starting to play guitar himself. He was hanging around, and I think we just asked if he wanted to play with us."

"Mark Arm introduced me to Jeff, and within five to thirty seconds, I think he wanted to punch me, because I had recently been introduced to the exciting world of sarcasm," Gossard says. "That to me was the greatest joy anyone could ever have: watching Monty Python movies and making flippant statements and joking about anything that could

possibly be joked about even if it didn't make sense. He couldn't have been more serious. But for whatever reason, he still sort of thought it might be a good idea for me to try out for Green River, because I guess he heard that I had a Marshall amp. That was sort of an interesting first encounter. I didn't realize that I was pissing him off. Of course, he didn't tell me that until years later."

Ament may not have much cared for Gossard's sense of humor, but he couldn't deny that the new addition made Green River's sound a lot heavier. "At that point, Steve was going for more of a jangly kind of garage kind of 13th Floor Elevators thing," Ament says. "Sure enough, I think Stone sat down and learned the songs with Steve and Mark, maybe a little bit before we had our first practice, and it sounded great. It sounded more like what I think all of us had hoped that the band was going to sound like."

OTHER INGREDIENTS

By the time Ament and Gossard had begun to establish themselves musically in town, guitarist Mike McCready had already been gigging in Seattle bands for more than five years, first with Warrior and then with Shadow. Gossard and McCready had actually attended the same middle school and frequently geeked out together on their shared love of hard rock.

"I think we were fourteen when we first met," McCready says. "I had my band, Shadow, and he was the funny, sarcastic guy that used to come around, and we'd always laugh. He hadn't started playing guitar yet. In Seattle back in the early eighties, the punk rock crowd and the metal crowd hung out, because there weren't a lot of us. So we'd see each other at parties. He was a rock fan. He liked Iron Maiden. We used to trade rock pictures. That was our thing. It sounds so silly now, like, 'I got this one Michael Schenker; I'll trade it for two David Lee Roths!' We loved David Lee Roth and Van Halen."

At the time, there was another established Seattle band called Malfunkshun, and its larger-than-life lead singer, Andrew Wood, would soon touch the lives of the future Pearl Jam members in profound ways. Wood was just fourteen when he and his brother Kevin formed Malfunkshun in 1980, but

at that young age, he already had all the makings of a unique rock personality.

"It was probably one of the first live shows I'd gone to. I was probably a junior in high school; maybe a senior," Gossard recalls of his initial exposure to Malfunkshun. "There Andy was in lingerie, with gloves and tights and high boots and a boa. They played these slow, heavy, kind of Sabbath songs, which at that time, nobody was playing. It was glam and punk and then this tribute to Sabbath and Kiss. Seeing bands like that would inspire a group of twenty people, all moderately drunk to heavily drunk, to go crazy in their own little world in downtown Seattle and have it be one of those nights you talk about for years.

"Andy wasn't a rock star yet, but he was going to be a rock star," he continues. "You saw him and were like, 'I'm on your team. I want to be anywhere near you.' And that's how most people felt about him. It was so easy for Andy to gather people around him and have people just sitting around laughing with him, wanting to share time with him. It probably was a burden for him, just because he had so much charisma in that regard."

But offstage, Wood grappled mightily with substance abuse, prompting a trip to rehab in 1985 that put Malfunkshun on hold. When he completed the program, he moved in with another talented local singer named Chris Cornell, whose band Soundgarden had formed just a year earlier.

"The first guy that I called on the phone to see if he wanted to be my roommate wasn't Andy—it was Stone Gossard," Cornell remembers. "He was living at home, I think, and he answered the phone, and he's like, 'Yeah, no, I'm good, I don't really want to change my living situation right now.' He was at home, so I thought that was a little weird, but I thought, Whatever, that's great. He said, 'But Andy just got out of rehab, and he might need a place.' I didn't really know him, but I thought, Well, that would be interesting. He seems like an interesting guy. I called Andy up, and he's like, 'Sure, I'm coming over.' My brother Peter, who was my roommate at the time, was leaving and had already paid some rent. He meets Andy at the door and goes, 'Yeah, I already paid rent for the next two months, so you're going to have to pay me first.' Andy goes, 'Sure, I'll play ball with you.' And he walks in, and that

GODFATHER

KODAK SAFETY FILM 5063

GEORGE GEORGE   JOEY ANTHONY   EDDIE VEDDER   DAVE SILVA

BAD RADIO   CONTACT (619) 460-

GREEN RIVER
SHADOW
SLAUGHTERHAUS 5

AUG 24   SATURD
GORILLA   EN

Hollywood, Ca.   (213) 463-65

23

was it. He moved in, and next thing you know, Malfunkshun is rehearsing in my living room."

BOUNTIFUL RIVER

Meanwhile, Green River was becoming a local must-see, finagling its way onto bills with underground rock titans like the Dead Kennedys and Sonic Youth, and attracting the attention of burgeoning New York indie label Homestead Records. Dissatisfied with the band's musical direction, Steve Turner quit in the summer of 1985 to enroll in college, but the band was undeterred and embarked on its first tour in October.

Although the crowds were generally sparse and at times nonexistent, it was a watershed experience for the musicians to play in famed venues like New York's CBGB. It was also eye opening to be in the thick of the myriad punk- and hardcore-inspired music scenes throughout the country, particularly in Detroit, where a Halloween gig opening for Glenn Danzig's post-Misfits band Samhain turned ugly. "I was wearing this pink shirt or something and literally got pulled offstage and got pummeled," Ament says. "The Detroit punks were having none of it."

Before the end of the year, Green River's debut EP, *Come On Down,* was released by Homestead. Years later, it would be described as the very first "grunge" release, but at the time, *Come On Down* was simply the kind of rock 'n' roll that could make you bounce around the room one second and nod your stoned head along with the sludgy beats the next.

ENTER MATT CAMERON

Seattle had its fair share of good drummers in the 1980s, but nobody quite like Matt Cameron, who, on the advice of a friend, had moved from San Diego in 1983 to pursue a career in music. "I drove up in a Datsun truck, and it broke down in central California, so we had to sleep at this mechanic's house for two days," he says. "I didn't know if the move was going to be permanent or not, but in the back of my mind, I was preparing myself for that to happen. My first reactions were really positive. Coming from San Diego, which is a huge, enormous place, Seattle seemed small and more closed in. The people that were

doing it were also the people that were supporting the other groups. It definitely felt like being in a club."

Cameron had started taking drum lessons at age nine and by thirteen was doing his best Peter Criss impersonation while playing in a Kiss cover band. "We were called Kiss. We almost got sued by Gene Simmons," Cameron says. "He had his eyeball out there for all the Kiss imitation groups at the time." At fifteen, Cameron found himself singing the song "Puberty Love" in the notorious 1978 B movie spoof *Attack of the Killer Tomatoes* at the behest of director John De Bello, who'd gone to school with his older sister. And like Ament, Gossard, and McCready, Cameron was wowed by teenage exposure to the greatest rock bands of the era, especially a December 16, 1977, show by Queen at the San Diego Sports Arena on its News of the World tour. "Still to this day, I think that's the greatest show I've ever seen," he says. "It was just life changing."

Once settled in Seattle, Cameron played in a couple of bands before joining Jack Endino, Daniel House, and Ben McMillan in Skin Yard in 1985, and often crossed paths and shared local bills with Green River's Ament and Gossard. By early 1986, the Seattle scene had coalesced enough to warrant its own compilation, *Deep Six,* which C/Z Records issued in March. In addition to Green River and Skin Yard, the album included tracks from the Melvins, Malfunkshun, Soundgarden, and the U-Men.

"No one had really made a proper professional recording before," Cameron says. "We had a two- or three-night concert to celebrate that record, and I think that's where I saw Malfunkshun play and met Andy for the first time. I thought they stole the show. They were just incredible live." Adds Gossard, "The Malfunkshun song on that record, 'With Yo' Heart (Not Yo' Hands),' you hear Andy Wood's mojo working in regards to blending punk and metal and FM rock."

In June Cameron left Skin Yard to join Cornell, guitarist Kim Thayil, and bassist Hiro Yamamoto in Soundgarden, beginning a creative partnership that would last more than a decade and launch the band to worldwide popularity alongside fellow Seattleites Nirvana, Alice in Chains, and Pearl Jam.

"Kim and Chris and Hiro were in a band called the Shemps," Cameron says. "They did Doors covers, and they weren't

that good, but I remember watching the singer and thinking, Oh my God, this guy's amazing! When I heard they formed Soundgarden, I would definitely try to catch their shows. They were one of those groups that from the very inception had a sound. When their other drummer, Scott Sundquist, decided he didn't want to tour, I called Kim up right away and said, 'Dude, I want in.' Chris was like, 'Yeah, let's get him,' because he'd heard me play before. So it wasn't necessarily an audition, but I learned a bunch of their songs, and in about a week's time, we were playing at the Ditto Tavern."

EXIT GREEN RIVER

Just before releasing the seven-inch single "Together We'll Never" b/w the Dead Boys' "Ain't Nothin' to Do" on its own ICP label in November 1986, Green River aligned itself with Bruce Pavitt, whose *Subterranean Pop* fanzine had helped spread the independent rock gospel across the country in the early eighties. Now Pavitt was looking to start his own record label, and joining forces with Green River seemed like the perfect way to launch it. The only problem: Pavitt was perpetually out of money. Indeed, it took until July 1987 for the newly rechristened Sub Pop to release the five-track Green River EP *Dry As a Bone,* which the group had recorded the prior summer with Jack Endino.

Dry As a Bone further honed the band's dirty, punk-tinged sound, prompting Pavitt to call it in promotional materials "ultra-loose grunge that destroyed the morals of a generation." Mark Arm had been using the term *grunge* to describe local music for several years by that point, including in a 1981 letter to the Seattle fanzine *Desperate Times,* but as championed by Pavitt, the term soon took on a life of its own.

However, Green River wouldn't be around to enjoy the ride. Once again, due to Sub Pop's financial instability, the label was sitting on a full-length album from the band, titled *Rehab Doll,* but had no plans to release it anytime soon. In addition, Ament and Gossard found themselves continually butting heads with Arm over the band's musical and career direction, and after an October 24, 1987, show opening for Jane's Addiction at the Scream in Los Angeles, Green River dissolved acrimoniously.

Green River

"There was always that kind of contingent in the Seattle scene—'hipper than thou' types," Cameron says. "Jeff and Stone got labeled as the commercial element of the scene, or whatever. That's all bullshit, because they weren't trying to write a certain way. It's just how everything came out, and they were being true to their artistic instincts, and I always appreciated their instincts. Writing a good rock chorus is one of the hardest things you can do as a songwriter. Having it sound big and melodic and powerful and having that come across on the radio or in a performance, man, that is not easy."

Despite its short life span, Green River's musical influence would be felt strongly in Seattle and beyond in the years to come, primarily thanks to its blend of punk and hard rock. "At that time, those two things were usually separated very extremely in terms of the social stigma attached to liking one or the other," Gossard says. "The influence of bands like Motörhead helped bridge the heavy metal world and the punk world. All of a sudden, you could take the experimental amateurism of punk rock and the thrill of playing in a bar, but also touch on some of the things that made heavy metal so powerful and exciting. We were really do-it-yourself. We made records right away without knowing much about how to do it. We designed our own album covers and paid for our own tours. And, we were on Sub Pop, which became an enormously influential label. Our stuff is always going to be looked at in terms of what came after it, and, of course, all the stuff that came after it is hugely influential. Green River probably was influential in its own way, but nobody would have ever heard of Green River if Nirvana hadn't shown up. Nirvana captured that whole phenomenon of combining the art of punk and rock and making it sound brand new."

Ament and Gossard wasted no time moving forward. The pair had begun jamming informally with Malfunkshun's Andy Wood and Regan Hagar before Green River officially split, and by the end of 1987, the new group, provisionally named Lords of the Wasteland, was gigging in public. "I think we played a hair salon once, doing covers," Gossard says. "It was just an extension of being in the same practice place. Everybody recognized Andy's talents at that point,

so I wanted to play with him as soon as I could."

Hagar had no reason to think that the new band would interfere with Malfunkshun. But shortly after the first Lords of the Wasteland show, he realized that both acts could not coexist. "Andy and I were still in Malfunkshun, and we walked down to the shared space where Green River, Malfunkshun, and now Lords of the Wasteland practiced," he says. "And there were Jeff and Stone with Greg Gilmore, the number one drummer in town. Andy and I just turned around and left. I got the phone call that night: 'Greg's going to take your place in this band, and we hope everything is all right.' I was young, and my ego was plenty intact. I made it through that, and we maintained our friendship, because Malfunkshun was still going in my mind. Next thing you know, this new band is getting label interest and everything was snowballing for them. It happened very fast. There was no more Malfunkshun. There was no time for it."

MIKE'S MOVE

For Mike McCready, then twenty, and his band Shadow, time had run out to hang around Seattle in the hopes of making it big. In late 1986, the musicians packed up and moved to Los Angeles to try to score a record contract. There they toiled for more than a year, subsisting on ramen noodles and ponying up their savings to secure bookings on "pay-to-play" bills at venues like the Roxy and the Whisky a Go-Go, often during the least desirable time slots imaginable.

By early 1988, disillusioned with the Los Angeles experiment, Shadow moved back to Seattle and split up. McCready put his musical dreams on hold and enrolled at Shoreline Community College. "There were ten-thousand-plus bands down there, and the odds of a band making it were very small," he says. "I guess my parents' voice was in the back of my head going, 'You have to have something to fall back on.'"

THE MISSING PIECE

Back down in San Diego, there was another struggling musician on the verge of a breakthrough. Eddie Vedder was born in Evanston, Illinois, but moved to San Diego as a preteen and spent parts of his adolescence there and in the Los

Angeles area. Vedder had appeared in TV commercials and print ads as a youth, and his passion for theater acting grew as he reached high school. But his true obsessions were surfing and rock 'n' roll; Vedder had both met surf legend Mark Richards and attended his first Bruce Springsteen concert a few months shy of his thirteenth birthday.

For the next decade, Vedder worked odd jobs (construction, waiting tables, night watchman, petroleum company) and played in a succession of forgettable bands, almost always as a rhythm guitarist and not as a lead singer. Most of his energy was devoted to making his own crude four-track demos at home on a Walkman and a boom box, until he scrounged up enough money to buy a professional quality Tascam four-track machine in 1984. "I rode that thing like a horse," he says. "I really learned to write at a time when popular music just wasn't speaking to me. Writing my own songs was a way to create music I wasn't hearing on the radio or anywhere else."

Vedder also made fast friends in the San Diego music scene, where his eagerness to devote his life to rock 'n' roll impressed his peers. "I worked in the middle of the night and that's how I made my living," he told *Just Rock* magazine in October 1991. "I was always this musician and I didn't want to work nine to five. In the day, it felt like I was an artist that didn't have a job. I would stay up all night and read and write. When I would get home to my little apartment complex, everybody would have gone to work, and I could make as much noise as I wanted. So I would then record everything that I had written."

In late 1987, Vedder responded to an ad in the alternative weekly *San Diego Reader* placed by the local band Bad Radio, which was looking for a lead singer. Vedder's demo tape submission included a cover of Bruce Springsteen's "Atlantic City," and it was good enough to score him an in-person audition.

"The studio they practiced at was run by this Russian cat, Valery Saifudinov, who had a metal band called Flight 19," Vedder says. "Somehow I went in and got the job. At the same time, some friends of mine who were in college were helping run a club that was total goth. In San Diego, there wasn't much of a live scene. The only time people would go out to see a band was if they were on MTV. You couldn't get anything

MALFUNKSHUN

SOUNDGARDEN

Deranged Diction

MALFUNKSHUN & MY EYE
Thursday, July 3
at the CENTRAL

DEEP SIX
GREEN RIVER
MALFUNKSHUN
THE MELVINS
SKIN YARD
SOUNDGARDEN
U-MEN

PREMIERE
OTHER LOVE ONE
SPECIAL GUESTS
AY · APRIL 22
HOTEL
Alaskian Way So
AND OVER

ANOTHER PYRRHIC VICTORY

THE ONLY COMPILATION OF DEAD SEATTLE GOOD BANDS

GREEN RIVER
H-HOUR
MALFUNKSHUN

GREEN RIVER

THE LOVE BONE EARTH AFFAIR
DESMOND AND THE JUPITER CHILD SAT LOUDLY UPON THE
GAZEBO SCANTILY CLAD IN CHARTREUSE REGALIA REMINISCING
THE TIMES OF OLD WHEN U COULD BUY 3 BLACKYROLDS 4
A TASTE O EUCALYPTUS AND USE THE CHANGE FOR SOME
PURPLE PIE PETES OR A STREET SCAMP BABY'S SMOOTH DOG LOVIN.
AS THRU FADES AWAY ☀ (BUTTERFLY OF DESMOND) LANDREW THE LOVE CHILD
AND HIS HOLY ROLLERS MEET THE LOIN QUEEN PARADER FOR A SMELL OF SASSPARILA.
STONE & BOOTSY GIGGLE AND WAIL WHILE JEFF & GILLIKUTTI SHAKE AND WIND THEIR WAY
2 THE FARAWAY QUARTERS OF THE QUEENS JEZEBEL HOUNDS ≈ YOU TOO
CAN B SET FREE BY THE DIOMOND BRACELETS ○ LOVE & JUST BELIEVE IN THOSE
TATTOED SOUL EYES & CATCH A RIDE WITH THE LADY WITH THE WITCH HAZEL EYES
TO THAT PLACE WHERE MOTHER LOVE BONE WAITS FOR YOU...
BEWARE ECO DOGS for the CAPRICORN SISTER HAS RISEN ✶

MOTHER LOVE BONE

AS A BONE

MOTHER LOVE BONE

HAVE YOU SEEN ME?
570-1590

BAD RADIO

GREEN RIVER

THURS: FEB. 23
BAD RADIO

BAD RADIO

AD O

GREEN RIVER

BADBAD RADIORADIO
THIS THURSDAY JAN. 12   THIS THURSDAY JAN. 12

MALFUNKSHUN

KROSS
WITH GREEN RIVER
SOUND GARDEN
MALFUNKSHUN

OINGO BOINGO

27

happening locally, it seemed, although there was a good band called Night Soil Man, and another called Donkey Show. I started doing the flyers for this thing called Red Tape. We'd take over a sports bar, Visqueen the whole place, get a smoke machine, and hang up some paintings. All of a sudden, I had a way to get a gig. I had an in."

THIS IS MY KIND OF LOVE

In Seattle, Ament and Gossard hurried their new band—now called Mother Love Bone, and rounded out by guitarist Bruce Fairweather—into Reciprocal Recording Studios to record demos in February 1988. Because Chris Cornell and Andy Wood were still living together, Matt Cameron got an early taste of the group and was impressed by how quickly the disparate elements of Malkfunkshun and Green River had blended into something fresh.

"That's when I really started appreciating Stone's songwriting," he says. "I think that was a band that really pushed his pop sensibilities—the kind of big rock chorus sensibilities that he was able to completely master down the line." Wood reveled in the creative process, inspiring his new bandmates to think of Mother Love Bone as more than just a rock 'n' roll band. "Andrew Wood was an artist more than anything," Ament says. "This was how he was going to find joy in life: writing and recording songs."

"He had that attitude that anything is possible," adds Cornell.

In an ironic stroke of timing, just as Mother Love Bone was getting going, Sub Pop finally released Green River's *Rehab Doll* in June 1988, eight months after the band's split. "When it came time to put the record out, Bruce Pavitt was like, 'Well, I don't have any money. Can you guys help me press up these records?' We saved our money for four or five months and everybody chipped in, like, two hundred or three hundred dollars," Ament says. "We pressed one thousand records and helped pay for a couple of ads in fanzines like *Forced Exposure* and *Matter.* I remember the day that the records came in. We went over to Bruce's apartment, and there were five or six boxes of five hundred records. I think the other five hundred went to some distribution company, and that was kind of the start of Sub Pop. The amazing thing is, in the midnineties, we got paid

back that initial investment. We all got, like, four hundred dollars each back, in twenty-dollar bills. I fucking spent it every day. I'd buy a piece of pizza and go, 'This is on Bruce Pavitt.' It was the best four hundred dollars that I spent, because that was fucking a lot of money back in those days."

SIGN ON THE DOTTED LINE

Although Mother Love Bone had little in common with the sound or style of the decadent Los Angeles rock scene that had turned Jane's Addiction and Guns N' Roses into two of the biggest bands in the country, major labels started sniffing around in the summer of 1988. Unprepared, Ament turned to an acquaintance named Kelly Curtis, who'd dropped out of high school in the 1970s to serve as a roadie for revered Seattle rock band Heart, and was currently working at a local management company.

"They didn't know anybody that had any kind of connections in L.A. with lawyers, managers, or record companies," Curtis says. "I'd come from the Heart background, which didn't seem to make obvious sense to any of us, other than that I'd had some experience in the music business. The deal was, would I help them meet some people? I said, 'Sure.' So we took a trip to L.A. to set up some meetings with lawyers and labels. I'm not sure if we met with managers or not, but it kind of just revealed itself over time that I should just be doing it. We were getting along well enough to just keep going. It just kind of naturally evolved."

In Los Angeles, Curtis introduced Mother Love Bone to lawyer Michele Anthony, who was already representing Soundgarden and Alice in Chains. "Kelly invited me to one of their shows at the Troubadour in L.A., and I absolutely fell in love with them," says Anthony, who soon signed on to represent Mother Love Bone. "I loved the music they were making. And I loved Andy. He was such a character. I remember him telling me how he was going to spend his money. His list was everything from nail polish to a house. He couldn't wait to play arenas so he could buy bigger houses. He thought big. An arena would have been too small for him."

Before long, Mother Love Bone found itself at the center of a label

bidding war, ultimately signing with the PolyGram Records imprint Mercury. "We called it the 'Seattle restaurant tour,'" Ament recalls. "We'd take the guy from Atlantic Records out and order bottles of Bordeaux—like, four-thousand-dollar dinners. We were just having the time of our lives. We'd done, like, twenty of these dinners with ten different labels, and we said, 'We've got to do something here.' Right at the last minute, Michael Goldstone showed up from PolyGram, and PolyGram had the best roster at that point. Geffen had Guns N' Roses and Junkyard and all these bands that were kind of happening in L.A. It seemed like they already had too many good bands. So we ended up signing with PolyGram."

In January 1989 Mother Love Bone recorded its debut EP, *Shine,* at Seattle's London Bridge Studios. Released on March 20, it included what would become the band's signature song, the eight-minute epic "Chloe Dancer/Crown of Thorns."

"It's a song that Andy and I wrote together, so it's a combined musical effort that showcases both of our tastes," Gossard says. "It's simple. And the lyric has that bittersweet quality to it. It's haunting and beautiful, but at the same time, it's colorful. It has the flavor that Andy loved to bring to everything that he did."

Starting in March, Mother Love Bone set out on an extensive North American tour with the leather-and-hairspray-loving English rock band Dogs D'Amour. The shows were often poorly attended, and traveling in tight quarters led to inevitable intraband arguments. But Wood had a knack for winning over even the most jaded of audiences, and he and Ament

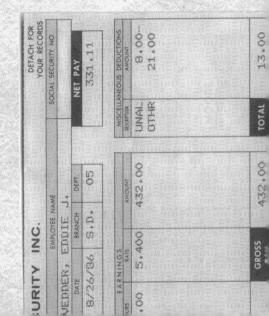

found themselves bonding over a shared love for obscure music and sports.

"He was so into sports, even though he wasn't athletic at all," Ament says. "He had those Coleco electronic football games, and he had pages of notebooks with teams and standings. He'd play hundreds of games a week and catalog the scores and highlights. The whole Mother Love Bone tour, that's what was going on in the backseat of the van. A coat would go over the top of the two of you, and you'd just pass this thing back and forth."

By the end of 1989, Mother Love Bone had wrapped work on its debut album, *Apple,* which was recorded both in Sausalito, California, and Seattle. Steeped in classic rock influences but distinguished by Wood's commanding vocals, *Apple* portended a big year ahead for the band. But Wood's reemergent drug habit, which now included the occasional dabbling in heroin, hung over Mother Love Bone like a dark cloud. Around Thanksgiving, friends staged an intervention, after which Wood voluntarily entered inpatient rehab at Valley General Hospital in Monroe, just northeast of Seattle. For the moment, Mother Love Bone was in limbo.

THE FINISHING STROKE

In San Diego, Eddie Vedder and Bad Radio kept plugging away, although Vedder was still finding the confidence to let loose onstage. Often, he'd stand rooted firmly in place, barely looking at the audience. "We'd do a local battle of the bands, where if you play on Friday and win, you play the next Friday," Vedder says. "And then if you win that, you get your song played on the radio, once. Then maybe you'd get three hundred dollars' worth of shitty gear. Still, we'd win them. It's interesting, looking back. I was fearful of rejection, but whenever I got it going and put myself out there, I was given positive reinforcement."

On November 21, 1989, Vedder couldn't have picked a better moment to be proactive. That night, he met former Red Hot Chili Peppers drummer Jack Irons for the first time during a Joe Strummer show at the Bacchanal in San Diego. Irons had played drums on former Clash vocalist/guitarist Strummer's then new album, *Earthquake Weather,* and was on tour with him as well.

"On that tour, I actually met my wife-to-be in San Francisco, and then a day or two later I met Eddie," Irons says. "I didn't know him before the San Diego show, but he later told me he'd help out at shows and get in for free. Then he could meet the guys he was interested in meeting. He knew who I was from the Chili Peppers days, and that night he introduced himself. Then the power went out, and he had the lighter. I just remember becoming good friends from that point on. I was living up in L.A., and he would come up and hang out with me and my wife. We'd go play basketball. Eventually he became friends with all my friends."

"I loaded in Joe Strummer's gear that night," Vedder says. "I remember listening to a Red Hot Chili Peppers bootleg in my Toyota Corolla with Jack, although it was Cliff Martinez playing drums, not Jack. Fifteen minutes into Joe's set, the opening band sabotaged the power in the club over a money dispute. I got flashlights and took everybody backstage, and I'm holding the light for Joe as he's rolling a spliff with tobacco and weed. Mind you, I did not smoke cigarettes then, so it blew my head off. It took ninety minutes to get the power back on. I took a Polaroid with Joe after the show, and he signed it. Little did either of us know that he would be quite responsible for our band's existence."

Pearl Jam has always preferred to let its music speak for itself. But what follows is their story of their first twenty years, in their own words.

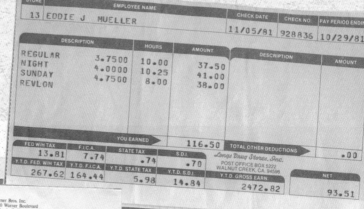

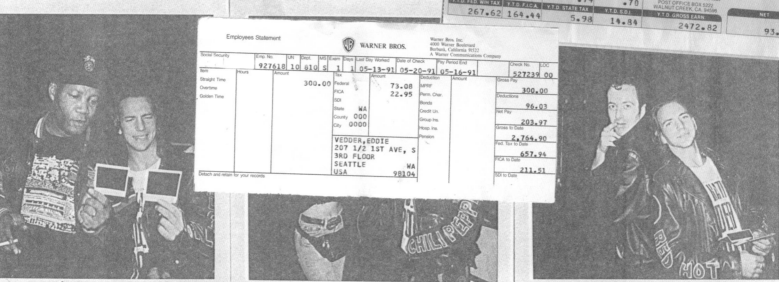

CHAPTER 1990

1990

It all seems so unlikely: the blend of birth, death, joy, tragedy, and coincidence that gave the world a band called Pearl Jam. Months before, they'd put music on the back burner while they toiled at restaurants and gas stations. But however it was that these five unlikely cohorts found themselves writing songs together, they knew they were onto something deeper and more vital than anything they'd ever experienced. And from those humble beginnings in the dingy basement of a Seattle art gallery emerged a band that would irrevocably change the mind, body, and soul of rock 'n' roll.

February 11
Bacchanal, San Diego

Bad Radio, having recently won the San Diego State University Cultural Arts Board battle of the bands, plays its last show with Eddie Vedder and then dissolves temporarily. The group reforms later in the year with original vocalist Keith Wood and moves to Los Angeles in search of a record deal.

Jack Irons: I definitely went to see Eddie play once or twice. He would just sort of mention it. He was very nonchalant about it. He was shy. He wasn't saying, "This is what *I do*." I saw him once or twice and remember thinking he was a good singer. He definitely gave me some music to check out, which I thought sounded good.

Eddie Vedder: In Bad Radio, we got in fistfights, with me telling them they needed to work harder. I said, "I'm not going to put flyers on people's windshields before I go to work if you guys aren't going to help out." Or, "Where did those flyers go?" "Oh, they're still in my backpack," and it's the day after the gig. They made fun of playing for dead people at the goth night. I was just like, "Fuck you!" We got the gig and we may have even gotten paid fifty dollars. Usually we didn't get paid at all.

March 9
The Central, Seattle

Mother Love Bone plays its final show.

Jeff Ament: It was the same night as Lenny Kravitz's first show at the Backstage. Andy and I were bummed we couldn't go.

Stone Gossard: The band was struggling. It was very stressed out. We hadn't written much of anything in a while. The joy was gone. We were trying to live up to the record deal, but I don't think any of us felt like we hit it out of the park. We felt like we just went and spent $150,000, but is it great? We were listening to Guns N' Roses and wondering how we could compete against something like that. Andy had been clean and sober for months before he died. We knew he was in a struggle, but he was an optimist. He wanted to believe that he was going to see his opportunity as a sober person and as a person who was going to take a little bit more control of his destiny by being able to say what was important to him as an artist. He was in a band with a lot of type A male personalities. He probably felt bulldogged half the time in the band, just because between Jeff, Greg, and I, we had really strong views about where we wanted to go. And we weren't necessarily on the same page, either. It was fractured, and it was a struggle. But we always had laughs, and we could find ways to get through what we needed to get through.

March 19

Three days after being found unconscious at home by his fiancée, Xana LaFuente, Andrew Wood dies of a heroin overdose at age twenty-four, less than a month shy of the intended release of Mother Love Bone's debut album, *Apple*. The project eventually comes out on July 19 and is later repackaged as a self-titled release with bonus tracks in 1992.

Stone Gossard: I knew he was struggling. We had seen a lot of people struggling in Seattle at that time. We knew that he was

trying to be sober. But you can't really be a junkie and be superproductive. I mean, maybe somebody can, but he wasn't going to be able to do it, and we weren't going to be able to deal with it if he was going to be a junkie. I mean, I think we would have had to accept him as a junkie and, like, celebrate it on some level, which I don't think any of us were ready to do.

Jeff Ament: Andy and I had been working out at a gym down in Pioneer Square. I think the last rehab he'd been in was six or eight months before. He was on this program to get healthy and fit so he could go out and do his thing and run around the stage. That morning, we were supposed to hook up to work out, and he called and said, "Hey, man, I'm not feeling that good." His voice was kind of scratchy. Looking back on it, he was high, but at the time I didn't notice that. He sounded sick; no big deal.

That night, Greg and Bruce and I went down to the Oxford Bar to meet this guy who was going to possibly be our tour manager. I had a couple of beers and rode my bike home, and when I got there, there was a weird note on my door that said, "Hey, I think your singer's in trouble." I went in, and there were five messages from Andy's girlfriend, Xana, just hysterical. I got back down on my bike and rode back to the Oxford, and Greg and Kelly were there. We all got in a taxi and went up to Harborview Medical Center, but Andy was already on life support. Whenever people would start to get into drugs after that, I wished I had a picture to show them of Andy when he was in the hospital, because it was so horrible. I was in denial for a while. I was really pissed off at him and sort of detached from what had happened. I didn't really have the coping skills at that point to deal with it.

March 24
Paramount Theatre, Seattle

Andrew Wood's life is celebrated at a memorial service.

Jeff Ament: Things started to change with Stone and I after Andy died. I remember hanging out with him a lot and sometimes not saying a whole lot of anything. He wouldn't really talk about the fact that he was writing some songs, but I would hear it from other people.

Mother Love Bone

July 21
The Gorge, George, Washington

Mike McCready has a life-changing moment seeing Stevie Ray Vaughan in concert. McCready had moved to Los Angeles several years earlier with his band Shadow in search of a record deal, but returned to Seattle broke and disillusioned about a career in music. Lately, he was working at the Italian restaurant Julia's and taking classes at Shoreline Community College, and barely playing guitar at all.

Mike McCready: At the time, I was so depressed about life. I wasn't playing at all then. I'd given it up. While Vaughan was playing, it was very sunny. But as soon as he started "Couldn't Stand the Weather," these huge clouds rolled in overhead, and rain began pouring down. When the song ended, the rain stopped! It was like a religious experience, and it changed me. It lifted me out of the negative mind-set I was in, and it got me playing again. I thank him forever for that.

Summer

After reconnecting in February at a house party, Stone Gossard and his old middle school friend Mike McCready begin playing music together in the attic of Gossard's parents' house. Before long, McCready is campaigning for another old friend to join them.

Jeff Ament: I met Mike when he was in Shadow. Their singer, Rob Webber, was changing into his outfit for a gig one night right across from the restaurant that I worked at, so he invited me over to the show. When I walked in, there was a skinny little kid wearing baggy spandex onstage, playing an Eddie Van Halen "Eruption"-style solo with his foot up on the monitor—shredding. But I thought, This is so ridiculous. Look at that kid. He looks like he's eleven. I was like, "Man, I'm going to hate these guys. This is going to be awful," because I was a hardcore punk rock dude at that time. Over the course of the next couple of years, some of their friends started hanging out with some of our friends, and we started having parties together. Mike was always at these parties playing guitar, just fucking shredding Stevie Ray

Vaughan licks. I'd never been in a room next to somebody who had that much dexterity or who could play blues in that way. After Andy died, I heard that Stone and Mike were playing together, and I was like, "That's fucking awesome." We'd had cool guitar players before, but we'd never had a guy that could step out like that. Mike has that ability. He can just fucking blast it into outer space.

Mike McCready: Stone was the most sarcastic, caustic guy that I knew. When he'd come around, he'd have us in stitches. Jeff told me that being from Montana, if someone is sarcastic to you, you just punch them, you know? And I think that was what almost happened when Jeff and Stone first met. Mark Arm intervened. There was the deep sarcasm or the deep kind of Seattle passive-aggressiveness that goes on, which probably was not part of Jeff Ament's world in Montana.

Stone and I had just started playing together, and I recall we were riding out in a VW Rabbit to bring our guitars to have them looked at. We had just started, just he and I, the Pearl Jam thing, and I was like, "We've got to get Jeff in this band." And I remember Stone was like, "Pfft." He wasn't into it. I think they had some stuff to work out that was unresolved from certainly Andy dying and the whole Love Bone thing. But knowing how well those two guys worked together, seeing how they put records out, how they marketed themselves, how they wrote songs together, I was like, "We've got to have Jeff in this band." They went and had a dinner, and then the next thing I know, Jeff's coming around, and I'm like, [*whispering*] "Fuck yeah!" Hopefully, I was instrumental in that happening. I was kind of adamant about it.

Stone Gossard: I met Mike McCready probably when I was in seventh grade. I got to hear about this band called Warrior, and it was these kids who were in sixth grade or seventh grade that had Marshall stacks and Flying Vs. And I could not believe that. I was like, "Wait a minute, there's guys already playing in bands?" I was just getting turned onto Led Zeppelin at that point. Years went by, and I saw him playing along to some blues records at a party. I think he was jamming over some Albert King or

something. That wasn't really my strong suit. I was just looking in my past and saying, "Mike McCready! I know him. He's good." We didn't think about it too much. We just did it. We would see each other periodically before this, but he was just getting back into seeing music live, and we were running in the same circles again. We'd always enjoyed each other, so it was natural that we reconnected.

The only song that was Love Bone's was "Alive," which was then called "Dollar Short." Andy actually had lyrics for that. I don't think we ever recorded a full version of it, although there may be a bootleg of it. I think we played it in Portland. It was the exact same arrangement of "Alive," but Andy had a completely different set of lyrics for it. Mainly it was my arrangements and just showing them to Mike.

Jeff Ament: Some friends of mine were in this band War Babies, whose bass player didn't work out. And I immediately got thrown into playing some shows and recording a bunch of songs with them. At that point, I kind of thought maybe I'd go back to art school. You know, I kind of thought maybe we had our one shot at being a rock band. It seemed like it was going to be impossible for lightning to strike anymore. I still felt that love of doing some sort of graphic work or being a painter. I only went to college for two years, and I kind of felt like that was unfinished.

When I started playing with War Babies, I just fell in love with playing music all over again. Richard Stuverud—who I still play music with to this day—he was the drummer in that band and we just had a blast, man. We'd get together early and totally rework the songs, and I'd play him some Clash or Prince tunes and say, like, "Man, let's get this out of the AC/DC realm and give it a funky Clash groove, and it'll make it more interesting." Right around that time, Stone said, "Hey, I'm thinking about recording these songs. Do you want to come play bass on these songs?"

As things started to progress a little bit, we were doing some promotion for the Mother Love Bone record, and we were hanging out a lot. I'd always start to hint toward, like, if we're going to do this, I want to do this in a better way. I felt like the past bands that we were in, there was a lot of passive-aggressive behavior, and I was just over that. I was old enough

that if I'm going to be in a band, I want to be in a band with guys that I can be open with, that I can trust. We went out and had dinner at the Queen City Grill in Seattle, and we sort of gave each other new boundaries and guidelines and things that we expected out of one another in terms of how we treated each other. And it was huge. It was kind of the first time that we were really honest and open with one another about how we felt about each other.

Late July

Eddie Vedder joins L.A.-based musician buddies like former Red Hot Chili Peppers/then Eleven drummer Jack Irons, Flea, Cliff Martinez, and guitarist Dix Denney on a camping trip to Yosemite National Park. On the drive home, Vedder hears a Mother Love Bone tape for the first time in Irons's car.

A page from Vedder's journal, dated July 23, 1990, reads: "'Move 'em out, rawhide.' The sun is rising to greet us as we move along this winding fwy north towards our takeoff point in Yosemite Valley. We improvised a 4-hr. shuteye session at a functioning house/arcade. Speeds up to *70* miles per hour. Jack's car is big . . . Very big and black. Dusty black. And it's got a break in the front grill from a previous mishap which gives it a large toothless grin. I feel very safe in this car."

Jack Irons: He definitely got the reputation on that trip as "Crazy Eddie." That kind of energy showed up in the first few years of Pearl Jam, when he was still young and could do that to himself. He was just having fun and was a bit of a daredevil.

Eddie Vedder: I took every dare that there was along the trail. If there was a slide to slide down, I slid even farther. I did things that I wouldn't ordinarily do but I have done ever since. It changed me. There was this long rock slide. The guy from Thelonious Monster and the Weirdos, Dix Denney, was in front of me. He had started down on a lower part of the slide and I already picked up great speed right behind him, so I evaded him by going to the left—and what I did was send myself off into some huge rapid that was just pumping away like it had done for years and years. I think I heard all ten of the

guys on the side [*makes gasping noise*], even above the sound of the rapids, and I knew I was in trouble. I just went for it. The story goes that everyone held their breath and didn't see me bounce up for a while. And finally, about twenty yards upstream, I popped up like a cork, and everybody applauded.

August

Without a permanent singer or a drummer on board, Ament, Gossard, and McCready record instrumental demos at Seattle's Reciprocal Studios of the songs that would later become "Alive," "Once," "Footsteps," "Black," "Breath," "Even Flow," "Animal," and "Alone." Soundgarden's Matt Cameron accepts Gossard's invitation to play drums; McCready's former Shadow bandmate Chris Friel also drums on some of the tracks.

Matt Cameron: I thought it was going to take a long time for those guys to heal. And I was surprised and really inspired by how quickly they got back to doing some more music. Instead of having that be an event that might seal their fate in a negative, they drew inspiration from it somehow, albeit maybe a darker inspiration. They definitely kept making music, and, ultimately, that's when I first started playing with those guys: for all these songs that Stone had written after Andy passed away. I was struck by how the music was sort of different from Mother Love Bone. It had a little more emotional resonance. Stone wrote these enormous chord charts that were about as big as that wall, with, like, "G-B-E-D," just so we could know where we are. Jeff and I always give him shit about his enormous chord charts.

During a trip to Los Angeles, Ament and Gossard had given a cassette with five songs from the just-finished recordings to Jack Irons, whose style they'd long admired, in the hopes that he would join the nascent band.

Jeff Ament: Stone and I decided that we'd help promote the Love Bone record when it came out, and it was kind of an arduous process because you're in L.A. doing press and talking about Andy. Everybody wants to know the dirt on what happened and why Andy died.

But during that time, Stone had written these songs, and we sort of had the idea that maybe we wanted to keep trying to make some music. So we were looking for a drummer, and we were looking for a singer. Jack Irons, who played in the Chili Peppers, was one of our favorite drummers at that time. And we hooked up with him with the idea of trying to get a band going around him. We went out and played a pickup basketball game with Jack and John and Dix Denney from the Weirdos. Flea and maybe even Anthony Kiedis were there. During that weekend, we told Jack, "Well, if you're not interested, if you know any other drummers or any other singers . . ."

Jack Irons: My wife and I made a decision that we wanted to have a baby. It was around that time that my wife got pregnant, and I didn't have any money. I got offered a tour with Redd Kross, who were willing to pay me one thousand a week for nine weeks. That was nine thousand more than I had, so I said, "Okay. That's what I'm going to do." Now, right around that time, Stone and Jeff got in touch with me. They were staying at a hotel in Los Angeles and asked if I could come visit them. I wasn't that familiar with Mother Love Bone. I was an L.A. guy, and they were Seattle guys. That was before everything started busting open and the Seattle sound was becoming the world's sound. They said, "Do you want to start a band with us?" And I was just like, "I can't." They were interested in me from the point of view of having been in the Chili Peppers. I think that's what attracted them to me. Stone said, "Well, we have a demo tape. Why don't you check it out, and certainly if you know any singers, pass it along."

Mid-September

While in Los Angeles to attend the Concrete Foundations rock convention, Ament and Gossard invite Vedder to their room at the Hyatt Regency hotel for a quick face-to-face meeting, having been told by Jack Irons that he might be a good fit for their new project. Visiting from San Diego, Vedder drives over to the hotel from Irons's house in Los Angeles. To this day, none of the principal parties can remember whether Vedder had already received the instrumental demos or if Irons handed them off to him

shortly afterward, before leaving on tour with Redd Kross.

Jeff Ament: It's possible that he'd just gotten the tape and hadn't listened to it yet.

Eddie Vedder: Maybe I'd sent the tape with my vocals, and they hadn't heard it yet. That's the only thing I can think of.

Stone Gossard: Ed just popped up, and we said hello. But was that before we gave him the tape, or after he gave us something to listen to? I know Jeff and I had one meeting with him before he came to Seattle.

Eddie Vedder: One thing I do remember saying at the meeting in the hotel was, I was always into three-piece and four-piece bands. In a five-piece, it starts getting hard to remember everybody's name. This is quite embarrassing looking back, but I said, "There's no way I could ever play the leads, but if you wanted it to be a four-piece, I could learn the rhythm parts if Stone wanted to do the solos." In essence, I was suggesting getting rid of Mike McCready, although, of course, I didn't know him and hadn't seen him play. I was like, "Personally, I've always liked a four-piece," not knowing that I was dissing not only Mother Love Bone but also their new group. [Laughs] They were probably like, "Ugh. Who is this fuckin' knucklehead?" Sorry, Mikey!

September 13

Adding his vocals atop the instrumentals on his four-track recorder, Vedder's three compositions are a mini-opera named Momma-Son, consisting of the songs "Alive," "Once," and "Footsteps." In "Alive," the narrator is informed by his mother that the man he thought was his father is, in fact, not—a turn of events Vedder had experienced in his own life. In "Once," the narrator becomes unhinged and murderous ("Once upon a time, I could control myself"), and by "Footsteps," he's reflecting on his wasted life from a prison cell. That day, Vedder had surfed at Pacific Beach, written the songs, and then mailed the music, which he'd recorded over a Merle Haggard's Greatest Hits cassette, to Jeff Ament in Seattle.

Eddie Vedder: Jack gave me the tape, the instrumentals, and I took it to work, and it was the midnight shift. So I listened to it a bunch and went in the water that next day. Had to surf. It was in my head. And then I wrote, like, three songs, I think that day, and then sent it off at, like, four o'clock before I had to go back to work, because I had an early shift that day. Whatever artwork was on there was just scribbled. It has my phone number on it, in case they wanted to call. Subtle.

It all came together as a piece, just in the water. It was really foggy that day, too. I remember you couldn't even see the waves coming. You couldn't even see twenty feet, so you were really just waiting. And maybe I was a bit too far out, 'cause I just drifted off, and maybe . . . now that I think back, I don't remember surfing a lot that day. I just remember being out there. I don't remember the waves I caught that day. And, you know, surfers remember their waves. I didn't catch any waves that day, but, well, one—one big one.

September 19

Vedder's cassette arrives in Seattle and wows Ament, Gossard, and McCready, who call and invite him to immediately fly up to Seattle for an audition.

Jeff Ament: We got a tape that had "Alive" and "Once" and "Footsteps" on it. And they're pretty much exactly the way that they ended up on the record. I think he just stayed up all night and wrote this crazy trilogy of songs that kind of centered around this one particular character. On first listen, I thought, Wow, this is really good. I listened to it two more times and thought it was awesome. So I called Stone and said, "I think you need to come over here and tell me for sure."

Stone Gossard: Ed's choices were definitely different than what I would have expected. Ed's stuff is so driven by lyrics. He had to find the melody for the lyric to have an impact. I think I was used to singers that would just find the melody first and then match it with some words.

Mike McCready: I think that it was fate or something. There had to be some sort of luck and timing and fate. We gave a tape to Jack Irons, and he randomly

knew Ed from a hike, you know? And then Ed would go surfing and put lyrics to three songs. There's something else in the universe happening other than it being planned out. Because you can plan as much as you want, but life is going to happen the way it's going to happen. There's one guy we tried out before, and then Ed. Boom. You couldn't have planned that out. There's no way. It's just too fantastic of a story how that happened.

Eddie Vedder: The whole process took twelve hours. I could have not done that. I could have blown it off and not written those songs.

Jack Irons: Somewhere along the line on the Redd Kross tour, I heard Eddie was already up in Seattle. It was pretty much that simple.

Matt Cameron: Here's a funny story. I never got a proper tape of the sessions I did with those guys. After I did the demos, I didn't really hear what the outcome was other than once Eddie had arrived in Seattle and started working with the group, that's when I knew that they had a new singer. When I learned the song that eventually became "Alive," and I heard the playback and the mix of it, I felt like that could be a really, really great vocal song. When I heard what Eddie had done with that, it was a perfect addition to the music that we had made. Some singers just have an instinct that can't be taught. I felt a connection there, which felt perfect for the music.

October 7
Pacific Amphitheatre, Costa Mesa, California

The day before his maiden voyage to Seattle, Eddie Vedder attends the Gathering of the Tribes festival, a musically diverse event that predates Lollapalooza by a year and is organized by the Cult's Ian Astbury. The event features performances by Soundgarden, Iggy Pop, the Cramps, Ice T, the Indigo Girls, and Public Enemy, among others. Vedder watches Soundgarden's set fifty feet from the stage in the mosh pit. Little does he know that barely twenty-four hours later, he'll be sharing a microphone with Chris Cornell.

1990

October 8

Eddie Vedder arrives in Seattle to play for the first time with Ament, Gossard, McCready, and newly added veteran local drummer Dave Krusen. "Black," "Just a Girl," "Breath," "Alone," "Oceans," and "Release" are among the first songs hammered out at the practice space in the basement of Galleria Potatohead. This initial visit lasts for seven days, with Vedder begrudgingly returning to San Diego due to his work commitments at a gas station.

Jeff Ament: I remember when Ed first came to town. Right before he got on the plane to come down, he said, "When I get there, I want you to pick me up, and I want to go straight to the practice studio, and I don't want to fuck around." I just want to plug in the instruments and get at it. I don't want to sightsee and I don't want to get anything to eat or whatever." And that's sort of what we did those first five or six days. We'd wake up, and we'd get a cup of coffee, and we'd go to the practice studio and play music until we got hungry. Then we'd go down and get a veggie burrito, and we'd come back, and we'd stay at it. Then maybe we'd go out to Cyclops and get a little dinner, get a couple drinks in us, come back, and maybe bring a bottle of wine back with us. It was kind of an all-day affair. It was sixteen hours of making music, and we'd do that for five days.

Eddie Vedder: I do remember there being a real connection made on the phone with Jeff, and talking about artwork; how he was into artwork. And the responsibilities as a band member, or working with people. It's not a slacker job, or it's not a rock star thing. It's about music, it's about art, it's about all these things in common, which is probably why we ended up roommates when we first started touring. We just connected and became really close. I stayed at his house when I first came out, and he put up with a lot, because it was a bit hard for me at the beginning, coming up. He was the shaman. He was the one I was following or staying close to. He was like the ballast. It was good to have.

Stone Gossard: Well, we were practicing. You go in there and run down the list of songs. Ed worked on five or six songs, and we had another four or five

we were putting together. We'd play him something, and he'd say, "I'll have something for it tomorrow." Jeff starts talking immediately about playing a show at the end of the week. We didn't really have time to begin to worry about what we were going to be, other than, we need eight songs. We were just off and running; throwing out ideas, jamming on stuff, and hitting the record button. Ed's fully possessed personality didn't come out until after we'd toured for a few months. As he got to know the crowds and interact with the live environment, he transformed. He had an incredible voice and was a hard worker, and he could write on the fly. But in terms of that complete losing-his-mind thing, that didn't happen for a while.

Dave Krusen: Stone had some songs that he'd demoed, and we started working on those, but also, that whole time we were working on new stuff. Eddie had some lyrics for "Alive" and maybe another one that he'd come up with already. As fast as we were working on those songs, new songs were cropping up. It was the fastest, most creative thing I've ever been a part of. It was so quick, and ideas were flowing so fast. I just remember Eddie had papers laying all over the place and was constantly scratching down lyric ideas.

Mike McCready: Half of Ed's head was shaved, and he had a Butthole Surfers shirt on, with shorts and Doc Martens and a leather jacket. I was excited to meet him, because when I first heard him on the demo, I was like, "Who is this guy? Is he real?" It was too good to be true, in my mind, how good "Alive," "Footsteps," and "Once" sounded.

October 13

The new band records ten songs ("Even Flow," "Once," "Breath," "Release," "Just a Girl," "Alive," "Goat," "Alone," "Oceans," and "Black") and a handful of improvs or unfinished ideas, including one which would later turn into "Yellow Ledbetter," live to digital audiotape to officially chronicle its first week together.

Jeff Ament: We knocked out ten songs, and that ended up being the bulk of the first record. So that first week was pretty good!

October 14

After having been warned repeatedly by Vedder not to be late, Mike McCready picks the singer up at five in the morning and drives him to Sea-Tac Airport for his early-morning flight back to San Diego. That night, Vedder works behind the scenes for concert promoter Avalon Attractions at James Taylor's concert at the Open Air Theater on the campus of San Diego State University. Five or six days later, he returns to Seattle to continue work with Gossard, Ament, McCready, and Krusen.

October 22
Off Ramp, Seattle

The new band, temporarily dubbed Mookie Blaylock after one of the New Jersey Nets player's trading cards made it into the tape case of the instrumental demos, plays its first concert in front of approximately two hundred people. The set list consists of "Release," "Alone," "Alive," "Once," "Even Flow," "Black," "Breath," and, as an encore, "Just a Girl," which would appear only once more on a Mookie Blaylock or Pearl Jam set list.

Jeff Ament: It was really intense. It was really introverted because everything was so new, and we wanted to make sure we were playing our parts right. I think Eddie was kind of freaked out because he was singing in front of these guys that had been in this big Seattle band. Everyone was really nervous even though it wasn't a big show. It was rough, but it felt so good to get up and play.

Dave Krusen: The very first show, I remember being really nervous mostly because the songs had been worked up so fast that I was worried I was going to miss a part. I remember being really excited to play a show. Eddie was very kind of shy that first show. He had a hat pulled over his face, pretty much. The first night was very subdued compared to what it ended up progressing into.

Stone Gossard: Kim Thayil from Soundgarden came up to me after and said he particularly liked that song "Evening Flow." You know how the evening just flows? [*Laughs*] There were probably one hundred fifty people there, but I don't remember anything about the

T-Shirt design by Jeff Ament

show other than that. I don't think we knew our songs very well.

Mike McCready: I remember not wanting to do a show, because Jeff and Stone were still under contract with PolyGram. I thought if we showed people how good we were, they wouldn't let them out of the deal. So I thought it was a bad idea, but Stone was like, "Aw, fuck it. Let's go do it." Randy Johnson, the star pitcher from the Seattle Mariners, was there. So were the guys from Soundgarden. It was really crowded. The place was a dump. But it was exciting. We opened up with "Release," and I remember it being weird, because I thought we should open up with something heavier. Ed's inclination was to draw them in slowly. It was just tiny and hot and fun and over really quick. I remember Ed being very, very shy and just standing there. I also remember realizing that my dreams were starting to come true.

Chris Cornell: It definitely to this day was absolutely the best inaugural show I've ever seen in my life. Hands down, no comparison. And it has nothing to do with my perception of how great they are as a live band now. I remember exactly what I was thinking then, and it was that they were absurdly great. The only other thing I remember about that show was standing next to Kelly Curtis, who had been through hell with what happened with Andy. He was beaming and he said, "Well, I'm a happy guy right about now." He knew and I knew we'd just seen an incredible show and that Pearl Jam was a phenomenal band.

Nancy Wilson: Eddie was sounding really good, but he was looking at his shoes most of the show. He was really thrown into the deep end, in front of a big Seattle crowd. They'd just lost Andy Wood, so people had their scorecards out. They were standing in judgment. I'm sure he felt the sharpest edge of that. He wanted to be worthy in some way. His spirit was coming from such an emotionally honest and powerful place, and he navigated it like a true surfer.

October 23

After a second week of rehearsals and their live debut, the members of Mookie Blaylock convene at Galleria Potatohead

to record new versions of the same ten songs and other odds and ends they'd put to tape on October 13. The band then heads to the Seattle Kingdome to take in an NBA preseason basketball game between the Seattle Supersonics and the Chicago Bulls. Chicago wins 102–90.

Last Week of October

With Vedder still in Seattle for a few more days before returning to San Diego, Stone Gossard and Jeff Ament fly to New York. There they meet with Mother Love Bone's PolyGram A&R representative, Michael Goldstone, who'd recently been brought to Epic by Sony Music executive VP Michele Anthony, who'd been Mother Love Bone's lawyer. Manager Kelly Curtis, also on the trip, experiences a bit of a mishap:

Jeff Ament: Stone and I were meeting Michele and Michael for dinner, but Kelly never showed up. He'd been picked up walking down the street because the police thought he looked like some criminal that was wanted! This was before cell phones, so we were like, "What the fuck?" We didn't find out about it until the next morning.

Kelly Curtis: I was never arrested, but I was in a cell for a couple of hours until I was put in this lineup. It was the weirdest thing. It was all short, balding guys. The police never said anything to me. I was just let go after the lineup. Those guys carried on without me, for sure.

Later on the same trip, Curtis successfully negotiates Gossard's and Ament's exit from their PolyGram contract, clearing the way for their new band to sign with Epic.

Kelly Curtis: Rick Dobbis was newly running PolyGram at that point. We thought, there's a new guy here who has no history with us, so maybe if we begged to get off, he'd let us go. We hired the lawyer, a guy named Richard Lehrer, that had negotiated Dobbis's new deal. We thought there'd be a relationship: like, at least this lawyer knew this guy and would help us. We'd had this long thing where we were trying to get money to record demos and PolyGram wasn't giving us anything, but we were still contractually bound to them. Jeff and

Stone and I went there and asked if we could please go. Our singer had died and nothing was going on. We didn't tell them we'd found the most amazing singer and were almost done with a record. Michael had left PolyGram by that point, and Michele had gone to Sony. He said, "Yeah, I'll let you go." We were going to meet Michele and Michael downtown at a restaurant to celebrate. Stone and Jeff and I were in the restaurant, and Rick Dobbis came in. We thought this was going to fuck everything up. He'd see we were talking to Sony and then renege on our deal. He came up to us and asked us how dinner was, and we said it was great, although we hadn't eaten anything; we'd just ordered beers. One of us had to go outside and wave off Michael and Michele.

Michele Anthony: When I joined Sony, one of the first things I did was bring in Michael Goldstone. Almost immediately, we started hatching a plan to bring Jeff and Stone's new band to the label. There was a really strong, core family feeling about it, even before they came.

November 13
Off Ramp, Seattle

Formed as a tribute to the late Andy Wood, Temple of the Dog—a hybrid of Mookie Blaylock and Soundgarden, featuring Jeff Ament, Stone Gossard, Mike McCready, Chris Cornell, and Matt Cameron—plays its first and only complete show while in the midst of recording its self-titled debut album.

Jeff Ament: We'd only had a couple of rehearsals, so we were superfocused on trying to play the songs right.

Mike McCready: Man. The solo is super-sloppy on "Reach Down"!

December

Eddie Vedder packs all his belongings in his truck and moves permanently from San Diego to Seattle, where he alternates between crashing in Kelly Curtis's basement and at the band's rehearsal space.

Stone Gossard: On the way up from California one time, he drew a picture

for me on a flight. I think it was a poem. I was like, "I don't think anyone has ever given me a piece of artwork." His sensitivity to that kind of stuff was so great. It was completely off my radar. I think it took me years to understand Eddie. "Release"—he was really coming from a different place that I didn't fully understand.

Jerry Cantrell: I was living at that time with Kelly Curtis and his wife. They kind of adopted me, and I lived in their basement in two separate houses. I remember when Eddie came up. He was staying at the house, too, so we were both camped down in the basement for a while. I really dug him right off the bat.

December 16

Mookie Blaylock is interviewed on Seattle radio station KISW-FM. During the chat, the band explains how it came to meet Eddie Vedder and, as a treat for people calling in with suggested band names, gives away tickets to a show the following week opening for Alice in Chains at the Moore Theatre. The demo for "Once" is played at the end of the segment.

December 19
The Vogue, Seattle

Mookie Blaylock plays its second show alongside Bathtub Gin and El Steiner.

Eric Johnson: The very first couple of shows, Eddie was really shy. He looked a little different than Seattle guys, too. He was wearing shorts, so he looked like a surfer. His voice was so incredible from the beginning, though. Everybody in town knew Jeff and Stone. But Eddie was a brand-new guy, and a lot of eyes were on him.

December 22
Moore Theatre, Seattle

Mookie Blaylock opens for Alice in Chains. At the end of the set, Chris Cornell jumps onstage with the band to perform a couple songs from the *Temple of the Dog* album, culminating in him hoisting Vedder onto his shoulders.

Chris Cornell: Eddie was on my shoulders, and I think we were both sort of climbing around the rafters. I remember kind of running and him yelling at me because it wasn't that comfortable running and someone bouncing their shoulder into your stomach.

Jerry Cantrell: Chris was that kind of a guy. Most of us in Seattle have always been pretty supportive of one another. There wasn't a lot of taking potshots or trying to derail each other. It was mutual admiration. And that's a powerful thing for Chris to do, but he loved those guys.

Nancy Wilson: In Seattle, there's a sense of community that's not competitive. It's very enlightened, if you ask me. Chris Cornell could have shut Eddie out and said, "No, Soundgarden gets all the glory now." But he got up onstage with the newcomer and built his confidence. It helped Eddie grow those wings pretty fast.

December 31

The members of Mookie Blaylock, joined by friends from Soundgarden and Alice in Chains, celebrate New Year's Eve with an old-fashioned hootenanny at the Seattle-area ranch of writer-director Cameron Crowe and his wife, Heart's Nancy Wilson. Some of the group heads back into town for a bash featuring a performance by eighties hit makers the Romantics, thrown by friends of Kelly Curtis from the local concert promotion scene. A member of Mookie Blaylock who will go unnamed has a bit too much to drink, prompting the others to coin the phrase, "There's no such thing as free champagne."

Nancy Wilson: We did it just like the Indians used to do: We sat around and played acoustic instruments, remembering songs that we knew or making new ones up. I remember going to sleep just before the sun came up. The next afternoon, I went to the kitchen, and there was a note from Jerry that said, "Look at the elephant." I had a little mechanical elephant windup toy that twirled; it was a gift from Chris Cornell. Apparently Jerry had been fixating on it overnight, and in the morning he was feeding champagne to the horses.

Temple of the Dog

Andy Wood's death from a heroin overdose in March 1990 had a cataclysmic impact on the Seattle music scene that had nurtured his musical ambitions to the brink of stardom. For Jeff Ament and Stone Gossard, it not only meant the loss of one of their best friends but also the end of Mother Love Bone, the band to which they'd devoted the past two years of their lives.

Chris Cornell, Wood's former roommate and musical sounding board, got the call that his friend had overdosed while in New York on the way back to Seattle from a Soundgarden European tour. Wood was being kept alive by life support machines, but doctors informed his family that he would never regain consciousness.

"Andy's girlfriend, Xana, said, 'You can't unplug him until Chris gets here,'" Cornell recalls. "So I immediately got on a plane to Seattle, and I walked in, without sleep, into a hospital room with his close family, most of which I'd never met, and everyone in his band and all of his friends and his brothers.

"Up to that point, I think life was really good for us, as just a group of musicians in a scene making music. The world was sort of our oyster. We had support, and we supported each other. Andy was kind of like this beam of light above it all. And to see him hooked up to machines, that was, I think, the death of the innocence of the scene."

Soundgarden had to return to Europe for more shows almost immediately, and Cornell began channeling his grief into new music, writing two songs about Wood titled "Say Hello 2 Heaven" and "Reach Down." "We were invincible," he says. "No one was going to die, and if they were, it wasn't going to be him. And if it did happen, it wasn't going to happen like that. The impossible suddenly was happening irrevocably in front of us, and

we were all sitting there having really no tools to deal with it. I think that's where the songs came from, because the next few weeks of my life were just a horror."

On "Reach Down," Cornell imagined he was "creating a dialogue" between himself and Wood, and Wood "is telling me everything's okay. I kind of envisioned him making it to where his dream was, which was to be on a stage playing in front of an audience the size of the US Festival: 'Reach down, pick the crowd up, carry it back in my hands.' He's reaching down to his enormous throngs of adoring fans and pulling them up to him, and now the circle is closed, and he has achieved his dream."

Cornell quickly recognized that he had no next step in mind for what he was writing. "I felt like, 'Well, why am I writing these songs, and what am I going to do with them when they don't sound like Soundgarden songs to me at all?' Because they didn't," he says. "I just had this notion that it would be great as a tribute to Andy, just to try to get people to think about him. Maybe I could record these two songs with the members of Mother Love Bone, and we could release them as a single," possibly on local label Sub Pop Records.

That summer, upon arriving home from abroad, Cornell recorded demos of the two tracks, copied them onto a cassette for Gossard and Ament, and dropped it off at Kelly Curtis's office. "And then I think I just lost my nerve. I didn't pursue it at all," he admits. Several weeks later, Ament called and voiced his wholehearted approval of the works in progress.

"He was very complimentary about the songs and super-encouraging about it," Cornell says. "That gave me the confidence to say maybe we could record it. Jeff wasn't hesitant. He was like, 'Yeah, we could do that. Maybe we

could come up with another song or two and do Andy solo songs so people can hear him.' That was really exciting to me, that people could hear Andy's songs. That was my mission.

"I think Stone really liked that idea, and immediately I heard from Jeff again. He said there'd been some grumblings about the idea from family or friends of Andy's. They'd voiced a concern that maybe we were sort of trying to exploit Andy. And that didn't feel so good. Jeff responded like, 'Well, fuck it. We'll just make our own record.' He said it in that style of thinking like Andy would. That's all it takes, somebody to say, 'No, we'll just do it.' I work really great in that kind of an environment. If there's encouragement and passion behind something, I will work tirelessly. So I just started doing that, writing more songs."

Ament's excitement about the project was also driven by his interest in helping Cornell make music that sounded different from Soundgarden. "I loved Soundgarden, but I saw an opportunity for us to be Chris's band and get as weird as we could," he says. "I decided to play fretless bass on a lot of the stuff, to pull it a bit out of the 'rock' thing. There's a lot of harmonics and weird playing styles. The way Chris wrote the songs made it seem like he wanted it to be a bit more of an art project."

Simultaneously, Ament, Gossard, and Mike McCready were jamming on the material that would eventually appear on Pearl Jam's debut album, *Ten,* which to Cornell seemed to be of a piece both musically and emotionally with his newest creations like "Wooden Jesus" and "Your Saviour." But there was a momentary hiccup when Cornell realized he'd had an unpleasant experience years earlier involving McCready's prior band Shadow.

"I had originally thought it'd just be

Mother Love Bone and me," he says. "I think Jeff told me, 'Stone has this guy, Mike McCready. He's a great guitar player.' Then the volume went down a little bit: 'He's in a band called Shadow,' maybe hoping I wouldn't remember the name. Actually, before I'd met anyone in Soundgarden, I was looking at the *Rocket,* the monthly magazine that had want ads. In it somewhere was a band called Shadow; they needed a singer. I called the guy; it wasn't McCready. I drove to his house in Bellevue, and he gave me a cassette. He lived at home. I didn't get a good vibe from him. I put in the tape and didn't get a good vibe from the tape. Later I remember I got a call from the guy, who said he wanted his cassette back. He wanted me to drive back across the lake. I said, 'No, I'm sorry, I don't really want to be in the band.' And he said, 'Well, I want my cassette back.' Really? Your low-bias cassette with no label on it? You really need that back, huh? So I got this attitude when I heard 'Shadow,' but I trusted Stone. There was no way this guy was not going to be good."

With McCready and Soundgarden drummer Matt Cameron, who'd also played on the Gossard-Ament-McCready demos, on board, initial rehearsals for the Wood-inspired project took place in early October at the Galleria Potatohead Gallery on Second Avenue in Seattle's Belltown neighborhood. When it was clear that there was now more than enough material for a full album, the musicians, now calling themselves Temple of the Dog after a lyric in the Mother Love Bone song "Man of Golden Words," shifted to London Bridge Studios to get down to business.

"We probably had four Temple rehearsals," Gossard says. "The ones that Chris wrote were pretty well formed, and I had three arrangements that became Temple songs as well, including one that Jeff cowrote, 'Pushin' Forward Back.' Chris is just a master. He was a pro at that point already. He just took those arrangements, snapped them together, and we were off and running."

Wanting it to match his image of Wood playing to a massive festival crowd, Cornell had conceived the eleven-minute "Reach Down" as "a Neil Young guitar opus; a 'Fuck you' to the world of people who don't want to hear a guitar solo." When McCready attempted an uncharacteristically timid lead during an early rehearsal, Cornell urged him to dig deeper and let loose.

"I said, 'We're going to come to it again, and I'm going to leave the room as it starts. Just solo until I come back. Don't stop until you see me.' I left for a really long time," he says. "You could tell from listening that everybody had sort of run out of ideas, and they just wished it would end. So we let it go, and we didn't play it again until we were in the studio. I think I did the same thing in the studio—I just left and came back. We're rolling the tape, and it's guitar solo time right away. He starts playing, and nothing's happening. We're like, 'No, no, no, no, no. This is your time to shine.' And he does it again, and I started thinking, Maybe he's not awesome. We all converged on him at once and said, 'You're being polite. This is your moment to go fucking berserk.' And then he went out of his mind. You can tell he's trying to remember every trick he's ever learned. Fifty seconds of the solo would go by, and he'd try to up the last, and keep going until his headphones flew off. The last minute of the solo, he's not playing to anything. It was the first time I think any of them had seen that. We were like, 'Holy shit! He's out of his mind. He's got problems that are going to come out again somewhere, so good luck, guys. But that was awesome.'"

Ament says he appreciates "Reach Down" because he can envision both Wood and Cornell as the subjects of the song. "Andy was the guy who could reach down and pick anybody up," he says. "But in a sense, Chris was the guy reaching down and picking me and Stone up and saying, 'Come on, guys.' That was pretty important to me at the time. Even when Stone and I decided to play together again, I wasn't one hundred percent sure it's what I wanted to do, and I don't think Stone was, either. Being able to play with all these great musicians had a big impact on me in terms of deciding whether I was going to play music again or whether I was going back to art school. So, thanks, Chris and Matt."

The song that would become the album's centerpiece, "Hunger Strike," was birthed from Cornell's admitted obsessive-compulsive dislike for odd numbers. At a certain point during the writing process, there were nine songs completed, "and I hated that," he says. "So I had this other song that I whipped up so we could have ten, because I just have to have ten. And it was 'Hunger Strike.'

"The song basically had one verse and then these chunky chords and a repeating chorus. I think it was the only song I wrote in my life stoned, because that never worked for me. I was never a big pot smoker. But I'd smoked pot for whatever reason, and I was revolving around on the arpeggio and just came up with the melody. I wrote the lyrics pretty quickly. I couldn't write any more lyrics to that concept. That verse was it. It said everything you could possibly fucking say about that feeling in it. I might've tried to write a second verse, but it probably was awful, and I just thought it was done and that it will just be an oddly arranged song that's a deep album track.

"I was wanting to express the gratitude for my life but also disdain for people where that's not enough, where they want more. There's no way to really have a whole lot more than you need usually without taking from somebody else that can't really afford to give it to you. It's sort of about taking advantage of a person or people who really don't have anything."

On the same day that Eddie Vedder arrived in Seattle to play with his soon-to-be Pearl Jam bandmates for the first time, Cornell had scheduled a Temple of the Dog rehearsal. Aside from saying

a quick hello to Cornell in the hallway, Vedder kept to himself while the group ran through its songs. But when they started playing "Hunger Strike," he made a move that would change his life forever.

"So we're in the rehearsal and I showed them the song, and we get to the chorus," Cornell says. "There's a low part and a high part. I'm going to sing them both now, so they get it. It's the magic of overdubs, and I can do both parts, and it will sound great. No problem. So I'm doing it: 'Going hungry, going hungry, going hungry.' I'm not doing it good. The high part's hard to sing anyway, but I'm doing it. All of the sudden, I feel this shadowy presence over my shoulder. And there's only one mike, and the chorus comes around again, and he sort of moves his shoulder in just to let me know he's got a plan. And I don't know him. We had said hi. And it wasn't in a way that was intrusive or egotistical. It was literally almost like he had pity on me and was just trying to help me through this moment, because I was having a hard time. So he hit the 'Going hungry, going hungry, yeah.' I sang the high part, and then he hit it again. All of a sudden, a lightbulb went off in my head and I thought, 'Fuck, his voice sounds incredible in that deep register. That low part where I'm singing, mine's not that convincing.' I thought, 'Wait a minute. What if I sang the first verse alone, just the guitar and me, and then the band drops in, he sings it, it's the same verse, but it's a different guy, so it'll be like a real song with two verses?'

"Now still in my mind I thought, 'This'll just be a better song number eight,' you know? I think I had to write the words down, and we tried it there, and it was fucking jumping off immediately. It went from, 'Oh yeah, this works, we like this,' to 'This is, like, a really great song.' Eddie's singing on it changed the feeling of the lyrics, too. It suddenly became more gospel. It became more meaningful to me. At the time, I thought it was because someone else was singing it.

"I suppose that was the moment where I felt like I knew him," Cornell says. "I'm a guy who's sitting here trying to produce a record, and I've got this song that I want to sound great, and I don't want to be embarrassed, and he just made it sound better than I was doing on my own."

Vedder says he could hear Cornell trying to sing the two parts, and halfway through the song, he "just kind of stepped up and did it. And I remember being a little nervous about doing it, but he was really happy about how it sounded, which was great. The fact that he asked me to be on that record, I mean, that's the first time I was ever on a real record. So that could be one of my favorite songs that I've ever been on, or, for sure, the most meaningful. It was the first time hearing myself on a record, and it was such a great song."

"Turns out he sings harmony really fantastic," Gossard muses. "Best background singer in all of rock, Eddie Vedder. It literally was, like, the most fluid, musical, and just instantaneously good-sounding thing that any of us had ever been involved with. And still to this day, it's probably one of those moments. That was when everything magical was happening. Take Chris Cornell's songwriting and his voice and his lyrics, and Matt Cameron, and then for them to ask us to be part of that, we were just in heaven at that point. Chris already asked us to play on his songs, so him inviting Ed to participate, too, was just like another huge, generous, gracious gesture that said, 'I'm not only going to help you guys with this record and these songs I wrote, but I'm also going to write some lyrics to some songs that you wrote, Stone and Jeff, and I'm going to even ask your new singer, who I haven't really heard his voice yet, to sing on it, too.'"

Cameron adds, "Not only did Eddie rise to the occasion, but he matched Chris and Stone's chops in the studio and understood the type of record we were making—a very hard thing for someone outside of our scene to relate to at that time."

Although he didn't know it at the time, Vedder's intersection with the Temple world had actually begun back in September, when he received a cassette featuring the three Gossard-Ament-McCready-Cameron instrumentals from his friend Jack Irons. He overdubbed his own lyrics and vocal melodies onto the tape, transforming a track that Gossard had named "Troubled Times" into the song "Footsteps"—and, in the process, securing the audition in Seattle. Around the same time, Cornell, unaware of Vedder's existence, much less the fact

that he had some of the same music in his possession, wrote an entirely different song atop the instrumental and called it "Times of Trouble." The latter appeared on the *Temple of the Dog* album. Perhaps in the interest of not confusing people, Pearl Jam didn't unveil "Footsteps" until the spring of 1992.

As Vedder became acquainted with the Seattle music scene in the days that followed, Cornell was a frequent guide and companion. The first night they hung out, Vedder recalls ending up "in a little park with him and his friend Eric, chasing his dog Bill in the mud with a twelve-pack of the cheapest beer you could buy, which is called Schmidt. That was the party. It was like, 'Wow. This is what they do for fun up here—chase a dog in the mud with cheap beer? This is going to be great.' And that went on for years."

"Sometimes," Cameron muses, "I wonder if that was a void that Chris felt from Andy's passing, like having another equally talented singer that he could bounce ideas off of or just basically relate to. I've always wondered about that. He really embraced Eddie when he first moved up here, and I know Eddie felt a real mentorship with Chris's relationship in the beginning stages. I think that gave him a lot of confidence to really tackle a lot of the music that was in front of him. Chris had a bigger role than he knows with the genesis of *Ten* and Pearl Jam starting out."

Temple of the Dog played just one official show, on November 13, 1990, at the Off Ramp in Seattle, and breezed through the recording of a self-titled album before year's end. After the spring 1991 release of the project, the members would reconvene a handful of times to perform Temple songs at one another's shows throughout the next year. But by the end of 1992, Pearl Jam and Soundgarden were among the most popular rock bands on the planet, and despite "Hunger Strike" turning into a huge rock radio hit amid grunge mania, Temple of the Dog retreated into the background.

Still, its significance to the principal parties looms enormously even twenty years on, with Ament convinced that the Temple album remains "one of the best things that any of us has done, in terms of a group of songs."

"What came out of a tragedy gave birth to something that was really impactful and hugely positive in my life,

which would have never existed if we didn't have that trust and camaraderie with each other," Cornell says. "I was in a band with Matt, and he was always my first choice as someone to play drums on something, but I'd never played music with Stone or Jeff, I'd never met McCready, I don't think, and I'd never met Eddie. So that would have never happened."

"That record continues to be a high-water mark in terms of how the Soundgarden sound and the Pearl Jam sound could blend together to have its own sound," Gossard says. "We never sounded heavier, and Soundgarden never sounded groovier or more laid back."

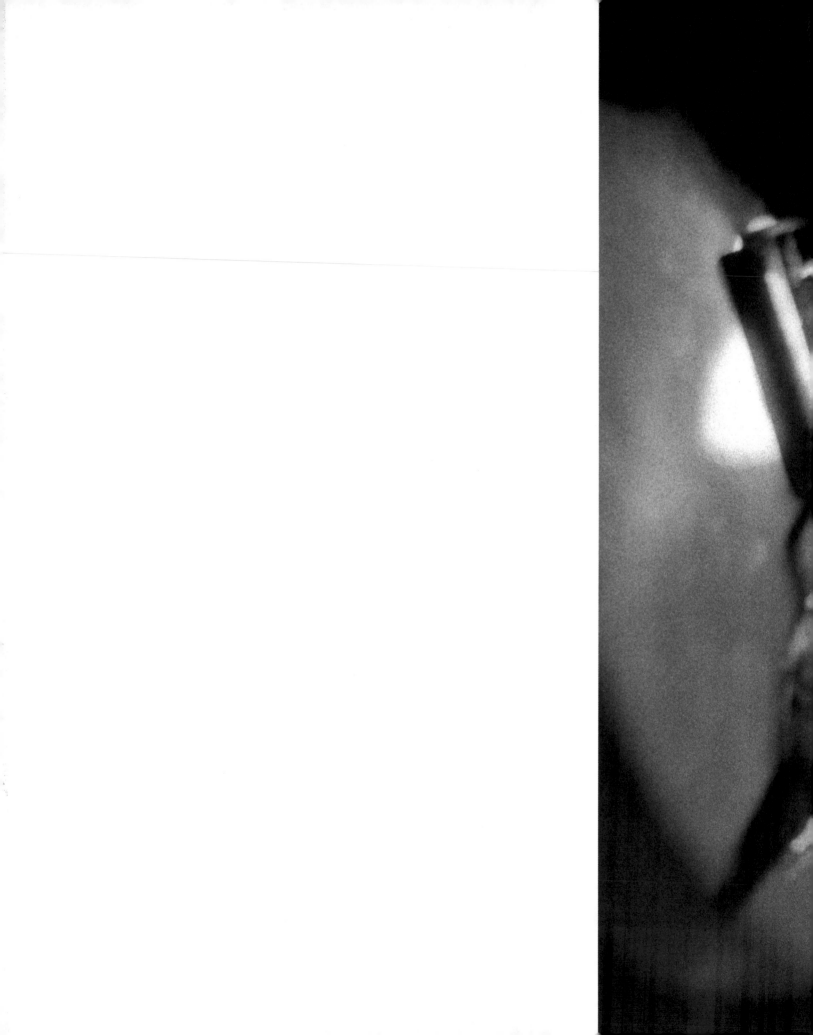

CHAPTER 199

1991

Pearl Jam didn't even have a real name as it set off on its first real tour in early 1991, but it had the music that was about to form one of the most iconic albums in recent rock history. At this point, success was still incremental, whether it was winning over radio programmers one at a time or conquering club audiences in small towns with ever more dazzling live performances. Once *Temple of the Dog* and *Ten* were in stores, and Pearl Jam was on board to appear in and contribute music to a Cameron Crowe film about twentysomethings in Seattle, it wasn't long before the band was at the cusp of full-on superstardom. But there was no time for Pearl Jam to rest on its laurels. Instead the band pushed forward with all its might, taking along millions of fans on what was about to become an all-encompassing trip.

Early January

Eddie Vedder, Stone Gossard, and Mike McCready give a brief interview on Seattle radio station KXRX-FM and play the demos for "Once" and "Even Flow."

January 10

Harpo's Cabaret, Victoria, British Columbia

In its first show outside of Seattle, Mookie Blaylock opens for Alice in Chains. Confronted with a disinterested, noisy crowd, Vedder hurls the base of his microphone stand at the back wall of the venue in the middle of the set.

Jeff Ament: We were a little concerned. We didn't want to decapitate anybody before we made a record. [*Laughs*] It didn't take him that long to come out of his shell, that's for sure.

January 29

Mookie Blaylock records demos of several songs with producer Rick Parashar at Seattle's London Bridge Studios. "Alive," "Wash," and a cover of the Beatles' "I've Got a Feeling" are chosen for release in April by Epic as a promotional single because they best represented the vibe of the new band.

Jeff Ament: We knew "Alive" was going to be an album track. We thought "Wash" had potential but that maybe it would

develop a little bit more. "I've Got a Feeling" was just a light moment in the studio. *Let It Be* was the first full album that I ever bought, so pretty much every song on that record takes me back to being eight years old. I loved that Ed took lyrical liberties with the "Everybody had a good time" part and included Andy in it. It was a profound transitional group of songs. It sort of made it okay that we were moving on. Ed was very sensitive to what he was getting into.

February 7

Florentine Gardens, Los Angeles

Mookie Blaylock begins a brief West Coast tour supporting Alice in Chains, offering the first live performances of "Garden" and "Brother," the latter of which would not be played again for

another eighteen years. The song is eventually released as an instrumental on the 2003 compilation *Lost Dogs* and then with vocals on the 2009 reissue of *Ten*.

Jeff Ament: It was good for us to get out of town and out where nobody knew anything about us. The first three or four shows were in Seattle, and all eyes were on the new guy. That was the best thing we could have done.

Jerry Cantrell: Being a fan of Green River and Love Bone, and also being friends with those guys, I thought Mookie Blaylock was kind of unfocused at first. Maybe not from Stone's and Jeff's situation, but just the band jelling. It was certainly a different sound, which, of course, they were trying to create. What I remember was, I liked the band and I liked the music. Like with anything different, especially from people you know, it takes a minute to grab on to it. Things had happened for us, and we were on our way. These guys were starting again. We just wanted to give them as much support as they'd given us in the early days of our band.

February 25

Off Ramp, Seattle

Cast as one of the stars of Cameron Crowe's new Seattle-centric film, *Singles*, Matt Dillon hits the town with Eddie Vedder, Jeff Ament, and Stone Gossard after this Mookie Blaylock–Alice in Chains show.

Cameron Crowe: I was trying out the camp counselor thing: "Let's all go to this

club and check out these bands." It really was the hell version of John Hughes. Here I come into the club with all these actors, and we sit in the corner. It was so packed, and people were throwing beer bottles, and after a little bit, [actress] Kyra Sedgwick says, "I really get the 'wonderful' scene going on here. I'm going to go home now." Then the costume girl goes, "Great. This is *great*. 'Bye!" It ended up being Matt Dillon and [actor] Campbell Scott hanging until the very end, slam dancing.

Mark Arm: I went and saw a Mookie Blaylock show at the Off Ramp. I would keep tabs on them from a distance. It was like we were spying, but there was genuine interest in what our friends were doing. We had that shared history.

March 10

Eddie Vedder and Jeff Ament are interviewed on Seattle radio station KISW and announce that Mookie Blaylock is changing its name to Pearl Jam, as well as entering Seattle's London Bridge Studios the next day to begin recording its debut album for Epic Records. Demos of "Release" and "Once" are also played.

Jeff Ament: Stone and Ed and I went to New York to sign the contract with Sony, and we saw in the paper that Neil Young was playing Nassau Coliseum with Sonic Youth and Social Distortion on February 22. So we got in a van, went out to Nassau, saw the show, and Sonic Youth was really incredible at that show. Neil played only about eight songs, but it was, like, a three-hour show. We were kind of panicked trying to figure out a band name, and he was having these long jams, and we just threw *Jam* at the end of *Pearl*. Kind of a stupid name, but it has a lot of meaning. There's some weight behind it even though it doesn't sound like there's any weight behind it.

Vedder loved perpetuating the made-up story that the band name was inspired by a special recipe from his "Great-grandma Pearl."

Eddie Vedder: I've got some Indian in me, and it turns out that she used to make this kind of hallucinogenic preserve. I wish it was passed down through the family. If it was, it was stopped about a generation before me. I never got to taste any myself. But I'm still in search of that elusive recipe for Pearl jam.

March–April

Eddie Vedder, Stone Gossard, and Jeff Ament shoot their scenes for *Singles* in Seattle, portraying members of the band Citizen Dick, led by Matt Dillon's character, lead singer Cliff Poncier. Their most extended appearance is in a scene where the band members are sitting in a coffee shop and discover a local newspaper review that trashes Poncier for his "pompous, dick-swinging swill." In an attempt to not hurt his feelings, they don't read the story out loud, but Poncier can tell the review is negative. The piece ends with mention of Poncier being "ably backed" by Gossard, Ament, and Vedder, after which Vedder says to a dejected Poncier, "A compliment for us is a compliment for you!" Ament lends Dillon several pieces of his clothing to help flesh out the role of Poncier.

Jeff Ament: When we were originally in the movie, we were nobody. The record wasn't even out yet. We were just, like, some guys in a rock band that Cameron knew in Seattle that could play this small part in the movie. I was involved in the art department, and we all helped Matt Dillon prepare for his role. Over the course of that next year before the movie came out, we blew up, and all of a sudden the focus of the movie wasn't so much on this little neighborhood movie in Seattle—it was about this movie that had Pearl Jam in it, and Alice in Chains and Soundgarden and all these Seattle bands. It was probably kind of fucked for Cameron, because all of a sudden it was out of his hands. It became a movie about something else.

Eddie Vedder: If it weren't for *Singles,* I don't know how I'd have felt good about leaving my job back in San Diego. There was some security there, no pun intended. Working with the movie was an adventure. To see all that happening in this town—it was right when I was up here and starting to learn about it, and there was a movie being made about it and bringing all these people together. But also I think I got a thousand dollars for giving Matt Dillon three guitar lessons, and that's kind of what kept me going.

Ed's bank balance

April 16

Temple of the Dog's self-titled debut album is released by A&M Records.

Jeff Ament: We didn't have any real expectations for the first Pearl Jam record. If anything, we felt like doing Temple would help reintroduce us a little bit. Both records were good records, and we were excited to be putting music out. Only a couple months before that, I didn't know if I wanted to play music at all.

May

Epic Records sends the promotional sampler featuring "Alive," "Wash," and "I've Got a Feeling" to members of the Mother Love Bone and Soundgarden mailing lists. Inside is the first Pearl Jam fan newsletter, handwritten by Jeff Ament, which introduces Vedder, Krusen, and McCready as "new guys," and on the

1991

cover of the sampler is the Jeff Ament–drawn "Stickman," soon to be tattooed on thousands of fans across the world.

Jeff Ament: I drew the stickman the night after Kelly Curtis told me that we needed artwork for the giveaway cassette for "Alive." The "art" really just represents how I was feeling at the time, playing in the best band I'd ever been in, and all of us were in such a creative zone. It didn't really have anything to do with the song. That's how we did it in those days: lots of twenty-four-hour deadlines. The band did it all. Good and bad, it was ours.

Michele Anthony: By the time they were signed to Epic, Kelly, Michael, Jeff, Stone, and I already had history and a bond from Mother Love Bone and the experience of Andy's death that created a foundation for trusting and respecting each other. Pearl Jam, from the start, always had a clear vision for who they were musically and who they wanted to be in the world. A big part of my role in their life, even though I was running the larger company with Tommy Mottola, was really to keep everyone out of their way and to listen to their ideas. I thought I could do the greatest service to them by helping them implement their vision.

May 25
RKCNDY, Seattle

Pearl Jam performs at a show to celebrate the end of production on the Cameron Crowe film *Singles.* This is drummer Dave Krusen's last performance with Pearl Jam.

Dave Krusen: I've been a recovering alcoholic now for years. But then, I was a really bad alcoholic. I couldn't quit drinking, which led to other stupid activities. Pearl Jam gave me so many opportunities to get it together, and they were so nice about it and never got on my case or sat me down and confronted me. They gave me every opportunity in the world, and I just couldn't stop. I had so much going on at the time. I had a relationship I was in that was not going well, and I was about to have a baby. I was sticking around to try and quote-unquote do the right thing, which ended up not being the right thing. At the time, I thought I was doing the right thing.

At the RKCNDY show, I ended up

getting so drunk that I got into a big melee at this after-party. I got into an argument with my girlfriend, which led to a fight with some other guy, which led to the police coming, which led to me disappearing for two days in a blackout. Finally, the band getting ahold of me and just going, "You know, you've got to get some help because obviously your drinking is so out of control." I had a really bad attitude about it, and then I finally went, "You know what, you're right. I'm going to go to rehab."

Mike McCready: We tried out Brad Wilk from Rage Against the Machine, who I think was a friend of Eddie's at that time, over in Surrey, England, while we were mixing *Ten* and it was cool, but it didn't mesh. He was a really heavy drummer, as you know from Rage Against the Machine. It just didn't really work out with our situation.

July 4
RKCNDY, Seattle

Pearl Jam returns from mixing its debut album outside London to play a hometown show with new drummer Matt Chamberlain, formerly of Edie Brickell & New Bohemians, who had been recommended by a friend of Epic A&R executive Michael Goldstone. The group then heads out on a six-show tour, including its first gigs in New York.

Matt Chamberlain: They flew me out to Seattle. At the time, I was living in Dallas, where Edie was. I got to Seattle, and I think we rehearsed for about a week. It wasn't very long, because I remember feeling like I had to cram for it. They had this little space in Belltown, right by the Crocodile Cafe. It was in the basement of this blacksmith/metal-working shop—this total dive-y, rock band rehearsal space. Stone and Jeff picked me up at the airport, then we had some food and went straight to the space. There was a little side room down there. This guy comes out, with his hair sticking up, looking like hell. It was Eddie. He was living in the space and had just gotten food poisoning the night before, so he was in horrible shape. They had flown my drums up. I unpacked them and set up, and we basically just jammed on the songs for a week. In the meantime, they took me out to all these really fun places, and we

hung out with all these interesting folks. What a great time to be in Seattle.

We had an Econoline van with a trailer. We drove through the desert, and the AC broke. We stopped a lot so everybody could cool off. Somehow we ended up in Boston, and I think we did drive all the way across the country for that show.

July 12
JC Dobbs, Philadelphia

"State of Love and Trust" is performed for the first time at this show.

Matt Chamberlain: By the second or third song, people were moving closer to the stage. By the end of every gig at any of these places, people would be like, "Fuck yeah!" and be totally into it. Converts. At that time, Eddie took it so seriously. After every show, he'd be drenched, speechless. He wouldn't talk for a while. He was jumping around like a nutcase for an hour. It was a cathartic experience for him at the time. The one thing I remember about him that made me kind of laugh . . . I thought it was so great. He wore a Butthole Surfers T-shirt from the *Locust Abortion Technician* album: the one with the disturbing image of the Ethiopian children. He wore that shirt, and he had these army shorts with a hole in the butt that he would gaffer tape up. And white Doc Martens. He would wash his clothes in the hotel room. Everybody was broke. I had to loan Stone twenty bucks at one point because he didn't have enough money for lunch.

July 13
The Marquee, New York

Pearl Jam's first show in New York is played before a music industry–heavy crowd in town for the New Music Seminar. Four nights later, the group plays the legendary Lower Manhattan venue the Wetlands Preserve, with Motörhead front man Lemmy Kilmister among the audience members.

July 21
Cabaret Metro, Chicago

Pearl Jam opens a six-band bill alongside Naked Raygun, Urge Overkill,

Ned's Atomic Dustbin, the Jayhawks, and Soul Asylum, celebrating this famed Chicago club's ninth birthday.

Matt Chamberlain: In Chicago, nobody knew who the fuck Pearl Jam was. We soundchecked, and the doors opened immediately afterward. We were first on a bill of several other much more established bands. I remember watching Urge Overkill; they were killing it.

August 3
RKCNDY, Seattle

The day after "Alive" is released as a single in the United States, Pearl Jam returns to RKCNDY to shoot a black-and-white video for the song during a show. Josh Taft, a longtime friend of Stone Gossard's, serves as the director; the band insists on recording the audio live rather than miming to a prerecorded track, which was unheard of on MTV at the time. The clip captures the unbridled energy of the band's early gigs, with fans stage diving throughout and Eddie Vedder hanging upside down from part of the lighting rig. A mini–Temple of the Dog reunion takes place later in the show, with Chris Cornell singing on "Reach Down" and "Pushin Forward Back." The "Alive" video is eventually released in September.

Jeff Ament: We were seeing our friends make videos, like Soundgarden and Alice in Chains, and it seemed absolutely ridiculous to be spending so much money. One video could be as much as an entire recording budget. We went to Josh and said, "We don't want to spend more than twenty thousand dollars," and he said he could do it. The lighting budget was minuscule, and it was probably a three- or four-camera shoot. And we wanted the music to be live, so it was a little bit more representative of what it was like to be at one of our shows. Lip-synced videos had run their course, from our perspective. That way, if it failed, we didn't break the bank on it, and the record company wouldn't drop us for blowing three-quarters of a million dollars on two videos.

Matt Cameron: It was intended to be a video shoot, although they did film the entire show just in case. It was so bizarre. In Seattle, they had a huge local following, from years of the band members playing in town. RKCNDY also wasn't that big, and it was packed with all the locals, drunk and partying and jumping on each other.

Dave Grohl: I moved to the area in 1990, so I missed Green River, Mother Love Bone, and a lot of the legendary Seattle bands before the city blew up. But I remember the first time I heard Pearl Jam. I was living in West Seattle and got in my van to drive down to the 7-Eleven, and I heard "Alive" on the radio. It was funny, because before I knew who it was, or anything about the band, I just pictured these really big, fat, hairy dudes. That's the first thing that came to mind. I imagined that they looked like Poison Idea or Canned Heat or something: this band of big, hairy dudes. I don't know why. Maybe because it sounded like classic rock 'n' roll to me. It didn't sound punk rock to me; it sounded like a rock 'n' roll band. That was just before *Nevermind* came out. And it was just before everything blew up.

August 15

Drummer Matt Chamberlain opts to not continue touring with Pearl Jam. Earlier in the month, before his decision was final, he suggests as a potential replacement another drummer he was familiar with from Dallas, Dave Abbruzzese, who flies up to Seattle to check out Pearl Jam in time to see the "Alive" video shoot at RKCNDY. When Chamberlain confirms he is leaving the band, Abbruzzese quickly returns to Seattle and is hired to join Pearl Jam. Shortly thereafter, Chamberlain joins the house band on NBC's *Saturday Night Live*.

Matt Chamberlain: The deal was, they wanted me to jump on board with them and tour the entire album cycle. I literally had just gotten off the road and gotten out of a band situation. I didn't have anything to do with Pearl Jam. I was just there to help out. I didn't even know these guys. And then they basically asked me to uproot everything in my life and join their band that was in a van, still. Basically, I just had no connection to them on a personal level or musically. It could have been any drummer—they just needed one. Had I known it was going to generate millions and millions of dollars, maybe I'd have given it a second thought. But I think I made the right decision. It just wasn't my thing. They were on a mission, but I was just there to help out for a second. I was just an innocent bystander.

They were asking for drummers. I thought I could help them out. They didn't know of anybody that would fit the bill, or they would have called that person. I knew this guy in Dallas. I remembered seeing him play around town in a band—kind of like a funk-rock thing, as a lot of people were doing back then. I thought, "Wow. This guy has this John Bonham thing going on, but also this great feel." It made an impression on me. I didn't really know him that well, from this small Dallas club scene, but for some reason he popped into my head when Stone asked. They never had a cattle call audition because they were so desperate. They just needed someone who was available and willing to move up there. Luckily, Dave was way into it. They flew him up. My drums were still there after the "Alive" video, and he actually kept using them for a while because it was expensive to get equipment up there. Luckily, he worked out. I don't think they even auditioned anybody else. They sent him a tape, and he said, "This is the shit! I love it!" He lost his mind, and he got the tattoo on his arm of the little stickman. I was like, "Excellent! I hooked somebody up."

August 19
RKCNDY, Seattle

Pearl Jam celebrates the impending release of its debut Epic album, *Ten*, with another RKCNDY show, Matt Chamberlain's last with Pearl Jam.

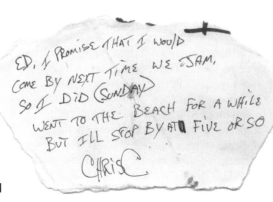

ED, I PROMISE THAT I WOULD COME BY NEXT TIME WE JAM, SO I DID (SUNDAY) WENT TO THE BEACH FOR A WHILE BUT ILL STOP BY AT FIVE OR SO
CHRIS

1991

August 23
Mural Amphitheatre, Seattle

Pearl Jam concludes the 1991 schedule for the Sounds of Seattle concert series at this outdoor show in front of approximately four thousand fans, marking the debut of new drummer Dave Abbruzzese.

August 27

Ten is released. In its first week, the album ships fewer than twenty-five thousand copies in the United States, not even close to enough to appear on the *Billboard* 200 album chart. *Ten* does not make that chart until the first week of January 1992, when it creeps on at no. 155.

Kelly Curtis: The thing I remember the most is that with this kind of music, there wasn't really a radio format for it. No one knew what to do with it. There were people at Epic, like Michele Anthony and Harvey Leeds, that championed this new style. But they couldn't get any radio interested in it. Goldstone was pretty relentless in keeping it alive, too. At the time, Nirvana was out, and huge. It took a while for us. The biggest hurdle was radio. Was it alternative? Was it rock? What was it? It took them actually getting people out to a show and sticking with it for months. That came from the top at Sony. In most cases, a band would have a two- or three-month window, and you'd be done. But they stuck with it for six or seven months. I think that came from Michele and her relationship with Michael. They kept hammering away and

getting people to come see the band. Then things started happening station by station, and you could feel a groundswell beginning.

Michele Anthony: In 1991, "alternative" was Natalie Merchant and Depeche Mode. It wasn't what we think of alternative radio now. Pearl Jam didn't easily fit into the alternative format. Guns N' Roses was the bridge between the hair bands and the music that would come later out of Seattle. It seems incredible now to hear Pearl Jam and Nirvana as not fitting in a rock format, but a lot of those stations were still playing Warrant and classic rock. We were literally caught between formats for a good nine months. The way out of that was to make people believe. How do you do that? Make them see a show.

October 3
Concrete Foundations Forum, Los Angeles

Members of Pearl Jam join Soundgarden's Chris Cornell and Matt Cameron for an impromptu performance of Temple of the Dog's "Hunger Strike" at this annual hard rock convention.

October 4

Pearl Jam films a video for "Jeremy" with director Chris Cuffaro at a Los Angeles warehouse. A teenage actor plays the part of the real Jeremy Wade Delle, a sixteen-year-old Texas high school student whose classroom suicide inspired the song. Because "Jeremy" is not a single at the time, Epic declines to pay for the video, and it is eventually shelved. To date, it has been released only on Cuffaro's website.

Jeff Ament: We loved Chris. We shot photos with him at least a couple of times. This may have been the first video he ever did. It was a heavy collaboration with him. It was shot in very high-contrast black and white and was a little bit more of a big shoot; we were in a soundstage with tons of people around. I remember not being totally unhappy with that video. A lot of the reason behind it not coming out was driven by the record company. They thought if we made a proper video for "Jeremy," it could reach

a lot of people, and they were obviously right.

October 6
Hollywood Palladium, Hollywood, California

Pearl Jam performs alongside Spinal Tap, Alice in Chains, and Soundgarden at *RIP* magazine's fifth anniversary party, with Vedder noting that it will be "a year ago tomorrow" since he first met his bandmates. Another Temple of the Dog miniset occurs at the end of the show for the songs "Hunger Strike," "Reach Down," and "Pushin' Forward Back."

October 16
Oscar Mayer Theatre, Madison, Wisconsin

Pearl Jam begins a two-month North American tour supporting Smashing Pumpkins and the Red Hot Chili Peppers. An appreciative Eddie Vedder tells *ROX* magazine, "I'm proud the Chili Peppers have taken two new bands out instead of someone who would guarantee more ticket sales. It's a great opportunity for us and it's good for the crowds. It's a good mix of styles, very Neapolitan, three distinct flavors, something for everyone. I'm the luckiest Chili Peppers fan in the world."

Jeff Ament: I remember being out on a van tour when somebody told us the Chili Peppers wanted us to tour with them. It couldn't have been a better thing to happen for us at that time. We knew we'd be opening. We only got thirty minutes, so we knew right off the bat that we had a lot of catching up to do. I'd go out to the bus before the show, bring my bass out, and play superhard. I almost got a sweat before we went onstage. Ed was in there a lot singing in the front while I was in the back. We sort of felt like, if we don't bring it, we could get booted off this tour a week or two in. We went a bit crazy trying to make sure that didn't happen.

Michael Goldstone: To me, it all seemed to come together around the tour they did with the Pumpkins. Things had built slowly to that point, but the gigs started to become legendary. The Limelight and Wetlands gigs were when the East Coast

lulaz
Ampitheatre

press began to get on board. Through touring, the word of mouth was really spreading.

October 26
Normandy High School, Parma, Ohio

Before its evening gig at the Cleveland Music Hall, Pearl Jam plays local radio personalities in a game of basketball, portions of which are broadcast on TV. Vedder and Ament get their picture taken with Cleveland Cavaliers fan favorite and then announcer Jim Chones.

November 8
CBGB, New York

Pearl Jam plays a surprise show at this legendary New York rock venue primarily for fan club members and members of the media. "Black" is played as an unusual opener by request.

Stone Gossard: Green River played there in 1985 in front of, like, ten people, all workers. I remember the bartenders liked us.

November 9
Tower Records, Rockville, Maryland

Pearl Jam plays a five-song, thirty-minute acoustic set at a local record store in the afternoon before its show on the American University campus in Washington, DC. At the latter, "Leash" is performed for the first time.

November 12
Madison Square Garden, New York

Jeff Ament attends a New York Knicks home game against the New Jersey Nets, for whom Mookie Blaylock is playing. Afterward, "he was walking down the corridor at the end of the game, and I, like, reached over and yelled his name and handed him a shirt. He looked at me really puzzled. I don't know what he thinks of it all." Ament later sends Blaylock a gold record, and he returns the favor with a pair of tennis shoes spray-painted gold. The pair also play a couple of games of H-O-R-S-E, which Blaylock wins handily.

November 14
Tower Records, Yonkers, New York

Another in-store acoustic performance of five songs. During "Alive," Vedder changes the lyrics to joke about the ravages of playing seven shows in seven days: "'Is something wrong?' she said / 'Of course there is / I have no voice,' he said." A few hours later, Pearl Jam plays "Alive" and "Porch" at a second acoustic in-store at CD World in Menlo Park, New Jersey, with Dave Abbruzzese drumming on his own legs.

December

Rolling Stone asks Vedder to contribute a letter for its Year In Review issue. He writes, "Finally, music gets to the point. Ian sings, 'We are all here . . .' Perry sings, 'These are the days . . .' Cornell sings, 'The wreck is going down,' and he's right. Wake up, or die in your sleep."

December 10
City Coliseum, Austin, Texas

Vedder continues to hone his climbing antics at his own peril.

Eddie Vedder: I saw these girders, these beams at the top of the ceiling, and I just had to climb up there. When the security guards tried to grab me, I said, "I'm in the band and I can do what I want," and I went. It was stupid, but when you can climb the barriers and get to the rooftop, it's a beautiful thing."

December 11
Trees, Dallas

After opening for the Smashing Pumpkins and Red Hot Chili Peppers at the Bronco Bowl, Pearl Jam plays its own headlining set at another club across town. Vedder relates the true story that inspired "Jeremy," which occurred in nearby Richardson, and mock apologizes to local band Dr. Tongue for having stolen Dave Abbruzzese from them.

December 15
Club DV8, Salt Lake City

Jeff Ament injures his ankle after jumping onstage during this show.

Jeff Ament: It was the one show after the first leg of the Chilis tour on our way home for ten days off for Christmas before we finished up the West Coast with the Chilis and Nirvana. I severely tore ligaments and was laid up the entire break, and hobbled around most of the tour after Christmas.

Eric Johnson: That was about the third trip to the emergency room on this tour. He was jumping around, and I swear you could hear his ankle pop over the music.

Christmas

Pearl Jam releases its first fan-club-only seven-inch vinyl single with two new tracks, "Let Me Sleep (It's Christmas Time)" and "Ramblings."

Jeff Ament: Initially, we had the idea of the fan club in Mother Love Bone, and it was probably one hundred or two hundred people. I'd handwritten letters or postcards back to most of those people. With the single, Kelly Curtis had a handful of the Beatles fan club singles, and he remembered getting those when he was a kid. I thought that was a really cool thing. The idea with the first couple with "Ramblings" was to do a fucked-up, demented version of the Beatles' greetings on the B-sides of the singles. Then it got to a point where with "Ramblings," nobody really took that to the next level. There was no clear vision of what it was going to be. We thought maybe we should put a proper song or a more experimental song on the second side.

December 27
Los Angeles Memorial Sports Arena, Los Angeles

The first of four shows with Nirvana subbing in for Smashing Pumpkins on the Red Hot Chili Peppers tour. Pearl Jam had snagged the slot after Soundgarden turned it down to tour with

Guns N' Roses instead. With Pearl Jam first on the bill, Vedder is intent upon making an impression on the audience, and runs from the stage to the back of arena and then back to the stage, but not before tripping on a row of seats and doing his best to appear unharmed.

Jeff Ament: At some of the early shows that fall, like in Madison, Wisconsin, there were only a couple hundred people in the theaters. But within a couple weeks, they were more and more full. By the end, when we did the West Coast run with Nirvana, the places were packed when we went on. It changed in a pretty short period of time.

Dave Grohl: I heard "Alive," and I realized it was that band, like, "Oh! It's *that* band." I walked out, and Eddie was up in the fucking rafters somewhere. I knew then that they were going to be fucking huge. It's a funny time to try to make sense of, because everybody's band seemed to be going from running out of gas in your van on the highway to selling out twenty-thousand-capacity arenas. But there was something about the connection they had with the audience, whether it was musical or lyrical or the energy that was going back and forth. It was undeniable. It was only a matter of time.

December 28
Del Mar Pavilion, San Diego

Vedder ups the ante with his stage acrobatics and gets himself into a nearly insurmountable jam during a climb into the rafters in the midst of "Porch."

Eddie Vedder: Sometimes, I'd get to the part where I might start climbing the walls, and in that case, the only thing to climb just happened to be one hundred feet high. [*Laughs*] I thought, Well, that seems a little intense, but it's really all I've got to work with, so let's see what happens here. There was an I-beam I could wrap my hands around, but then I got to the top and went to put myself hanging upside down by fingers and feet, and it was like an

H-beam. Literally, what I was hanging on to was just past my first knuckle. It was muddy and wet with the steam coming off the crowd. Luckily, I weighed only about one hundred twenty pounds at the time. I was really working against gravity. I think I had a good fifty feet to go until I could hit another chain that the lights were hanging off of. I knew I had family in the audience, and I couldn't die in front of my brothers. I think I scaled down to the light rig, got a mike cord, swung down that back to the stage, and when the song was over, I went to the side and came really close to vomiting. That was one where I thought, That got pretty fuckin' stupid. But I was channeling something different. I got to that place you hear about where the mom lifts the car off the two-year-old kid. It was that kind of adventure.

At that point in life and having at long last the opportunity to play for bigger crowds, I really and truly felt like I had nothing to lose. No thoughts of what may be waiting in my future. It was all about the *now*. And that was part and parcel with whatever message the group and I had to impart to the audience at that instance. Risking your hide to evoke that emotion became part of the program. Usually instantaneous, but on good nights, I kind of figured it was going to go that route. I wasn't going to forget those nights of our band firing, and I suppose I didn't want the crowd to forget, either.

Mike McCready: He went hundreds of feet in the air, and he's in the middle of the audience. It was kind of like, "Okay, he's doing it again," because he did that all over the place. But he really went far that time. I'd seen him do that a whole bunch of times, and it made me nervous every time he did it, like, he's gonna die. At least he didn't kill himself.

Eric Johnson: That was easily the scariest thing I've ever seen at a concert. You could see the condensation on the beam and Eddie's fingers sliding. I was right under him the whole time. I thought maybe I could try to break his fall, but that's about it. I think Eddie really wanted to put himself out there. He'd give everything for a show, almost like he was playing for a championship every night. He'd always go into the crowd during "Porch," and I began to hate that song because of it. It would give me an ulcer.

December 31
Cow Palace, Daly City, California

Pearl Jam's whirlwind first year of existence concludes with a New Year's Eve show alongside Nirvana and the Red Hot Chili Peppers. The group roars through its thirty-minute set, with Vedder clearly moved by the moment: "If I wasn't in this band," he declares, "I would still make sure I was here tonight." Before "Porch," someone begins playing the riff from Nirvana's "Smells Like Teen Spirit." "Just remember, we played it first," Stone Gossard jokes.

Jeff Ament: I sort of felt like they were the biggest shows of our lives at that point. We were up there with Nirvana, and there was a competitiveness and a little bit of tension between us at that point. Nirvana bassist Krist Novoselic came out and told us there was a community jukebox between the backstage trailers, and he got upset that we were playing Crosby, Stills, Nash & Young songs and Beatles songs. So he put a sign on the jukebox telling us what we couldn't play. I was just, like, ready to fuckin' tangle with him. Like, "Great! Perfect. Bring it on." We promptly loaded the thing up with everything he said we couldn't play, so he'd come over and bump the jukebox during our songs. Eventually it just got unplugged.

Mike McCready: We were on the tour bus after the show, and we heard that *Nevermind* was going to knock Michael Jackson off the top of the charts. I remember a friend of mine jumping on our bus looking for Kurt to congratulate him, without realizing she was in the wrong place. There was such a groundswell of kids going crazy when we were playing, and everything was blowing up. I felt we were good enough to achieve all the things Nirvana had, too.

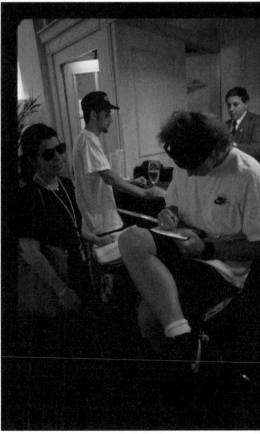

1991

Ten

It all started out so innocently that day in Los Angeles in September 1990, when Jack Irons handed his friend Eddie Vedder a tape featuring five instrumentals by a Seattle band so new that it had no drummer or vocalist, much less a name. "I can't join them," Irons told Vedder, "but they're looking for a singer. Let me know what you think."

About a month later, Vedder was in Seattle jamming with Stone Gossard, Jeff Ament, Mike McCready, and Dave Krusen on the songs that would make up *Ten,* one of the most popular albums of the late twentieth century and a watershed moment for the musical revolution that came to be known as grunge. Alongside Nirvana's similarly iconoclastic *Nevermind, Ten* sold more than thirteen million copies, ushered in a new era of previously unfathomable commercial success for alternative rock, and turned the group we now know as Pearl Jam into a worldwide phenomenon.

The three songs Vedder overdubbed onto that cassette back in San Diego and sent back to Seattle became the thematically linked Momma-Son trilogy of "Alive," "Once," and "Footsteps." Upon his arrival in the Pacific Northwest, the band beat those tunes into more fully realized versions. It also began crafting the foundations for future *Ten* tracks "Even Flow," "Release," and "Oceans," as well as songs like "Breath" and "Yellow Ledbetter," which didn't make the cut for the debut album but would figure prominently in Pearl Jam's career at a later date.

"We would spend four or five hours working, get something to eat, and then another four or five hours working," says Ament of the pace of the first rehearsal sessions. "It was the first time any of us had felt so strongly about creating music

as a band. We loved the songs we were making together and could sense its potential."

"It all just fell together," Vedder says. "No one really compromised toward each other at all. It was kind of a phenomenon, in a way. We'd all played music for at least six, seven, eight years and been in different bands, and we were feeling something that we'd never really felt before, with the honesty and the way it was all coming out."

"Black," which evolved from a Gossard demo titled "E Ballad," confirmed everybody's instincts that the quintet was onto something special: music through which they could channel their wildest, deepest dreams and darkest thoughts. On "Black," the narrator attempts to pick up the pieces of a broken relationship, at first in an almost lighthearted, observational style, but his thoughts become heavier and more emotional as the song crests to a gripping finish: "I know someday you'll have a beautiful life / I know you'll be a star / In somebody else's sky / But why can't it be mine?"

That sentiment later struck an immediate chord with teenagers experiencing their first brushes with love, breaking up, and adult emotions. "It's about first relationships," Vedder says. "The song is about letting go. It's very rare for a relationship to withstand the Earth's gravitational pull and where it's going to take people and how they're going to grow. I've heard it said that you can't really have a true love unless it was a love unrequited. It's a harsh one, because then your truest one is the one you can't have forever."

Vedder plunged even further into the formative experiences of his life on "Release." Hearing Gossard noodling around with a droning riff and his

bandmates beginning to craft a song around it, he walked to the microphone and poured forth with raw emotion about the father he never knew: "I'll wait up in the dark for you to speak to me / I'll open up / Release me."

"They started playing it, and I just started singing it," Vedder says of "Release," which was nearly ten minutes long at first. "And then afterward, it got me all tore up. And I went in the little hallway, and then Jeff came out and said, you know, 'You okay?' And I was having a bit of a moment. Most of the words were done on the first take. I went back to the hotel, sat at the windowsill, and got the rest. I realized, we all got together in that room, and I was still thinking of stuff with my dad and loss. And they're thinking about the situation with Andy and everything. We were strangers, but we were coming from a similar place, and all that kind of came out in the first batch of songs."

The dreamy "Oceans" came to life after Vedder left the band's rehearsal space to feed a parking meter but got locked out in the process. As if it were a scene out of a movie, it started to rain. Trapped outside, Vedder could hear Ament's bass line permeating the concrete basement. He just happened to have paper and pen on hand to jot down some words inspired by his love of surfing. "This is why the vocal melody matches the bass exactly," Vedder explains. "It was all I could hear."

And while "Black" and "Release" were pure Vedder autobiography, "Alive" was one of the singer's first attempts to craft a new story based around actual events, in this case the nearly decade-old revelation that the man he thought was his biological father was not. The anthemic chorus ("I'm still alive!") belied the reality that Vedder had actually met his father on several occasions but knew him only as a family friend, and that the man had died of multiple sclerosis in 1981, before Vedder had a chance to see him again.

"It was a work of fiction based on reality," Vedder says of "Alive." "In some ways, that was a way to get it out. By no means was it a nonfiction story. It was just certain ways that I felt. Who knows why it came out at that time? I have no clue or remembrance."

Following his second weeklong stint in Seattle, during which the band recorded more than a dozen songs and ideas and played its first show under the name Mookie Blaylock, Vedder had to go back to San Diego to tie up loose ends before moving up north for good. Once he returned, the band wrote another half dozen new songs as strong as the material that had already been put to tape.

"As fast as we were working on those first songs, new songs were cropping up," remembers Krusen, who had joined forces with Gossard, McCready, and Ament only a few weeks earlier and was still very much getting to know them. "It was the fastest, most creative thing I've ever been a part of. It was so quick, and ideas were flowing so fast. I just remember Eddie had papers laying all over the place and was constantly scratching down lyric ideas. Stone and Jeff had a lot of really good drum ideas. It wasn't frantic, like, 'We've got to get this done in a hurry.' And it didn't freak me out in the sense that I was like, 'Oh my God, this is the best band ever.' I was more taken aback by the whole thing. It was really amazing."

Because he was given a minimum of direct feedback during rehearsals, Vedder was initially unsure if Ament and Gossard were happy with what he was contributing. "A song would end, and they'd talk to Dave: 'Well, it needs to shift here, or get to this part quicker. Want to try it again?' The next time, they'd say, 'Dave, lay off the hi-hat.' It was all about the rhythms and the groove," he says. "Finally, they'd be finished, and I'd go, 'Real quick, am I doing all right?' And they'd say, 'Yeah, yeah, you're fine.' 'Okay! I'll just keep going.' I did bring my guitar, but I don't think I ever played it [laughs]."

For Gossard and Ament, the sessions were quickly proving that despite whatever personal differences remained between them from their time together in Green River and Mother Love Bone, they'd stumbled onto something that seemed powerful enough to transcend it all.

"At that time, Jeff and I had played in a lot of bands together and had gone through the roughest of times together," Gossard says. "We had a real fruitful relationship in terms of, everything we did kept succeeding on a certain level beyond our skill. But Jeff and I have always had this adversarial relationship. I have nothing but gratitude about it now, because we just laugh at each other and go, 'Thank God we worked it out.' But we generally are juxtaposed about any particular issue. If I'm not being a contrarian, he is. It's all been muted now because what we probably thought of as our new band that we might try to control together immediately was taken over by Ed. So we both learned the greatest lesson of all, which was, just as you're fighting over the scraps of control, you meet somebody with so much mojo and charisma and artistic energy that your argument becomes pointless. There was some great irony there."

During Vedder's second trip to Seattle, he and Ament were responsible for two pieces that illustrated the musical versatility of the new project. "Deep," one of the earliest examples of the band's ability to craft heavy-duty rock 'n' roll that also had great grooves, was inspired by a story Ament told Vedder about walking down a Seattle street with a beautiful view of the city, only to look up at an abandoned apartment building and see a man shooting heroin. "I think about why people need those other things in their lives to keep them happy or keep them going," says Vedder. "I guess I was kind of addressing that in the song."

As the band accumulated more and more material, Vedder started making a habit of staying behind at the rehearsal space after everyone else had left for the night to "make noise" and record vocals. "The one night Jeff stayed back with me, we made a bunch of noise and got into this ambient groove" that the musicians dubbed "Master/Slave." One portion of the ominous-sounding piece was chosen to open the album, while a second, longer section was added to the end of "Release." Says Vedder, "That's a good thing to go to sleep with. After you've listened to the record, it kind of lulls you."

Originally written on acoustic guitar and then transposed for twelve-string bass, Ament's "Jeremy" and "Why Go" added two more multifaceted rock songs to the mix and provided additional showcases for Vedder's deeply affecting narratives.

Ament says, "Ed had been reading a newspaper when we were starting to jam on 'Jeremy' and basically wrote the entire lyrics off of one article" about a Texas teenager who'd committed suicide in his high school classroom on January 8, 1991.

"It ended up being this superheavy, heavy lyric. I still didn't really understand songwriting at that point. Pretty much that whole song is in A—there's not really any major chord changes. It sort of goes against the rules of how to write a pop song. A lot of it was the emotion that was coming off of Ed."

On "Why Go," inspired by a young friend of Vedder's who'd been committed to a psychiatric facility after being caught smoking pot, the singer lashed out at selfish parents who weren't willing to weather the difficulties associated with raising a family. "The adolescent gets put there because his or her parents were told by a psychotherapist that they needed to be there," he says. "At that point, the kid fully rebels and freaks out. It came out in the song: Why go home to this person who put you in here? After months or even years, the insurance would run out, and they'd say, 'Yep, she's fine. She can go home now.'"

Written during one of his solitary stints late at night in the rehearsal space, "Porch" became Vedder's only individual songwriting credit on Ten. Although only three and a half minutes on record, the song quickly blossomed into one of the band's best concert jams, often reaching ten minutes in that setting despite being played significantly faster than its studio version.

"There are times in your life when everything seems poetic," Vedder says of the song. "Sometimes, everything you see drives you to explore further thought, or at least write it down. There are songs everywhere asking to be written. At that time, things like 'Porch' just seemed to come out. My cells were vibrating."

Shortly after finalizing a deal at Epic Records, Pearl Jam hit London Bridge Studios in Seattle in late March 1991 to record *Ten* with producer Rick Parashar, who'd also worked on the *Temple of the Dog* album. It's somewhat amazing to consider that the band had been together for only five months and played about twenty shows by then. But Pearl Jam knew exactly what it wanted to accomplish at this point in the process, from the diversity of the material to how the budget was going to be allotted.

"We were all in agreement that we wanted the record to be as diverse as it could possibly be," Ament says. "That's why we fought so hard about having 'Oceans' and 'Release' and 'Master/Slave.' We didn't want to be pigeonholed. At that time, things seemed really clear to me on what we were doing and where we were headed with it. I don't think I've felt that clarity since. We didn't want to waste a lot of time, and everybody was kind of in that same zone. The only thing in our lives at that point was making that record."

Ament and Gossard were particularly intent on not making the same mistakes they felt they made during the early days of Mother Love Bone's tenure on PolyGram. "I think especially early on, you're really trying to hold on to what the identity is. That was the good thing of going through what we went through with Mother Love Bone," Ament says. "I mean, because we were so new to the major-label world, we kind of gave in a lot of times to how they wanted things done. We spent a lot of money on stupid things, and we spent way too much money making the Mother Love Bone record."

To be sure, the band told Goldstone it would absolutely not spend "two or three hundred thousand dollars" making *Ten.* Instead Ament recalls drawing the line at $75,000 and insisting upon using the rest of the advance to buy good instruments, a good PA, and to pay rent on Pearl Jam's rehearsal space—"things that were going to allow us to be a better band. The fact that we got this second chance, which is incredible anyway, that we hooked up with Ed and kind of immediately wrote some songs that we thought were really good, and people were interested in it, we just weren't going to fuck up again. We

weren't going to let a second chance get away."

Once Pearl Jam was comfortably ensconced in the studio, things moved fast and smooth, with a few exceptions. Band members claim that "Even Flow" was attempted anywhere from fifty to one hundred different times, mainly owing to tempo irregularities and Krusen's inability to get comfortable on his drum stool. "They had to edit the middle because I was speeding up at the end. It was just a nightmare," he says.

"Alive" was also a trouble spot, simply because the band was already in possession of a killer version of the song from its demo session with Parashar in late January. Ultimately, that version is what wound up on *Ten.* Says Krusen, "We'd captured that song at that moment, and it was really good."

In early June, Pearl Jam traveled twenty-five miles south of London to Dorking, England, to mix *Ten* at Ridge Farm Studios with Tim Palmer, who had also mixed Mother Love Bone's *Apple.* Abroad for the first time in his life, Vedder was enchanted by the rustic atmosphere and found himself wandering the grounds in the middle of the night, unable to sleep. Vedder did miss home, however. His inner basketball freak got the better of him, so he arranged for VHS tapes of the ongoing NBA finals between the Chicago Bulls and Los Angeles Lakers to be express mailed to him—only to find that they wouldn't play on the UK's PAL system.

Looking back, Vedder says *Ten* still sounds as distinct to him as it did while Pearl Jam was making it. "It was music I'd never really heard before," he says. "It wasn't so much 'grunge rock' as it was 'groove rock.' That early Jeff and Stone songwriting period is really about the groove. It was guitars and guitar pedals, but it had this thing about it that I hadn't really heard before. It wasn't Jane's Addiction or the Cult or the Chili Peppers or U2 or Sonic Youth. It was this different thing. To have this new framework with its own identity was really exciting. It felt like it was our own."

"Pretty much my whole musical career, I'd been in bands with incredibly imaginative lyricists," Ament says. "But Ed was the first lyricist that I felt like I really related to on a gut level. I just felt like I could really relate to what he was singing about, and how. I felt a real

camaraderie with him that I'd really never felt since the first band I was in. He was somebody I trusted wholeheartedly. It almost didn't seem real at the time. I was so excited to play with him.

"With things like 'Black' and 'Release,' I don't think he'd ever put those feelings into words before, and we certainly hadn't been involved in anything that had put those sorts of things into words. We were feeling the same things—coming to grips with death, loss, loneliness, and all that stuff, and really starting to understand it. Everybody was pretty raw at that point. Luckily, Stone had been picking up his guitar and channeling that hurt into songs."

1992

Pearl Jam wasn't quite a household name in 1992, but one would certainly have been hard pressed to find an American teenager who didn't own *Ten,* much less know every word to "Jeremy," "Alive," "Black," or "Even Flow." With its music becoming omnipresent, the band began to use its notoriety to further causes it held dear, from voter registration to abortion rights, and even put together a free hometown show in Seattle to give back to the community that embraced it so warmly. Indeed, Pearl Jam found itself standing strong amid a group of bands for whom rock 'n' roll meant much more than merely commercial success. But alternative rock was also an increasingly valuable commodity, and Pearl Jam was about to experience just how far people were willing to go to claim their own piece.

January 2
Salem Armory Auditorium, Salem, Oregon

Pearl Jam completes its run on tour with Nirvana and the Red Hot Chili Peppers. The trek was to conclude the following day in Seattle but was canceled due to both Kurt Cobain and Anthony Kiedis being ill. Instead Pearl Jam plays a club show that evening at Seattle's RKCNDY.

January 4

Sandwiched between Jon Bon Jovi's cover of Elton John's "Levon" and Van Morrison's "Why Must I Always Explain?" "Alive" debuts at no. 45 on *Billboard*'s Mainstream Rock chart, where it eventually spends twenty-five weeks before peaking at no. 16.

Bruce Springsteen: The first songs I heard of Pearl Jam's, I believe, were "Alive" and then "Jeremy." The thing that struck me most was Eddie had an unusual voice for hard rock music. It contained within it a folklike tremolo that was unique in that form. I always thought that tremolo created an intimacy in the midst of what could be a violent sound that reached your heart. I knew coming out of the alternative scene was going to make the road they found themselves on a difficult and conflicting journey. The paradox of wanting to speak so personally and then suddenly have so many who want to listen throws you back on yourself. It's just the way it is. But every young artist has to draw their lines at a place they're both comfortable in giving and protecting their heart. I knew from that tremolo and the power of their band that Eddie and Pearl Jam were

going to find themselves smack dab in the middle of it all.

January 17
Moore Theatre, Seattle

With Vedder bitterly complaining about the "movie lights" throughout, Pearl Jam's show at the hometown Moore Theatre is filmed once again by Josh Taft, with footage eventually used for the "Even Flow" video. In it, Vedder climbs to the venue's balcony during the guitar solo break and famously leaps backward into the outstretched arms of the audience. Due to a technical glitch during the show that rendered the live audio unusable, the audio track for the clip is a rerecorded studio version of "Even Flow" with Dave Abbruzzese on drums that was tracked the previous fall, as opposed to the *Ten* version. At this show, the band also for the first time covers the Who's "Baba O'Riley," which eventually becomes one of its most powerful show closers.

Eddie Vedder: I remember thinking that other bands could play "Baba" that I'd been in, like little shit bands, and there's no way you could even come close. So maybe once I get around some good musicians, I thought, "Well, maybe I'll bring this idea up again." I just wanted to hear it live. Somehow I got onto the idea that Mike McCready could play the synthesizer part on his guitar. And then it was on.

January 24
Hollywood Palladium, Hollywood, California

Pearl Jam performs alongside Fugazi, L7, Lunachicks, and Torture Chorus at

a Kim Gordon–emceed benefit for Rock for Choice, which L7's members founded the previous year to raise awareness of abortion rights. Eddie Vedder had recently become enthralled with Fugazi's striking punk-powered hardcore sound, as well as the band's staunchly antimainstream bent and insistence on charging only five dollars for its always all-ages shows. At the show, he meets Fugazi's members for the first time and forms a quick and long-lasting bond with singer-guitarist Ian MacKaye, even accompanying him for a late-night meal at Denny's afterward.

Ian MacKaye: There was a lot of excitement about them, which, to me, was coming out of nowhere. I didn't know them at all. They wanted to bring in special lights, like a follow spot. Fugazi's lighting show is pretty much white light. For years, we had these two halogen work lamps. I'm surprised people didn't sue us for blinding them. Anyway, I remember Eddie jumping into the crowd and being carried all the way to the back of the room and back again, with a spotlight following him the whole time. I think the promotion people were like, "Let's accentuate that! That's the energy we need to go with!"

When Eddie and I spend time together, it's just easy. We just fall into it. We don't really stay in touch. We don't check in with each other. But the friendship is a kind of to-be-continued thing. You pick up where you left off. He's a deep guy. He's so supersensitive and supertalented. Every time I see him, something else gets revealed. He sent me a note in calligraphy, and I was like, "Where'd that come from?" It made me feel like an artless fool! We even went out paddleboarding on the Potomac River. Can you imagine? That was hilarious! I also brought him to play softball, and he was a ringer. He made me feel like a clumsy oaf.

January 31

Pearl Jam shoots footage in Los Angeles intended for a video of "Even Flow" with director Rocky Schenck, but the band is dissatisfied with the outcome, and none of the material is ever released. Instead the performances filmed earlier in the month in Seattle by Josh Taft comprise what eventually becomes the official "Even Flow" video.

PENSACOLA
w/ DONITA SPARKS,
DEE PLAKAS &
HER HUSBAND KIRK

ROCK FOR CHOICE PRESENTS
CONCERT TO MARK THE ONE YEAR ANNIVERSARY OF THE MURDER OF DR. DAVID GUNN

PEARL JAM · L7
FOLLOW FOR NOW

ROCK FOR CHOICE

WED. MAR. 9 · PENSACOLA CIVIC CENTER
PENSACOLA, FLORIDA

THE RIGHT TO HAVE SAFE, LEGAL
OUR FREEDOM
ER! WE WON'T GO BACK
TY FOUNDATION. AND FUND.

K BUSH IN '92

Pearl Jam &
U.S. tour 1992

Pearl Jam
U.S. tour 92

Pearl Jam
U.S. tour 1992

this one

this one (for back of each best shirt

music for rhinos
music for rhinos
music for rhinos

---

13 MAERZ '92 12:46 SONY MUSIC FRANKFURT   49 69 1305216 P.2

.305216 P.1

43999 - Holidex: UTR NL

① ALIVE SHIRT · SET LIST BACK — all the same except doing white stickman in a flesh tone   (BLACK - t-shirt)

② CARTOON · new tour dates BACK (included here) switch colors around on front, on our clothes, hats, etc.   (WHITE - t-shirt)

SHIRT — drop white border around [PEARL JAM] filling with grey or white

back   (BLACK - T-shirt)

HIRT / BLACK back — more white in candles for presence
outfit back   (BLACK T-shirt)

UP / MASTER / SLAVE BACK (warmer red, grey, silver, twin
     (BLACK T-SHIRT)

DESIGN · RHINO BACK

     (BLACK - T-SHIRT)

-92 TUE 19:37 MARK~ALAN PROD. INC.   P.0

Press schedules.   Nat'l radio to tape shows.
                          After show in Café.

PEARL JAM EUROFAX
FEBRUARY 12 1992

1. ERIC CAN YOU GET ME THE ANSWERS TO YESTERDAY'S QUESTIONS: PARASHAR CREDIT FOR STATE OF LOVE AND TRUST, B-SIDES FOR EUROPE.

2. IF YOU GUYS ARE SERIOUS ABOUT TAKING SOME SORT OF VACATION I NEED TO KNOW WHO WHAT WHERE AND ECT....

3. LOOKS LIKE THESE SOUNDGARDEN SHOWS WILL HAPPEN IN TEXAS. WE ARE IN THE PROCESS OF WORKING OUT THE LOGISTICS NOW.

4. REGAN WANTS TO PLAY WITH YOU GUYS IN SEATTLE.
   Tribe one night (Bless another night.
5. CAMERON'S MOVIE NOW COMES OUT IN JULY (DRAG) DO YOU WANT ME TO STILL PURSUE SATURDAY NITE LIVE? Wait to see when Mat
   Don't feel like pushing it.
6. ERIC CAN YOU SEE WHAT THE RATE IS IN MILAN AND TRY AND GET FRAN THE SAME.

7. FIND THE ENCLOSED START OF THE NEW RIDER FOR THE US TOUR. PLEASE CHECK IT OUT AND ADD OR SUBTRACT AND GET IT BACK TO ME.

8. ALSO ENCLOSED IS THE ESSAY INFORMATION FROM SPIN FOR EDDIE.

9. DANNA COOK WILL BE AT THE LONDON SHOW AND SHE HAS A LAM ALREADY.

HOPE EVERYONE IS WELL.

PS T-SHIRT DESIGNS ARE DUE SOON AS WELL AS SINGLE ART WORK FOR EUROPE.

KELLY

Record is at   457,000
   5 day   108,700

B·sides.   Yellow Letter (the need the tape of the
            4 version.) B-side to Evenflow..
            And Dirty Frank — Mixed? Eddie
            needs to be present for mixing.

PEARL JAM
EUROPE 1992

CITY	VENUE	CAPACITY
TRAVEL		300
TRAVEL		300
SOUTHEND	ESPLANADE CLUB	
LONDON	BORDERLINE	300
OFF		500
STOCKHOLM	KOOL KAT	300
OSLO	ALASKA	
COPENHAGEN	MUSIC CAFE	1000
OFF	LOCOMOTIVE	750
PARIS	MELKWEG	
AMSTERDAM		500
OFF	REVOLVER	
MADRID		400
OFF	SORPASSO	300-1000
MILAN		600
OFF	INTERNATIONAL 2	400
MANCHESTER	RIVERSIDE	
NEWCASTLE	CATHOUSE	300
GLASGOW		500
OFF	ROCK CITY	300
NOTTINGHAM	EDWARDS NO. 8	400-850
BIRMINGHAM	QUEENSHALL	
BRADFORD	U.L.U	
LONDON		500
		600
ARCH		450
GRONINGEN	VERA	1000
DEN HAAG	PARD	
NIJMEGEN	DOORNROOSJE	600
UTRECHT	TIVOLI	1000
EINDHOVEN	AFFENAAR	
ROTTERDAM	NIGHT-TOWN	600
		650
OFF	LUXAR	400
KOLN	LOFT	
BERLIN	MARKTHALLE	750
HAMBURG		1000
	BATSCHKAP	

Stone Gossard: Yes, this was my idea. Some of it was filmed in a zoo after dark, and the rest of it was us jamming on the side of a cliff. It was way more "big rock" than we wanted. I'm not sure it will ever be seen.

Jeff Ament: It was awful, and we knew at the time that it was awful.

February 3
Esplanade Club, Southend, England

Pearl Jam plays its first show in Europe, an unannounced gig in a seaside town about forty miles from London. *Ten* isn't scheduled for release for another three weeks but is already doing robust business as an import, as is the commercial single for "Alive," available in four different formats. In Southend, Eddie Vedder is genuinely surprised to discover how many fans know the words.

Kelly Curtis: At the time it was blowing up, it had become different than Pearl Jam and the music. It had become this Seattle thing, and that was the point that the band started saying, "No more." All the records were stickered with "the Seattle Sound." That was really annoying to everybody. In those days, the directive for an international release came out of New York. If Sony decided it was an important record, everybody in the universe got that message. It's different now. Every territory runs itself. It might have been that the record had quicker success internationally because it's a little more sophisticated musically, and they weren't as tied to a format or style. It was easier for fans there to just love it, as opposed to in America, where there was a struggle to find a home for the music.

February 4
BBC Television Centre, London

Pearl Jam plays "Alive" on its maiden television appearance on BBC Two's *The Late Show.* Later that day, the band gives its first official concert in front of an industry-heavy audience at the Borderline, a tiny London club in the basement of a Mexican restaurant.

February 10
Virgin Records, Paris

Pearl Jam squeezes into a Paris record store for a four-song acoustic performance.

February 19
Albani Bar of Music, Winterthur, Switzerland

The day after an unbearably hot and cramped show in Milan, Italy, Pearl Jam arrives at this venue outside Zurich to find that the room is even smaller and decides to take the performance in a new direction. The result reached mythic status among Pearl Jam fans, as it has never surfaced among bootleg collectors, and even the set list is not known.

Jeff Ament: We showed up at this club, and the stage was about as big as our normal drum riser. We looked at it and wondered how we could play a show in there and fit all our gear in. Somebody said, "Why don't we play an acoustic show?" There were some people from the label there, and they got us some acoustic guitars. We'd probably played seventy or eighty shows as a band on *Ten* at that

point, so it was a really refreshing take on things. The audience sang the songs back to us, because we had a little teeny PA.

Mike McCready: I mean, it was really small. I just remember being cramped onstage and Ed standing there and Jeff and I sitting next to each other. And I remember being kind of uncomfortable playing acoustic because we were so used to the power of electric. But I also knew that the songs were good enough to be acoustic because early on we had played some of them that way when we first started.

February 21
International II, Manchester, England

Pearl Jam's tour bus is robbed following this show.

Eric Johnson: Our truck driver Henrik was napping on the couch of the bus when he woke to find a guy looting backpacks

MTV UNPLUGGED

3/16/92

'92

PEARL JAM

and briefcases. When the large and imposing Henrik rose and confronted him, he pulled a knife on Henrik, rethought his position, and ran. Later that night, I made a comment to some T-shirt bootleggers, and as I was being verbally assaulted, I saw another guy make a cell phone call, and within seconds, a horde of seriously nasty fuckers came running. I was so happy to leave Manchester alive that night.

February 28
Union of London University, London

Fed up with the proliferation of stage diving and crowd surfing at the European shows, Eddie Vedder tells the crowd early in the show, "See your boots there? The big, shiny metal buckles? See these people's heads here? Because they are people's heads, and these aren't fucking casaba melons. Everybody, it's a beautiful thing when you lie down on top of the crowd looking like Jesus Christ. But, I swear, all I wanna do is crucify you when I see you smashing people's heads."

March 2
Paard, Den Haag, Netherlands

Eddie Vedder's younger brother Jason Mueller plays bass with Pearl Jam during a show-closing jam on the Beatles' "I've Got a Feeling," which teases bits of Jane's Addiction's "Jane Says" as well as Temple of the Dog's "Hunger Strike" and "Say Hello 2 Heaven."

March 9
The Loft, Berlin

Pearl Jam covers Neil Young's "Rockin' in the Free World" for the first time at this show. During the encore, Vedder tells the audience, "Just one thing, so it's clear: We are not the sound of Seattle. There are many sounds of Seattle."

Jeff Ament: We started playing "Rockin' in the Free World" at the end of our first album tour cycle, and it came out of only having eleven or twelve songs to play at that time. After playing one hundred shows, we were looking for anything else to play. There's a third part in that song that's sort of like a little bridge: an A section before the chorus. We didn't play that section probably the first ten or fifteen times that we played that song. And it was only when we ended up playing that song with Neil that we had to properly learn the arrangement. Every single person in the band saw that song being played on *Saturday Night Live* when he first wrote it, playing it with Steve Jordan and Charley Drayton. It's one of the few times where music on television actually really worked. What was going on in that room actually translated across the TV, and that just doesn't happen on TV very often. That song was a part of us, part of everybody in some sort of a way. We didn't have to practice it. We all kind of knew it.

ALL ACCESS

24

ALL ACCESS

22

ALL ACCESS

PEARL JAM

nikko hotels internatio

PEARL JAM

EUROPE 1992

Eddie —

whats up..
Im in Rm.
unda Tate.
I'm trying fo
Pink Floyd Ter
tor tor. if you
To go...

Reservations: 1-800-NIKKO-US
Fax-A-Res: 1-800-544-4455
New York • Atlanta • Chicago • San Francisco • Los Angeles • Hon

1992

PF

ERIC JOHNSON GROU

Guest name	Bag Tag	Check In	Check i	
Eric Johnson Party				
Mr Kelly Curtis				
Mr Hugh Mility	6	6-Mar	8-Ma	
Mr Juan Badapple	1	6-Mar	8-Ma	
Jim Rockford	2	6-Mar	8-Ma	
Dr Hugh Jeego	3	6-Mar	8-Ma	
Guy Jantic	4	6-Mar	8-Mar	1223
Eric Johnson	5	6-Mar	8-Mar	1225

March 13
Nachtwerk, Munich

Pearl Jam performs *Ten* in its entirety and in sequence for the first and only time to date on the last show of the European tour.

March 16
Kaufman Astoria Studios, Queens, New York

Pearl Jam heads directly to New York at the conclusion of its first European tour to tape an episode of MTV's hugely popular *Unplugged* series. The offer had actually come in the day after the impromptu acoustic show outside Zurich.

Jeff Ament: We were like, "We just did it!" Had they called a week before, we wouldn't have known if we could have pulled it off. But in Zurich, it seemed like it was all right musically. We had very little experience as an acoustic band at that point, so part of us wished we could do it over. Nirvana did theirs a couple of years later and obviously spent some time on it. We literally got off the plane from Europe, spent all day in a cavernous sound studio in New York, and did the show that night. It was just kind of what it was. It's pretty powerful, and Ed's singing great. Yet it's kind of naive, which is kind of awesome.

The set list for the taping features "Oceans," "State of Love and Trust," "Alive," "Black," "Jeremy," "Even Flow," and a grand finale of "Porch," during which Vedder falls off of his stool, gets up, and pretends to use it as a bodyboard, and then scrawls "Pro Choice!!" in black marker on his left arm.

Mike McCready: People seemed to like the *Unplugged* performance a lot, but I didn't really like that that much. It was like, "We're a rock band. We play loud." I was fighting it, trying to make it sound heavier than it really was. I love acoustic now. But back then, I was more, "Let's bring the power of this band."

March 25
First Avenue, Minneapolis

Pearl Jam begins a North American headlining tour with support from Jack Irons's band Eleven. Three nights later at Chicago's Cabaret Metro, with U2's the Edge and Larry Mullen Jr. looking on,

Smashing Pumpkins drummer Jimmy Chamberlin and bassist D'Arcy Wretzky join Pearl Jam to cover the Pumpkins' "Window Paine" and the Beatles' "I've Got a Feeling." From the stage, Vedder begins a tradition of taking Polaroid photos of the audience each night, telling the *Washington Post,* "I just want to remember all this. It's happening so fast."

April 11
Studio 8H at 30 Rockefeller Plaza, New York

Pearl Jam performs "Alive" and "Porch" on a Sharon Stone–hosted episode of NBC's *Saturday Night Live.* Vedder wears a homemade T-shirt depicting a coat hanger on the front and "No Bush in '92" on the back, and adds pro-choice lyrics to "Porch." The group also appears in a skit leering at Stone from the other side of the room in a nod to her then current infamous leg-crossing scene from the movie *Basic Instinct.*

Eddie Vedder: A lot of young people expressed thanks that I made a statement. It was really no big deal. That's how I feel, and I thought maybe I would say something. I had a blank T-shirt ten minutes before I went on, so I just put a piece of tape on it and a certain symbol. It wasn't planned.

April 12
Limelight, New York

The night after *Saturday Night Live,* Pearl Jam plays at a former church turned concert venue that usually plays host to dance parties, in front of a crowd featuring *SNL* stars such as Chris Farley, Adam Sandler, David Spade, and Mike Myers. The group returns to this spot in 2006 to tape an episode of VH1's *Storytellers.*

April 28–30
City Coliseum, Austin, Texas; Bronco Bowl, Dallas; Unicorn Club, Houston

Pearl Jam opens three shows for Soundgarden in Texas. Vedder gives everybody another huge scare while climbing an I-beam in Dallas.

Eddie Vedder: In the beginning, the urge to stage climb was from being in the crowd waiting for the next band to go

on, and there'd be thirty minutes as a set change, and I'd be looking at the venues and the theaters and the balconies and the shapes of the rooms, and I thought, God, it would be great to be able to climb up there, and I bet you could go from that point to that point. Like, if you had the opportunity, wouldn't that be a great thing to do? And then all of a sudden you had the chance to do that; like, you had the mike and you had the stage and you could do that. And then once you got up there, you realized, Wow, no one's been up here for a long time! There were inches of dust. Who knows what had happened in that building for years? But I definitely went to places that no one had been to in a long time.

Matt Cameron: He got to the very top of this thing, and it's probably, like, an eighty-foot fall or something, and I was just thinking, He's really going to hurt himself if he continues doing these types of performances. But he has that sort of mental toughness, like he's able to visualize his next step. That might have saved him from a big injury. But I'm glad he's not doing that anymore.

May 5

Ten is certified platinum by the Recording Industry Association of America for US shipments of one million copies.

Eddie Vedder: We're not concerned with how many people buy our albums—but we are concerned with how closely people listen to our music. It's nice to be able to share our art with people, and that's a rare opportunity. Now, so many people have bought our record and the whole thing has become so mind blowing that I don't even care anymore. It doesn't matter to me how or why people bought our record or if our success had anything to do with some "Seattle wave." We're a band, and our music is an art. We're not on tour to sell records—we're on tour to share our art.

May 11
KLOS-FM Studios, Los Angeles

Eddie Vedder and Stone Gossard take questions from fans on the nationally syndicated radio show *Rockline,* explaining why Pearl Jam won't be performing any Mother Love Bone songs live ("Andy Wood and Eddie Vedder are

certainly not the same people. It just wouldn't feel very comfortable, I don't think," Gossard says) and discussing the inspiration behind some of the material on *Ten*. The duo also performs acoustic renditions of "Alive," "Even Flow," and, in its live debut, "Footsteps." Referring to the Momma-Son cycle of "Alive," "Once," and "Footsteps" that won him his job in Pearl Jam, Vedder tells listeners, "Put those three songs together and try to figure it out, and then write me, and I'll tell you if you're right."

May 13

MTV Unplugged premieres. Although heavily bootlegged, the performance is not commercially released until it is included on DVD with the deluxe reissue of *Ten* in 2009.

May 17
Roseland Theater, Portland, Oregon

The ballad "Angel," with music penned by drummer Dave Abbruzzese, is performed for the first time.

May 18

Citing concerns over crowd size and lack of adequate security, the Seattle Department of Parks and Recreation withdraws its permit for a planned free Pearl Jam-Seaweed "Drop in the Park" concert at the city's Gas Works Park five days before the event is to take place. The band had gone to great lengths to keep the show safe and the expected forty thousand fans under control. Undaunted, Pearl Jam begins planning a makeup event for early fall elsewhere in Seattle.

Eddie Vedder: All these skateboarders were en route to the park when the show got canceled, so we rerouted them to this giant piece of property owned by a friend of ours, about forty-five minutes outside of the city. It ended up being this massive party with a bonfire and a couple hundred people that were already at Gas Works waiting for the show to start. Gas Huffer, Zeke, and 7 Year Bitch played, and I seem to remember singing some songs, too.

Jeff Ament: The city has always had a big disconnect with what was going on here musically. At that time, they really

didn't want to have anything to do with it. We were really, really excited to put on the show initially, but it took six months or something for us to finally figure out a way to do it. Most of it was us kind of giving in to the fears the city had about what was going to happen at this "grunge concert." All we wanted to do was put on a free show for the town.

Kelly Curtis: In hindsight, it was probably a blessing. I don't think we would have been prepared for the size or the amount of people that were coming. At the time, it was frustrating, because the city stopped us a week out and said we couldn't do it. I think the city just realized that a free Pearl Jam show could have been out of control, and the park could not have handled how many people showed up.

June 5
Nürburgring, Nürburg, Germany

Pearl Jam begins its second European tour by playing its first major festival gig at Rock Am Ring Festival in Germany before fifty thousand fans. The audience is even larger three nights later at the Pinkpop Festival in the Netherlands, where Pearl Jam's set is broadcast on Dutch television.

June 18
Volkshaus, Zurich, Switzerland

The songs "Alive," "Once," and "Footsteps," known as the Momma-Son trilogy, are performed together for the first time. Eddie Vedder informs the audience, "I never told anybody about this before. I don't wanna ruin any interpretations of the songs that you have, but it's about incest, and it's about murder, and all those good things. And if you can picture it in your mind, the third song takes place in a jail cell. So this is our own little mini-opera here." The trilogy is played again at the next two shows in Vienna (June 19) and Paris (June 22).

June 25
Moderna Museet, Skeppsholmen, Stockholm, Sweden

Pearl Jam performs in a venue on the grounds of Stockholm's Museum of Modern Art, where the show was moved

from a much smaller club. Vedder starts the show alone with debut covers of Police's "Driven to Tears" and Hunters & Collectors' "Throw Your Arms Around Me." Afterward, the band is crushed to learn that someone had broken into its dressing room during the show and stolen numerous personal items, including several of Vedder's journals filled with lyrics and song ideas.

Jeff Ament: They took whatever was laying around, including Ed's whole suitcase, which had more than one journal in it. It was most of what he'd been working on over the previous three or four months; most of his life was in there.

Eddie Vedder: After that, I got really good at writing in a way that only I could read. In case anybody ever wanted to look at my notebooks posthumously, they wouldn't be able to know what I was thinking.

June 26
Roskilde Festival, Copenhagen, Denmark

Tensions from the break-in the night before boil over during this massive festival gig, as several band members become embroiled in a tussle with security. Afterward, citing exhaustion, Pearl Jam opts to scrap the remaining seven dates of the European tour, including a gig the next night on a Turkish festival bill alongside Nirvana.

Jeff Ament: We were trying to keep it together, but it was already starting to get

EUROPEAN SCHEDULE

JUNE/JULY

CITY/VENUE

Nurburgring ROCK AM RING
Finsbury Park Festival
Off
PinkPop Festival, Holland
+ hotels (one night)
Off
Stuttgart Kongresszent[?]
HAMBURG Docks
Off
BERLIN WUHLHEIDE
BREMEN SCHLOSSPARK
NUREMBERG Serenadenh[?]
Off
MILAN City Square
ZURICH Volkshaus
VIENNA Rockhaus
Off
PARIS Elysee Montm[?]
Off
STOCKHOLM Museum [?]

ROSKILDE, Denmark [?]
TURKU, Finland Festival
+ hotels
OSLO, Norway, Isle of Calf $10,000..
Festival

[?]TE - YOU WILL HAVE TO USE DUPLICATE BACKLINE AT TURKU [?]
should go Denmark - Oslo on June 27th.

        Off

    LONDON Astoria Theatre   £ 5,000 v[?]
    Off
    EUROCKEENES, France Festival $10,000 F[?]
                                   + hotels [?]
    TORHOUT, Belgium Festival $10,000 [?]
    WERCHTER, Belgium Festival $10,000 [?]
    Direction: Rod MacSween, Barry Dickins +hotels [?]
    Proprietors: Grinland Ltd
    Registered office: 12 Thayer Street, London W1M 5LD

PINKPOP '92

HALLO VENRAY   10.30 - 11.00
BUFFALO TOM   11.15 - 11.55
PJ HARVEY   12.20 - 13.00
ROWWEN HEZE   13.20 - 14.00
FAMILY STAND   14.30 - 15.15
SOUNDGARDEN   15.45 - 16.30
DAVID BYRNE   17.00 - 18.00
PEARL JAM   18.30 - 19.30
LOU REED   20.00 - 21.00
THE CULT   21.30 - 22.30

Wijzigingen voorbehouden

Toegang tot een frontstage-area slechts met toestemming van de optredende artiesten en kan zelfs ontruimd worden. Voor elke area geldt het principe "vol is vol". Bij misbruik volgt intrekking van deze pas. Access to one of the frontstage areas is at the discretion of performing artists or security.

CORTIS MGMT.   TEL:206-292-8141   Aug 12 92   17:13 No.004 P.06
AUG-12-'92 WED 16:51 ID:MSK MUSIC&TAX 9TH FL TEL NO:310 312-3789   #918 P05

obviously go down if labels are required and minors are not allowed to buy our records. Sales to adults will also go down if record stores decide to put labeled recordings in a hidden section of the store or if they decide not to carry those recordings. The loss in sales if this law is enforced against each of us as individual musicians or all of us collectively as a group could significantly harm our livelihood.

DATED this _____ day of August, 1992.

"PEARL JAM"

_____
STONE GOSSARD

_____
JEFF AMENT

_____
EDDIE VEDDER

_____
MIKE McCREADY

_____
DAVE ABBRUZZESE

83

weird. Nirvana was on the bill, too, and this was when the Nirvana versus Pearl Jam thing was at its pinnacle. Courtney Love was on the phone the whole time next to me calling random people, super fucked up. It was surreal. Stone and I talked, and then we called Kelly to tell him we had to come home. It felt like something that could potentially unravel in a really bad way. During "Deep," Ed went into the crowd, and when he came out, security didn't know it was him. Eric Johnson went to get him, and security started wailing on them. I think Mike may have jumped in, too. I thought, Oh my God. It can't get any worse. Deciding to go home let us know that making a buck at that point wasn't the most important thing. The most important thing was keeping our sanity and staying in control of the thing we were driving.

June 26

The soundtrack to Cameron Crowe's Seattle-centric film *Singles* is released on Epic Soundtrax, featuring the previously unreleased Pearl Jam tracks "State of Love and Trust" and "Breath."

Jeff Ament: "State of Love and Trust" and Mudhoney's "Overblown" were pretty good representations of what was going on in Seattle and in music at that time. They matched up with the movie pretty well. I think that song was also Ed responding to the angst of being in love when you're too young to really know what to do. "Breath" had been around since Stone's earliest Pearl Jam demos. It wound up being a midtempo rocker number with a big ending, and in some ways, it may have resembled "Alive" too much. There were too many epic-ending songs with big guitar solos and hooky choruses on *Ten*. But thank God it found a home on that soundtrack, because it's worthy.

June 27

With *Ten* nestled in the Top 10 of the *Billboard* 200, the self-titled *Temple of the Dog* album debuts at no. 181 on the chart fourteen months after its original release. Three weeks later, the Eddie Vedder–Chris Cornell duet "Hunger Strike" creeps onto *Billboard*'s Modern Rock Tracks chart at no. 24.

July 18–19
Shoreline Amphitheatre, Mountain View, California

Pearl Jam begins its stint on the second Lollapalooza music festival alongside Soundgarden, Ministry, Ice Cube, the Red Hot Chili Peppers, Lush, the Jim Rose Circus Sideshow, and the Jesus and Mary Chain. For many teenagers, this is not only their first Pearl Jam show but also their first experience at a rock festival, and the band's electrifying performances make a profound impression. And with Pearl Jam usually slated second on the all-day bill, band members get to spend copious amounts of time watching the other musicians and enjoying the camaraderie. In particular, Vedder cements a quick bond with Jim Rose, often participating in an onstage stunt drinking "bile beer." He and Soundgarden front man Chris Cornell also play a handful of surprise acoustic sets on the second stage, and at one particularly rainy show in Cuyahoga Falls, Ohio, on July 29, join fans in joyously and repeatedly sliding down the mud-soaked

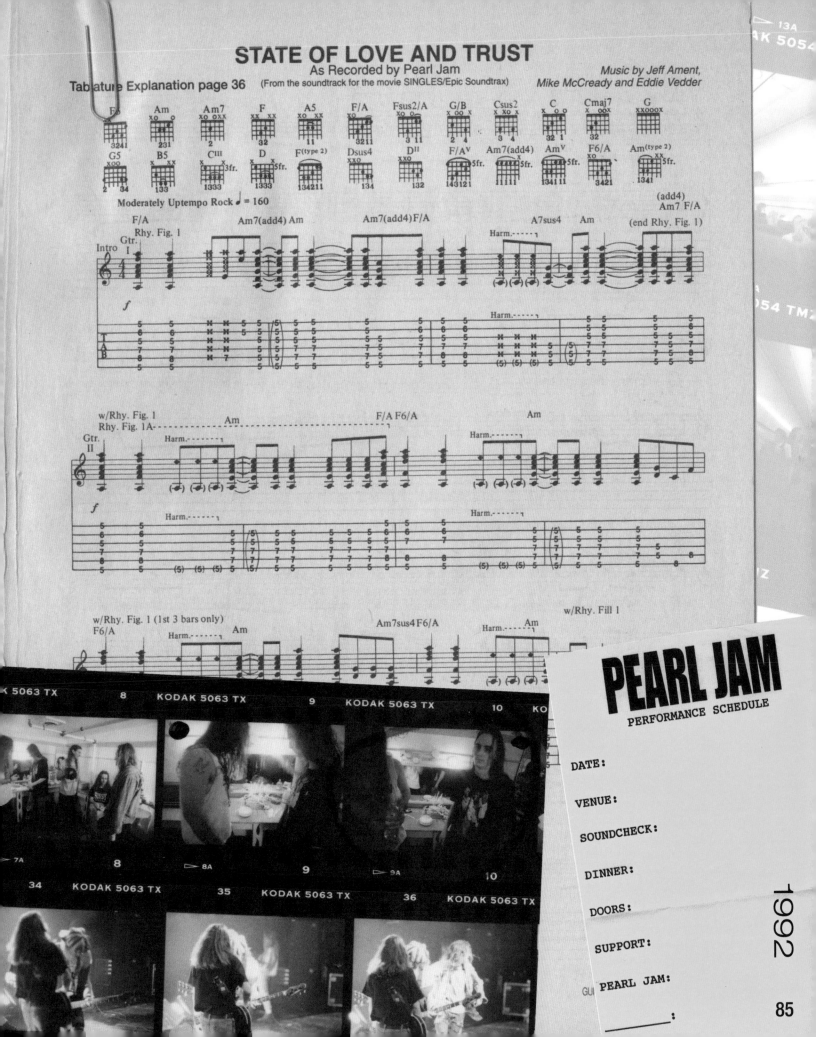

STATE OF LOVE AND TRUST

As Recorded by Pearl Jam

(From the soundtrack for the movie SINGLES/Epic Soundtrax)

Tablature Explanation page 36

Music by Jeff Ament,
Mike McCready and Eddie Vedder

lawn section. Vedder continues to shock concertgoers with his stage climbing antics and finally eases up on them after being roughed up during a show in Ontario, Canada.

Eddie Vedder: Playing to people that you'd never played for before, it was like, "You know what? We're going to play, we're going to take this to some level that people aren't going to forget. And if that means risking your life to do something that they won't forget, in some kind of adolescent Evel Knievel way, we're going to do it." And it was pretty incredible that if you did something like that, people really paid attention, so much so that they would move to catch you at the end. I'd act like I was going to jump this way, and then I'd switch to the other and watch the whole crowd sway over to make the grab.

Jeff Ament: A couple of weeks before the tour, there was an opportunity for us to renegotiate, not just the money but the time slot. But we were like, "Naw. We don't want any added pressure to this situation. We want to have fun." That was the angle that we took. And it was fun. At most of the shows, Al Jourgensen from Ministry was walking around with a bottle of Maker's Mark bourbon with ten hits of acid in it. Good times were being had. We could get superfocused at two in the afternoon, rock out for thirty minutes, and then just have fun. We still have an absolute blast playing shows, but I don't know if we've ever had more fun on a tour. We were playing intense shows. But within an hour, I'd be playing basketball with Flea and Ice Cube. It was a big party atmosphere and not very competitive at all.

Matt Cameron: On that particular tour, we really witnessed how the live audience was reacting to Pearl Jam. And it was just amazing.

Chris Cornell: I think it was one of my favorite tours of my career, because we shared a lot of camaraderie. It's like your buddies you grew up with that you played in front of ten people with for years, and now you're on tour together playing for twenty-five thousand people a night. And it seems to also mean something culturally. It's not just that they're spinning my single on the radio.

Culturally, it's changing the way people think about rock music. That was pretty phenomenal.

But suddenly there was a responsibility of, if people are saying we're kind of the new guard, does that mean we have to act a certain way? Do we have to act responsible? Are there some rules to that? Should we not say something that might make a kid want to go get drunk or smash something? Is that bad? Is there a social responsibility to our roles? And if so, should that be something you sit down and figure out in kind of a left brain way, or is that something you should just allow to happen?

A great example is that me and Eddie went into the hotel room of someone on our crew. And he's sort of giving me and Eddie shit, saying we're piss poor excuses for rock stars, because we didn't do anything rock star–like. There was a little practice amp on the floor of the room, and Eddie and I kind of looked at each other. Eddie and I were going to show him, *No, actually you're wrong!* I threw the amp through the window so hard that it crashed through the glass, cleared the roof, and landed down in the alleyway below. Then what starts out as just having fun becomes the social responsibility of, what if it hit a car or a person? Also, my name was written on a piece of tape that was on the amp, and I didn't want to go to jail. So, immediately I ran down to the alley and took off the tape. The cops came to the room, and he made up a great story about how he'd slept with a girl the night before, and her boyfriend came, forced his way into the room, and then threw the amp through the window. Great liar! How did he come up with that? And the cops bought it, and that was it. I don't think we ever really tried to prove to anyone again that the new guard of rock star wasn't going to be outdone.

August 1

With a commercial single for "Jeremy" having been released about a week earlier, the song's video, shot in June in London and directed by Mark Pellington, premieres on MTV. In it, teenage actor Trevor Wilson portrays the titular figure, harassed by his classmates and misunderstood by his parents. In the final scene, Jeremy enters a classroom, removes a handgun from his pocket, places it in his mouth, and pulls the trigger as the screen flashes light, then cuts to black. The other students are then shown, motionless and splattered with Jeremy's blood.

Eddie Vedder: It means you kill yourself, and you make a big old sacrifice and try to get your revenge, and all you're gonna end up with is a paragraph in a newspaper: sixty-three degrees and cloudy in a suburban neighborhood. That's the beginning of the video. In the end, it does nothing; nothing changes. The world goes on, and you're gone. The best revenge is to live on and prove yourself. Be stronger than those people. And then you can come back. That's kinda what I did.

Jeff Ament: Luckily, we picked Mark Pellington to do it. He was a great collaborator. It reminded me of working with Cameron Crowe, in terms of how seriously he took our input. Mark felt that song deeply and visually represented it.

August 14
Lake Fairfax Park, Reston, Virginia

Vedder misses the bus to this gig and has to hitchhike several miles to the venue, leaving his bandmates scrambling as their set time approaches. Chris Cornell gamely goes onstage and is about to sub for Vedder on vocals, telling the crowd, "I don't know all the lyrics to any of these songs," just as Vedder rushes in to relieve him and start the show with "Once." Cornell returns to sing "Hunger Strike" for the first time ever with Pearl Jam, a collaboration that would happen only once more in the next eleven years.

August 21–22
Southern Tracks Recording Studio, Atlanta

Having remixed "Jeremy" earlier in the year for its music video as well as for a radio version, up-and-coming producer Brendan O'Brien hits the studio to record music with Pearl Jam for the first time while the band is in Atlanta for Lollapalooza. The August 21 session happens immediately after Pearl Jam's early-afternoon set at Lakewood Amphitheatre and continues the following day. The band tracks demo versions of "Leash" and "Rats," as well as a cover of the Dead Boys' punk classic "Sonic Reducer," which comes out at the end of the year on a fan club single. Also put to tape is a version of the Who's "Baba O'Riley," which remains unreleased.

Brendan O'Brien: I felt a lot of pressure, right or wrong, because I thought I was on the hot seat to see what I could do. It was Pearl Jam Nation at that point. At any moment, I was expecting a call telling me they were going with any number of other bigger-name producers. Why wouldn't they? But they stuck with me. My whole thing was to keep it moving and make it fun, and they seemed to enjoy themselves. I really remember understanding how good Eddie was. I knew he was a really good singer who could write great lyrics, but when a man can stand in front of a mike and sing, that's not a particularly easy thing to do, and he was absolutely great at it. I remember saying to him after hearing "Baba," "I didn't know you had that in you!" It was a real moment for me in understanding Eddie's true potential. I also could tell that they were wonderful guys who I really wanted

to be around. I hadn't always had that experience as an engineer. At that point, I'd only produced a couple of things.

September 9
Pauley Pavilion, Los Angeles

Pearl Jam begrudgingly performs "Jeremy" at the MTV Video Music Awards after initially insisting on playing a cover of "Sonic Reducer." Later in the show, in a moment that would become somewhat mythical in later years, Eddie Vedder and Kurt Cobain reportedly dance together under the stage while Eric Clapton is performing "Tears in Heaven."

Eddie Vedder: There was a lot of stuff that got said, but none of it really matters. There was a person we both knew, who told me that Kurt asked about me a lot, asked how I was doing and what I was like. That made me feel good, because so much bullshit was getting written about us. We ended up talking a few times. And this one time, he told me flat out, just delivered me a whole paragraph on the respect he had for what I did, and he realized it was pure. After the MTV Awards, I remember going out surfing the next morning and remembering how good that moment felt and thinking, Fuck, man. We were going

through so much of the same shit. If only we'd talked, maybe we could have helped each other.

Dave Grohl: It was like, "Okay. God! Can we get on with this already? Jesus Christ!"

Kelly Curtis: Things were huge, but at the same time, it was scaring the band to death, especially Eddie. It was just everywhere. After "Jeremy" won those awards, the label wanted to keep going. But the band was just done. It was too much for them. The label told us we had to go with "Black," and that it was the biggest song. The most pressure I got was from Sony Music CEO Tommy Mottola, who called me and said that if we didn't release "Black," it would be the single biggest mistake I ever made in my life, and my management career would be over. So, obviously it was coming from way up. I think Michele and Michael understood, even though I'm sure it was frustrating for them. That was a heavy phone call for a young manager trying to do the right thing. But the band was absolute in its decision. It was easy to say no to that, because that's what they'd decided. I wasn't going to side with the record company.

I remember a lot of managers showing up and sniffing around. I don't think I even had a credit card at the time. There were a lot of people wanting to help me or drive me out; people with powerful resources behind them. But the band backed me up forever. And at the same time, there were a few managers out there that were very encouraging, like Paul McGuinness [U2, among others] and Elliot Roberts [Neil Young, Tom Petty, Joni Mitchell, and others]. They told me I was doing the right thing and to hang in there and just ride it out. I can only imagine all the offers that were coming in. Ed was offered a Calvin Klein underwear ad. And I seem to remember something about pajamas. But it's kind of a blur.

Michele Anthony: All of a sudden, "Alive" and "Even Flow" were getting airplay. "Black" was the obvious quote-unquote ballad on the album, so, of course, a lot of people within the company wanted it to be the next single. They felt it was capable of crossing beyond the alternative and rock formats. But that

was anathema to the band and Kelly. I agreed with them, and that's why Tommy made the call.

Michael Goldstone: There was a lot of pressure on them to put "Black" out as a single. But it was a really smart decision to not oversaturate people with *Ten.* "Black" became more of a single in people's minds. Sometimes songs end up being singles even though they were never actually released as singles.

Eric Johnson: They really wanted to take control of everything that was happening to them, so you can imagine how it would feel to get things like a request from the record company for

"Black" to appear on a heavy metal compilation.

Stone Gossard: Ed was just so on the edge that he made the decision to pull everything back. It's like, "I can't, I need to stop, I don't want to do it." I think everybody went, "Okay, this is going to be interesting. Let's see what happens." We all thought if we weren't going to be going down the same path, the mania would probably go away. I don't think any of us were like, "I'm going to quit." The wisdom of the decision wasn't evident for a while.

1992

September 10
Park Plaza Hotel Ballroom, Los Angeles

Pearl Jam and Alice in Chains play a premiere party for *Singles* that is taped to air at a later date on MTV. Director Cameron Crowe has to plead with the bands to perform at the show, having been told by the film's distributor, Warner Bros., that the already-one-year-in-the-can *Singles* might not be released otherwise. By any measure, the event is an unmitigated disaster and is broadcast just two times. Indeed, Pearl Jam's very sloppy live performance of "State of Love and Trust" has to be meticulously edited and combined by Brendan O'Brien with the song's studio version to make it broadcast worthy.

Jeff Ament: It was a classic Hollywood clusterfuck. We'd played a show at the same venue as Green River, and it was where they did the Guns N' Roses "Welcome to the Jungle" video. We were sort of maybe a little bit ticked off that on our one day off, we're in the middle of this clusterfuck of a show, and it's not really a full show. We're only going out and playing for forty minutes or something. So we're downstairs, and there's a bottle of tequila. We hardly ever drank before the show, and we ended up polishing off this bottle of tequila right before we went out onstage. We were fucking wasted. And we went out, and it's just chaos. The sound was bad onstage, and they covered the stage with this plastic for some reason. I don't know if there was some fancy carpet underneath it that they didn't want to get dirty. I remember Ed couldn't hear, so he's telling them to turn the monitors up. And nothing's changing. And finally he runs over, and he grabs the light board—he's actually looking at the wrong end of the stage—and he picks it up and fucking dumps the whole thing, thinking that that's the monitor rig. And it was actually the light rig. The monitor rig was on the other side of the stage. At the end of the show, we get downstairs, and they go, "Uh, the fucking police are here looking for you. They're going to arrest you guys because there's a riot, and a fire marshal got punched out." They scooped us into a van and snuck us out the back way, and somebody cleaned up our mess. I don't know how they ended up showing it.

Eddie Vedder: Actually, I have more memories than you would think I'd have. The monitors weren't really working that well, so I kept looking over and asking, "Turn the monitors up. I can't hear anything!" At some point, after a while, I just got really upset. They had this pipe and drape thing, and I took it, and I pulled it off and threw it down. And then I looked over, and it wasn't our soundwoman at all. It was the lighting person, and I kept wondering, like, "Why is it getting brighter in here?" [*Laughs*] There were some long soundchecks that day, so I drank one bottle of wine, and then there was another that I opened to give to friends, and they weren't drinking, so I drank that one, too. Was there a fire marshal?

Cameron Crowe: It was the first time I'd seen Eddie like this. I think he'd been going through a lot of problems adjusting to his success, and he was drunk. Very drunk. They took the stage, and they tried to play their set, and there was immediately a security altercation in the crowd. Eddie started to talk about the stage being slick, I think because beer had been spilled, and he said, "This stage is fucking slick, like Hollywood." I began to see the studio executives and their families starting to stream for the exits. Some fights were breaking out. It was like nothing I really was prepared for, particularly coming from these guys, but it was memorable. However, there was nothing that was airable for the TV show that was supposed to come out to promote the movie. I think they put something together, but the show was a disaster.

Stone Gossard: The way Ed was going to deal with it was just, "I'm going to just get as fucked up as I can possibly get because I can't wrap my head around what's going on and I don't feel like I'm in control of it."

September 11–13
Irvine Meadows, Irvine, California

The Lollapalooza tour ends with three eventful shows outside of Los Angeles, culminating on September 13 with a Temple of the Dog reunion for "Hunger Strike" and "Reach Down" during Pearl Jam's set. At the September 12 show, members of Rage Against the Machine join Pearl Jam for "Rockin' in the Free World," as does Eleven drummer Jack Irons, who is wearing a blond wig and introduced as Kurt Cobain by Vedder. The *Los Angeles Times* doesn't get the joke and writes in its review that Cobain joined the band onstage.

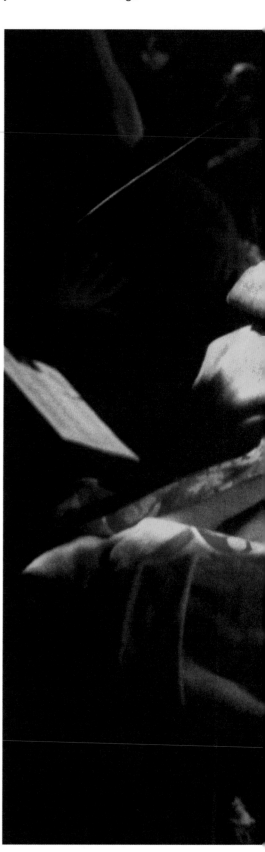

92

September 20
Warren G. Magnuson Park, Seattle

Pearl Jam makes good on its pledge to organize a free hometown concert following the last-minute cancellation of a show at Gas Works Park in May. Dubbed "Drop in the Park," the event also features performances from Seaweed, Cypress Hill, Pete Droge, and the Jim Rose Circus Sideshow. Approximately thirty thousand fans show up, three thousand of whom register to vote on-site. Recordings of the show are released for the first time as part of the 2009 deluxe reissue of *Ten.*

Jeff Ament: That taught us a lot about how to put on your own show. There were definitely things we didn't do right. The barricade was too small. It broke at one point during Cypress Hill's set. We were definitely getting into something we didn't have the experience dealing with, but it was still great. There was definitely a celebratory vibe to that show, and relief. It took months of us working with the city to pull it off.

Kelly Curtis: Even when we did come back later to do Drop in the Park, which took a lot of planning and help, we still barely got out of that alive, as far as it nearly turning into a disaster. But it didn't.

1992

DROP IN THE PARK
48 ← TYPE
24 DROPLET CAN LAM OVER LETTERS

33,000 enjoy
a free day
with Pearl Jam
Hit band rocks Seattle park
SoundLife 9

48 ← TYPE
24
42 KB
8 W I T H
20 PEARL JAM
14 SEAWEED · DEPENDERS
8 PEACE, LOVE, + GUITARS
12 PETE DROGE · SHAWN SMITH
8 L A Z Y   S U S A N
24 MAY 23, 1992

DROP IN THE PARK
MAGNUSSON PARK
SEPT. 20 1992
W I T H
CYPRESS HILL
S E A W E E D
ROBERT ANTON WILSON · LAZY SUSAN
PETE DROGE · SHAWN SMITH
MASTER OF CEREMONIES JIM ROSE

DROP IN THE PARK
PEARL JAM
SEPTEMBER 20, 1992

Times   Monday, September 14, 1992

from his home to Tahoma
Junior High School, where the
boy was airlifted to Harborview
Medical Center.

**Pearl Jam fans
dash for free tickets**

■ SEATTLE

Motorists jumped medians
and drove on sidewalks as more
than 10,000 people scrambled
for free tickets to a concert by
local band Pearl Jam.

The dash began at 8 a.m.
yesterday when rock radio
stations announced the Seattle
Center Coliseum as the site for
the ticket giveaway. The concert
is Sunday at Magnuson Park.

Tickets were distributed in
packets of two, and by noon all
10,000 packets were gone,
coordinator John Hoyt said.

September 25–26
Andrews Amphitheatre, Honolulu

Pearl Jam winds down its touring activity in support of *Ten* with two Honolulu shows and a third on September 27 in Maui. While relaxing on the beaches of Hawaii, the group shoots a video for "Oceans" with director Josh Taft, but the clip is released only internationally until its inclusion eight years later on the DVD *Touring Band 2000*.

Jeff Ament: It was very low-key, but still, we were on vacation spending a whole day with a cameraman. It felt like a big celebration at the end of the tour, and I think the video comes off that way. There's a lot of smiles, and it looks beautiful.

October 16
Madison Square Garden, New York

Eddie Vedder and Mike McCready perform "Masters of War" at a star-studded tribute concert celebrating Bob Dylan's thirtieth anniversary in the music business, which is broadcast on Pay-Per-View. The day before, they meet Neil Young for the first time, during rehearsals for the show, which also includes Eric Clapton, George Harrison, and Tom Petty. Vedder spends an epic night out at an Irish bar with the musicians afterward and seeks advice from Dylan for how to deal with all the attention. Dylan tells him, "Don't read anything in the paper. Don't watch TV. Get away."

November

Eddie Vedder writes an article about abortion for *Spin* magazine's November issue.

> The fact is that those people handing down decisions on the abortion issue are not the ones who will have to live or die by it. Ten years old. That's the age my child would have been. And I would not be here in Glasgow. I wouldn't be in this band or traveling. And I wouldn't have seen the liberal ways in which other countries we have visited deal with this issue. I wouldn't have been asked to write this piece. The fact that I've been through it on all levels is the only reason I accepted. Perhaps I'll have a child in the future, when I can provide properly. Who knows. But as individuals in this "free" country, we

> must have the right to choose when that time is right. This is not a game. This is not a religious pep rally. This is a woman's future. Decide on the issues and vote—male or female—for this is not just a women's issue. It's human rights. If it were a man's body and it was his destiny we were deciding, there would be no issue.

November 1
Shoreline Amphitheatre, Mountain View, California

Pearl Jam performs for the first time at Neil Young's annual Bridge School Benefit, which raises funds for a school for children with severe speech and physical impairments. The band offers acoustic versions of "Footsteps," "Jeremy," "Black," "Alive," the ultrarare "Angel," and Steven Van Zandt's "I Am a Patriot," as well as the debut performance of future Pearl Jam classic "Daughter," which the band had written during Lollapalooza and fleshed out one night in Denver in the back of the tour bus.

Jeff Ament: The first time we got asked to play the Bridge School was one of the most powerful musical experiences we've ever had. A few months later, Neil asked us to go to Europe with him.

Eric Johnson: The first time they did Bridge School, we were standing in front of the hotel waiting for the van to take us to the venue. We see Neil drive up in this gigantic, old black Cadillac with the license plate "Pearl 10," which, of course, he'd had years before there was ever a Pearl Jam or an album called *Ten*. It was a beautiful moment.

Christmas

Pearl Jam releases its second fan-club-only seven-inch vinyl single, "Who Killed Rudolph?" including the Dead Boys cover "Sonic Reducer" it had recorded earlier that summer with Brendan O'Brien in Atlanta, and "Ramblings Continued."

December 31
The Academy, New York

Pearl Jam celebrates New Year's Eve with a support slot for Keith Richards and the

X-Pensive Winos in front of five thousand fans in New York. The show opens with an extremely fast rendition of "Wash," which is never played in this style again, and also features the brand-new "Daughter" and a jam based around Ted Nugent's "Stranglehold," prompting Mike McCready to reassure the crowd, "They forced me to play it. I think Ted Nugent is a stupid idiot." McCready and Eddie Vedder join Richards and his band, plus guitarist Robert Cray, for a show-closing performance of "Goin' Down." This concert is later released as a free bonus CD with fan club orders of Pearl Jam's self-titled 2006 album.

Jeff Ament: I remember hanging out with some friends from New York at that show up in the balcony. One of my friends said, "Oh, see those two people in the front row? That's Marc Jacobs and Anna Sui." I said, "Is that the guy who came out with a grunge line? A three-hundred-dollar corduroy jacket?" This friend of mine goes, "I dare you to go ask him that to his face." "How much?" "A dollar." I went down, did a fake fashion twirl, and went, "Hey, Marc, what do you think of this for the next line?" I was probably wearing red velvet shorts and tights. We were young and full of shit and energy. We weren't afraid to open up for Keith Richards, even though we respected him as much as anybody at that time. Eddie flipped off the Marky Mark billboard from the Times Square big screen, too, that night. Perfect.

No. _Brown_
STYLE _70's Jacket_
SIZE _MED_
PRICE _____

No. _____
STYLE _____
SIZE _____
PRICE _$.24⁰⁰_

Receipt for corduroy jacket

PEARL JA

102

CHAPTER 1993

1993

"Grunge" was at the peak of mainstream attention in 1993, and Pearl Jam was at the center of the storm.

Hunkered down in a California studio to record its second album, *Vs.*, the band enjoyed a brief respite from the static. As the ride got bumpier, Pearl Jam took solace in simply doing what it thought was right regardless of conventional wisdom, including eschewing videos and interviews to promote the new album. The band also toured and bonded with industry veterans like U2 and Neil Young, who provided role models for how to forge an enduring career without becoming bogged down by all the ancillary distractions. But no matter how hard it tried, Pearl Jam could not escape that it was arguably the most popular band in the world, a fact made plain by the record-breaking first-week sales for *Vs.* that October. To be sure, Pearl Jam had to invent a way forward for itself without getting swallowed by the maelstrom, but figuring out how to do it would be the most difficult undertaking of its career.

January 12
Century Plaza Hotel, Los Angeles

Eddie Vedder inducts the Doors into the Rock and Roll Hall of Fame, telling a humorous story about stunts the prefame band members pulled to avoid being drafted for the Vietnam War (pretending to be gay, feigning insanity). Afterward, he fills the late Jim Morrison's shoes and handles lead vocals for intense versions of "Roadhouse Blues," "Break On Through," and "Light My Fire" with surviving members John Densmore, Robbie Krieger, and Ray Manzarek, who were performing together for the first time since 1978.

January 23
Hollywood Palladium, Hollywood, California

Vedder plays "Porch," the Bad Radio song "Homeless," and a cover of Hunters & Collectors' "Throw Your Arms Around Me" at his first solo show as a member of Pearl Jam. The concert, which also features 7 Year Bitch plus Seattle bands Screaming Trees and Green Apple Quick Step, commemorates the twentieth anniversary of the US Supreme Court's *Roe v. Wade* decision legalizing abortion.

January 25
Shrine Auditorium, Los Angeles

Pearl Jam wins favorite new artist (pop/rock) and favorite new artist (heavy metal/hard rock) at the American Music Awards.

April 27

Stone Gossard's side band Brad, which also features Satchel's Shawn Smith and Regan Hagar, releases its Epic debut album, *Shame.* The musicians jammed together for the first time after the 1992 Lollapalooza tour and, with help from bassist Jeremy Toback, quickly recorded eleven songs that October at Avast! Recording Co. in Seattle. But with Pearl Jam in the throes of preparing for its second album, Brad goes on hiatus.

Shawn Smith: At the time, Pearl Jam was the biggest band on the planet. It was over the top, the whole thing. There was never a thought of anything beyond making one album.

Stone Gossard: We started out, and the band was trying to use the name Shame. Some guy in L.A. owned the name, and he had a band, but he wasn't really using it. He was thinking about it and wanted to keep it. Months went by, and he still wasn't using it. We offered him ten grand or something for the name. I think he found out I was in the band and wanted more money. At some point, we gave up. His name was Brad, so we just decided if he was going to keep that name from us, we were going to take his name! I think he later started a band called Stone, but I don't think they were very popular.

May 13
Slim's, San Francisco

With the album still provisionally called *Five Against One* basically finished, Pearl Jam, billed as the David J. Gunn Band in an attempt at a surprise, returns to live duty for the first time since New Year's Eve '92. "So, which one of you couldn't keep a secret?" Vedder jokes with the

BRAD

beyond-capacity crowd. "These are some new songs," he says. With that, the outside world is introduced to "Animal," "Go," "Blood," "W.M.A.," "Dissident," "Rearviewmirror," and "Rats," plus "Better Man" and "Whipping," both of which wouldn't be released until the third album, and "Hard to Imagine," which wouldn't officially see the light of day for another five years. The band also riffs on Cyndi Lauper's "Girls Just Wanna Have Fun" and AC/DC's "Dirty Deeds Done Dirt Cheap."

Jeff Ament: That was before the Internet, so we didn't have to worry about bootlegs getting out at that time. It's

too bad you can't do more of that now; work through songs without the rest of the world hearing them within an hour. We were working on rough mixes that morning, so we loaded up our gear and drove into San Francisco. Right after the show, I drove all night and the next day to Las Vegas to see the Grateful Dead and Sting with my brother.

June 26
Sentrum Scene, Oslo, Norway

After two surprise shows in Missoula, Montana, and Spokane, on June 16–17

Pearl Jam embarks on a three-week European tour, which includes a blend of headlining shows and dates supporting both Neil Young (backed by Booker T. & the MG's) and U2.

June 28
Sjöhistoriska Museet, Stockholm, Sweden

Neil Young and Pearl Jam perform Young's "Rockin' in the Free World" for the first time together during the encore of Young's set.

Mike McCready: Just being able to see Neil Young with Booker T. & the MG's every night from the front of the stage was amazing. They're the greatest band in the world. I've never seen one better; so tight, but laid back and groovy, too. One night we were playing "Rockin' in the Free World," and I was standing right next to Steve Cropper. Steve looks at me, nodding for me to play a lead. So I do a lead, and then he does one and nods back for me to do another. So I do another lead, and suddenly he plays this fucking lead that just ripped my head off. All I could do was laugh and go back to playing rhythm. It was like he was testing me: "Okay—you're still not shit."

1993

Eddie Vedder: Neil and I were sitting and talking once, sometime around the second record, and he said, "Don't get away from the band. I bet there's a lot of people telling you to do something on your own." And I thought to myself, No [*laughs*], I haven't heard that at all! So, don't worry. I'm sticking with these guys.

Neil Young: This was right when the "grunge movement" was everywhere, but there was a lot of turbulence around it, with all this Nirvana versus Pearl Jam stuff. I just told them to forget it. Ignore it completely and don't pay any attention to it. It didn't make any difference what other people thought.

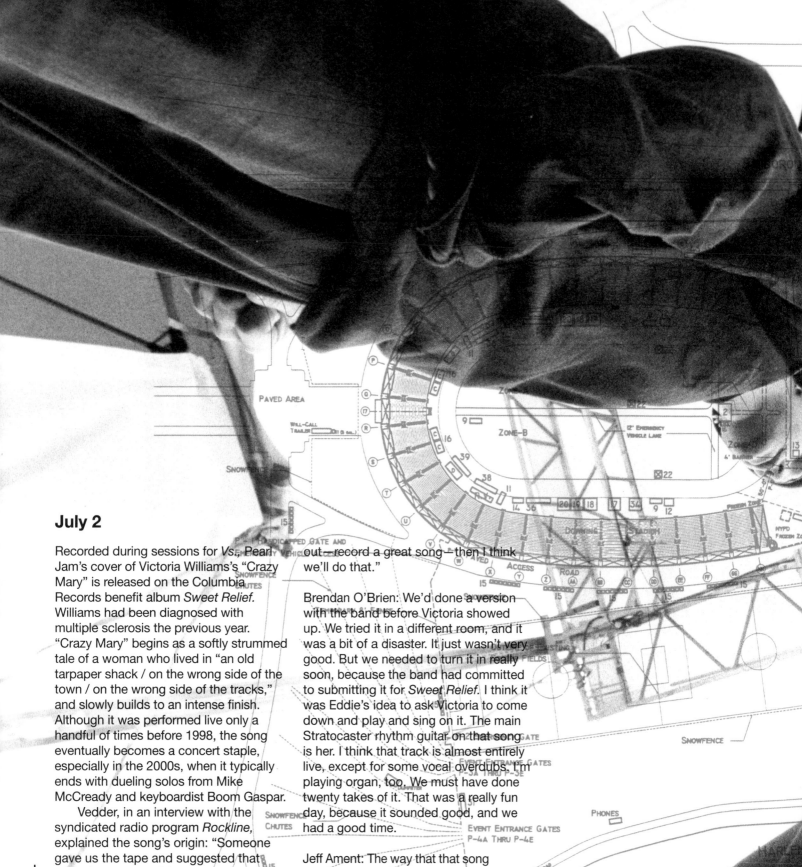

July 2

Recorded during sessions for *Vs.*, Pearl Jam's cover of Victoria Williams's "Crazy Mary" is released on the Columbia Records benefit album *Sweet Relief*. Williams had been diagnosed with multiple sclerosis the previous year. "Crazy Mary" begins as a softly strummed tale of a woman who lived in "an old tarpaper shack / on the wrong side of the town / on the wrong side of the tracks," and slowly builds to an intense finish. Although it was performed live only a handful of times before 1998, the song eventually becomes a concert staple, especially in the 2000s, when it typically ends with dueling solos from Mike McCready and keyboardist Boom Gaspar.

Vedder, in an interview with the syndicated radio program *Rockline*, explained the song's origin: "Someone gave us the tape and suggested that song. It was one of the moments you stop taking for granted that fact that you are living and have the use of all your limbs, and so forth. Something that no one should take for granted, and if all we had to do was record a song to help her out—record a great song—then I think we'll do that."

Brendan O'Brien: We'd done a version with the band before Victoria showed up. We tried it in a different room, and it was a bit of a disaster. It just wasn't very good. But we needed to turn it in really soon, because the band had committed to submitting it for *Sweet Relief*. I think it was Eddie's idea to ask Victoria to come down and play and sing on it. The main Stratocaster rhythm guitar on that song is her. I think that track is almost entirely live, except for some vocal overdubs. I'm playing organ, too. We must have done twenty takes of it. That was a really fun day, because it sounded good, and we had a good time.

Jeff Ament: The way that that song was written fits perfectly in Boom's wheelhouse. The first time he played it with us, it was like, "Oh shit. That *is* Boom!"

Mike McCready: Boom has a real blues-based background. On that song, he told

1993

me, "Start off slow, and build," because a lot of times, I will play superfast and go, "Why did I do that?" From his advice, I start it off slow. He starts the solo, and I walk over kind of slowly to him. We kind of just nonverbally communicate. He'll do a riff, and I'll try to replicate it on guitar. We go back and forth, back and forth, and then hook up on a common chord. It's so fun.

July 2–7

Stadio Bentegodi, Verona, Italy; Stadio Flaminio, Rome, Italy

Pearl Jam opens four shows in massive stadiums for U2 on its highly conceptual Zooropa tour, playing in front of audiences that are inattentive at best and openly hostile at worst. Vedder seems to feed on this ambivalence, which matches his own mixed feelings about this stage in U2's creative evolution. Bemused, Bono is near the front of the crowd on the second night in Rome to watch Vedder perform with the words "Paul Is Dead" gaffer-taped onto his T-shirt (a pun on the U2 front man's real name, Paul Hewson) as well as a fly mask (seemingly a dig at the U2 song "The Fly").

Eddie Vedder: U2 was one of my favorite groups of all time. I'd seen them from the *War* tour to this new, intensified Technicolor version on such a large scale in these European stadiums on Zoo TV. I felt like in order to watch the band, I had to cup my hands over my eyes. I didn't want to be watching the biggest screen ever invented. It was rare that Bono was within twenty yards of any other member of the band. I felt like it was my duty as this old-school follower to tell one of the guys, "This shit ain't working!" But after every song, 80,000 Italians are clapping, screaming, and losing their minds. So who was I to say?

A couple years later, I sent a picture of our stage diagram to the Edge as a joke. It was like four stick figures drawn on a piece of paper. The only other thing written on it was "35 feet across." That was basically our setup. That was the detailed diagram we were operating on. I'd heard U2 was working on a record and practicing in a garage, so I sent it to Edge. I said, "I heard you're working on new stuff that sounds organic, so here's a diagram of our stage, should you want to borrow it." It was so tongue-in-cheek, it looked like I had a toothache when I wrote it. But I got back a three-page, beautifully handwritten letter from Edge, who has incredible penmanship. He addressed it in quite a serious matter. By the time of *The Joshua Tree,* they were taking the opportunity to push the stadium rock 'n' roll experience to another level, and they felt that was their duty, whether it was going to work or not. At that point I understood that these weren't decisions they were making out of fashion, or simply being clever. It was like an edict they'd created as a new philosophy for the group; to really explore the avenues of connecting to people on a large level.

Nancy Wilson: That tour tested the foundations of the basic Seattle artistic integrity law at that time. The commercialization that U2 was seriously poking fun at with *Zooropa* was kind of cynical, but it was so big that it was hard to interpret for guys like Eddie and Pearl Jam, who had basically exploded the megacorporate facade of the whole eighties music scene. Eddie and Bono spent a lot of time in corners, talking all night. They had philosophical issues to discuss. Eddie was really having trouble grappling with it. He felt he needed to understand it, and he couldn't, but I think Bono finally got him there.

Eric Johnson: After the last Rome show, I'd heard there was going to be a fireman's strike in the city starting at eight o'clock the next day, and that no planes were going to be allowed to fly out. We had a show to get to in Dublin with Van Morrison and Neil Young, so that was the only thing on my mind. Bono invited the guys to hang out after the show, and I begged them to at least give me a phone number where I could reach them, because we had to leave the hotel at six o'clock to get out ahead of this strike. Of course, at six thirty, Eddie wasn't back yet, nor was Jeff or Stone. And nobody at the hotel spoke English, or didn't want to. The phone was ringing behind the front desk, and this old guy won't answer it. Thinking it was the guys, I just went back there and started answering it. If anybody was speaking Italian, I'd just hang up. Eventually they all rolled in, smiling. Somehow we made the flight.

August 1

Bad Religion's seventh album, *Recipe for Hate,* is released on Epitaph Records and features Eddie Vedder singing on "American Jesus" and "Watch It Die."

1993

August 2–3
Community Center, Berkeley, California

Vedder meets his idol Pete Townshend for the first time when Townshend is in the Bay Area for solo shows to promote his album *Psychoderelict*.

Eddie Vedder: The first night I met Pete, I kind of laid some stuff on him. But he was so gracious. I was terrified, because he was just the most important person to me musically, and probably in other ways, too. Maybe even psychologically. He'd just played these two long solo shows, probably three hours each. I had tried to sneak in and out of the gigs, and then someone said right before the second one that he really wanted to meet me. So then I thought, Well, I can't turn him down. The first couple of songs were nerve wracking because I really wanted to avoid that situation. He was singing "Rough Boys," and he saw me. I was in the fifth row. And he stopped singing and just, like, looked at me. I heard the bootleg recently, and it really did happen. I thought he came back and sang, "I want to bite and kiss you," but the actual lyric is, "We can't be seen together." So I go back, and the first thing he said was, "I waited so long to meet you." He said, "The last time I really remember enjoying playing live was back when this picture was taken." And I looked at it, and it said, "1976." I was like, "Pete, that's in 1976." He goes, "I know. I know. That was the last time."

Pete Townshend: The very first meeting we had, he said, "Help me. I don't know whether I want this." I think I said, "I'm not sure you have a choice. Once you've been elected, you have to serve as mayor. [*Laughs*] You don't have a choice." I think that helped him, because at that time, I think part of him wanted to go and be a bum on the beach in Maui.

September 3
Universal Amphitheater, Universal City, California

"Jeremy" wins video of the year, best group video, and best metal/hard rock video at the MTV Video Music Awards, while director Mark Pellington wins best direction in a video. Pearl Jam premieres "Animal," still more than a month away

from official release on *Vs.,* and plays "Rockin' in the Free World" with a surprise guest, tour mate Neil Young. Vedder tells the crowd that if it weren't for music, he may have wound up turning the gun on himself like the protagonist in "Jeremy."

Eddie Vedder: Our mind is on music, which is probably a really good thing for everybody. We'd love to do things on MTV and just have it kind of be a different form of public access. You know, I don't have MTV. I don't have cable. And so I don't even know—that's how it was at the awards—I just didn't know what it meant, really. It was a strange form of appreciation I showed, I know.

Neil Young: I don't even know what I was doing there, to tell you the truth. But it sounded like a good idea, and we rocked. We rocked it good.

September 10

Pearl Jam's collaboration with Cypress Hill, "Real Thing," is released on Immortal/Epic Soundtrax's *Judgment Night* soundtrack. The song has never been performed live by Pearl Jam.

October 18

Vedder and Ament spend ninety minutes answering questions from fans and premiering music from *Vs.* on the national radio call-in show *Rockline.* Although they bristle at such straightforward queries as "How would you describe the music on your new album?" (Vedder: "We wouldn't. We'd listen to it. Or tell you to listen to it"), they clearly have fun interacting with their audience and letting their guard down. At the end of the session, Vedder and Ament make up a little ditty on the spot about the then ubiquitous "Bee Girl" from the Blind Melon video for "No Rain." Vedder also gives out his home phone number, saying he wants to keep the conversation going with fans and also drive his annoying downstairs neighbor crazy with the constant ringing.

October 18

In an interview with MTV News, Nirvana front man Kurt Cobain says he has

"always hated" Pearl Jam's music but that he and Eddie Vedder have "had a few conversations on the phone, and he's a person I really like. I didn't like him then when I was talking shit about him all the time. Well, now I can appreciate him. I realize that the same people that like our band like their band. So why create some kind of feud over something as trite as that?"

Dave Grohl: I grew up listening to everything from the Beatles to Bowie to Neil Young to Slayer to Minor Threat to ABBA. So I've always appreciated the differences in music. But 1991 was a funny time. It was a changing of the guard. The kids were finally having their say, and they were bored and tired with that same version of rock 'n' roll that had been so popular in the eighties. Guns N' Roses and heavy metal and all of that shit just seemed so dishonest and played out. It didn't seem real. Here we were, these three guys that grew up in shitty, middle-class neighborhoods, that were attached to this American hardcore version of punk-rock morals and ideals. Even U2 seemed like a bunch of dorks to us.

When Nirvana first started getting a lot of attention, it was important to us that we try to explain to everybody that there was a different way of doing things. You don't have to put on makeup. You don't have to wear stage clothes. You don't have to play up to the rock 'n' roll cliches that a lot of people had grown accustomed to. In that way, we were kind of antiestablishment. But I think that sometimes, that sort of stubborn morality would get in the way of appreciating music. I think what happened with our so-called feud with Pearl Jam was that Kurt was vocal about his dislike of their music, to the point that it made it seem like our bands hated each other. Kurt's musical taste was one thing. But I think his appreciation of the people and of the band was another. Kurt was extremely opinionated and really vocal about that kind of shit, sometimes to a fault.

Peter Buck, R.E.M. guitarist: I moved from Athens, Georgia, to Seattle in 1993 and started crossing paths with the Pearl Jam and Nirvana guys. Actually, I was Kurt's next-door neighbor. He used to call occasionally just to talk about stuff. But it was so overwhelming. The

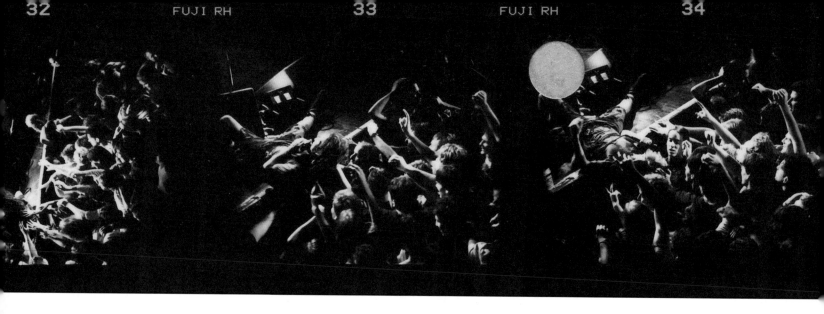

Athens scene is so laid back. Even when R.E.M. got popular, it wasn't that big of a deal. In Seattle, it was heavy duty. All of a sudden, these guys I'd vaguely met were as famous as Elizabeth Taylor. It was really hard for everybody to deal with. Every night at the Crocodile Cafe, there'd be thousands of kids who you could tell hadn't heard a hard rock record until the year before. I remember thinking, I don't know how these guys are dealing with it.

October 19

A week after its vinyl release, *Vs.* is issued on CD in North America by Epic Records.

Michele Anthony: Michael Goldstone and I had to follow the band around Italy that summer to gather the artwork and lyrics for the album, which at the time the band was doing completely by hand. None of it was done by the end of those shows, so we followed them to London, and then to Ireland. Tommy Mottola, the president of Sony at the time, finally told us, "Look, you can't just fly all over the world with Pearl Jam." We were prepared to come back empty-handed, but Eddie promised to have them for me at breakfast the day we were supposed to leave. And sure enough, at eight that morning, he met me in the coffee shop of the hotel and handed me everything. I carried them back to New York in a bag like they were CIA papers.

Tim Bierman: I owned a record store in Missoula, Montana, called Rockin' Rudy's Record Rental. Because Jeff was a Missoula guy, Pearl Jam frenzy hit

there as hard as it hit anywhere. We had a midnight release party at the store, and hundreds of people were lined up outside waiting to get in. I think we sold over four hundred copies of *Vs.* Jeff actually called me after midnight from somewhere on the road to check in, and I was able to hold the phone out to the crowd. It was literally like a concert. People were hooting and hollering and screaming congratulations. In a little town in Montana, it was pretty crazy to feel that big groundswell.

October 25

A close-up concert photo of Vedder, eyes closed and bellowing into a microphone, graces the cover of *Time* magazine alongside the headline "All the Rage: Angry young rockers like Pearl Jam give voice to the passions and fears of a generation." Vedder had refused to be interviewed for the piece and did not give his consent for his photo to be used on the cover.

Eddie Vedder: Kurt and I only spoke on the phone a few times, but we discussed this during one of them. *Time* wanted to interview both of us, and we just decided we didn't want to do it. We agreed that we didn't want or need any more attention at that point, then they still put me on the cover. I heard later that he was upset about it, which made me even more infuriated about the situation.

Chris Cornell: One thing about Eddie's attitude, which was always extremely consistent from the very beginning, was that he wanted Pearl Jam to be a band

that goes out and tours in a van and pays its dues and plays clubs and makes albums, and has a slow, natural life. Somewhere in there, he wants the whole world to know who they are, but he was very, very specific about not wanting it to be right this second. All of that would come out later when you would hear criticisms about him complaining about the enormity of the success. I would hear people say, "Well, he wasn't that way in the beginning. He wanted to dominate the universe, and now they're a big success and he's complaining." That's not true. He was actually very shy about the idea that they would immediately go out and have huge commercial success.

You've got to really hand it to everyone in Pearl Jam that they managed to stay together and figure out a way to exist as a band. When they became TV stars because of the first three videos, and specifically "Jeremy," they made a decision to not do that anymore. Anything it was that they seemed to be uncomfortable with, they changed their approach and stuck to it and never, never faltered from it, no matter what happened. That's pretty rare. I can't name off the top of my head another band that's actually ever done that.

October 25
Off Ramp, Seattle

Pearl Jam plays a surprise hometown show and then another two days later at the Catalyst club in Santa Cruz, California. The gigs serve as warm-ups for a two-month North American tour in support of *Vs.* Set lists vary dramatically

from night to night—"Oceans" sets
a low-key tone on October 30 in San
Jose, while "Go" is like a dynamite
explosion to start the next day's show in
Berkeley—and nearly every song from
the new release is in heavy rotation.
Pearl Jam is also already playing songs
like "Whipping" and "Last Exit," which
will figure prominently in album number
three, and is well on its way to making
staples of covers like "Rockin' in the Free
World" and the Who's "Baba O'Riley."

October 26

Vs. debuts at no. 1 on the *Billboard* 200
and sets a new record with first-week
sales of 950,378 copies in the United
States, according to Nielsen SoundScan.
In fact, *Vs.* sells more copies that week
than the nine other albums in the Top
10 combined. Industry observers seem
alternately flabbergasted and overjoyed,
prompting a host of "grunge is here
to stay after all"–type of stories in the
mainstream press. Pearl Jam is officially
the biggest band in the world, but the
celebration is muted.

Tim Bierman: I was just starting to hang
out with Jeff and the band. We were
on our way to the show at the Warfield
Theater in San Francisco. Eddie wasn't
there, but everybody else was. They were
stressed out already, and Kelly seemed
kind of nervous. He told the guys they'd
sold one million copies of *Vs.* in the first
week. I was expecting everybody to
jump up and congratulate each other,
but instead they just stared out into
the street. I was really confused. I was

1993

thinking, All of a sudden they may be the biggest band in the world, and they're scared by it. It made me watch the show with a different perspective, and that's kind of when I really got it.

Jeff Ament: Partly, we didn't understand it. In a perfect world, we hoped to grow a little more slowly than we did. The more we fought it, the bigger we got. We stopped doing interviews and all this other stuff, but we're still breaking sales records. We all came from nothing, or not very much. And all of a sudden, the world is your oyster. You go from not being able to get a show in town at the two-hundred-capacity club, and now you have every band in the universe saying, "Do you want to go on tour with us?" It was great, but it was weird. The overriding feeling was of guilt, like, do we deserve this yet? There may be a time when we deserve it, but we didn't think it was that quickly.

October 28

Pearl Jam's first cover story in *Rolling Stone,* for which Cameron Crowe spends time with them during *Vs.* sessions, in Seattle, and on tour supporting U2, hits newsstands.

November 5
Empire Polo Fields, Indio, California

Pearl Jam plays an instantly infamous show before twenty-five thousand mud-encrusted fans at the future site of the Coachella Valley Music & Arts Festival, which had never previously hosted a rock concert. The crowd starts throwing shoes onstage during sets by the opening bands, and continues to do so throughout Pearl Jam's performance. Before the first encore, Vedder shouts that he and Ament "are going to the front gate, and

when you exit, we are going to beat the shit out of every barefoot person here!" The version of "Blood" from this show is released on the CD single for "Daughter," while the improv rant "Fuck Me in the Brain" shows up on the third Ten Club holiday single.

November 6
Mesa Amphitheatre, Mesa, Arizona

"Yellow Ledbetter" is performed live in its complete form for the first time at this show, proceeds from which benefit two groups opposed to building enormous telescopes on sacred Apache Indian ground.

November 9

Credited as M.A.C.C., Mike McCready, Jeff Ament, Chris Cornell, and Matt Cameron cover Jimi Hendrix's "Hey Baby (Land of the New Rising Sun)" on Reprise Records's Hendrix tribute album *Stone Free.*

November 30
Aladdin Theater, Las Vegas

With Mudhoney on hand as the opening act, a mini–Green River reunion featuring Gossard, Ament, Mark Arm, and Steve Turner takes place for the first time since the band broke up in 1987. The musicians, augmented by Urge Overkill drummer Chuck Treece, play "Swallow My Pride" and "Ain't Nothin' to Do" in the first encore. Later, an Elvis impersonator named "Terry Presley" duets with Eddie Vedder on Ol' Blue Eyes' "My Way."

Jeff Ament: After Green River broke up, there were some things said from their perspective about us that were hurtful and totally not truthful. I couldn't help but stand on the other side of the line that was drawn and say, "We're better."

1993

CO & terry presley, Elvis' cnsin, VEGAS w/ MUDHONEY

Stone Gossard: Jeff and I sort of made a conscious choice about parting ways with Green River, so I'm not exactly sure why Jeff would have been stung as much as they might have been stung. [*Laughs*] I remember feeling like, "Wow, they really jumped onto something that sounds good right away." I was very happy for them. I was glad Steve and Mark had found each other again and were making music that sort of sounded like what I think probably was more natural for both of those two guys to be making.

Mark Arm: That was definitely the time when we reconnected. Pearl Jam were huge. It was a weird thing, because the focus wasn't on the band so much as it was on Eddie. We played with them in Colorado, and I remember kids chanting, "Eddie! Eddie!" before they came on. It wasn't like they were chanting, "Pearl Jam! Pearl Jam!" But clearly he was speaking to a lot of people at that point.

December 7–9
Seattle Center Arena, Seattle

Pearl Jam basks in having almost made it through an extraordinary year with three triumphant sold-out shows at the hometown Seattle Center. Vedder jokes that the Momma-Son trilogy of "Alive," "Once," and "Footsteps" is like Pearl Jam's version of *The Nutcracker Suite,* and offers the endearingly casual farewell, "We'll see you guys around town," before the penultimate song of the last show.

December 13
Pier 48, Seattle

The year 1993 is supposed to end on a high note, with a special moment of camaraderie between the two biggest bands from Seattle—and possibly the world. MTV rolls tape for its *Live and Loud New Year's Eve* special, which was to feature Nirvana and Pearl Jam, plus the Breeders and Cypress Hill. The stream of negative comments from Kurt Cobain about Pearl Jam had eased up in recent months, and there seemed to be no better way to put the whole episode in the past than for the bands to share the stage on this night. But just hours before the taping begins, Vedder falls ill and Pearl Jam cancels. Ament and Gossard do drop by, however, and even jam with Cypress Hill on "Real Thing." Nirvana plays a dazzling set that goes on a half hour longer than planned to make up for Pearl Jam's absence. Had Vedder made it out that night, it would have been the last time he'd see Cobain alive.

Jeff Ament: Stone and I just wanted to be part of the show however we could, so we played with Cypress Hill. I remember going up to Kurt and Courtney and saying, "How's it going?" and she said something like, "Why are you here? I thought you'd be playing basketball." I was like, "Okay, have a good night." That was pretty much my typical interaction with Kurt. I watched a little bit of Nirvana and then left.

1993

1993

1993

130

LM-OFFRAMP-03

"Where's Eddie?"

It was afternoon, mid-April 1993. Sessions were well under way for the second Pearl Jam album at the Site, a state-of-the-art studio in San Rafael, California, favored by the Keith Richardses of the world. Even though they bashed out four new songs right off the bat, including two incendiary rockers that were double the speed of anything on *Ten*, it had taken the band a while to get comfortable here. The idea was that getting out of Seattle, where things had become more than a little crazy, would be good for everybody.

Right now, there was a more immediate problem: There was no sign of Pearl Jam's lead singer. Vedder had vocals to sing and lyrics to write. But he hadn't shown his face at the Site for several days. Fed up with the cushy surroundings at the studio (there was a chef on duty at all times) and feeling a good deal less than creative, he had taken to disappearing into San Francisco, thirty miles to the south, or just parking his truck nearby and falling asleep in it. And when he was at the Site, he hunkered down in the studio's sauna, turning it into his room.

Sure, there was work to do, but you couldn't blame Vedder for needing some space and time to process exactly what was going on. *Ten* had by this point sold 4.7 million copies, and you couldn't scan an FM radio dial without hearing two or three songs from the album playing simultaneously. The music spoke to teenagers around the world—some of whom just thought grunge was cool, some of whom were sure that Eddie was singing directly to them.

The band was finding some solace in the music being made at the Site under the watchful eye of producer Brendan O'Brien, to whom it had been introduced by members of the Red Hot Chili Peppers. Jeff Ament and Stone Gossard were particularly enamored with O'Brien's production on the Black Crowes' smash hit 1992 album *The Southern Harmony and Musical Companion,* and after a trial run in Atlanta during an off day on the Lollapalooza tour the previous summer, all parties agreed that they should work together on the second Pearl Jam album a few months later.

"My job was to try and keep everybody feeling as creative as possible," O'Brien reflects. "I encouraged us to meet every morning. It was like, 'Okay. Tomorrow, nine thirty, pep talk in the kitchen, and then we're going to play softball.' We did that for quite a while. It was a way to get us all together to have fun.

"The idea was to camp out at the Site, work the songs up, and record them one at a time," he continues. "That way, we wouldn't get too far ahead of ourselves. But I don't think anybody anticipated that Eddie wasn't going to relate to it very well. He didn't like that Stone would show up in a robe and slippers to rock. So there came a point about halfway through where there was a group of songs for which he had no lyrics, and he let me know he had to go off and disappear for a while."

"It would have been nice if somebody with some perspective would have made us recognize this, but we just got way too far ahead of Ed at that point," Ament says. "We'd come up with a couple of songs, and he'd be working on lyrics. He'd come back, and there'd be another song. That went on for ten days, where we had fifteen song ideas, and he's still working on the fourth or fifth song. We should have been more sensitive to that and left him to do his thing."

"On the first record, we were living in a basement, and I was pissing in Gatorade bottles and putting quarters in the parking meter so my truck wouldn't get tickets," Vedder says. "On the second one, I felt too far away from the basement. It was a hard place for me at that point to write a record. Especially with lyrics, I didn't want to be writing about hillsides and trees among luxurious surroundings. I was more into people and society, chaos and confusion, and answering the question, What are we all doing here?"

On the songs already put to tape, Vedder was channeling his unease with being anointed spokesman for a generation. "I am lost, I'm no guide / but I'm by your side," he promised on "Leash," which Pearl Jam had been playing live since late 1991. (Perhaps pointing right at those for whom grunge was a commodity to be bought and sold, he screamed, "Get out of my fuckin' face.") "Rats," set to a loping funk groove, theorized that the furry little rodents might actually be more admirable than humans. On "Blood," Vedder shredded his throat as he pleaded, "It's . . . my . . . blood!" as if to say, "What more can I give?"

The door opened, and Vedder walked in. He certainly hadn't slept in a bed with sheets the night before, and he had a pretty bad case of poison ivy from wandering around in the nearby hills. No words were exchanged as he made his way into the vocal booth, nodding at his bandmates along the way. "Let's try 'Daughter,'" he said.

Written by Gossard, the track was hatched the previous summer in a hotel bathroom in Denver ("because it sounded better," according to Vedder) and later on the band's tour bus during Lollapalooza. It was played live for the first time, with rough lyrics, at the end of the year during

Pearl Jam's first appearance at Neil Young's Bridge School Benefit outside San Francisco.

The song was a chilling peek behind the curtains of a home where a young girl suffered unnamed abuse at the hands of her parents. On the reference tracks, Vedder was originally singing "Don't call me brother" instead of "Don't call me daughter" during the chorus. When he made the switch, the song took on an entirely different meaning. "'Don't call me brother' has this kind of hippie connotation, but 'Don't call me daughter' was just straight up deep," O'Brien says with a laugh.

"I look at that as one of the best songs I've written and one of our best collaborations," Gossard says. "It was figuring out a weird tuning that all of a sudden just made the guitar feel different. When I talk about how many different perspectives and how many different stories Ed's got to tell, one of the most important things is his ability to write from other people's point of view, and in particular from a female point of view. That song is just instantaneous in its impact. It's like you only have to hear it once. You know the whole story, or you at least sense the whole story."

Vedder's storytelling was just as evocative on songs like the largely acoustic, waltz-tempoed "Elderly Woman Behind the Counter in a Small Town," on which the titular narrator is moved to take stock of her stuck-in-a-rut life after encountering an old flame. The lyric "hearts and thoughts they fade / fade away" conjures the opportunities never seized, and later in the song, the line "I just want to scream / Hello!" reveals how buried the subject's true desires have become. Ironically, it became an instant crowd-participation moment at concerts, with Vedder often yielding the last word to the roaring audience.

Vedder had written the chords shortly after waking up in the studio one morning, and the words spilled out just as quickly—he recalls the entire song was composed in less than thirty minutes. Gossard happened to be sitting outside reading the paper, told Vedder he'd liked what he'd heard, and by the end of the day, "Elderly Woman" was in the can.

Album closer "Indifference" marries some of Vedder's most emphatic lyrics ("I'll swallow poison, until I grow immune /

I will scream my lungs out till it fills this room") with the most restrained music Pearl Jam had ever written. One could almost picture the band performing in a circle surrounded by candles, seeking strength from its unwavering conviction to "keep taking punches / until their will grows tired."

On "Dissident," Vedder crafts a tale that has been interpreted both literally (a political refugee is taken in by a woman who then betrays him) and as a metaphor for sexual abuse. (The singer once told a live audience, "A woman's word is sacred, and no means no, and that's what a 'holy no' is.") And on "Glorified G," he makes an entire song out of a tossed-off comment by drummer Dave Abbruzzese, who unwittingly told his bandmates that he'd recently purchased a couple of guns.

Outraged, Vedder exclaimed, "You bought a gun?" Abbruzzese replied, "In fact, I bought two," which became the first line of the track. Recalls McCready of the song, which was born out of a jam where he, Gossard, and Ament were playing parts that didn't seem to work at all with one another, "Dave said he had guns at his house, but that they were 'glorified versions of pellet guns,' and Ed ran with that."

Abbruzzese was also responsible for the album's blistering opening track, "Go," which started life as something quite different. "We were sitting around a campfire at the Site hanging out at night," McCready says of the track, which is actually about a car on the verge of breaking down, and not a toxic relationship, as the lyrics imply. "Dave had an acoustic guitar in dropped-D tuning, and he came up with this riff. He didn't have a pick, either. It was odd to have a drummer playing guitar but also to have such a cool riff. We worked on it a little bit that night, and the next day, we finished it in the studio."

Because this was Pearl Jam's first album with Abbruzzese, who'd joined just before the release of *Ten* in 1991, Ament had been on a mission to make their rhythm section as tight as could be, and the results were evident on songs like "Rats," "Leash," and "Go."

"I remember playing along with tons of records beforehand, like Fela Kuti, the Police, and some reggae stuff, really trying to soak up something different," Ament says. "It was a little bit like we

were making our first record all over again, because it was with a different drummer and a new producer. And Dave had really different strengths as a drummer than Dave Krusen. The groove shifted on the second record."

With time ticking to finish the album, there was one song in particular that just wasn't working to the satisfaction of Vedder and O'Brien. Vedder had brought in the propulsive "Rearviewmirror" virtually complete, and for the first time in the Pearl Jam catalog, the song featured him playing guitar. The verse riff was something he'd been noodling on for years. His singing radiated intensity as he described leaving a bad situation far behind—"Saw things so much clearer / Once you were in my rearviewmirror"—a perfect match of music and lyrics.

But Vedder was unhappy with his vocal takes, and O'Brien was not satisfied with Abbruzzese's playing. On one of the last days at the Site, both Vedder and Abbruzzese finally nailed their parts, after which Abbruzzese threw his sticks against the studio wall, a sound audible on the recorded version. Later, he punched a hole through his snare drum and tossed it over a hill near the studio.

"I had everything to prove there, and those guys were coming off a ten-million-selling record, so they were feeling the pressure," O'Brien says. "Myself, I was thrilled with the idea of following up a big record. But there was a moment at the end where it was just time to leave that place. It was time to go.

"There was still a little bit of work to be done, but I'd made all the roughs," he continues. "Eddie, for whatever reason, maybe because of the way the first album was finished, felt like that was it, and that he wasn't going to get an opportunity to fix things and have his say. He was very emotional and upset about us leaving with things undone. I had to explain to him, 'I'm not going to fuck you over here. We're going to finish this the way we're supposed to finish it. But we all need to get out of here!' He was really worried the album was going to get thrown out there without him having the chance to change things. It was a trust thing with him that he needed to get past."

Another major unresolved issue at that point concerned a stunning track titled "Better Man," which dated back to Vedder's pre–Pearl Jam project

Bad Radio. A slow-building, midtempo composition that begins with only Vedder's voice and guitar, "Better Man" is a vivid story song about a woman trapped in an abusive relationship. Cowering in bed at four in the morning as her man stumbles home, the woman wrestles with the "lie" that she "still loves him" and how she wants to leave him but "can't find a better man." And though the music builds to an anthemic finish, the resolution of the tale is completely ambiguous: "She loved him / She don't want to leave this way / She needs him / That's why she'll be back again."

O'Brien had heard Pearl Jam play the song during preproduction rehearsals in Seattle and was immediately smitten. "After they finished, I was like, 'Awesome! That's a hit! That's fabulous. Why haven't I heard that before? It wasn't on any of the tapes I had,'" he recalls. "They all just looked straight down, and the whole room was deflated. I knew I'd said the wrong thing.

"It was a very personal song for Eddie, and one of the first songs he'd written," he continues. "He didn't want to hear that it was a big smash hit. I learned something very valuable. At that point, I didn't know Eddie that well. I said to him, it would be great to see what you've got going on lyrically. He had all his lyrics

taped to the posts in the rehearsal room. He goes, 'Sure, no problem.' As I'm leaving that day, he sticks a Polaroid in my bag and says, 'Check this out later.' It was a Polaroid he'd taken of the lyrics on the post, and the note says, 'Here's those lyrics you were asking about.' It was kind of brilliant, but it was also him serving notice, like, We're not going to talk about that song right now. In due time, but not now."

Still, O'Brien couldn't resist suggesting Pearl Jam try recording the song at the Site. "I was certain the world was going to love it, and I was certain that Pearl Jam needed it," he says. But when they did, "it was tentative and not

really working out." What happened next still raises O'Brien's blood pressure.

"Eddie told me he'd decided to give the song to Greenpeace for a charity record, and that Chrissie Hynde from the Pretenders was going to sing it," he says. "I was like, 'What? What? We can't give one of our best songs away!'" Adds Gossard, "That was the beginning of Ed's 'Now that I know Brendan wants to do it, I don't want to do it.'"

O'Brien reluctantly agreed to produce a separate "Better Man" session at George Lucas's nearby Skywalker Ranch, but for reasons none of the key parties is willing to discuss, Hynde never showed up. O'Brien then decided to stop pushing for its inclusion on the Pearl Jam album, content enough that at least it wasn't going to appear anywhere else for the time being.

"I have to be honest with you: I've never thrown a session in my life, but I kind of did that day," O'Brien says. "I didn't work real hard to make it sound good. It was a weird setup anyway, and the band was uncomfortable. I made no effort to help them, because I didn't want that song going away. I had no intention of Chrissie Hynde doing that song. It was like, over my dead body! That was *our* song."

When it came time to choose a name for the album, the band gravitated toward *Five Against One,* inspired by the first line of the song "Animal." Gossard wrote the main instrumental riff for the funky track back in 1990, and it appears on the original pre–Pearl Jam instrumental demo tape he made then with Ament, McCready, and Cameron.

Gossard loved the proposed title and its nod toward the struggles the band was enduring not only in its attempts to make a great sophomore album but also to come to grips with the five very different personalities that made up Pearl Jam. At the last minute, however, the band decided to call the album *Vs.,* even though some cassettes had already been pressed with *Five Against*

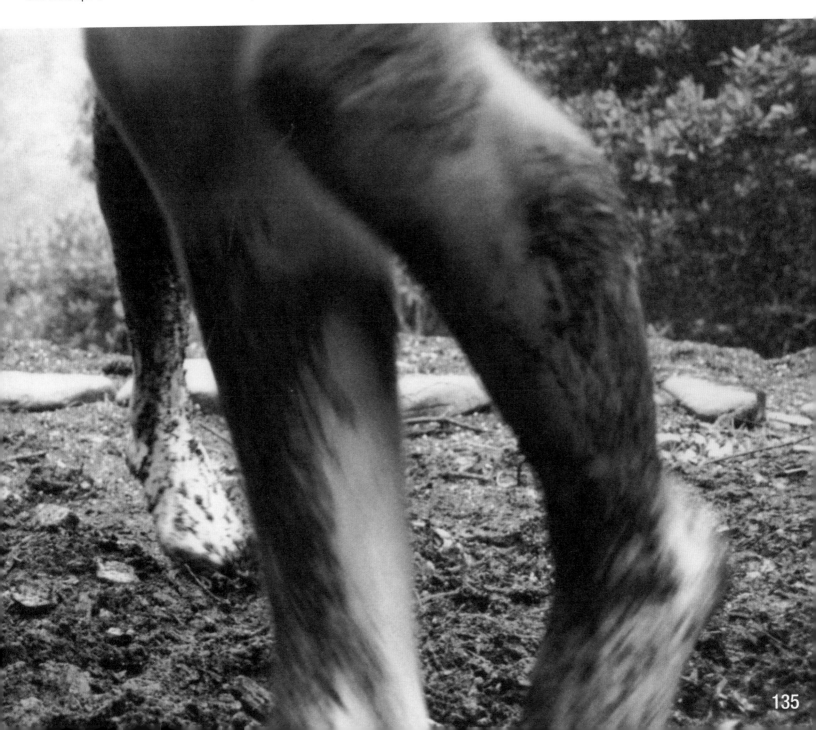

One as the title. For the cover, the band chose Ament's black-and-white close-up photograph of a sheep trying to stick its head through a wire fence.

"I think *Five Against One* was perceived as a bit harsh, within the band," he says. "I threw out *Vs.* last minute, but it turned out being a cool title. It did sort of feel like us against the world a little bit. We were poor twenty-seven-year-old victims at the time. [*Laughs*] We were testy artists, always pushing the boundaries as far as we could go."

Indeed, that zest for continual forward momentum is at the heart of *Vs.* "As *Vs.* started to come together, I realized *Ten* wasn't representative of how we wanted to sound," Ament says. "I remember going into the control room and being blown away at how incredible it sounded. We were actually becoming a good band. We could get superheavy, weird, and experimental, and also mellow. We were achieving our goal, which was to be a band that could play a lot of different styles."

"It's maybe my favorite Pearl Jam record," Gossard says. "It felt more like we could be this super hard rock band, have these folk songs, have a ballad, have this song that's kind of a groove kind of song and a midtempo rocker. I think our first record has that to some degree, but *Vs.* continues the experiment of *Ten* in a way that shows that we're not going to be just one thing. We're not going to be AC/DC and just give you the meat and potatoes every song. We have multiple songwriters and different perspectives."

1993

CHAPTER 1994

1994

Pearl Jam didn't name its second album *Vs.* for nothing. In 1994 the fight had spread to several fronts: fame and celebrity, consumer rights, philosophical approaches to music and business, and the commercialization and homogenization of rock 'n' roll. The suicide of Nirvana's Kurt Cobain, who struggled mightily with success, brought many of these issues to a head. But solutions and new perspectives began to emerge, in the form of alternatives to playing in Ticketmaster venues, rewarding fan club members with the best seats in the house, and creating dedicated Pearl Jam radio broadcasts. With Ticketmaster, Pearl Jam was in for an epic, down and dirty battle with the potential to cost its reputation, and its bottom line, dearly. But it seemed as if the band was at its most powerful when backed into a corner, and Pearl Jam was prepared to keep swinging.

February 23–24
Carnegie Hall, New York

Eddie Vedder is an unannounced performer at two star-studded concerts dubbed Daltrey Sings Townshend in celebration of Who front man Roger Daltrey's fiftieth birthday. At the first show, many attendees have yet to return to their seats after intermission and thus miss Vedder's acoustic performances of "The Kids Are Alright," "Sheraton Gibson," and "My Generation." The next night, word has spread that Vedder will be playing, and he receives a standing ovation following a set of "Let My Love Open the Door," "Squeeze Box," "Naked Eye," and "My Generation." Later, with help from Jim Rose, Vedder destroys his dressing room on a whim and attempts to write the lyric "I hope I die before I get old" from "My Generation" on the wall in his own blood. Carnegie Hall, in turn, sends him a bill for $25,000 in damages.

March

Pearl Jam announces its intention to keep ticket prices for its upcoming summer tour below $20. In doing so, the band challenges what it feels are unjust service fees being charged by Ticketmaster, the dominant ticketing agency in the country.

March 6–7
Paramount Theater, Denver

Pearl Jam begins the second leg of its North American touring in support of *Vs.* and debuts two brand-new songs: the rip-roaring punk rocker "Spin the Black Circle" and a three-chord screed on the commodification of the band's music, "Not for You."

March 9
Civic Center, Pensacola, Florida

Pearl Jam performs on the one-year anniversary of the murder of Pensacola-based abortion provider Dr. David Gunn, with proceeds benefiting Rock for Choice. Setting the tone for the evening, Eddie Vedder opens the show with a solo performance of Tom Petty's "I Won't Back Down" and later tells the audience, "All these men trying to control women's bodies are really beginning to piss me off. They're not in touch with what's real. Well, I'm fucking mean and I'm ugly, and my name is reality." Dr. Gunn's son, David Jr., also speaks during the encore. Anti-abortion pamphlets are distributed in the venue parking lot, one of which reads, "If you continue on the road you are on, rejecting Jesus Christ, you will have a front row seat in the hottest concert in dark, burning, eternal hell. When the doors close, you are in forever."

March 10–13
Chicago Stadium; New Regal Theater, Chicago

In Chicago to play two shows, one exclusively for fan club members, Pearl Jam goes head-to-head with Ticketmaster for the first time. As Stone Gossard later testifies before Congress, "Ticketmaster insisted on imposing a $3.75 service charge on top of the $18 price of a ticket to our concerts. We negotiated with Ticketmaster's general manager in Chicago and obtained an agreement to identify that service charge separately from the actual price of the ticket. Then, just as tickets were to go on sale, Ticketmaster again reneged. It was necessary for us to threaten to perform at another venue before Ticketmaster backed down and agreed to sell tickets that separately disclosed its service charge. Even then, Ticketmaster told us that its concession only extended to our Chicago shows and we should not expect them to be willing to do it elsewhere."

The fan club gig at the 2,500-capacity New Regal Theater quickly becomes legendary in fan circles for its set list full of then rare and unreleased songs ("Hard to Imagine," "Yellow Ledbetter," "Alone," "Last Exit"), as well as the last performance of Dave Abbruzzese's "Angel." Vedder leaps from the balcony during "Porch," remaining motionless afterward for nearly a minute before rising back to his feet to sing the last chorus.

March 14–15
Fox Theatre, Saint Louis

Vedder guests with opening act the Frogs at both shows; on the second night, he is lowered from the rafters on wires while wearing gold wings and joins them to sing a few bars of "Jeremy." Another new song that would later become one of Pearl Jam's most beloved, "Corduroy," is played for the first time at the second show.

March 17
Elliot Hall, Purdue University, West Lafayette, Indiana

A bomb scare delays the start of what Vedder later that night says "might be the best show we have ever played."

CARNEGIE HALL
ED'S DRESSING ROOM
DALTREYS BIRTHDAY

141

March 19
Masonic Theater, Detroit

While trying to pursue another strategy for keeping ticket prices and service fees low, Pearl Jam again comes into conflict with Ticketmaster over the ticketing for this show. As Gossard later testifies before Congress, "In Detroit, we decided to try to bypass Ticketmaster by distributing tickets through our fan club and by a lottery system. We were informed that Ticketmaster threatened the promoter of this concert with a lawsuit for violating its exclusive Ticketmaster agreement by allowing this method of distribution to occur, and also temporarily disabled the promoter's ticket machine so that it could not print tickets for the concert for that time." According to Ament, Pearl Jam received approximately six hundred thousand ticket requests for this show in a four-thousand-seat venue.

March 20
Crisler Arena, Ann Arbor, Michigan

"Jeremy" opens a show for just the fourth time ever and last to date. Yet another new song, the ballad "Nothingman," debuts here.

March 22
Cleveland State University Convocation Center, Cleveland

Eddie Vedder pays tribute to Pete Townshend by performing his decades-old solo track "Sheraton Gibson," which contains several references to Cleveland. The song has never reappeared on a Pearl Jam set list.

March 24–25

In response to Pearl Jam's public statements about attempting to circumvent using Ticketmaster for its planned summer tour, North American Concert Promoters Association executive director Ben Liss sends a memo to members saying, "Pearl Jam is putting out feelers once again to require promoters to bypass Ticketmaster on their dates later this summer. Ticketmaster has indicated to me they will aggressively enforce their contracts

with promoters and facilities." The next day, Liss sends a second memo with stronger wording, informing promoters that Ticketmaster CEO Fred Rosen "intends on taking a very strong stand on this issue to protect Ticketmaster's existing contracts with promoters and facilities, and further, Ticketmaster will use all available remedies to protect itself from outside third parties that attempt to interfere with those existing contracts."

March 26
Murphy Athletic Center, Murfreesboro, Tennessee

Legendary Booker T. & the MG's guitarist Steve Cropper joins Pearl Jam for a cover of the Otis Redding classic "(Sittin' on) The Dock of the Bay" and sticks around to jam on "Rockin' in the Free World."

March 28
Bayfront Amphitheater, Miami

Approximately twenty-four thousand fans cram into what is intended to be an eight-thousand-capacity venue in downtown Miami; many bust through a metal fence to sneak in. Vedder dedicates "Not for You" to "all those fuckers who were charging more than eighteen dollars for your fucking ticket."

April 2–3
Fox Theatre, Atlanta

Pearl Jam hunkers down in Atlanta to play two sold-out shows at the venerable Fox Theatre and track the first session for its third studio album with Brendan O'Brien. The April 2 show includes a live improv-jam dubbed "Out of My Mind," which later appears as the B-side to the "Not for You" single. With Epic Records footing the bill, the April 3 show is offered live on a free, nonexclusive basis to radio stations around the country—three hundred wind up broadcasting it—and is arguably the most memorable of Pearl Jam's career to that point. For many new fans, it's the first show they've ever heard and/or their first bootleg. The twenty-six-song set includes the live debut of "Satan's Bed" as well as future staple "Better Man," described by Vedder as "a new song, but it was written a long time ago." After the show, Vedder spins

records by Sonic Youth, Mudhoney, Daniel Johnston, Eleven, and Shudder to Think during a DJ set that presages the long-form broadcasts Pearl Jam will host in 1995 and 1998.

Jeff Ament: That was sort of the beginning of us thinking about the live bootleg thing. That balance of playing the songs well plus it being this visceral experience that we knew we presented as a rock band, I just remember trying to figure out how to balance it out. How do I play my instrument in a way that comes across good on a radio, on a live tape, and also play a real rock show? We were listening to ourselves differently from that point on. It made us a better band to put us under the microscope like that. It gave us the confidence to put out every show,

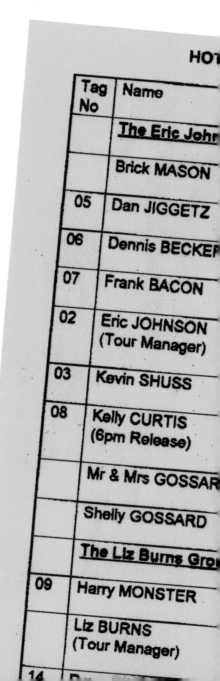

Tag No	Name
	The Eric Johr
	Brick MASON
05	Dan JIGGETZ
06	Dennis BECKEF
07	Frank BACON
02	Eric JOHNSON (Tour Manager)
03	Kevin SHUSS
08	Kelly CURTIS (6pm Release)
	Mr & Mrs GOSSAR
	Shelly GOSSARD
	The Liz Burns Gro
09	Harry MONSTER
	Liz BURNS (Tour Manager)
14	

143

knowing there'd be some mistakes, and we'd be okay with it.

April 8
Patriot Center, Fairfax, Virginia

Nirvana lead singer Kurt Cobain is found dead in his Seattle-area home of a self-inflicted gunshot wound to the head. Cobain had escaped from Exodus Recovery Center in Los Angeles on March 31, flown back to Seattle, and holed up in his house before killing himself. During the postshow DJ session on April 3, Vedder pleaded directly to his fellow front man, whose whereabouts at that time were still unknown, "Please be all right."

That night, the stunned members of Pearl Jam play a tense, emotional, but rarely somber show. "Sometimes, whether you like it or not, people elevate you . . . and it's very easy to fall," Vedder tells the crowd. "I don't think any of us would be in this room if it weren't for Kurt Cobain." Having destroyed his hotel room earlier in the day upon learning about Cobain's death, Vedder accepts Fugazi singer-guitarist Ian MacKaye's offer to spend the night at the famed Dischord Records house in Arlington, Virginia.

Ian MacKaye: I have a memory of listening to music, drinking tea, and doing a lot of talking. Eddie was deeply saddened by Kurt's death and, I think, trying to get his mind around the ramifications that would surely follow.

Eddie Vedder: Kurt still resonates in my life. It always comes up around a campfire, or playing music with a few guys in a room or in a garage, for no particular reason. Maybe there's a basement party with just a few people, of which he had known. I always think, He would have liked this. If he stuck around, this would have been a good night for him. But I didn't know him that well. We were going through similar things. And I understand there were certain things that were in the press; certain things that were maybe motivated by the press and other things that I think he was sincere about. I honor whatever he said, because I had the same feeling, and I've had the same feeling since of, like, people kind of copping their trip. Had Nirvana not been the first band to come out of Seattle and have the attention spike so high, I still

think that things would have happened up here, but not quite the way they did. I always admired and respected him and felt a kinship. I would hear there were some competitive feelings there, and I kind of thought that was good.

Mike McCready: I was pissed at him for a long time. I didn't know him or anything, but I'd seen Nirvana, and I thought they were great. But then they were talking shit about us all along. Jeff and Stone were always like, "Don't say anything. Just let it go." And they were right on that inclination. That's what the press would love. Kurt was comparing us to Poison, and I took that personally. It's sad that he went out the way he did. It was just like, "Why can't we all be in this together?" because we had this camaraderie with Soundgarden. We all wanted to be successful. We were all ambitious, but we didn't step on each other to get there.

Jeff Ament: Stone has said something to the effect of that when Kurt was judging us, it had an impact on us and how we did things. That might have been true for him, but not me. I had a lot of musical peers at that time; people in my life that I really respected. Kurt wasn't one of them. I didn't even know him. The most disappointing thing to me at the time was that I wanted to be more friendly with him. He came from a fucked-up, homophobic small town, and so did I. I felt like there were things we could relate to with one another. Those handful of times when I went up to him to initiate a conversation, I got nothing back. Then he died, and as far as I was concerned, that was it; a lost chance. Having lost Andy a few years previous, I wanted to reach out to Dave Grohl and Krist Novoselic to somehow tell them that it was going to be okay.

The first time I saw Krist after that was probably eight or nine months later. I was with my friend Curtis, and we were going snowboarding. Curtis had just gotten a new Ford Explorer, and he wanted to drive me up to Stevens Pass in the Cascade Mountains in Washington State. The road conditions got superbad out by Monroe. We hit some ice and wound up going backward into a ditch at fifty-five miles an hour. The car rolled over. We were both upside down in his truck, looking at each other, like, "Are you all right?" We walked up to the edge of the road, and the thickest, most beautiful snowflakes were coming down. There

was nobody in sight. I looked back at the car, wondering, Are we dead? What the fuck is going on? All the sudden, this truck pulls up, and it was Krist. I was like, "Maybe we *are* dead!" Krist stayed there with us for a little bit and then drove into town and told the cops that there was a wreck. I think about that a lot, and just how absolutely happenstance it was that he was the first person to find us after what I thought was a near-death experience.

April 9

Pearl Jam accepts an invitation to tour the White House and meets personally with President Bill Clinton. Although they discuss Kurt Cobain's death, the conversation turns to basketball, as Clinton's beloved University of Arkansas Razorbacks had just won the NCAA men's championship.

Eddie Vedder: We were there specifically to find out whether some of the US military bases that had recently been shut down could be used as concert sites. It would have been a way to avoid using Ticketmaster, and it would have been a boon to local economics. I was also asked if I felt okay assisting in an official response to Kurt's suicide, but at the time I was too shell-shocked to offer any help.

Jeff Ament: We went with Mudhoney, and somebody came in and said, "You five people go with him"—the five people being us—and, "You eight guys go over here." The Mudhoney guys got the B tour, and we got the A tour. We saw the war room, the Oval Office, and hung out with Clinton. I have a roll of film of that somewhere. It was pretty incredible. We were cracking jokes. I'd just been to the Final Four in Charlotte, North Carolina, which he attended to see Arkansas play. Every single person that went to the game had to go through a metal detector, but there were only four or five of them in the arena, and I gave him shit about having to miss the first five minutes of the game because of it. Then he proceeded to talk about the Secret Service and how hard it was for him to make the adjustment; like, he couldn't drive his Mustang around. We weren't afraid to ask him anything, and he wasn't afraid to talk about anything. He was just one of the guys.

145

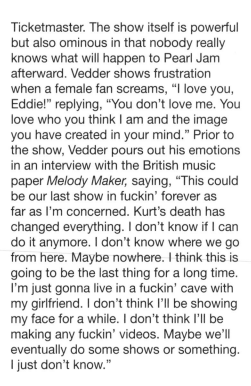

April 10–11
Boston Garden, Boston

At the first show since Kurt Cobain's suicide, Eddie Vedder tells the crowd that Pearl Jam is still feeling the effects of the news. "I've gotta admit, we've got a lot on our minds. It is tough to play. I personally felt we shouldn't play at all. It is really very odd—it's just like that empty feeling." During the second show, "Immortality" is played for the first time, with very different lyrics than what would wind up on the version from *Vitalogy.* Vedder smashes a hole in the stage with his mike stand during the show-closing "Rockin' in the Free World" and disappears into it as the song ends.

April 12
Orpheum Theater, Boston

On the second-to-last show of the spring tour, Pearl Jam allows its crew to create the set list, resulting in a fan-favorite performance featuring several new songs ("Immortality," "Not for You," "Better Man"), old favorites in odd places ("Release" as the encore opener, "Even Flow" second in the set), and ultrararities ("Dirty Frank," plus a cover of the Beatles' "I've Got a Feeling").

April 16

Pearl Jam performs an unheard-of three songs on NBC's *Saturday Night Live:* the still unreleased "Not for You," "Daughter," and "Rearviewmirror." At the end of "Daughter," Eddie Vedder adds a line from Neil Young's "Hey Hey, My My (Into the Black)," the song from which

Kurt Cobain used the line "It's better to burn out than fade away" in his suicide note. As credits roll, Vedder opens his jacket to reveal a large *K* written just above his heart on his T-shirt, and holds his hand there somberly. Unbeknown to his bandmates, Mike McCready was heavily intoxicated for the live broadcast.

Mike McCready: We ended with "Daughter." I remember talking to Stone the next day, and he asked, "What'd you think of 'Daughter'?" And I thought in my mind, We played "Daughter"? I essentially blacked out on TV. I don't remember it. Those are the things I'm not proud of. It's just what I had to go through. That was a heavy time, for sure; some darkness. But that's how I dealt with it, for better or for worse.

April 17
Paramount Theater, New York

This late addition to the tour itinerary winds up being Pearl Jam's last full live performance for nearly nine months, as well as Dave Abbruzzese's final concert as the band's drummer. The majority of the tickets are given to local fan club members, with the rest being distributed through local radio station giveaways, a procedure that also causes issues with

Ticketmaster. The show itself is powerful but also ominous in that nobody really knows what will happen to Pearl Jam afterward. Vedder shows frustration when a female fan screams, "I love you, Eddie!" replying, "You don't love me. You love who you think I am and the image you have created in your mind." Prior to the show, Vedder pours out his emotions in an interview with the British music paper *Melody Maker,* saying, "This could be our last show in fuckin' forever as far as I'm concerned. Kurt's death has changed everything. I don't know if I can do it anymore. I don't know where we go from here. Maybe nowhere. I think this is going to be the last thing for a long time. I'm just gonna live in a fuckin' cave with my girlfriend. I don't think I'll be showing my face for a while. I don't think I'll be making any fuckin' videos. Maybe we'll eventually do some shows or something. I just don't know."

May 6

Unable to find suitable venues to perform in that do not have exclusive contracts with Ticketmaster, and frustrated that the company would not agree to limit its service charge to 10 percent of the face value of each ticket, Pearl Jam cancels its summer tour, with manager Kelly Curtis telling *Billboard* that "the band's committed not to tour until they find an alternative" to what it perceives as Ticketmaster's unfair service fees.

Representatives from the US Justice Department approach the band about filing a memo with the department's antitrust division, which Pearl Jam agrees to do. In it, the band asserts that Ticketmaster, through its extensive, exclusive contracts with major concert venues, controls a monopoly over the marketplace, and that the company has pressured promoters not to handle Pearl Jam shows. On May 31 a Justice

Department spokeswoman tells *Billboard* that the antitrust division is looking into "the possibility of anticompetitive practices in the ticketing industry," thereby launching an investigation.

Stone Gossard: Because of our dispute with Ticketmaster and feeling, really, that the only way we could tour was to sort of go outside and try to do it on our own, and given the amount of time we had and our feelings about security and whether we could actually put on a safe show consistently, we just felt that it wasn't appropriate, and we should deal with this issue first and focus on recording music.

June 30

Stone Gossard and Jeff Ament testify in Washington, DC, before the Information, Justice, Transportation, and Agriculture Subcommittee at congressional hearings regarding possible antitrust action against Ticketmaster. The crux of Gossard's and Ament's testimony is that because Ticketmaster has exclusive contracts with nearly every major concert venue in the United States, bands have no meaningful alternative to distribute their tickets, giving Ticketmaster the power to exercise excessive control over things such as service fees.

Stone Gossard: "Our interest is really quite narrow. We simply have a different philosophy than Ticketmaster about how and at what prices tickets to our concerts should be sold. We can't insist that Ticketmaster do business on our terms, but we do believe we should have the freedom to go elsewhere if Ticketmaster is not prepared to negotiate terms that are acceptable to us."

Although several congressmen seem genuinely interested in conversing with the musicians on the topic, others ask absurd questions ("What does Pearl Jam mean?") or interject that they've been practicing Pearl Jam songs on guitar.

Congresswoman Lynn Woolsey even tells Gossard and Ament, "You're just darling guys." At one point, an exasperated Ament excuses himself to go to the bathroom.

Kelly Curtis: The biggest misconception was that we sued Ticketmaster or that we came to the Justice Department, but none of that happened. We bitched about Ticketmaster because at the time, our tickets were twenty-five or thirty dollars, and Ticketmaster was charging ten or twelve in service charges. We didn't understand that. Our big complaint was, at least separate the prices, so people know what we're charging for tickets. Ticketmaster was superpowerful, and I think they thought of us as snotty-nosed brats. If we were so stupid as to charge so little for our tickets, then they would take the money. How the Justice Department got involved was, I think, due to the publicity that was being generated by our boycott and what we'd said. Doing the congressional hearings—and I'm sure Stone and Jeff feel the same way—was just a joke. I remember thinking afterward that it was a humongous waste of time and just posturing.

Stone Gossard: Anytime you're invited to testify, you have no idea where the energy is coming from to make that happen. You can think, "Oh yeah, they really want to hear our testimony about this particular thing," but there's a lot of manipulation going on at that level. When you're on that big of a stage, it's not in your control. You're sort of playing a part to some kind of larger drama, and I think that's what we walked away knowing.

Mike McCready: We had a lot of bands saying, "We're with you, Pearl Jam." And they all bailed, every one of them. A lot of big-name bands bailed on us. We were out there twisting in the wind by ourselves. I think that maybe that showed some integrity, and people thought, "Okay, they're really doing this for the right reasons. They're trying to keep the prices low."

Eddie Vedder: The guys went to the Holocaust Museum after they testified, and it was a free ticket. However, you had to reserve them. So on a free ticket to the Holocaust Museum, there was a three-dollar service charge from Ticketmaster. Just the idea that they were getting a service charge for a free ticket at the Holocaust Museum, I think that's a pretty symbolic story about who we were up against.

August 1

Dave Abbruzzese is fired from Pearl Jam after a breakfast meeting with Stone Gossard.

Stone Gossard: Dave Abbruzzese is a gentleman. He is a nice guy and a fantastic drummer, and he added a lot to the band. But he was one individual in a situation where five people had to work it out. There comes times when if a personality conflict is not resolved, sometimes you have to make changes. He was in a situation where the band felt they had to make a change, and I helped facilitate that, because I'm part of the whole. It was a missed opportunity for him, for sure, in terms of not figuring out a way to identify that there was a problem and to move through it; to put yourself in a position where you're not being kicked out. I think anyone who listens to those records realizes he is a great drummer. It wasn't his drumming that was the problem. The problem was that he needed to fit in with a group of five very different, strong personalities and do it in a way that worked with those five personalities. I'm sorry that it didn't work out. I wish that it had.

Mike McCready: Dave Abbruzzese was integral in getting us to the level where we were at because he was a really good drummer, and we were out there touring with him. I can't say that he wasn't an integral part of us kind of being huge. He fit in at first, and I got along with him. But I think Dave and Ed never really got along.

Brendan O'Brien: I remember the very last day I saw Dave. He was at the studio in Atlanta, and we were taking a break from *Vitalogy*. Eddie was having a hard time figuring out how to get his guitar sound going. I knew he was a big Pete Townshend fan, so I went and found him a beautiful gold-top '69 Les Paul. He came to the studio on one of the last nights we were there, and I said, "Hey, I got you something." He didn't know what to say. He really was about to cry. He and I at that time did not have a great relationship, but this was a really nice moment between us.

The next day, I see engineer Nick DiDia shaking his head. He goes, "Dude, you have to figure something out." Dave was running around because he had to leave early to do something. He says to me, "I knocked this guitar over. I'll pay to have it fixed." He'd knocked the headstock off. It was a complete and total accident. I remember saying, "Maybe you should hang around and talk to Eddie about it." But he's like, "I've gotta go." Eddie came later, and I showed him the guitar. The look on his face was one of such contempt. I'll never forget it. I felt so bad. Right after that, Kurt died. We were supposed to get back together and finish, but we took a long break. They didn't tour. Everyone was thrown for a loop. During that time, Dave was fired. I don't know that Eddie can ever really look at that guitar the same way. I had it repaired for him beautifully, but it was sort of a metaphor for their relationship. And that was not lost on Nick and I.

Early September

Rumors begin circulating on Usenet and the Pearl Jam forum on America Online that Nirvana drummer Dave Grohl has agreed to replace Dave Abbruzzese in Pearl Jam.

Dave Grohl: I never talked to anybody in the band about playing drums for them. They never asked, and it was never even a question or an issue. Just after Dave was kicked out, I was in New York, and I was walking down the street with my girl. Some guy walks up and goes, "Hey, Dave. Will you sign my drumhead?" So I signed it, and it had Dave Abbruzzese's signature on it. I said, "Oh, you've got Dave from Pearl Jam." And he goes, "Yeah, he's right up the street doing an in-store." So I said to my girl, "Let's go say hi." I didn't know that there were rumors going around that I'd joined Pearl Jam. So I walk into this drum shop, and he's there signing shit. There's a line of people, and I walk past, and not really anybody recognizes me, and I'm like, "Hey, Dave. What's up?" And he looks at me like he'd seen a fucking ghost. He said, "Hey, is it true that the guys asked you to play drums for them?" And I'm like, "No! Why? Fuck no!" It was the weirdest timing.

Draft of June 29, 1994
DCLAN 0027588.01

ORAL REMARKS OF STONE GOSSARD
TO THE INFORMATION, JUSTICE,
TRANSPORTATION AND AGRICULTURE SUBCOMMITTEE
OF THE HOUSE COMMITTEE ON GOVERNMENT OPERATIONS

Mr. Chairman, members of the sub-committee, my name is Stone Gossard and with me is Jeff Ament. I play guitar and Jeff plays bass in Pearl Jam.

I would first like to thank you, Chairman Condit, … this hearing today. We, and I am sure many …icans feel very strongly about the subject of this …d we appreciate your efforts to shed light on this …

All of the members of Pearl Jam remember what it …o be young and not to have a lot of money. Many of …n's fans are teenagers who do not have the money to … $50 or more that is often charged for tickets today. …, given our popularity, we could undoubtedly … to sell-out our concerts with ticket prices at that level, we have made a conscious decision that we do …t to put the price of our concerts out of the reach … fans.

… these reasons, we have attempted to keep the … to our concerts to a maximum of $18. In … have also tried to limit any service charges …mposed on the sale of those tickets to a

Exhibit A

VENUE	TICKET PRICE	SERVICE CHARGE (PHONE)	SHIPPING CHARGE (PHONE)*	SERVICE CHARGE (OUTLET)
	$80.00-35.00	$7.25	$2.50	$5.00
Forum	$35.00-23.50	$6.25	$2.00	$4.25
s	$27.50	$6.25	$2.00	$4.25
Forum	$50.00-30.00	$6…		$4.25
Jr.			…00	$4.25
			…00	$4.25
				$4.00
				$4.00
				$4.00
				$4.00
				$4.00
				$3.75
				$3.50
				$3.00
				$3.00
				$2.25
				$3.00

ERIC

HOUSTON
3542 Timmons
Houston, TX 77027

THE TICKET CO.

ATLANTA
3145 Peachtree Rd. N.E. # 109
Atlanta, GA 30305
(404) 365-6555
Fax (404) 365-8333
(800) 730-7373

RICHARD J. MALEK — DATE 2/21/94
CUSTOMER'S NAME
COMPANY
STREET ADDRESS
PAID
CITY, STATE & ZIP CODE
PHONE 804-3621
CARD NUMBER: Card on file

QTY	SHOW DATE	EVENT	SECTION	ROW	SEAT	PRICE EACH	TOTAL AMOUNT
2	4/3	Pearl Jam	FF	15EE	(2)	300	600—

ALL SALES FINAL
PLEASE CHECK YOUR TICKETS BEFORE LEAVING.
THANK YOU
TOTAL 600—
GRAND TOTAL 600—
NO REFUNDS OR EXCHANGES UNLESS THE EVENT CANCELS. IN THE EVENT OF … HANDLING FEE WILL BE CHARGED. ALL REFUNDS MUST BE MADE … PLEASE NOTE: ALL CHARGES WILL BE MADE

…ic - I showed this to Kelly.
… said to make you a copy so you
… find this fan on concert night.
… wasn't complaining about the
…ice, said he's sure he'll get his
…oneys worth. But ~~the~~ just
…anted to inform us of whats
…oing ON. It's gotta be
…legal. They are making more $$
…an the band.

Thx

…Y SHOULD …lag over the … Pearl Jam's …mony before …Representa- … pushed the …laint against …he national …entative for …tified, deny- …ompany has …ncert indus- …journ among …iced a more

PHOTOGRAPH BY STEVE BARRETT/CONTACT PRESS IMAGES

JAM SESSION: Gossard, right, and Ament are sworn in

know … And M… son, a … that h… Pearl … ing to … Peters … it." Pe… own q… Recor… questi… micro… I've g…

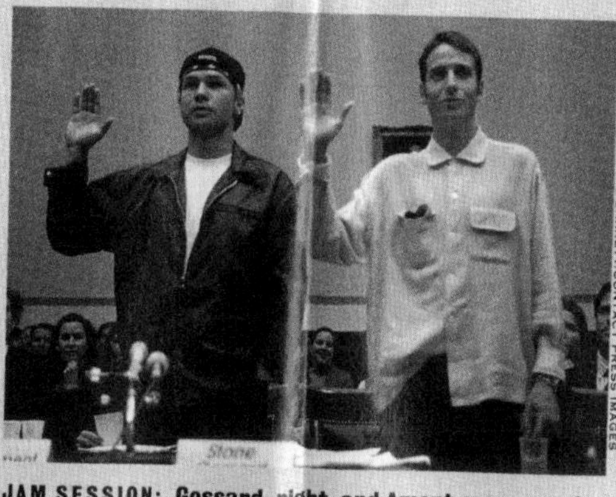

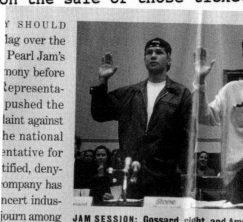

October 1–2

Shoreline Amphitheatre, Mountain View, California

Although no formal announcement is made that he's officially joined the band, former Red Hot Chili Peppers/Eleven drummer Jack Irons makes his first public appearance with Pearl Jam, playing during the band's second performance at Neil Young's annual Bridge School Benefit. On night one, the band plays "Let Me Sleep (It's Christmas Time)" from the 1991 fan club single for the only time to date. "Bee Girl," a song that Eddie Vedder and Jeff Ament had performed live on the air during their 1993 *Rockline* interview, is played for the first time the next night. Pearl Jam also offers stripped-down renditions of "Corduroy," "Not for You," and "Immortality" from the soon-to-be-released *Vitalogy* album, and joins Young both nights to cover the song "Piece of Crap" from his then new album *Sleeps with Angels.*

Neil Young: We were making up verses on the spot. Eddie had some that were really great. That version of that song, there was something going on that I really enjoyed. It showed me what the possibilities were.

November 22

Pearl Jam's third studio album, *Vitalogy,* is issued on vinyl by Epic two weeks ahead of its CD release. The following week, the album debuts at no. 55 on the *Billboard* 200 after shifting thirty-five thousand copies, making it the first vinyl album to chart on sales in that format alone in more than a decade.

Michele Anthony: At that point in time, CD was all the rage, and most companies were not putting out vinyl on any releases. But it was very important to the band that the albums came out on vinyl. Pearl Jam was one of the first bands we made vinyl for in the nineties.

December

Jack Irons is officially hired as Pearl Jam's new drummer.

Jack Irons: Pearl Jam had many phases of drummers. Each of those times, I was in the mix with the conversation and had conversations with them. It was definitely an opportunity they made available to me on a few occasions. But they were taking off so fast and they were so big that I was scared of committing my life

to it. I didn't fare too well in the Red Hot Chili Peppers after really intense touring. In '94, I had moved out of L.A. My longtime band Eleven had just finished a tour with Soundgarden. My son was three or four, and my wife and I had made a pact to get out of L.A. by the time he was of school age. I saved just enough money to get this cabin in Northern California. My wife moved us up there while Eleven was on tour with Soundgarden. I was there in June, July, and August. Then I heard Pearl Jam fired Dave, and I told my wife that maybe the time was right, and maybe those guys won't be touring like they did two years ago. So I reached out to Eddie and told him I'd like to get in the mix and give it a try. The difference in '94 was that I wasn't the only choice anymore. They were definitely going to have auditions, and each guy had a guy in mind they wanted to work with. But it helped me that I was Eddie's guy.

When it got to the point where it looked like I was the most likely guy to get the gig, I spent a bunch of time with Stone. We rehearsed in his basement studio. We never really confirmed that I was totally in the band. I went and did the Bridge School shows, but I didn't really feel confirmed until we started touring a few months later.

Mike McCready: We tried out Richard Stuverud, Jack Irons, and Josh Freese. I wish we could've tried out Chris Friel, but we just didn't do it. We had great jams with them. With Richard, I remember having a fantastic jam in Stone's basement. I think Ed felt like Jack was the guy that kind of made it all happen, you know? Jack gave the tape that he got from Stone to Ed, so Ed wanted to repay that favor. Ed wanted that to happen, so it did, and we all liked him. He's a killer drummer.

December 6

Vitalogy is released on CD. The following week, it leaps to number one on the *Billboard* 200 after selling more than 877,000 copies in the United States, the second-largest opening-week sum only behind *Vs.,* which sold a then record of more than 950,000. *Vitalogy* spends five consecutive weeks atop the chart.

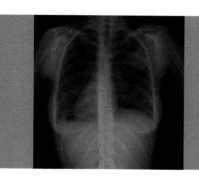

Vitalogy

The late-October 1993 release of *Vs.* turned Pearl Jam into the biggest rock 'n' roll band on the planet. It also spawned a feeding frenzy that took a huge toll on the group's day-to-day sanity. Everybody wanted a piece of Pearl Jam, and many were willing to capitalize on its fame with total disregard for the band's ideals. The most notorious example was the October 25, 1993, *Time* magazine story for which Vedder refused to participate, yet still found his face on the cover under the headline "All the Rage."

For a time, at least, Pearl Jam found solace in its creative drive. Indeed, before *Vs.* was even released, the band was playing an angry, bulldozing new song called "Whipping." And within weeks of the album's arrival, the pounding rocker "Last Exit" and the chugging, psychedelic "Tremor Christ" had been aired. By the spring of 1994, there was more than enough material for album number three.

That was sweet salvation to Pearl Jam's ever-growing fan base, as well as the staff of Epic Records, which had been engaged in a delicate tap dance with the band over its refusal to participate in traditional forms of promotion. Luckily, even with few interviews and even fewer (read: zero) music videos, *Vs.* managed to break the debut-week record for most copies sold in the United States. And there was no reason to think its follow-up would fare any differently.

"Most of the record was cut over the course of the *Vs.* tour," says Jeff Ament of sessions in New Orleans, Seattle, and Atlanta, once again with producer Brendan O'Brien at the helm. "Part of that time was us not wanting to waste a lot of time in between records, plus knowing that the record company wanted another one. It's kind of amazing when you look back, but we really didn't have more than a couple of weeks off for the first four or five years of the band."

In addition to all the new songs, the band was still in possession of "Better Man," for which O'Brien had campaigned vigorously but unsuccessfully to appear on *Vs.* The only problem was that although Vedder gave in to trying the song in the studio again this time around, he still had no real interest in releasing it.

"We did it in New Orleans, and Eddie just was not digging it," O'Brien says. "At this point, he needed me to back off." Then, on April 3, 1994, during Pearl Jam's satellite broadcast of its show from Atlanta's Fox Theatre, "Better Man" was played live for just the third time, and the free world got a chance to hear the song O'Brien had been raving about.

"It was an awesome performance of the song," O'Brien says. "The next day, I told the band how great it sounded. I asked Eddie, what if we took this drum, bass, and electric guitar track and built the song from that? He thought it was a great idea. It made total sense to him. He became invested in it, and it ended up sounding great."

But "Better Man" wasn't in the can yet, and it took a feat of tape-editing wizardry by engineer Nick DiDia to end the saga. "We'd already mastered the album, and at the last minute, Eddie called me and said, 'I know you're going to hate this, but I have to take that song off the record. It's really important to me.' The first chorus was so big and so happy, and he couldn't handle it," O'Brien recalls. "So I said, 'Do me one favor. Come to Atlanta, and let's fix the first part of the song. Let's at least try it.' So he came, and we recorded the first verse and chorus, which is just me on organ and him on guitar and vocals. Nick somehow cut that onto the other master right before the drums come in, and it became the record."

"Even when we'd tried it before, it didn't have the right feel and the right lift," Vedder says. "Then we started playing it live, and, finally, we got the vibe right. It just never happened in the studio."

"He was resistant to that song on a certain level because I think he felt like it wasn't rocking enough or something," Gossard says. "And it's such an undeniable melody, undeniable lyric, undeniable arrangement. It's an instant classic. It just is. It's just the nature of that song and his voice and the lyric and that perspective. It's unique." Adds Ament, "Arguably, it's the biggest song that we have."

That "Better Man" became one of Pearl Jam's most popular songs and a veritable rock radio standard in spite of Vedder's ambivalence is a turn of events about which Gossard often gently chides him.

"He's definitely one to put stuff on the shelf and say, 'Oh, it's not right.' And sometimes I think he knows it's really good and he's just tying his arm behind his back because, I don't know, it's worked for him or something," he says. "I never had that intuition. My intuition has always been, 'I want to write the greatest song I can write, and I want to work on it right now, and I want to put it out next week, and I want everybody to love it.'"

Vedder's almost keeping "Better Man" buried was a testament to his burgeoning leadership role in Pearl Jam. On the band's first two albums, Vedder was the focal point of Pearl Jam more for his singing and magnetic personality than his songwriting. But by the sessions for the third album, his writing output was dwarfing that of his bandmates.

"It wasn't a hostile takeover," Vedder

says with a laugh. "It's not about our personalities. It's not about so-and-so and so-and-so. It's really about the direction of the music and maybe there being more fast songs or more intense or more experimental or whatever. You're trying to reach a different destination with the songs that you're creating. If you've been used to having your hands on the wheel, it's probably tricky to give it up. To be honest, I think that I felt that anything we put out was highly representative of me, and because I was kind of becoming the most recognizable guy in the group, I needed to be more represented musically. And if that meant me creating the songs that were going to accomplish that, then I had to do it. If we were writing songs that were absolutely where I was coming from, then great. I think it was just me needing to be as proud as I could of the music we were making. Everybody should be able to put their songs in, and at first I was just the singer guy. And when I did more of the songwriting, it's going to take up real estate on the record. I can't remember if it was painful. I feel like it just had to be done, and I'm glad it didn't split us up or anything."

Opines Gossard, "This was the first record where I wasn't saying, 'Okay, I've got another one. I've got another one. I've got another one. I've got another one.' I mean, Ed didn't even say we were going to do this a different way; it just was. We were making a record in a different way. I was writing a few songs, but all of a sudden everybody was starting to write, and he was writing more.

"And at that time, I was like, 'Wait a minute, I'm the guy. Let me get in there and do this thing. I know how to do this thing.' At that point, it was really good for me to bring one riff, and then everyone could just pile on top of it. I wish I could have been more conscious of how things could evolve if you let them, you know what I mean?"

"A guy with that kind of impact on people, it's only natural that that person takes more of a role," O'Brien says of Vedder. "He started playing guitar more, which wasn't an easy transition. How do you squeeze everybody in? I think Stone around that time became a little disenchanted with the whole process, because no longer was Eddie the guy Stone found. He was *the* guy!"

In retrospect, Ament chalks up the changing dynamic more to Vedder's work ethic than any overt power grab. "He was working harder at writing songs than we were," the bassist says bluntly. "He had the ability to write a complete song at the time, and the rest of us really didn't. It's certainly easier to write lyrics to your own music than somebody else's because you understand the rhythm, the spaces, and the way you write melodies. I still don't know if he was consciously exerting wanting to take over the band or take the reins or the power. I think it was more like, 'Hey, man, I've got seven complete songs here. What do you guys have?' and we only had little riffs or two-parter things. It was a natural progression. But it led to the rest of us wanting to write pieces of music that lent themselves to being complete songs and that were more arranged from the beginning."

Still, several songs were born out of riff fragments and ideas, particularly "Spin the Black Circle," a rush of pure punk that became the album's first single, much to the raised eyebrows of Epic executives.

"Unbeknown to me, I was listening to demos Stone had given me with the pitch on the wrong setting on my Aiwa tape player," Vedder says. "I had come up with something in the truck with the tape player in my hand, but then I realized it was playing at a superhigh pitch. I turned it down, and it was really slow. I was like, 'Oh, fuck.' I pulled Stone off to the side and said, 'I think I've stumbled onto something. There's a killer song here if you'd play it this fast,' and I played it to him. He thought I was totally insane. But without putting up a fight, they tried it, and that's what it became."

The beautiful Jeff Ament ballad "Nothingman," which the bassist had initially demoed with drummer Richard Stuverud, found a similarly accidental path toward completion during a studio session in New Orleans.

"I heard that David Bowie and Brian Eno worked twelve-hour shifts on this one album where they went back and forth playing on each other's material," he says. "I had this idea that Ed and I could do that over the course of the week. We weren't going to do twelve hours, but the plan was to do eight and eight or something. We had a studio booked and two different engineers. On the first day, I laid down the music for 'Nothingman,' and he came in and wrote the words. It took so much out of him that he was done. So I stayed in there the rest of the time and screwed around. It was the best thing I'd ever done. I came out of that with six or seven pieces of music, a couple of which I later finished on my own."

Frequently on the album, Vedder vents his frustration at the co-opting of music for what he viewed as purely commercial means. "Corduroy" was inspired by the artist seeing a replica of his favorite thrift store jacket selling for hundreds of dollars by a store eager to capitalize on the grunge zeitgeist. (Hence the line "they can buy but can't put on my clothes.")

Even the TV soap opera *General Hospital* got into the act, casting future pop superstar Ricky Martin as a brooding, long-haired singer decked out in unmistakably Vedder-ish army T-shirts. "The music was getting co-opted at every turn," he says. "At the time, that freaked me out. He was, like, the handsome version of me. Now, I doubt anybody remembers that was Ricky Martin. Who knew he could dance?"

The seething, three-chord "Not for You," which the band debuted on *Saturday Night Live* months before releasing it, made clear in no uncertain terms that Vedder considered rock 'n' roll sacred, and he had no problem saying, "Fuck you," to those he thought didn't feel the same.

Says Vedder, "We were so fortunate after the first record to put away enough to live meagerly for the rest of our lives, so that you could actually say, 'No,' and say, 'Look, we don't need it. I don't need it.' We had straight ways of doing things we wanted to do with ticket prices and quality artwork with the record. I mean, just simple things. When you get in these situations where it's, like, you against them, it's not us from this band that sold a lot of records. It's, like, music fans and people who want to protect the purity of music, if it exists, against these people who unabashedly care about their profits. They're selling it like soap, you know? I felt like establishing something in that song: 'This music doesn't belong to you.' You know, 'You don't feel it like we do, you don't even know what's really going on here. You've never stood in line for a show. You haven't bought a record for years."

The struggle to remain whole in the face of Pearl Jam's sudden fame is most evident on "Immortality," a haunting, bluesy song with a an equally affecting McCready guitar solo. Although the song was written shortly before Kurt Cobain's April 1994 suicide, lines like "As privileged as a whore / victims in demand for public show / Swept out through the cracks beneath the door" made it easy for observers to believe that the song was about the Nirvana front man's all-too-brief life and tragic death. The poignant lyric "Some die just to live" also fueled speculation about the subject matter.

"It's not about Kurt," Vedder told the *Los Angeles Times* in 1994. "Nothing on the album was written directly about Kurt, and I don't feel like talking about him, because it might be seen as exploitation. But I think there might be some things in the lyrics that you could read into and maybe will answer some questions or help you understand the pressures on someone who is on a parallel train."

But for all of Pearl Jam's musical growth, the band's uneasy chemistry threatened its very existence. McCready was in the throes of a drug and alcohol problem so bad that he claims to barely remember significant portions of recording the album. At the urging of Gossard and Ament, he eventually checked into the Hazelden rehabilitation center outside of Minneapolis that summer. In addition, relations between drummer Dave Abbruzzese and the rest of the band, particularly Vedder, had deteriorated to a point of no return.

"We were four guys that had the same kind of humor, and we're a little older and we're less flashy," McCready says. "Dave was kind of that way. He's kind of flashy—but a hell of a drummer. I mean, he plays fantastic on *Vs.* and also toured relentlessly with us. But I think there was an increasing rift between those two in ideology of what a rock star is, and everyone's version of what that is was different than his, I think, to be honest with you. He and Ed simply quit talking after a while. That summer, I went to Hazelden. We had recorded the third album in that blur for me. I had stayed in Minneapolis because we weren't doing anything, and next thing, I get a call:

'We're thinking of firing Dave.' To me, it was kind of a shock. I was kind of getting clear in my head for the first time, and I didn't realize all the dynamics that were going on between them."

"I know there were moments when it felt like we were making music that meant something. It felt important," O'Brien says of the tumultuous sessions. "But there was a lot of tension. I, personally, was stressed out almost the whole time. I was trying my best to keep it positive, but it was a stressful time. Eddie was taking the reins a bit, but he was uncomfortable in his own skin. That made it tough for everybody. They were sort of imploding a little bit internally, because the drummer was in the process of no longer being in the band. But we did almost the entire record with him, even though it was not a great situation."

Late in the game, the band gathered scraps of recorded ephemera to shape into interstitial music, such as the minute-long "Pry, To," on which Vedder half sings, half mumbles the phrase "P-R-I-V-A-C-Y, it's priceless to me," and "Aye Davanita," a "just screwing around" studio jam with a chanted nonsense lyric that O'Brien looped and stretched to three minutes.

"We got interlude crazy," O'Brien says. "Stone was very much into hip-hop, and we were also Urge Overkill fans. They'd done a record we loved called *Saturation* with a bunch of interludes. So we started taking bits and pieces and adding them to things."

Vedder also manhandles a thrift store accordion for the wobbly dirge "Bugs," on which the intrusive insects are a metaphor for his loss of perspective at the onset of superstardom. As he wrestles with how to proceed, he could easily be talking about his friends, his fans, or his career: "Do I kill them? Become their friend? / Do I eat them? Raw or well done? / Do I trick them? I don't think they're that dumb / Do I join them? Looks like that's the one."

In actuality, Vedder had poison oak at the time and "was itching out of my skin. The song really *is* about bugs." He told *Spin* in December 1994, "Back then I had my mind on the business at hand, and I probably wouldn't have felt so free to take up two hours of studio time working on Eddie's wank-off accordion piece. For a long time after recording it,

I was playing it for friends, saying it was the best thing we'd ever done. [*Laughs*] We just decided to do something that was fun to listen to and wasn't bombastic and wasn't everything that the band had become."

For months, a loose album concept had been brewing based on an 1899 health reference book that Vedder had purchased at an antique shop titled *Vitalogy,* or, in other words, the study of life. At first the band decided to christen the project *Life,* going so far as to stamp a promotional single for "Spin the Black Circle" with that title. However, Vedder quickly decided that he wanted not only to name the album *Vitalogy* but also to reprint the actual book cover and select images therein for the packaging.

As Sony's lawyers soon discovered, one version of *Vitalogy* was in the public domain but another was not, and it was no small feat to get clearances for the artwork the band wanted to use in time for the release date. "Literally, my conference room turned into a *Vitalogy* war room, with artwork spread everywhere," says then Sony executive vice president Michele Anthony. "We went through both versions to figure out which images we could use."

The final package for *Vitalogy* faithfully reproduced the cover and humorously out-of-date excerpts from the original book to emphasize the themes of particular songs. For instance, the medical textbook definition of *nightmare* is included on the page devoted to "Pry, To," while Vedder's dental X-rays accompany "Corduroy," and the lyrics to "Whipping" are written on a petition to then president Clinton demanding federal intervention into abortion clinic violence.

But according to Ament, the lavish design "cut into about thirty precent to forty percent of our royalties, because the manufacturing wasn't set up to do what we wanted" and because a great deal of the assembly had to be done by hand. In fact, the package didn't even fit on a standard CD shelf in record stores— another "We're doing it our way" detail which suited the band members just fine.

Vitalogy was essentially finished in the summer of 1994 when Pearl Jam parted company with Abbruzzese and replaced him with Vedder's longtime friend Jack Irons. Wanting Irons to

somehow be represented on the album, Vedder and the drummer bashed together seven-plus minutes of abrasive free-form jamming and laid on top of it audio recordings of patients from a mental hospital answering questions about their state of mind. The finished track, titled "Hey Foxymophandlemama, That's Me," provided an eerie end point to the project and quite an unusual recorded introduction to Irons as part of Pearl Jam. "Music is chemistry between people. That was just a jam," says Irons, who insists it was a coincidence that he

happened to play on what at the time was the strangest song Pearl Jam had ever put on an album.

As became clear when it debuted at number one on the *Billboard* 200 with first-week US sales of 877,000 copies—second only to *Vs.* for debut numbers—and then stayed atop the chart for another month, the American listening public was more than willing to tolerate the experimentation. Pearl Jam was as popular as it would ever be, but the satisfaction of such remarkable achievements still proved elusive.

"At the time, I thought, This isn't our best record. I remember feeling kind of disappointed or feeling, like, not connected to it at the end, and I didn't help finish it," says Gossard. "It was out of my hands for the first time. And in retrospect, thank God that we made a record that all of a sudden had this different energy. Now it's one of my favorite records, and it has on it songs that are some of the most important songs to our career and to me personally."

1995

As Pearl Jam struggled to make sense of Kurt Cobain's suicide and assimilate new drummer Jack Irons into its ranks, the group was even less visible around the release of its third album, *Vitalogy,* than it was for *Vs.* To escape, the band headed to the other side of the globe for its first shows in Asia and Australia. But in 1995 there was no place in the world untouched by Pearl Jam mania, and the shows often erupted into near riots. Upon returning home, Pearl Jam remained steadfast in its refusal to perform in venues under contract to Ticketmaster, choosing fields and fairgrounds in out-of-the-way locales instead of big-city arenas. In the end, the tour was a disaster that took five extra months to complete. But Pearl Jam was undaunted, and somehow even found time to record and tour with Neil Young, as well as start work on its own new album before the year was out.

January 8

Pearl Jam hosts Self Pollution Radio, a four-and-a-half-hour show featuring its own two-set, eleven-song performance and additional live cuts from Soundgarden, Mudhoney, Mad Season, and the Fastbacks, plus visits from Mike Watt, and Nirvana's Krist Novoselic. Originating from a rehearsal space that Eddie Vedder and friends kept in a rundown area of Seattle, the broadcast is offered on a free, nonexclusive basis via satellite to radio stations across the country. During it, Vedder officially announces that Jack Irons is Pearl Jam's new drummer. Vedder also offers the first taste of Nirvana drummer Dave Grohl's new band Foo Fighters in the form of the song "Exhausted," from the band's still unreleased self-titled debut album.

Eddie Vedder: At the time, there was so much attention being paid to certain groups from our area. We were going to play a live show on the radio, and then we figured out a way to do it where it wasn't just one station. In fact, it was any station, without commercials. We would just do it ourselves and put it out on the airwaves with a giant satellite parked out behind a little shit-hole rehearsal place, and whoever wanted it could have it. The idea was to make sure that the Fastbacks played and Mudhoney played and bands that weren't getting the same kind of attention that ours was but deserved it maybe twofold. And it worked.

Jack Irons: It was done in a really low-key way. It was just friends and musicians in a little house. At that time, I wasn't really aware of the popularity a band like Pearl Jam had, and I was pretty nervous for it to be going out on the radio, because I was the new guy.

Jeff Ament: We need to do that again! It was all the people we knew in town that were making killer music but weren't selling zillions of records. It was such a cool excuse to have a beer from the keg and hang out, and that was Ed's vision. I think it had to do with him not being from Seattle but then developing strong friendships with these great bands.

Eric Johnson: The sign might have said something about saw blades. It was literally a boarded-up, overgrown, mossy shit hole, on a sad ex-highway that ran through Seattle. There really wasn't anything cool or ironic about the place. It was a perfect hiding spot. You really didn't want to snoop around that area too much, as it seemed like a good place to find a body.

Kelly Curtis: All these separate radio stations wanted live broadcasts, so we thought, What if we just did it ourselves, but anyone could have it? We put it up there and let everyone know what the satellite coordinates were. It turned out pretty cool, and a bunch of other bands from Seattle got to be a part of it.

January 12
Waldorf Astoria Hotel, New York

In a speech that jokes about the proximity of Pearl Jam's table to that of Ticketmaster executives, with whom the band was still fighting, Eddie Vedder inducts Neil Young into the Rock and Roll Hall of Fame. Stone Gossard and Jeff Ament join Young and Crazy Horse to perform "Act of Love," a new song they'd record two weeks later during the sessions for what would become the *Mirror Ball* album. Vedder, Gossard, and Ament also guest with Young on "Fuckin' Up."

Eddie Vedder: He's taught us a lot as a band about dignity and commitment and playing in the moment. I don't know if there's been another artist that has been inducted into the Rock and Roll Hall of Fame to commemorate a career that is still as vital as he is today. Some of his best songs were on his last record.

January 14–15
DAR Constitution Hall, Washington, DC

Pearl Jam joins Neil Young and Crazy Horse, L7, and Lisa Germano at two benefit shows for Voters for Choice, a political action committee founded by VFC president Gloria Steinem and Kristina Kiehl devoted to abortion rights and electing prochoice candidates. Tickets are available only through a mail-in lottery; 175,000 postcards are received for the 7,400 seats. The January 14 show is Jack Irons's first full set with Pearl Jam in front of an audience, but some people boo when Gloria Steinem introduces him. Later, Vedder tells the crowd he appreciates their show of support for Dave Abbruzzese but that "Jack Irons saved the life of this band, so thank him." Earlier in the day of January 14, Vedder, Gossard, Germano, Steinem, and members of L7 appear at a press conference at the 9:30 Club to discuss abortion rights. "I know what it is not to be heard, so if I can raise my hand and speak out for some of these people who don't have a voice at the moment, then I almost feel a responsibility," Vedder says.

January 26–27, February 7, 10

Pearl Jam and Neil Young record what becomes the album *Mirror Ball* with

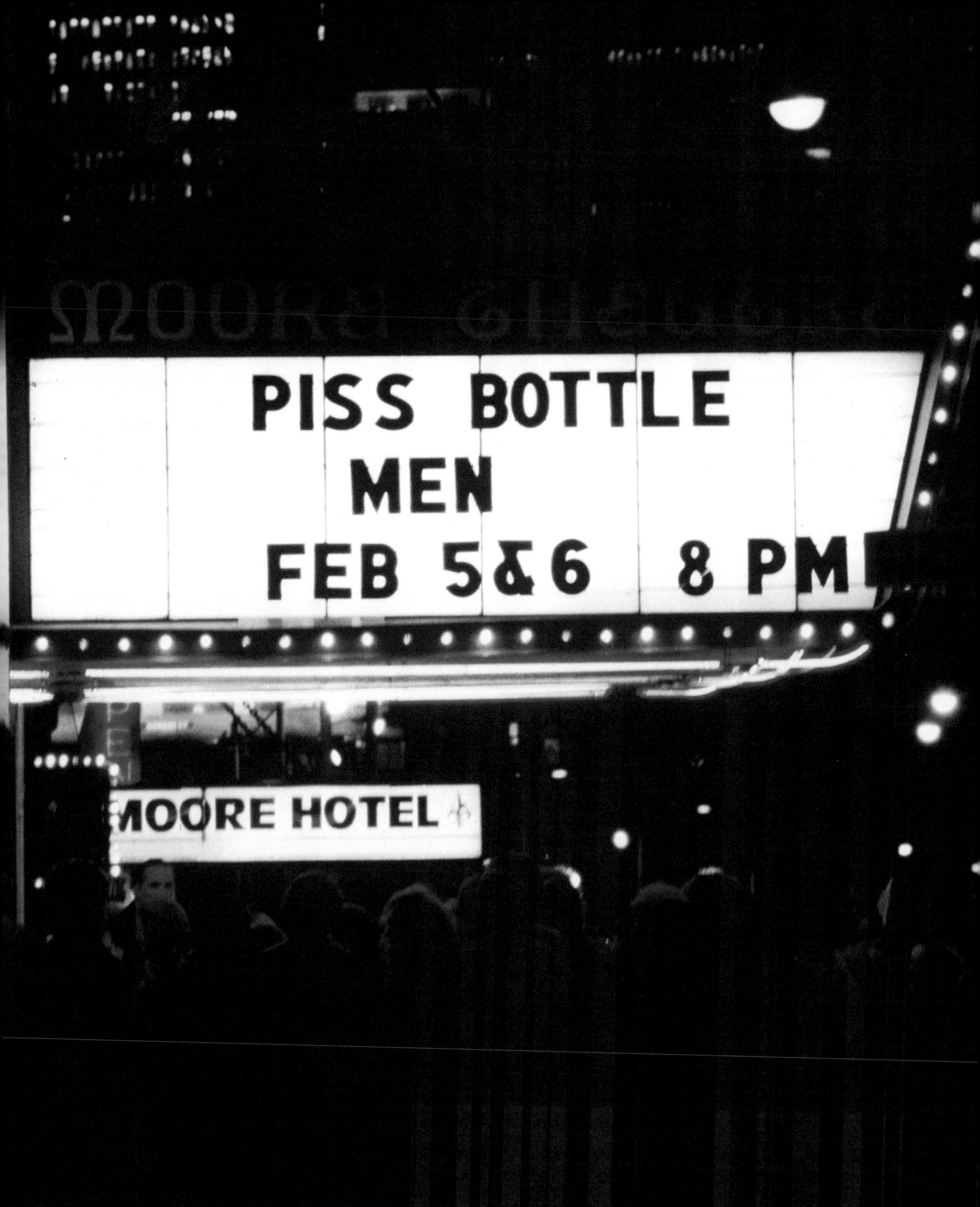
PISS BOTTLE
MEN
FEB 5&6 8 PM
MOORE HOTEL

producer Brendan O'Brien at Bad Animals studio in Seattle.

February 2

Vitalogy is simultaneously certified platinum, double platinum, triple platinum, and quadruple platinum by the Recording Industry Association of America (RIAA) for US shipments of four million copies.

February 5–6
Moore Theatre, Seattle

As a warm-up for its impending Far East tour, Pearl Jam, billed as the Piss Bottle Men, plays two hometown shows in front of local fan club members, who were mailed free tickets. "Lukin" is played for the first time at the February 5 show, as is a cover of Pete Townshend's solo hit "Let My Love Open the Door." In town to finish work on *Mirror Ball,* Neil Young joins the band at the second show to perform "Act of Love." On February 8, Pearl Jam gets in one more last-minute gig in Missoula, Montana, which features a one-off cover of Bob Marley's "Redemption Song." The opening act is Shangri-La Speedway, featuring Jeff Ament's longtime friend Tim Bierman, who would eventually become the manager of the Ten Club.

Tim Bierman: Jeff was kind enough to come out and play with us. We did a cover of "Bad Liquor," an American Music Club song, and the Stooges' "I Wanna Be Your Dog," with Jeff on guitar. Luckily, I knew enough people in the crowd that they kind of liked us and didn't turn on us, because they definitely could have.

February 18
Izumity 21, Sendai, Japan

Pearl Jam kicks off its first Far East tour, encompassing a month's worth of shows in Japan, the Philippines, Singapore, Thailand, Australia, and New Zealand. "I Got Id," having just been recorded during the *Mirror Ball* sessions, is played for the first time on February 21 in Osaka, Japan. Four days later in Manila, eight thousand fans pack the Folk Arts Theater, while thousands more sing along outside.

Jeff Ament: When we decided to do those shows, we wanted to make them affordable. Manila and Bangkok were anywhere from ten dollars to fifteen dollars. We lost a ton of money because we had to put gear on planes and boats. Then there'd be two days off with our entire crew. But those remain some of the most memorable things we've ever done as a band. You look out, and you see no white people. Not only are the people inside the venue singing, but thousands of people outside are, too. I remember Eric Johnson telling me in Manila that everybody outside was singing along to the show. They were forming human pyramids to see up over the edge, like, five people high. I remember walking around Manila and having people follow us. We had lots of interesting interactions on that tour, and I couldn't have been more stoked. We were in a band that was taking us to places we'd never have been able to go without it.

February 28

Former Minutemen/fIREHOSE bassist Mike Watt releases his solo debut, *Ball-Hog or Tugboat?,* featuring Eddie Vedder on vocals on the song "Against the '70s." The album sports a who's who of alternative and punk rock luminaries, including Nirvana's Dave Grohl and Krist Novoselic, Henry Rollins, the Pixies' Frank Black, J Mascis, Flea, and Sonic Youth's Thurston Moore.

Mike Watt: Eddie and I met at a gig; some benefit at the Hollywood Palladium. When he was living in San Diego, he'd seen me play in fIREHOSE. That night, I told him I could almost hear him singing the song "Dirty Blue Gene" by Captain Beefheart. Later on, I put out these "Get in the ring with Watt"–type of invites to people. They'd just come in without knowing the songs. It was kind of an experiment, because I didn't have a band then. I thought, If the bass player knows the song, anybody can play it. Eddie came in with all the words written down for that Beefheart song, but we went for another one I wrote instead. He'd found a wet suit in the trash in the alley, and I think it had bugs and shit in it. He had to pull it off because he was getting all itchy while he was singing.

March 10
Sydney Entertainment Centre, Sydney, Australia

Red Hot Chili Peppers bassist Flea guests with Pearl Jam on a ramshackle cover of Neil Young's "The Needle and the Damage Done," only after a birthday cake is presented to Jeff Ament, and his face is pushed into it. Flea sticks around for a cover of Pete Townshend's "Let My Love Open the Door," by which point the stage is covered with bits of cake.

March 14

Mad Season, comprised of Alice in Chains vocalist Layne Staley, Pearl Jam guitarist Mike McCready, bassist John Baker Saunders, and Screaming Trees drummer Barrett Martin, releases its Columbia debut, *Above.* The album is eventually certified gold by the Recording Industry Association of America for US shipments of five hundred thousand copies, and spawns the Mainstream Rock hits "River of Deceit" (no. 2) and "I Don't Know Anything" (no. 20).

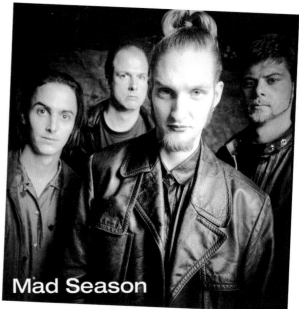

Mad Season

Mike McCready: We did all the Mad Season music in about seven days. It took Layne just a few more days to finish his vocals, which was intense, since we only rehearsed twice and did four shows. So, this has been the most spontaneous thing I've ever been involved in. This was done even quicker than Temple of the Dog, which took about four weeks.

March 16

Vs. is certified six times platinum by the Recording Industry Association of America (RIAA) for US shipments of six million copies.

March 16–17

Flinders Park Tennis Centre, Melbourne, Australia

After having attempted it eight nights earlier in Adelaide but stopping short because Vedder couldn't remember the words, Pearl Jam gets all the way through a cover of Split Enz's classic "I Got You." Dave Grohl makes a surprise appearance on drums during the show-closing "Sonic Reducer." The next night's performance at the same venue is broadcast on Australian radio station JJJ and once again finds Grohl guesting, this time on "Rockin' in the Free World."

Dave Grohl: My girl and I were close to Dr. Sharon Zadanoff, an acupuncturist and holistic chiropractor who was also really close with Pearl Jam. We thought we should go to Australia and surprise her. We fly all the way down to Australia, land in Sydney, drive to fucking Melbourne like idiots for sixteen hours, check into the hotel, and go see Pearl Jam. We walk backstage, and Jack Irons says to me, "Is there any way you could play a song tonight? My wrists are fucked up." This was my vacation. I hadn't played in front of people in a year. But I did "Sonic Reducer," which was really fucking fun. I'm not kidding; it was maybe the craziest I've ever seen an audience in an arena. At one point, the audience came spilling over the walls where the seats were up top to get closer to the stage. It was dangerous. It was fucking crazy.

March 21

The soundtrack to the film *The Basketball Diaries* is released by Island Records, featuring Pearl Jam (with Chris Friel on drums) backing the movie's subject, writer Jim Carroll, on the song "Catholic Boy."

March 22

Entertainment Centre, Brisbane, Australia

Dave Grohl is back again to drum with

Pearl Jam on Mike Watt's "Against the '70s," played here by the band for the first time, and "Sonic Reducer."

March 24–25

Mt. Smart Super Top, Auckland, New Zealand

Split Enz's Neil and Tim Finn join Pearl Jam at both Auckland shows to perform their songs "I Got You" and "History Never Repeats." On the afternoon of the second show, Vedder is carried several hundred feet off the coast while swimming with Tim Finn but is rescued by lifeguards.

Neil Finn: My son Liam, who was eleven at the time, was a very big Pearl Jam fan. *Vitalogy* had just come out. We got a message from the promoter that Eddie was quite keen to hook up. Would Tim and I want to come to the show and maybe get up and sing something with him? I may well have been into it anyway, but there was no way Liam was going to let me not do that.

   Eddie is a very charming guy, but he was quite stressed out in those days. There were a lot of security issues on that tour, and he was real nervous about the barricades at the front holding up. But he was very gracious and welcoming of us. We worked out two or three songs in his trailer, and doing them was fantastic. I must admit I had no idea Pearl Jam was such a good jamming, freewheeling band. I was deeply impressed from the side of the stage. It was a good introduction.

   There was a funny little upshot of that night. The review in the *Herald* the next day was very complimentary, but it made a disparaging comment about how the show ended with my brother Tim and I. It was an odd thing, but I think Pearl Jam may well have been intending to come back for an encore. 'History Never Repeats' ended up being the last song of the show. The review made a very snide comment that it was a nice gesture, but it made the show end with a whimper and not a bang, which I was really incensed about! I've had bad reviews before and I can cope, but I don't want to be the cause of a bad review for somebody else! I sent the guy a real nasty letter. That's the first and only time I've ever written a letter to a reviewer, and I gave him a real serve about it.

   After the first show, Eddie came home with us. Sharon, my wife, has a

good eye for people who are a little bit fraught, and we thought he might like to just hang out in a house. Liam was incredibly chuffed that he took his room. We hung out and went to the beach. It was a really nice twenty-four hours. Once he got to the house, he was very relaxed and funny. I think it was a burden for him back then, that instant fame. He had a very sane response to massive celebrity, which was to become wary of situations.

Tim Bierman: Three separate groups of people wound up at that beach. Jeff's friends, Stone's friends, and Ed and the Finns—like, twenty-five people. We met this guy traveling with us named Rob Lamb, a radio personality who was also a musician. He was half Maori and covered in tattoos. He'd had an epileptic seizure and crashed his motorcycle and lost a leg. Then he became addicted to morphine and got hepatitis C. He stripped down to his tighty-whiteys and was showing everybody how to swim in the surf. But the rip was unbelievable. Ed got out too far, and he knew what he had to do to get back to shore, but it would have taken him an hour. That's why he put his hand up and shouted for us to come get him. When Ed met Rob, whose radio show, ironically, was called *Leg of Lamb,* he was really serious. Ed was like, "Hey, Rob, what happened to your leg?" And he goes, "Oh, I just had some tattoos removed."

April 4

Pearl Jam aligns itself with upstart ticketing company ETM for a thirteen-date summer North American tour, which will play exclusively non-Ticketmaster venues. ETM provides fully automated phone lines with the ability to handle four thousand incoming calls at one time, bar codes on tickets to deter scalpers, and a flat combined service-and-handling fee of $2.50 per ticket. Prices are set at $18 for indoor venues and $21 for outdoor sites, with capacities ranging from Idaho's twelve-thousand-seat Boise State University Pavilion to the fifty-thousand-plus Polo Fields at San Francisco's Golden Gate Park. "Obviously, what we're doing is risky," manager Kelly Curtis acknowledges. "And I'm sure some people are really hoping that it fails. But I feel like we're doing the right thing."

April 12
Gibson's, Tempe, Arizona

Eddie Vedder joins Mike Watt to play guitar in his band for a North American tour in support of *Ball-Hog or Tugboat?* The club tour also finds Vedder, disguised in a wig and masquerading under the name "Jerome230," playing drums with instrumental noise rock band Hovercraft. For Watt's set, Vedder is flanked by former Germs/Nirvana guitarist Pat Smear and former Nirvana drummer Dave Grohl, who also plays before Watt with his brand-new band, Foo Fighters. Harking back to their earliest days as touring musicians, the artists travel by van and keep each other in stitches via CB radio during marathon drives to the next city. But Vedder's participation remains secret for only a few days, and the venues become filled either by Pearl Jam fans or Watt fans who resent the distraction of the former. After enduring heckling and coins being thrown at him, Vedder drops off the tour following a May 20 show in San Diego.

Dave Grohl: The conversation started about maybe going on the road: What if I played the drums, Eddie played guitar, and Watt played bass? It'd be a good band, right? I was just starting up the Foo Fighters, so I thought maybe the Foos would come out and open, and I'd play drums with Watt. It'd give us a chance to start over and do it right, rather than putting out a record, booking a tour, and getting on a jet to play in front of twenty thousand Nirvana fans each night. Let's do what comes natural to us, which was practicing in a shitty little room and jumping in a van with Mike Watt. It made perfect sense. With Hovercraft being there, too, it was very much a tight little family that we had for that month and a half. It was a perfect first tour with the band. That's when I feel like I actually met Eddie. He's a real funny, gentle, kind dude. It's easy to look at people like Eddie, Springsteen, or Leonard Cohen and imagine them with the weight of the world on their shoulders 24/7, when in reality, they're just really nice guys. Eddie's fucking fun to hang out with. I mean, the guy's ticklish.

Mike Watt: I can imagine people who went to the gigs to see Eddie would have been like, "Who is this weird dude on the bass?" It was kind of naive, maybe, for us to think that people would just take it as dudes playing. The hype was something I wasn't used to. And the way I'd toured from the old days was that we'd play every night. When you're

1995

164

not playing, you're paying. That was kind of intense for them. But I think Eddie was feeling for me, too. God, I've had all kinds of shit thrown at me, including sacks of shit and puke, flashlight batteries, cups of piss. In Seattle, I did tell a kid off. Maybe he wanted to tell his friends at high school the next day that he'd worn a shirt that said "Fuck you Eddie" on it.

Eddie Vedder: It wasn't the coins being thrown and the Watt devotees suffering through some corporate rock star playing guitar that got to me. I can take that. It was more the press that was making me crazy. So much of the show to me was the mystery. You'd see Hovercraft, this freak-out band with a drummer wearing a wig, and then Foo Fighters, a band nobody had ever seen and with Dave Grohl singing and playing guitar

instead of drums. And the last set is an amalgamation of me, Dave, and Watt. This is pre-Internet. There were still secrets to be had. But if we played in Detroit, the paper in Toronto the next night would tell you everything that was going to happen. Watt had told me at the beginning, "If you ever need to pull the rip cord, do it." I wish I wouldn't have. I wish I would have stuck it out. The thing for me was like, "Are you kidding?" Getting harassed by the Watt faithful— he asked me to do this! Dave and I are showing our allegiance and our reverence to your hero. We're on your side! That was kind of ridiculous.

April 22

More than nine thousand fans purchase tickets through ETM for Pearl Jam's

June 16, 1995, show at the Casper (Wyoming) Events Center. The show was moved there from the original location of the Boise State University Pavilion due to logistical issues with ETM selling tickets there. A few days later, ETM transacts eighteen thousand tickets in less than ten minutes for two mid-June shows at Red Rocks Amphitheatre outside Denver.

April 28

Eddie Vedder, Pat Smear, and Dave Grohl back Mike Watt for performances of "Big Train" and "The Red and the Black" on the syndicated television program *The Jon Stewart Show*.

SAN DIEGO COUNTY SHERIFF'S DEPARTMENT

ENCINITAS STATION

SITUATION BRIEFING
PEARL JAM CONCERTS

PREPARED JUNE 5, 1995

San Diego County Sheriff's Department

Post Office Box 429000 • San Diego, California 92142–9000

William B. Kolender, Sheriff

John M. Drown, Undersheriff

June 5, 1995

Timothy J. Fennell, General Manager
22nd Agricultural District
2260 Jimmy Durante Blvd.
Del Mar, CA 92014-2216

Dear Mr. Fennell,

The Pearl Jam rock concerts planned for the 1995 Del Mar Fair have raised significant crowd control and public safety concerns for the Sheriff's Department. The band has a history of disturbances at its concerts and can be expected to draw tens of thousands of unticketed fans to the already crowded fairgrounds.

After reviewing the tentative security plans for these events and consulting with other public safety officials, it is my opinion that these events can not be adequately policed, given the anticipated crowds and environmental shortcomings of the venue. I have researched the history of this band and similar acts where disturbances have occurred and feel that even a substantial security and police presence will not reasonably insure the safety of both concert fans and other fair patrons.

I have discussed these issues with your Security Manager, Mike Murphy, and documented them in the attached situation briefing report. I strongly advise your board to consult with your legal counsel and carefully evaluate your civil liability in this matter in light of the attached information.

As your contracted provider of law enforcement services, I feel obligated to inform you of this information so that you can properly evaluate the risks of promoting this event.

April 29
Moore Theatre, Seattle

Mad Season plays a hometown concert that is released by Columbia on August 29, 1995, as the home video *Live at the Moore.*

Jerry Cantrell: To be completely honest, I was a little pissed off about Mad Season at the beginning. I was fiercely territorial of our thing, but the truth of it is, Layne wanted to do some other stuff, and that was a way for him to do it. I remember going to see them at the Moore. I was quietly against it, I guess. I was like, "Fuck! What are you doing, doing stuff outside the band?" But then I saw them play, and I got a whole new admiration for him doing that on his own, and with Mike McCready and those guys stepping out of their respective bands. There are a lot of creative people in Seattle. And even within a band, people have different musical views or things that don't get expressed within the band they're in. It was a healthy process for Layne to go through. I was very impressed with the record.

June 5

Citing unresolved issues involving security, the San Diego County Sheriff's Department asks organizers of the Del Mar fair near San Diego to cancel Pearl Jam's scheduled shows there on June 26–27, both of which have been sold out for weeks. In a statement, Pearl Jam manager Kelly Curtis says, "I am unaware of their specific concerns, but had they made them known, we could have addressed them months ago."

June 7
Moe's, Seattle

Pearl Jam backs Neil Young at a secret show to celebrate the impending release of their collaborative *Mirror Ball* album. Vedder appears only to sing backing vocals on "Peace and Love."

June 12

Pearl Jam cancels the June 26–27 shows at Del Mar Fairgrounds. In an angry statement to the media, Vedder says, "We did our job, set up the show, sold tickets. It's a long process. We're obviously ready to play. Not to make enemies, but it seems the officials in San Diego have overreacted, creating an impossible situation. It's a shame, really. Have a little more faith, assholes."

June 14

Pearl Jam announces that the Del Mar Fairgrounds shows have been moved to the San Diego Sports Arena, a venue under exclusive contract with Ticketmaster. The band is able to avoid using Ticketmaster services by honoring tickets originally sold for the Del Mar shows after the Sports Arena receives approval from Ticketmaster to do so. The same day, manager Kelly Curtis tells the *Los Angeles Times* that "it's impossible for a major rock group to put on a national tour under the current circumstances without Ticketmaster." Curtis also releases a statement saying that if the Department of Justice rules in favor of Ticketmaster, Pearl Jam "may be forced to perform in some Ticketmaster venues in order to reach their fans."

June 16
Casper Events Center, Casper, Wyoming

Although Curtis's comments two days earlier are being spun every which way in the press, Pearl Jam's first tour in more than a year begins smoothly, as the band opens the show with "Long Road," one of two new Eddie Vedder–penned songs recorded during the *Mirror Ball* sessions. "I don't know if you've heard. In New York and Los Angeles, in the papers, they're saying

Mr. Eric Johnson
Curtis Management
417 Denny Way #200
Seattle Washington 98104

Dear Eric:

On behalf of the Mid-South Coliseum Board and staff, I want to thank you for your cooperation to make our March Pearl Jam concert not only a success but an enlightening learning experience. This would never had been the case if not for the support and ideas from Eric Hausch and the entire crew.

Although I have many years of experience with general admission shows, the added crowd management dimension of body surfing and mashing was of great concern. Before your arrival our staff and representative from Mid-South Concerts met to develop our plan based on what we had heard. We were all extremely relieved when Eric offered such a thorough overview of what to expect and positive suggestions to our plans.

As a member of the International Association of Auditorium Managers (IAAM) and chair of the arena's portion of our July meeting, I am delighted to include Eric on our program. My peers are anxious to see your video of the GA floor activities and get answers to relieve their hesitation to ... events with mash pits and body surfing.

... never have I received this ... concern for their fans is ... back of house activities. It ... to working with you again.

The City of OKLAHOMA CITY

FIRE DEPARTMENT
GARY MARRS
Fire Chief

February 14, 1994

TO WHOM IT MAY CONCERN:

On November 23, 1993, Pearl Jam performed at the State Fair Grounds in Oklahoma City, OK.

In my twenty-one years of public safety service, I have never encountered a tour manager, staff and band members as concerned for the public's well being. All involved demonstrated a committment to the well being of all in attendance. The initial meetings with concert staff, the layout of the stage barriers, and Mr. Vedders positive comments and safety reminders to the audience, all worked toward a safe environment for people attending the concert.

Tour manager, Eric Johnson was easily available, cooperative, always positive and great to work with. He, along with all involved, made for a safe and pleasant evening. I would welcome Pearl Jam back to Oklahoma City any time.

Sincerely,

Jon A. Hansen
Jon A. Hansen
Assistant Chief

JAH/tf

pc

28th March 1995

Mr Eric Johnson
C/- Curtis Management
417 Denny Way #200
SEATTLE, WA, 98109
USA

Dear Eric,

On behalf of the entire staff and Management of the Br... like to congratulate you and your entire team on the ve... here March 21 and 22.

The experience of having Pearl Jam perform here was s... long time and would gladly have repeated again. Pear... more, with every single fan bursting with energy and c... we have ever experienced. Having placed ticket prices a... created the opportunity to fill the venue easily twice a... Brisbane another two nights would have not been u... beginning of the pro-active approach displayed by every...

From the point of view of managing public facilities, I,... degree of concern over crowd behaviour and risk r... unqualified publicity over the behaviour of some acts.... event coming to Brisbane. Once here, your tou... professionalism rarely seen with Rock Bands and embr... concerned with skilful precision.

I must single out Erik Hausch, your touring security ... operator I have yet encountered on a tour such as this. ... fan safety and enjoyment, as his paramount concern, ... equally concerned with. Our industry must have peop... concert industry to 'manage' with us the many issues rel... presentation, then get on with the job.

April 7, 1994

Mr. Eric Johnson
Curtis Management
417 Denny Way
Seattle WA 98109-4934

Dear Eric:

In the less than 24 hours I have had to reflect on last night's Pearl Jam concert here at the Civic Center, I ha... already concluded that the show was the best in my eight years here. Obviously, the band is terrific and rewarded its fans with a tremendous show for a very reasonable price.

The only thing that may have topped the quality of the show was the high degree of professional cooperation shared among you and your staff, Mike McGinley ... Metropolitan Entertainment and... in Springfi...

that we've surrendered to Ticketmaster," he tells the crowd. "That didn't happen. Take my word. That's a lie. So, that's New York and Los Angeles. We're in Casper, so we don't give a fuck about any of that stuff." After the gig, Vedder inaugurates a tour tradition by hosting a pirate radio broadcast dubbed Monkeywrench Radio from a van outside the venue, where he plays his favorite records and takes phone calls from fans. Frequently, Vedder rides in the van to the next show while the rest of Pearl Jam flies.

Eddie Vedder: I thought it would keep me grounded, but before too long, I was just isolated and really tired.

June 17
Wolf Mountain Amphitheatre, Salt Lake City

A torrential downpour accompanied by hail and lightning forces Pearl Jam to cancel this show. Vedder greets fans at the venue gates with a megaphone and promises that the band will "play twice as long" when it returns to make up the date.

June 19–20
Red Rocks Amphitheatre, Morrison, Colorado

Pearl Jam plays two highly unusual shows at the majestic outdoor venue near Denver. On the first night, the band debuts the fiery rocker "Habit," which Vedder had first played on the Mike Watt tour, as well as a cover of "Leaving Here," a Holland-Dozier-Holland song recorded by an early version of the Who dubbed the High Numbers. Pearl Jam plays seated for the first six songs of the second show, including a completely rearranged "Jeremy," a cover of Nick Cave's "The Ship Song," and a new song called "Falling Down," which was never performed again. Then the group ditches the chairs and goes electric.

Jeff Ament: We went through a phase, like, during our second, third, fourth records, where we tried to rework those popular songs and do different things to them. And we'd break them down or play them faster or just rearrange them different ways. And, you know, every single time, you'd go through a phase

where you'd kind of fall in love with a new version, and then, all of a sudden, you'd listen back to it at some point. You'd be like, "Man, the old version is way better." We were playing a different version of "Garden," and we ended up going back to the old version.

June 24
Polo Fields at Golden Gate Park, San Francisco

Suffering from a debilitating case of food poisoning caused by a room service tuna sandwich, Eddie Vedder makes it through only seven songs before telling the fifty-thousand-strong crowd he cannot perform any further. "This has been probably the worst set of twenty-four hours I've ever had," he says. "Lucky for you, I think Neil Young's here, so he's going to take over for a bit." Young does indeed emerge with a low-key "How ya doin'?" and proceeds to play fourteen songs backed by Pearl Jam, although the audience is less than pleased with the turn of events. At the start of the first encore, Jeff Ament is booed when he announces that Vedder will not be returning.

Eric Johnson: Eddie called me at six in the morning and said he wanted to go to the hospital. I went up to his room and got him, and I noticed a tuna sandwich with one bite taken out of it. He looked like death. I took him to the emergency room in a cab, and they did two full IV bags on him. I think we even checked ourselves out. When I showed up at the venue with Eddie, he was in the back of a town car. His knees were on the floor and he was grabbing the leather seat with his hands so hard that he was actually creasing the leather. It was insane. Neil didn't know anything about this. He showed up with some friends on Harleys, planning to do a song or two. It was so casual. I was already a little afraid of the crowd at the show because it was massive. It seemed a little volatile to me. When Neil realized what was going on, he came out and just wore them down.

Jeff Ament: During the first song or two after Ed left—and I can still sort of see this guy's face—there was this guy flipping me off the entire time. He was, like, ten feet from Neil. I was so bummed out. The crowd was showing absolutely

no respect to this guy who didn't have to do what he did. It wasn't a bar band from town. It was Neil Young! Are you kidding me? None of you have ever had a sick day in your life? Even if you did, you didn't replace yourself with somebody as good or better than you, at a moment's notice. It was probably one of my lowest points in the band.

Jack Irons: The humorous part of it is that Neil Young came out with us, and besides the songs from *Mirror Ball,* we only knew one or two songs, so we had to repeat a few. We did a lot of "Rockin' in the Free World" [*laughs*].

Mike McCready: Luckily, Neil Young was there. Once again, he's in our lives and helped us and saved us. We played about twelve songs with him when Ed had to cancel after three, and we had fifty thousand fans pissed off at us. Leading up to that, Jack, Stone, Jeff, and I were traveling in a jet. Eddie was traveling in a van, doing a radio show after every show after singing two and a half to three hours a night, which was a total disconnect on our part. We needed to sit down with him and go, "Look, you're doing your radio show, but you're exhausted. Are you embarrassed by us? Do you want to be in the band anymore?"

Kelly Curtis: That should have been a glorious day. Ed was sick as a dog. I remember him curled up in the dressing room on the floor, and Neil Young standing over him saying he had to suck it up and get out there. The show started, and he was singing great. I thought we were going to get through it. He's not a quitter. For him to just walk away in front of fifty thousand people—he just got in the car and left. We were faced with a tough decision. To cancel the show, we were scared there was going to be a riot. Neil, thank God, said, "Let's just go out there and wear them down." They played "Rockin' in the Free World" a couple of times. It turned into boos. People got tired and went home. Neil saved a riot, really.

Neil Young: That was quite a day. I remember Eddie lying on the floor. I suppose they could have done the show with him sick. If I'd have been able to produce that, I would have just had him on a cot, right by the mike, and let the other guys play the songs and shout out the lyrics. It would have been a beautiful piece of art. But he was so sick, we weren't thinking about art. It was more, "Holy shit. What's wrong with him?" I said, "I can play a couple of songs. We can do it." It was a surprise, but it was great. At the end, we did the same song again just to let people know how screwed up the whole thing really was. I was in a funny position, because I'm not Eddie. But I'm playing with his band, and playing songs the crowd doesn't know, and we barely know, either. It was an interesting musical experience.

June 25

After an intense band meeting right after the San Francisco show, Pearl Jam opts to cancel the remaining seven shows of its North American tour. In a statement, the band says the move was "brought on by the business problems and controversies surrounding our attempt to schedule an alternative tour."

Mike McCready: We had about a three- or four-hour meeting. We all agreed we needed to take some time off and figure it out. Ed was trying to maintain something that was more Fugazi or a do-it-yourself-type mentality, which he still maintains. And we try to do it to the best of our ability, but we weren't that band. We were a bigger band than that. There was a huge physical disconnect but also an emotional one. And nobody was really talking, around that time, about that. We were just kind of going along with it. But it reared its head in a show being canceled. We thought we were going to break up, essentially, I thought. I thought that was going to happen. But we didn't. We took some time off, and we got back together again. I think Ed realized that he needed to take some time off and maybe be less worried about what the image was.

Kelly Curtis: I remember Neil saying, "If it's not working, go home. You don't have to kill yourselves right now. You're going to have a career." He let the guys know it was okay to stop and save themselves. That meant a lot. So they just stopped and took a breather.

Michele Anthony: The whole point of taking on a tour of alternative venues was because Ticketmaster claimed it was not a monopoly and that there were choices in the marketplace. So Pearl Jam said, Let's try to do it without Ticketmaster. They really earnestly tried, but there were just too many obstacles. In my mind, their attempt to do that actually proved their point better than anything else. If Pearl Jam, who were at the peak of their attractiveness in the marketplace, couldn't pull it off, then nobody could. Did we get calls from Fred Rosen saying, "Can you speak to your band?" Of course. But were we going to get involved in that? Absolutely not. We all hoped the Department of Justice would have a better resolution.

June 27

Having had time to digest the ramifications of the tour cancellation two days earlier, Pearl Jam reinstates the July 8–9 shows planned as part of Milwaukee's Summerfest and a July 11 concert at Chicago's Soldier Field. Shortly thereafter, the rest of the scrapped dates are rescheduled for the fall.

June 27

Warner Bros.–Reprise Records releases the Neil Young–Pearl Jam collaboration *Mirror Ball,* although for contractual reasons "Pearl Jam" does not appear anywhere on the cover or in the liner notes. Instead the band members are simply listed by name.

Michele Anthony: There really wasn't a big brother artist at the time who could help guide Pearl Jam through this tough period, and Neil really stepped in and filled that role. I got a call from Kelly one day saying, "Great news! Neil wants to make a record with the band." I said, "That is great news!" But, he said, "It has to be on Warner Bros." By this time, I was so used to getting those calls from Kelly, because every few months there'd be another, "We can't do this, but we want to do this." I'm happy to say that each time, we were able to figure it out.

July 5

The US Justice Department announces that its investigation into alleged antitrust contracting violations by Ticketmaster is being dropped, with Attorney General Janet Reno adding, "We do not have a basis for proceeding." Industry observers opine that because venues willingly enter into exclusive contracts with Ticketmaster, the Justice Department had little basis on which to continue its investigation. In a statement, Pearl Jam says, "Ultimately, those who will be most hurt by the Justice Department's cave-in are the consumers of live entertainment. We will continue to work on behalf of our fans to keep our tickets affordable and accessible to everyone."

Eddie Vedder: We haven't lost anything, because we've learned from the experience. There's no way that we, personally, could have lost. It wasn't a chess game. It was basically a case of our trying to be responsible to the people who come to see the shows, in the same spirit as us making sure that we have a good barricade, to seeing to it that the T-shirts are sold at reasonable prices. Basically, it's showing respect to the fans. And, it's safe to say, a lot of these people—those who either run Ticketmaster or the arenas, or the promoters—haven't attended a show as a regular concertgoer in years. And that's for the record.

Kelly Curtis: It was an insane PR battle for Ticketmaster. I can't even imagine what they spent fighting us on it. They had teams of PR people and lawyers on the case. It seemed like it might have just been easier to do the right thing, but that was probably naïve on our part. Regardless, they will forever be tied to us on this issue.

Nicole Vandenberg, public relations manager: Although it's perceived that we lost the suit, which we never filed but agreed to participate in, we definitely won the battle in other ways: We were able to get our ticket prices separated from all the ticket service charges so people knew the difference between them; I think we made everyone more thoughtful about what goes into ticket price and what gets passed on to the fans; and it made us think more strategically about where and how we could better look after our fans through our fan club.

July 8–9
Marcus Amphitheater, Milwaukee

Two weeks after the San Francisco debacle, Pearl Jam returns to the stage as part of Milwaukee's annual Summerfest. Addressing the recent controversies, Vedder tells the audience at the first show, "I don't know what they're saying about us now, but whatever they said, they don't know anything. It's just nice to be able to stand here and communicate with you like this and share music. That's what it's really all about. It was being forgotten." At that gig, he brings local Neil Diamond impersonators Lightning & Thunder

opens uncharacteristically with "Act of Love" from *Mirror Ball.* Later, Red Hot Chili Peppers drummer Chad Smith joins Pearl Jam to jam on Jimi Hendrix's "Little Wing," which segues into the Funkadelic staple "Maggot Brain."

July 11
Soldier Field, Chicago

Pearl Jam wraps its tumultuous 1995 tour on a high note, delivering a thirty-one-song, two-and-a-half-hour set before forty-seven thousand fans at the legendary Chicago football stadium. Telling the crowd that Pearl Jam is

concert live from its van in the parking lot. Three unreleased songs appear ("I Got Id," "Lukin," "Habit"), and Brendan O'Brien guests on covers of Sly & the Family Stone's "Everyday People" and Pete Townshend's "Let My Love Open the Door." Feeling inspired by the show, the next day, the band begins recording songs that would eventually be released on the album *No Code.*

August 12
Sjöhistoriska Museet, Stockholm, Sweden

Minus Eddie Vedder but with Brendan

onstage during the encore to perform "Forever in Blue Jeans." After Vedder, in a wig, sunglasses, and gaudy jacket, sings "I Only Play for Money" with opening act the Frogs, the second show

playing on the same stage utilized by the Grateful Dead two days earlier, Vedder says, "We think it's only right that we play as long as they do." For the first time, Monkeywrench Radio broadcasts the

O'Brien on keyboards, Pearl Jam begins an eleven-date European tour with Neil Young in support of *Mirror Ball.* The trek includes the musicians' first-ever shows in Israel. The set lists feature six or seven songs from *Mirror Ball* plus a smattering of Young classics like "Mr. Soul," "Comes a Time," "Don't Let It Bring You Down," "Powderfinger," and "Cortez the Killer."

Jeff Ament: We played this frickin' Nazi amphitheater in Nuremburg and some crazy, crazy places. The shows in Israel were off the hook. We played a Roman amphitheater in Caesarea, which is north of Tel Aviv, right on the Mediterranean. They burned Christians there, like, every Sunday. We've got these big candles, and the sea's behind us crashing, and you're imagining them burning Christians. Neil doesn't say much, but every once in a while he would say something based on his thirty or forty years of being in bands and probably looking back and seeing all the right ways he did things and all the wrong ways he did things. We were lucky enough to hear it from this wise sage.

favorite bands, the Ramones. During the encore, Vedder stuns fans by announcing that moving forward, "Anytime you want to bring a tape recorder to one of our shows, you're more than welcome to. Maybe then you won't have to pay thirty dollars or anything like that to bootleggers. You can have your own tape, your own personal memory." The band also plays an apparently new song, "Open Road," for the first and last time.

September 17
Tad Gormley Stadium, New Orleans

An enormous crowd of forty-two thousand packs a college track stadium for this show. Vedder briefly leaves the stage fifteen songs in, and Mike McCready takes the mike for a jam based

around Jimi Hendrix's "Voodoo Chile." In town to supervise a new round of recording for *No Code*, Brendan O'Brien sits in on organ during "Better Man," and Joey Ramone joins Pearl Jam to sing "Sonic Reducer," a performance captured on the 1995 Ten Club holiday single.

October 13

Vitalogy is certified five times platinum by the Recording Industry Association of America (RIAA) for US shipments of five million copies.

November 1–2
Delta Center, Salt Lake City

Back in Utah to make up the June show scrapped due to heavy rain, Pearl Jam debuts two new songs that would become future staples of its live sets: the slide-guitar-heavy, midtempo rocker "Red Mosquito," and the furious, punkish "Brain of J."

November 4
Spartan Stadium, San Jose, California

Before the set from opening act the Fastbacks, Eddie Vedder premieres

September 13
Veterans Memorial Coliseum, Phoenix

The first of nine shows rescheduled in the wake of the San Francisco incident, all in non-Ticketmaster venues, finds Pearl Jam supported by one of Eddie Vedder's

NEIL Y. , BRIAN WILSON, ED BRIDGE SCHOOL LATE 9O's?

GREAT SHOT/POLAROID OF HOWARD ZINN RY ED. BOSTON

Stone, Jeff, Jack, and Mike with Neil Young and Brendan O'Brien

"Dead Man," from the as-yet-unreleased soundtrack to the Tim Robbins–directed film *Dead Man Walking,* starring Sean Penn. Fastbacks guitarist Kim Warnick and fellow opening act Ben Harper, playing his first show with the band, join Pearl Jam in the encore for a cover of the Byrds' "So You Want to Be a Rock 'n' Roll Star."

Ben Harper: Jeff had come to a few of my shows previous to that, and he's the one who introduced me to Ed and the boys. It was Jeff that put us on the bill. I will never forget it. For the first three songs, it was "Eddie! Eddie! Eddie!" I could tell it was only about twelve guys, but it felt like it was twelve hundred. On the next song, it was maybe six guys who felt like six hundred. And by the third song, it felt just like six guys. For the next forty minutes, it was gone. At the end of the set, Jeff was on the side of the stage throwing me the fist, like, "I was right! They like you!"

November 6–7
San Diego Sports Arena, San Diego

Pearl Jam completes its 1995 tour with two shows in Eddie Vedder's longtime hometown that were originally scheduled for late June. The band donates $50,000 from ticket proceeds to the ocean and beach advocacy group the Surfrider Foundation.

December 5

"I Got Id" and "Long Road," the two songs Eddie Vedder wrote during sessions for *Mirror Ball,* are released on Pearl Jam's *Merkin Ball* EP on Epic. Stone Gossard and Mike McCready are not at the studio when these tracks are recorded, leaving lead guitar duties to Neil Young. Brendan O'Brien plays bass on "I Got Id."

Christmas

Pearl Jam releases its fourth fan-club-only seven-inch vinyl single. No single was issued the prior year, so the 1995 edition is a double seven-inch with a gatefold sleeve consisting of "Sonic Reducer" live with Joey Ramone, "History Never Repeats" with Crowded House–Split Enz principals Neil and Tim Finn, "Swallow My Pride" with Mudhoney's Mark Arm and Steve Turner, and "My Way" with Elvis impersonator Terry Presley.

1995

Mirror Ball

Whenever Pearl Jam and Neil Young got together, be it to jam out at an awards show or team up for a series of concerts, something just seemed to click. Indeed, although they'd only known one another informally for a couple of years and hadn't spent more than a couple of weeks together over that period, Pearl Jam and Young had cemented such a strong bond by late 1994 that it seemed like the product of decades of friendship.

"In some ways, Pearl Jam seems older than I am," Young mused at the time. "There is a certain ancient wisdom in the way they fill the spaces and leave other spaces. It's not something they learned in this lifetime. In Pearl Jam, I have been given a great gift."

That October, Pearl Jam had chosen Young's annual Bridge School Benefit concerts outside San Francisco to introduce new drummer Jack Irons, himself a huge Young fan who was prone to blasting the anthology *Decade* while cruising around Los Angeles. Shortly afterward, the artists agreed to perform at two January 1995 benefit concerts for the reproductive rights advocacy group Voters for Choice in Washington, DC, right on the heels of Young's induction into the Rock and Roll Hall of Fame. Naturally, Eddie Vedder did the inducting.

First at the Hall of Fame induction in New York and then at the DC gigs, Young debuted a new song, a two-chord blast dubbed "Act of Love." Crazy Horse backed Young on the track at the Waldorf Astoria, but a few nights later, Young asked Pearl Jam to do the honors in DC. Eager to keep the collaboration going, Young informed the members of Pearl Jam that he'd like to come to Seattle immediately to record with them.

"When I played with them at the Rock and Roll Hall of Fame, we played really great," Young says. "I played with Crazy Horse at the DC shows, and we

didn't have good nights. It was mediocre, as I remember it. Crazy Horse has all the energy in the world, but everything has got to be right. And it wasn't right those nights. So I thought, Well, I'll see if Pearl Jam wants to make a record. They're excited, they have a lot of energy, and they're very solid and focused."

Longtime Pearl Jam producer Brendan O'Brien then got word from band manager Kelly Curtis telling him that Young would likely be calling him within the hour to ask him to produce the sessions.

"I'd spent up until age thirty-one or thirty-two with nobody calling," O'Brien reflects. "It went from nobody is calling, to Bob Dylan is calling. Elvis Costello is calling. Then Neil Young is calling. That was really an incredible moment. Ahead of time, he said to the Pearl Jam guys and to Kelly, 'I want to do it the Pearl Jam way. I want to use their guy and their studio.' He wanted our process for his record."

Says Young, "I decided rather than adding the complexity of using my own producer, that I'd use theirs. We got rid of everything individual on my side and all of my trappings, so it was just me going in there by myself. I don't even think I took a roadie. We saved a couple of days by doing that. Brendan already knew the sounds that the guys liked to hear. The whole idea was to do it as fast and as fresh as possible. I didn't want it to drag on."

It was actually that simple. On January 26 Young and the nonsinging members of Pearl Jam started rolling tape at Bad Animals studio in Seattle without so much as having rehearsed or talked about what the plan was. Initially, Young had only "Act of Love" and "Song X," a biting commentary on opponents of reproductive freedom set to a back-and-forth sea shanty cadence.

Jeff Ament recalls Young telling the band, "I want to just come to Seattle and just record it in your guys' deal. I'm just going to bring my amp and my guitar up, and let's knock it out." With the first two songs finished, Young said, "You know what? I think I'm going to have a couple more tomorrow."

"He had his boat up in Seattle—he went back to his boat every night for four or five nights and wrote two songs," Ament says. "He would come in with these big, long sheets of lyrics and a couple chord progressions. A lot of times, he'd come in with these three-chord songs that didn't change. 'I'm the Ocean' had six pages of lyrics taped together, with hardly any repeating lines in the whole song. He hung them on his mike stand. He'd written that the night before. He wrote the chords on a piece of paper, we jammed it two or three times, and that's what's on the record.

"And so we went from not knowing Neil very well to being in a room with him for five days, knocking out what ended up being the *Mirror Ball* record," he continues. "I had the flu for two of those days, so it all seems like a dream to me."

That Pearl Jam was suddenly for all intents and purposes being fronted by Young was a peculiar turn of events not lost on the participants, particularly Vedder, who was dealing with a scary personal situation involving an obsessive fan and was none too eager to leave the house, even for a unique situation like this.

"Neil is the only one that would be a big fan of the band and then get rid of Eddie," Stone Gossard says. "It would be cool to collaborate with Pearl Jam, but you'd think you'd want Ed involved. Neil likes to do things his way. It just shows you how an artist can be spontaneous and go, 'This is what my next project's going to be. Let's go make a weird record where I only play the songs for them three times and then they jump on board, and all I basically do is comp the chords. And then just when I think they've learned it, we're going to use the take from two or three takes ago, and that's it, done.' It just went by us so quickly, we never even had a chance to think about what we were doing."

Unlike his bandmates, Irons had never met Young before the 1994 Bridge School shows, and he admits being thrust into a studio with the rock legend was at times intimidating. "We did those gigs in Washington, DC. And at that time, I felt really confident. We were doing good with Neil," he says. "During the recording sessions, I was a little more nervous. It was a little more intimate. Here's Neil coming in and saying, 'Okay, we're recording on tape, and this is what I want.' I probably figured at the time that a guy like that knows exactly what he wants, because he's played with enough great musicians to call me out if it wasn't suiting him. But he wasn't like that at all. He was very supportive. He wanted to rock. It went really fast—maybe too fast."

While it may have been somewhat unusual for Pearl Jam, that pace was just fine with and actually preferred by Young, who remembers the sessions most for "this huge wall of sound we had going. My songs are really simple compared to Pearl Jam's. Mine are deceptively simple—sometimes just two chords. I play guitar much more than Eddie, so now there's another guitar in the mix, and they've already got two. In my history with three guitars, the only band that ever worked in was Buffalo Springfield. It mostly turns into a big mess. But everybody just played what they thought they should play. Stone and Mike are amazing guitar players, so that made it easy. It just happened; a little lead here, a little lead there."

The musicians had completed seven songs during recording on January 26 and 27. Young then briefly left Seattle but returned on February 7 with several additional tracks, which were put to tape that day and again on February 10. And with that, after four days in the studio, *Mirror Ball* was done.

On songs like "Throw Your Hatred Down" and "Downtown," Young's lyrics explore the generation gap between people of his post–World War II vintage and the twentysomethings making their mark on the 1990s—a gap he and Pearl

Jam had managed to bridge. "All these songs happened because of Pearl Jam, so I had this generation gap on my mind at the time," Young says.

Young looks back on a bygone era of rock 'n' roll on "Downtown," which references Jimi Hendrix, Led Zeppelin, and "hippies" who are only at the shows because "they want to be seen." "That's kind of like a teenybopper song," Young says. "But it's also kind of trippy and fun. It's maybe not up to the quality of some of the other songs. But it's very candid. It has a nice way of turning around and repeating itself."

Elsewhere, the seven-minute-plus jam "I'm the Ocean," with lines like, "I'm a drug that makes you dream," speaks to music's power as a unifying force. "Music is what brought Pearl Jam and I together," Young says. "And it's funny, because I can't play any of these songs with any other band. Even though some of them were just folk songs when I brought them in, they got played with this Pearl Jam drive and energy that really pushed them forward."

At the tail end of the *Mirror Ball* sessions, Vedder made his first appearance, helping Young finish the song "Peace and Love" and singing the powerful middle eight: "I took it all, I took the oath / I took it all, 'til I had most / I took what's left, I gave it breath / I had it all, once I gave it back."

"We listened back to 'Peace and Love,' and he liked the lyrics I'd written," Vedder says. "They counted the songs they had, and they had nine. Neil looked right at me and said, 'You write one, and we've got ten.' At that point, I hadn't written a song in three or four months. So I went upstairs to this little room and wrote 'I Got Id' in about twenty minutes. All it takes is someone like Neil to point at you, and it's on. It wasn't until probably three years later that I realized the chorus is kind of the same as 'Cinnamon Girl,' but I had no idea at the time."

The song was recorded with Young on lead guitar and O'Brien, subbing in for the flu-addled Ament, on bass. "The only people there were Jack, myself, Eddie, and Neil," O'Brien says. "The four of us got up there and did what ended up becoming 'I Got Id.' I remember thinking that it was kind of awesome. Right now, just for a minute, I'm in a band with Eddie Vedder and Neil Young [*laughs*]."

"Neil and Eddie were writing on the spot," Irons adds. "Neil would come in and just storm the room with this musical inspiration, so we went with it. Eddie got going with it, too."

Another new Vedder song, "Long Road," was his spontaneous musical reaction to receiving news of the death of Clayton Liggett, his drama teacher in high school in San Diego. Vedder grabbed his guitar and started playing a D chord over and over, almost like a bell tolling. Then the other musicians silently picked up their instruments and started playing the same chord. "We must have played that D chord for about four minutes," Vedder says. "When we finally hit the C chord, it was earthshaking. I went up to the mike, and the words just happened."

"With people like Neil Young, you learn from just witnessing," Vedder reflects. "All you have to do is watch and learn. It's not like lessons: 'Step two of this theory or that theory.' It's not even from conversations, like, 'Back then, I went through this or that.'"

Lessons or not, Young was happy to offer a sounding board for Pearl Jam, especially amid Vedder's struggle to keep the focus on music as the band's popularity soared. "All Eddie wanted to do was make music, but things got very out of perspective around that time. Everything he said became a big deal," Young says. "I'm glad he and Pearl Jam were able to put their heads down and just keep doing what they were doing."

Before the musicians began recording, executives from Reprise (Young's label) and Epic (Pearl Jam's) had agreed that "Pearl Jam" would

not appear on the cover of the album, because at that point it was assumed that Vedder would not be involved in the project. As such, "I Got Id" and "Long Road" were left off *Mirror Ball* and instead released at the tail end of the year on Pearl Jam's humorously titled *Merkin Ball* EP.

"We went back and forth on this, and Neil and I even had a couple phone calls about it," Vedder says. "We couldn't figure it out. We just wanted to avoid having a bunch of label negotiations, and it turns out that not having Pearl Jam mentioned was a decision we kind of regret, because it really was the coming together of both bands."

Ultimately, any effort to downplay Pearl Jam's role in *Mirror Ball* proved pointless when the album debuted in July at no. 5 on the *Billboard* 200, Young's best showing since his album *Harvest* reached number one in 1972. Some critics called the album half baked, but others praised its spontaneity and a "bang-it-out casualness" uncommon for a veteran such as Young.

On the heels of the infamous Golden Gate Park incident and before Pearl Jam's fall 1995 tour, the band—again minus Vedder but augmented by O'Brien on keyboards—backed Young for an eleven-date concert swing through such unusual locations as Israel and Austria. The bulk of *Mirror Ball* was performed during these shows, with Young classics like "Cortez the Killer," "Powderfinger," and "Down by the River" mixed in.

Young and Pearl Jam would play together again many times in the future, usually at his Bridge School concerts, but they all still remember the *Mirror Ball* experience as one of the most fulfilling of their careers.

Says Ament, "In some ways, I wish we could have had a little bit more time, but he showed us that you could write good and different songs in a really short period of time. And it couldn't have come at a better time for us. We were feeling the pressure of being a big rock band at the time, and in some ways, we probably put a lot of that pressure on ourselves. He made us realize it wasn't that important. It's not life-or-death stuff—it's just music." Adds Gossard, "I think he probably has been instrumental in why we're still a band, for sure."

MEAN FIDDLER PRESENTS

READING 95

PRODUCTION

Stage *Main*

Name *N. Young*

No. 3149

1995

176

PERFORM

NEIL YOUNG/PEARL JAM

STOCKHOLM, SWEDEN
Sjöhistoriska Museet, June 28, 1993

Grunge guru Young (left) and Steve Cropper

GLANCE, IT SEEMED A CLASSIC
...on-gap bill. On the one hand,
...as Pearl Jam, hard-edge champi-
...the Seattle sound whose fans
...a mosh pit in front of the stage;
...was Neil Young, an old-fashioned
...whose decision to use Booker T. &
...acking band seemed only to under-
...tesman status.

...e obvious disparities, what came
...lly in this pairing were the similari-
...g sense of narrative in the songs, the
...se of style, the close attention paid to
...namics. And
...acts finally
...for a show-
...ion of "Rock-
...ee World," it
...ost a match
...en.

...got into gear
...ening their set
...ly chugging ren-
..."Even Flow" that
...ly set the crowd
... With its dark
...keening chorus, it
...he perfect vehicle
...e Vedder to estab-
...presence and lay
...the audience. Once
...oundation was in
...Vedder had no prob-
...ilding upon it, draw-
...e listeners ever closer
...moved from the impas-
...d urgency of "Don't Go Out There" to the
... of "Jeremy."
...the front of

Hair apparent: Pearl Jam's Vedder

when to push a performer and when to
lie back. "This Note's for You," for
example, sizzled over guest drummer
Jim Keltner's fatback pulse, lending
extra authenticity to the tune's stylized
blues licks, while an encore rendition of
"All Along the Watchtower" was so
incendiary that one of the PA cabinets
was actually in flames at the song's end.
Yet Booker T.'s chirping B-3 rendered
their arrangement of "Harvest Moon"
more evanescent than the original, and
when Young sat at his piano for a heartbreaking run through "I
Believe in You," the rhythm
work was understated
enough to present the illu-
sion of a solo perform-
ance. —J.D. CONSIDINE

PETE TOWNSHEND

NEW YORK CITY
...on Theater, July 12, 1993

Psychoderelict: Pete Townshend

...M AN ENGLISH BOY," GOES THE
...pening lyric of *Psychoderelict*, the
...ew rock & roll concept album from
...hat medium's most celebrated prac-
..., Pete Townshend. Performing his
...opus at Manhattan's Beacon
..., along with old Who favorites and
...material from his solo repertoire, the
...an certainly exhibited a boy's physical stamina.
...ed in a natty, humidity-be-damned black suit,
...shend kicked off the American leg of his first full-
...ed tour as a solo artist by playing nearly three
...s without taking a break; and neither his energy
...his charm wilted a jot during that time.
...nitially conceived as a radio play with spoken dia-
...ue interspersed between songs that propel and

Psychoderelict...
uncanny ability to mar...
to brash indignation — "Whateve...
that lovely hippie shit?" High as...
— the music reflects his knack for
ly bittersweet melodies with fero...
Ballads like "I Am Afraid" and
and Then" gave Townshend a...
included six other musicians and...
ists, the chance to reveal a delica...
ty, while the more sonically and...
numbers were tackled with a few...

In addition to *Psychoderelict's*...
its effervescent chorus and jazzy...
most invigorating moments inc...

...deri...
Ope...
radi...
on...
who...
and...
ou...
wit...
co...
str...
cla...

around and doing windr...
threatening to remind y...
that trashing one's ax a...
hardly a new trick. Pe...
more a new trick than...
his muse and his sense...
say nothing of his cardi...
ator appears in little d...
der any time soon.

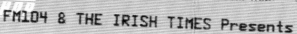

FM104 & THE IRISH TIMES Presents

NEIL YOUNG
THE MIRRORBALL TOUR
Plus Support
RDS (Simmonscourt)

DOORS OPEN 6.00p.m.
SAT 26 AUG 1995 7:30 PM

STANDING   C10*723
£0.00   INCL. BOOKING FEE

COMPLIMENTARY

177

CHAPTER 1996

1996

Pearl Jam continued to push the envelope in 1996, releasing its most experimental album, *No Code,* and once again foregoing music videos and interviews. Alone among its peers in its determination to tour without involving Ticketmaster, Pearl Jam also forged ahead with new ticketing company ETM for another tour in largely nontraditional venues. But without the proper infrastructure, the wear and tear of putting together shows from scratch was simply too much for the band to overcome. Not only was it costing the band significant energy to maintain the effort, it was taking the focus away from Pearl Jam's music. "We were still trying to circumvent everything, and it wasn't fun," Jeff Ament says. "After a couple of years of that, we said, 'Fuck this.' We need to make music and play music and do whatever we can to let people know where their money is going. But being the poster child for all of that, especially since we didn't have any help, was an impossible task." Indeed, Pearl Jam had gone to extremes with its touring strategy, but had yet to find a satisfying solution. Once again, it was time to step back, reflect, and think about new ways to make itself heard.

January 6

Columbia Records releases the *Dead Man Walking* soundtrack, featuring two Eddie Vedder songs, "Long Road" and "The Face of Love," performed by him with Pakistani *qawwali* vocalist Nusrat Fateh Ali Khan. Vedder befriends *Dead Man Walking* stars Sean Penn and Susan Sarandon, as well as director Tim Robbins, during the making of the film.

Eddie Vedder: Singing with Nusrat was pretty heavy. There was definitely a spiritual element. I saw him warm up once, and I walked out of the room and just broke down. I mean, God, what amazing power and energy.

January 25
Riverhorse Café, Park City, Utah

During the Sundance Film Festival, Eddie Vedder makes a surprise appearance with the Fastbacks to perform a cover of "Leaving Here" at the premiere party for *Hype!,* a documentary on the Seattle music scene that includes interviews with Vedder and future Pearl Jam drummer Matt Cameron, among many others.

Eddie Vedder: That was the only time I ever went to Sundance. Sub Pop rented a little chalet, and we jammed about fifty people in there. We stayed up all night.

January 29
Shrine Auditorium, Los Angeles

Pearl Jam wins American Music Awards for favorite heavy metal/hard rock artist and favorite alternative music artist.

February 20

Epic releases the double-disc benefit compilation *Home Alive: The Art of Self Defense,* featuring Pearl Jam's cover of "Leaving Here." Proceeds benefit Seattle-based Home Alive, a women's organization dedicated to providing access to self-defense information and techniques founded in the wake of the 1993 rape and murder of Mia Zapata, a member of the Seattle band the Gits.

February 28
Shrine Auditorium, Los Angeles

Pearl Jam wins its first Grammy, as "Spin

the Black Circle" is named best hard rock performance. Eddie Vedder gives the following speech while accepting the award:

"Well, we just came to relax. I just wanted to watch the show. I hate to start off with a bang. I'm going to say something typically me on behalf of all of us. I don't know what this means. I don't think it means anything. That's just how I feel. There's too many bands, and you've heard it all before, but, my dad would have liked it. My dad died before I got to know him, and he would have liked it. So, that's why I'm here. Thanks, I guess."

Eddie Vedder: I shouldn't have done it. I shouldn't have gone. I was in a bad mood, you know? We thought we could go down and just have fun 'cause we were making a record, and we were kind of together as a group, and we thought, Let's go down and let's just, like, laugh at it. We should do it once in our lives. And then you kinda got there and you realize, Man, fuck, this is it. This is supposed to be as good as it gets. I'm supposed to be really proud of this thing. And looking around, I wasn't proud of it at all. I was embarrassed to be there. I saw the Ramones the night before at Coney Island High, this little club in New York, and there I felt totally comfortable, you know? That was real. And then to go to this thing, it was so unreal, and not even surreal in a good way.

March 12

Stone Gossard guests on several songs on Los Angeles band Thermadore's Atlantic Records album *Monkey on Rico.*

April 9

Mike McCready guests under the name "Petster" with Seattle band Goodness for its cover of "Electricity, Electricity" from Atlantic's *Schoolhouse Rock! Rocks* tribute album.

June 11

Jeff Ament's side band Three Fish, which also features Tribe After Tribe's Robbi Robb and ex-Fastbacks drummer Richard Stuverud, releases its self-titled debut on Epic. A monthlong North American tour follows.

July 2

Interscope releases the benefit compilation *MOM: Music for Our Mother Ocean,* featuring Pearl Jam's cover of the Silly Surfers' 1964 single "Gremmie Out of Control."

August 6
The Palace, Los Angeles

At the request of Johnny Ramone, Eddie Vedder sings the Dave Clark 5's "Anyway You Want It" with the Ramones, which is the last song of their final show. The concert is released in November 1997 as the CD and home video *We're Outta Here!*

August 10

"Who You Are," the first single from Pearl Jam's upcoming album *No Code,* debuts at no. 8 on *Billboard*'s Modern Rock and Mainstream Rock charts. The track showcases the rhythmic drumming style of Jack Irons and surprises many with its gentler sound.

August 27

Pearl Jam's fourth studio album, *No Code,* is released by Epic. The set debuts the following week at no.1 on the *Billboard* 200 with US sales of 366,000, according to Nielsen SoundScan, making it the top-selling debut of the year to that point and the band's third consecutive chart topper.

September 14
Showbox, Seattle

Pearl Jam plays its first show since November 7, 1995, with a secret hometown gig to debut nine songs from *No Code.* Vedder tells the audience at the top of the show, "Good evening. Welcome to the R.E.M. record release party. Welcome to the Pearl Jam reunion tour. Have you heard the new record? Well, you're about to again."

September 16
Key Arena, Seattle

An equipment problem–plagued Seattle show is the proper kickoff to the band's No Code tour, which again is routed through non-Ticketmaster venues and alternate ticket purchasing and distribution systems such as the Philadelphia-based FT&T. As a result, Pearl Jam plays to smaller-than-usual crowds in such out-of-the-way locales as Toledo and Augusta, Maine. For the Seattle show, Pearl Jam is able to circumvent Ticketmaster by donating all its proceeds to the Seattle Center Arts and Peace Academies and the Northwest School.

Stone Gossard: We were standing up for what we thought was right, but the fact of the matter was that we couldn't play in the best venues, because Ticketmaster had exclusive contracts with them. It was very stressful, and I think it diminished some of the excitement about being in Pearl Jam at that time.

Jeff Ament: When you really understand how hard the crew had to work, we'd take on a lot of that frustration when we were trying to build those shows from the ground up.

September 20

Pearl Jam rocks through "Hail, Hail" on a commercial-free episode of CBS's *Late Show with David Letterman,* its first appearance on an American late-night TV show besides *Saturday Night Live.* The band also plays "Leaving Here" going into the credits, although only a few seconds of the song make it to air.

September 23

Pearl Jam's official website, Synergy, comes online at www.sonymusic.com/artists/PearlJam.

September 26
Augusta Civic Center, Augusta, Maine

Having chartered a jet from Italy to attend the concert, NBA star Dennis Rodman appears onstage during "Alive" to close

the main set. In an unusual ending, Vedder performs a solo acoustic "I Am a Patriot" by request from a fan who had sent him a letter.

September 28–29
Downing Stadium, Randall's Island, New York

Pearl Jam's first New York shows in more than two years are not in a sports arena but an aging multipurpose stadium on an island in the East River. Sold-out crowds of thirty thousand turn up for both. During a rain-soaked night one, Blues Traveler's John Popper guests on "Even Flow," and Vedder gives a heartfelt speech about how proud he is that so many people are bonding over Pearl Jam's music. At thirty-two songs and 168 minutes, the second show becomes the band's longest ever. During an 11-minute "Porch," Vedder blackens his eyes with burnt cork, wraps duct tape around his entire body, and leaps into the raging mosh pit.

Jack Irons: How many more fans can you play for? If we would have played Madison Square Garden that year, we'd have had to play four shows to reach the number of people who saw us in two. I can guarantee you that we would have not played four nights at Madison Square Garden. But where do you play if one hundred thousand people or more want to see you? How do you do that?

Eddie Vedder: When tickets were hard to come by and so much work had been done to organize the venues, security, Porta-Johns, et cetera, it seemed strange to stop playing after the normal hour and a half when you were at the peak of the journey. Everyone standing in their seats, amplifiers plugged in and working, and a half bottle of wine left to go: a perfect atmosphere to break out an obscure B-side.

October 1

The soundtrack to the Seattle music scene documentary *Hype!* is released by Sub Pop. It includes the version of "Not for You" recorded during Pearl Jam's January 1995 Self Pollution Radio broadcast, footage from which appears in the film.

"emancipate
yourselves from
mental slavery none
but ourselves can
free our minds"

Bob Mar...
-redemption s...

PEARL JAM

you have a voice

vote loud

october 11 is the last
day to register to vote
for the next elections
in north carolina

pearl jam
memorial stadium
charlotte, north
carolina
october 4, 1996
6:30pm

base price: 22.00
service fee: 2.00
total charge: 24.00 per ticket
handling fee: .50 per order

MEMORIAL STADIUM
CHARLOTTE, N. CAROLINA
1004   COMP
00051729089614

Three Fish

October 4
Memorial Stadium, Charlotte, North Carolina

In an attempt to register voters and vote out North Carolina's uberconservative Republican senator Jesse Helms, Pearl Jam teams with Gloria Steinem and Artists for a Hate Free America for this show in Charlotte. More than one thousand new voters are registered, some of them in the parking lot by a disguised Vedder, but Helms is ultimately reelected shortly thereafter. Brendan O'Brien joins the band to play bass on "I Got Id."

October 7
Fort Lauderdale Stadium, Fort Lauderdale, Florida

Twenty-five thousand tickets are sold for the tour finale in this eight-thousand-capacity venue. A young man in a wheelchair crowd surfs to the front and is lifted onstage during "Rockin' in the Free World," the second-to-last song of the show. The man, Mark Zupan, later goes on to captain the US wheelchair rugby team and is featured prominently in the 2005 documentary *Murderball.*

October 19–20
Shoreline Amphitheatre, Mountain View, California

Pearl Jam, augmented by Brendan O'Brien on Fender Rhodes electric piano, makes its third appearance at Neil Young's Bridge School Benefit, continuing an every-other-year tradition that began in 1992. Both shows feature a dramatically rearranged version of "Corduroy," and "Porch" is also played at the second show in a funky, altered form. "Nothingman" makes its first live appearance since before the release of *Vitalogy;* the version from night one appears on the 1997 compilation *The Bridge School Concerts, Vol. One* (Reprise).

October 24
Millstreet Arena, Cork, Ireland

Pearl Jam plays its first European show in more than three years, kicking off a monthlong tour in support of *No Code.* "Smile" is played for the first time four nights later in London.

November 3
Deutschlandhalle, Berlin

This show is broadcast around the world from a feed originated by Berlin's Radio Fritz. Afterward, on German radio only, Eddie Vedder spins a dozen of his favorite songs such as Shudder to Think's "Pebbles," the Who's "Sparks," and Lou Reed's "Sword of Damocles." He also takes calls from listeners, one of whom asks why the band waited until it was famous to stop making videos and doing interviews. His response:

"That's a great question. I don't think we understood those things from the start. I don't think we understood that you become a commodity. I don't think we understood that. We thought that that was how you got your songs to be heard, and in some ways, maybe it is . . . and I regret . . . Looking back, there's some things I would change, but I think that a band like Fugazi, who has a lot of these same beliefs . . . I think they're better because of it. I think we were naive in the beginning and we . . . and maybe we had faith, in that these things could be good. A video could be an art piece. An interview can be a way of communicating to a large amount of people at once. We lost our faith soon after that and decided to do whatever we could do to get around that."

November 5
The Vera, Groningen, Netherlands

Before European tour opening act the Fastbacks perform (at $4 a ticket) at this 217-capacity club, group members Kurt Bloch (bass) and Mike Musburger (drums) are joined by Eddie Vedder for a six-song set billed as the What. The trio plays the Who's "I Can't Explain," "The Kids Are Alright," and "Naked Eye," plus Pearl Jam's "Lukin," "Not for You," and "Rearviewmirror." Vedder joins the full Fastbacks in their encore for the Keith Moon–penned Who obscurity "Girl's Eyes" and "Leaving Here." On November 24 in Cascais, Portugal, the What appears again before Pearl Jam's set to play "I Can't Explain," "The Kids Are Alright," "My Generation," and "Young Man Blues."

November 15
Sports Hall, Prague, Czech Republic

The trucks carrying Pearl Jam's sound equipment are waylaid on Austria's snowed-in Brenner Pass, necessitating the show's start time to be pushed back several hours. Once they eventually arrive at the venue, the crew sets everything up in three hours instead of the usual ten, allowing the show to go off as planned.

November 17
Sports Hall, Budapest, Hungary

The *No Code* outtake "Black Red Yellow" is played for the first time, while Mose Allison's "Young Man Blues," popularized by the Who, debuts in the encore.

November 21
Sports Palace, Barcelona

Pearl Jam plays a seventy-minute soundcheck before this show that becomes a fan favorite in bootleg trading circles. The band practices the song "Parting Ways," which would not be released until the *Binaural* album in 2000, a sixteen-minute version of "Hard to Imagine," and a ten-minute exploration of "I'm Open."

November 27

Ten is certified ten times platinum by the Recording Industry Association of America (RIAA) for US shipments of ten million copies.

Eddie Vedder: When it got to be a double-digit platinum-selling record, there's serious guilt involved there, because you're seeing another band that made a better record than you did, or for whatever taste, you liked theirs better. Like, "Wow, I can really rock out to this." You'd see them in a club, and they'd had their record out for a year, and they'd sold fifteen thousand copies or something. The disparity's too huge.

And you're not responsible for it completely, but, so . . . I don't know, you do things. You start radio stations and do a radio broadcast and invite them on. And not out of guilt. Just saying, "Look, if we have the attention, let's use it, and, like, wave to everybody and then pull back. Here's a great band. Here's another great band. Here's a better band."

Christmas

Pearl Jam releases its fifth fan-club-only seven-inch vinyl single, "Olympic Platinum" with B-side "Smile" (live from the November 21, 1996, Barcelona show).

No Code

If there was ever proof that Pearl Jam wasn't the kind of band to bask in its own glory, it was evident on July 12, 1995. That was the day after the quintet played a marathon thirty-one-song set in front of forty-seven thousand fans at Chicago's Soldier Field, amid a heat wave that claimed six hundred lives in the Greater Chicago area. Seeking to capitalize on the residual energy from what was at the time one of its most memorable shows, the band booked time at the city's Chicago Recording Company to begin laying down new song ideas that had been bubbling up since earlier in the year.

But for drummer Jack Irons, getting right to work on his first Pearl Jam studio album since joining in late 1994 wasn't exactly what he had in mind. "I was feeling the effects of the heat and just coming into the studio right after such a major show," he remembers. "I was sort of bummed. I was like, 'Don't you guys chill out? Man, I'm tired!' Those guys were really into working at the time. To them, they could pound it on that stage, and the next day they'd be in the studio. I was like, 'How do you guys keep up?'"

"I don't think we'd quite figured out how to schedule ourselves at that point," Jeff Ament admits, adding that it was understandable Irons was exhausted, considering that as the drummer, he had the most physical job in the band. But for Irons, his own "little temper tantrum" led to creative inspiration.

"I asked my drum guy to set up my little drum set in a vocal booth," he says. "I said, 'I just want to practice in my own room.' I sat in there, and all of a sudden I started working on this thing that became 'In My Tree.' It was a teeny little room, with just enough room for me and this drum set, which was a toy bass drum and some Rototoms. It was

a practice set I would use backstage. Then, all the sudden, something cool was happening in there. I thought, Can we put some mikes in here? Brendan O'Brien and Nick DiDia threw up a couple of mikes. I recorded a bunch of me doing it and sat with it. Then when we came back to Seattle, we put it up and worked the song up from that opening drum bit. Eddie's the one who took it to the next level."

"In My Tree," with its tribal, galloping beats and cathartic chorus, and "Who You Are," another Irons-driven groove accented by sitar, piano, and hand claps, wound up as key breakthroughs to an entirely new type of sound on *No Code,* Pearl Jam's fourth studio album. The loose, rhythm-first tracks made good on the more stripped-down approach presaged by "I Got Id" and "Long Road," the two Pearl Jam originals recorded during the spring 1995 sessions for *Mirror Ball.*

"There was a lot of jamming going into *No Code,*" Irons recalls. "We'd get into the studio and start kicking it up. With 'Who You Are,' I liked to play that drumbeat a lot, and Stone came in and started kicking something over it. Next thing you know, there's a fairly loose track. Eddie sort of wrote right over it. I don't even think there were more than a few hours involved in cutting what became that basic track. Looking back, that was a very good session in Chicago. It was a defining moment for me as a drummer to create songs that way."

"Jack's drumming was funky," says Mike McCready. "It wasn't as hard as Dave Abbruzzese's. It was a little bit more groovy, so it lent itself to stuff like 'Who You Are.' It was very rhythmic and different than anything we'd experienced." Adds Ament, "I loved that

Jack approached every song differently with his drums. He'd change the setup of his kit depending on what we were working on."

A jam-first, collaborative approach was something that Stone Gossard had predicted would come to fruition several months earlier, when Irons was a brand-new addition. "You'll still hear more of Eddie's songwriting, but there will also be elements that'll enable everybody's personality to shine through," he told *Musician* magazine. "You'll hear that spontaneity, but I hope to spend more time arranging material and trying to get everybody involved in the songwriting process."

On the other end of the spectrum, Vedder brought in songs like "Habit" and "Lukin" essentially fully formed. "Habit," a wake-up call to a drug-addled friend set to furious, detuned rock, had been debuted during his stint on the Mike Watt tour earlier in the year. "Lukin" was actually the first new Pearl Jam song to be played live after the release of *Vitalogy,* having debuted at a February 1995 show in Seattle. Even faster and more punk inspired than "Habit," the track funneled all of Vedder's fury at his ever-eroding privacy into a sixty-two-second haymaker.

What turned into a week of recording in Chicago also produced initial versions of the Motown-style rave-up "All Night," which wouldn't see official release for another nine years, and the McCready slide guitar showcase "Red Mosquito," inspired by Vedder's having to bail out a few songs into a recent San Francisco show due to food poisoning. McCready actually played the lead part with Vedder's grandfather's Zippo lighter rather than a traditional slide bottleneck.

Once the band minus Eddie wrapped up an international tour backing Neil

Young in support of *Mirror Ball,* all five members ducked into a New Orleans recording studio for a quick session in the fall of 1995. Then work on the new album continued at Gossard's Studio Litho in Seattle. However, Ament didn't know that two of his bandmates had started recording until the day he arrived there.

"I was in Montana at the time," he recalls. "We'd set a tentative date to do some recording, which I thought was a week from this day, when Kelly Curtis called me. He said, 'I thought you'd be in the studio with the guys,' and that Stone and Ed were in the studio right now. I was like, 'Really?' By the time I got there the next day, they'd already recorded four or five songs with no bass. I had just spent the previous several months writing songs, so I thought there was some weird power trip going on. I don't think I ever really expressed my anger at that point, but I was pretty bummed. I think a lot of the anger was toward Stone, because it seemed like everybody else thought I'd been told.

"It's interesting, because there's also a lot of talk about there being a shift in power around this time," he continues. "Ed was in power, and Stone and I weren't. But I think really what was happening was that Ed was bringing complete songs in and nobody else was. The cream was floating to the top."

Everyone agreed that Vedder's "Off He Goes" was exactly that. O'Brien calls it "one of the most meaningful songs of theirs that I've ever worked on; it haunts me," while Ament says, "It's a song all of us can relate to." The delicate acoustic ballad is essentially Vedder's admission that he's "a shit friend": the kind of guy who breezes in and out of people's lives without apology, but, "before his first step, he's off again."

"That's when I first started figuring out how to isolate myself, and I got into some good stuff, writingwise. That and 'Around the Bend' were written in the same chair in a faraway place," Vedder says with a laugh.

Elsewhere, the hushed album opener, "Sometimes," finds Vedder searching for "my small self / like a book among the many on a shelf," while on "Present Tense," the lyrics suggest that the singer is lecturing himself to not dwell on his mistakes: "You can spend your time alone, redigesting past regrets / Or you

can come to terms and realize you're the only one who can't forgive yourself."

That type of personal storytelling and measured reflection on Pearl Jam's first five years of existence provides rich food for thought throughout the album. "Ed as a lyricist is just always so good, even at times when our music isn't quite standing up to the quality of his words," Gossard says. "*No Code* has some incredible lyrics, which opened some doors for him to points of view that he continues to explore now. There's a spirituality and humility to the lyrics that was brand-new then, and classic storytelling that continues to be part of what he does. He's always been so great at giving you another person's perspective."

"Present Tense" also serves as the conceptual center of *No Code,* making great use of the simpler-is-better motif. The McCready-penned song is a certifiable epic, ranging from a somber introduction to a soaring jam at its end, at once intense and calming. Similarly meditative is "I'm Open," which evolved from something Vedder used to play in his San Diego apartment years before joining Pearl Jam. "It was like a mantra," he says. "I don't know if it's about religion. I don't know if it's about a relationship. It's about being open to whatever is out there. It's saying, 'I'm here. I'm listening for the message.' Maybe it's asking for a song."

The experimentation on *No Code* is tempered on a series of showcases for Pearl Jam's awesome rock power. "Hail, Hail," with its insightful Vedder lyric "I sometimes realize I can only be as good as you let me," the sneering "Habit," and "Mankind," a sarcastic slam of C-list grunge imitators that marks Gossard's lead vocal and lyric-writing debut, delivered laser-focused insights and fist-pumping power chords in equal measure.

Pearl Jam also remains true to the profound influence of Young, especially on Ament's lone songwriting contribution to the album, "Smile." Vedder's lyrics were inspired by a note left in one of his notebooks by the Frogs' Dennis Flemion ("I miss you already / I miss you always"), while the ragged, four-chord choruses and harmonica solos make it the first Pearl Jam song perfectly suited to be played around a campfire.

As often happens in Pearl Jam, Ament thought he had "four or five

other ideas that were more interesting" than what became "Smile," but his "two-parter Neil Young nod of the cap" was the thing that most excited his bandmates.

"I felt like musically, especially with the way Jack was playing the tribal polyrhythms, that I could have contributed so much more to that record than I did," he says. "You could argue that there are two or three things on *No Code* that don't work that great, but the experimenting that we did, most of it came off pretty well. And a lot of that had to do with what Ed contributed. I've always related to him lyrically, more than any other singer that I've played with, and that record, particularly 'Present Tense' and 'In My Tree,' really touched something in me."

On the heels of the incredibly elaborate packaging for *Vitalogy,* Pearl Jam created an equally intricate cover design for *No Code,* consisting of 144 different Polaroid photos that form a square when the CD Digipak is unfolded. When the collage is viewed at a distance of a few feet, a black triangle with an eyeball in the center is revealed, and this logo appears throughout the package. Among the images are various eyeballs, including those of NBA star and Pearl Jam superfan Dennis Rodman, an ashtray full of cigarette butts, drawings, nature photographs, and the top of an apple. The design was steered by Vedder (under his alias Jerome Turner), who gravitated to the myriad hidden meanings that could be taken from the photos.

"It came from David Byrne and his fascination with Polaroids, which I adopted at an early age," Vedder says of the *No Code* art. "I used to spend half my paycheck from Long's Drugs buying Polaroid film and making collages. If it's not my top one, one of my top three record covers is the Talking Heads' *More Songs About Buildings and Food.* I'd show it to people after getting them really stoned: 'Isn't this the greatest cover ever?' They'd say, 'I don't get it!' 'Keep looking.' 'I don't get it.' 'Keep looking. Have another bong load.' It's actually 684 Polaroids of the group put together, even though it's just the four of them standing there. *No Code* was based on that idea. I found this forensic Polaroid camera in Atlanta. Normally, you can't take a Polaroid from any farther than four feet away and have it in focus. But this had a macro lens, so everything became art. A bowl of soup became art. Bird shit on a blue car looked like the cosmos. When you fold out the liner notes, you have the 'No Code' triangle, which means 'Do not resuscitate.' I thought that was symbolic of where we were with the group: If we're dying, let us die. Don't try to save us. We don't want to live as vegetables."

Indeed, as *No Code* neared release in late August 1996, Pearl Jam had played only twenty-two shows in North America in the eighteen months since *Vitalogy* hit stores, and the band's profile was arguably, although purposefully, at an all-time low. During the making of the album, Vedder gave his famous "This doesn't mean anything" acceptance speech after "Spin the Black Circle" won best hard rock performance at the Grammy Awards.

Those words, as well as the band's steadfast refusal to perform in venues under contract to Ticketmaster, give interviews, or make videos, won it the undying support of hardcore fans. But they also befuddled millions of others who just wanted Pearl Jam back in their lives. Thus it was no surprise that when the band decided to release the decidedly non-alternative-rock-sounding "Who You Are" as the first single from *No Code,* fans didn't know which Pearl Jam to expect anymore.

"It was a super-weird time in the band," Ament says. "We were in that mode of putting out a song like 'Who You Are' as the first single, when there were at least four or five other songs on *No Code* that were probably more appropriate."

"I felt frustrated on that record," O'Brien says. "That was the first one we did at Studio Litho. At first, nothing worked quite right. It was Stone's studio, and if I would complain about things not working, I'd be the asshole hassling Stone. Plus, I was always the guy trying to push them to be more universal. That's just my nature. If you bring me along to help, I'm going to try to get everyone to love you. On *No Code,* I wasn't sure what they had going on. In the middle of it, Eddie had this terrible stalker problem. He was becoming more introverted. And then he said, 'Let's all go to the Grammys.' We were not planning on going, but we were up for album of the year. We all sat in the front row, and Eddie said something I'm certain he's not thrilled that he said. Pearl Jam Nation just turned the channel right there. Then we put a record out that said, We're not thinking of you anyway [*laughs*]. It was a record that was meaningful to make, but somewhat indifferent to the listener. I recognized at the time that it was something that had to happen. It had a lot of merit and some amazing songs. But people's reaction to Pearl Jam around that time changed."

"It's a record that is semi-unprofessional," observes Gossard. "We were just kind of winging it and trying stuff that maybe didn't quite work, but sometimes that stuff sounds good ten years later. It's like Rolling Stones records like *Emotional Rescue,* where they're trying to be funky. It's like, 'Yeah, I don't know . . .'

"But you listen to it ten years later and go, 'Fuck! That's jamming!' It just goes to show that it takes a while to see that you're making the right moves. I don't think anyone in the band knew that *No Code* was the right record to make. I think we were like, 'I hope this is good.' It's not that experimental, but it's us. It's really us."

And that was more than enough for Vedder. "Taking that success level down a few notches was probably pretty helpful on a creative level," he says. "Because, you know, the more you think, the more you stink. The thought that a lot of people are going to be hearing and analyzing what you wrote was a tricky one. It made you question and double-think, as much as you didn't want to. I was never confident enough to not give a fuck."

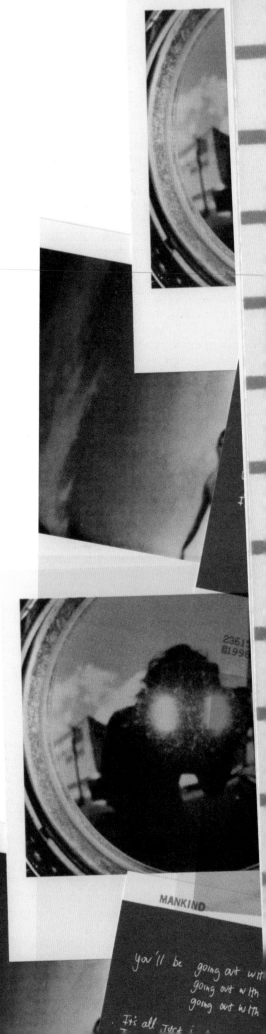

PEARL JAM

Hail, Hail

Who You Are

PEARL JAM

In My Tree

Smile

PEARL JAM

Off He Goes

Habit

PEARL JAM

Red Mosquito

Lukin

PEARL JAM

Present Tense

Mankind

PEARL JAM

I'm Open

Around the Bend

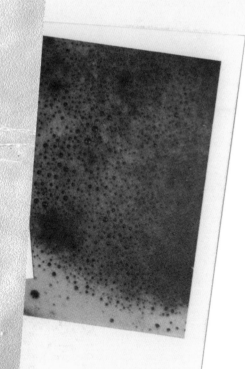

PEARL JAM
NO CODE

SPECIAL GUEST: FASTBACKS

MO. 3.11. 1996 BERLIN
DEUTSCHLANDHALLE

BEGINN 20.00 UHR

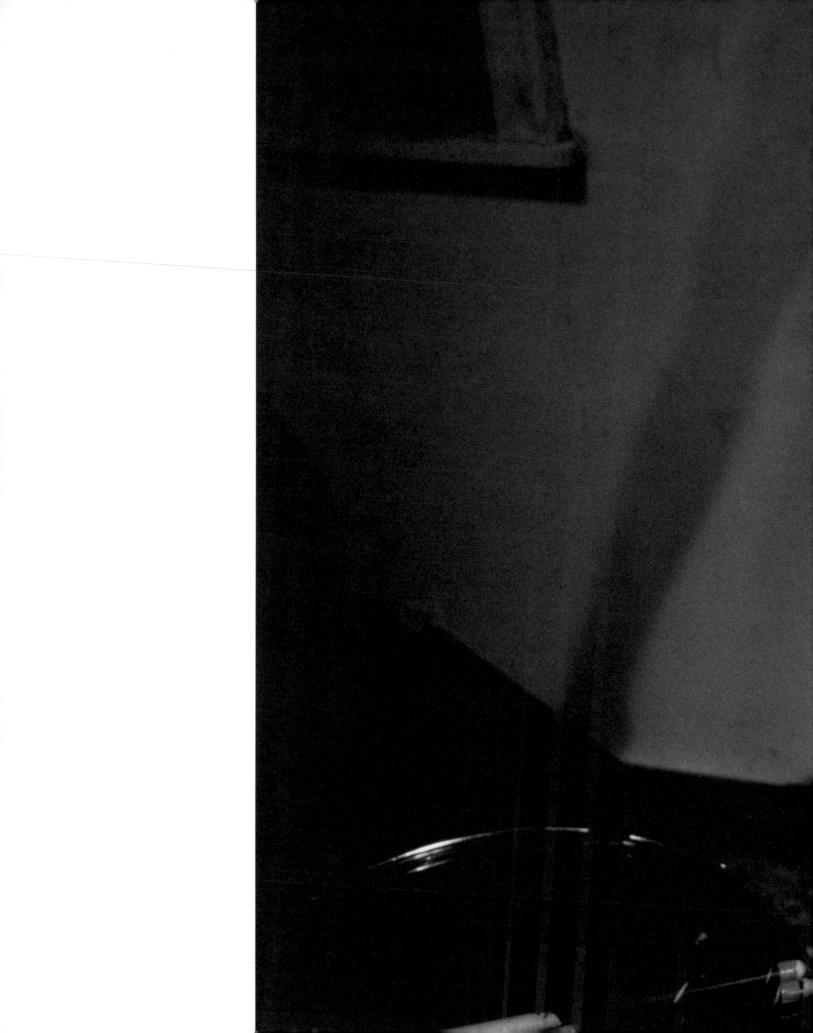

1997

On the heels of an extensive European tour at the end of 1996, Pearl Jam took a breather to reflect on its tumultuous past several years. Six months went by until a band member played in public in 1997, and even then, it was Eddie Vedder and Mike McCready making a fleeting appearance at a benefit concert. Instead the band was holed up in Seattle writing and recording music for its fifth studio album with Brendan O'Brien, who pushed, not always successfully, for Pearl Jam to focus on its most listener-friendly songs. During a break from the sessions, Stone Gossard and his cohorts in Brad regrouped, recorded a new album, and hit the road for the first time ever. And once the Pearl Jam album *Yield* was finished, the group eased back onto the stage in grand fashion by opening four stadium shows in Oakland for the Rolling Stones.

Stone Gossard: We felt we had some songs that potentially could be on the radio. Certainly I approached it feeling like, "We did the first one this way. Let's try to rehearse more, hone in on what it is that we're doing, and be a little bit more focused." I think that the result is mixed. "The Day Brings" is clearly a song that a lot of people attach themselves to, and I think there are some cool, weirder moments on that record where we took it to the next level. But I think if you ask anyone in the band, they would say that record's a little too safe; a little too calculated.

April 1

Mike McCready guests on *Breaking the Ethers,* the debut Epic album from instrumental rock outfit Tuatara. The group is comprised of R.E.M. guitarist Peter Buck, Screaming Trees drummer Barrett Martin, Luna bassist Justin Harwood, and Critters Buggin saxophonist Skerik.

April 8

Backed by Hovercraft, Eddie Vedder reads the Jack Kerouac poem "Hymn" on the Rykodisc spoken word tribute album *Kerouac: Kicks Joy Darkness.*

April 22

Jeff Ament makes an appearance on Tribe After Tribe's album *Pearls Before Swine* (Music for Nations).

June 8
Downing Stadium, Randall's Island, New York

Eddie Vedder and Mike McCready are surprise guests to open the second day of the second Tibetan Freedom Concert. Using guitars borrowed from the band Pavement, they perform the reworked "Corduroy" debuted at the Bridge School Benefit the previous fall, "Yellow Ledbetter," and an acoustic, sloweddown "Rockin' in the Free World."

Later in the show, they team with R.E.M.'s Michael Stipe and Mike Mills plus Patti Smith bassist Tony Shanahan to perform "Long Road," and McCready remains onstage to join the musicians for Suicide's "Ghost Rider" and Iggy Pop's "The Passenger." On both days of the concert, Vedder walks the grounds getting signatures on a petition to demand US government intervention into the Tibetan crisis.

June 15
House of Blues, Chicago

After watching the Chicago Bulls win the NBA championship two nights before, Vedder performs with his idol, Who guitarist Pete Townshend, for the first time during a Townshend solo show benefiting the Maryville Academy. Vedder sings "Heart to Hang Onto," "Magic Bus," and "Tattoo" with Townshend; the first two songs later appear as bonus tracks on Townshend's 1999 album *Pete Townshend Live: A Benefit for Maryville Academy.*

June 24

Stone Gossard's side band Brad releases its second Epic album *Interiors,* and two weeks later begins its maiden North American tour. A second round of dates follows in October. Oddly, over time, the album track "The Day Brings" becomes a staple for in-store play at groceries and drugstores.

Summer

Members of Pearl Jam and Soundgarden donate $400,000 to the Cascade Land Conservancy to aid preservation of 220 acres of wilderness in the Cascade Mountains foothills of Washington State.

November 4

Capitol Records releases a triple-disc compilation highlighting performances from the two Tibetan Freedom Concerts, including Eddie Vedder and Mike McCready's performance of "Yellow Ledbetter" from the June 1997 show in New York.

November 12
The Catalyst, Santa Cruz, California

Billed as the Honking Seals, Pearl Jam plays its first show in nearly a year at this eight-hundred-capacity venue and debuts three songs from the forthcoming album *Yield:* "Given to Fly," "Wishlist," and "Do the Evolution." Also played is "Brain of J.," which had made a lone prior appearance at the tail end of the band's 1995 tour. Before the first encore, Vedder calls Neil Young on a cell phone to wish him a happy birthday.

November 14–15, 18–19
Oakland-Alameda County Coliseum Stadium, Oakland

Pearl Jam opens four stadium shows for the Rolling Stones. The set lists go heavy on familiar tracks like "Corduroy," "Even Flow," "Alive," "Black," and

ED 27 MICK J. OAKLAND GIGS

KODAK 5054

"Better Man" but also include *Yield* cuts such as "Do the Evolution" and "Given to Fly." At the last show, the band makes it through a nearly complete take on the Stones' "Beast of Burden," played, according to Vedder, because the Stones hadn't been including it in their show. Later, during the Stones' set, Vedder duets with Mick Jagger on "Waiting on a Friend."

Jeff Ament: Those shows were after those two years of us doing things from the ground up. To just go open for the Stones, where it's their world and we just show up, was a pleasure. Not only were we playing with Mike's favorite band, but all of us grew up listening to tons of Stones stuff. Sitting and watching from the side of the stage, we got to see what things could possibly lie ahead for us, and maybe some things we wouldn't want to do, like have five other musicians onstage. They had a snooker table in Keith and Ron Wood's room, the bacon and mayonnaise sandwiches, Guinness on tap. It almost felt like Lollapalooza.

November 18

Pearl Jam's rendition of "Nothingman" from 1996 is included on *The Bridge School Concerts, Vol. One* (Reprise), a fifteen-track compilation from Neil Young's annual benefit concerts at the Shoreline Amphitheatre outside San Francisco. Released the same day, Eddie Vedder's guest appearance at the Ramones' August 6, 1996, farewell concert is included on the home video and CD set *We're Outta Here!* (Radioactive).

December 3

The Pearl Jam organization experiences firsthand how the Internet is changing the dissemination of music when Syracuse, New York, radio station WKRL-FM plays the entire unreleased *Yield* album on the air. A Syracuse University student promptly posts high-quality MP3 files of several songs online, resulting in quick cease and desist letters from Epic Records and the Recording Industry Association of America.

Christmas

Pearl Jam's sixth fan-club-only seven-inch single is a joint release with R.E.M's fan club. Pearl Jam contributes the Jack Irons song "Happy When I'm Crying," while R.E.M. offers "Live for Today." A snippet of "Happy When I'm Crying" eventually appears at the beginning of the song "Push Me, Pull Me" from *Yield*.

Jack Irons: I was getting a little pushy with wanting to do some of my weird stuff.

Peter Buck: When we were working on the R.E.M. album *New Adventures in Hi-Fi,* Eddie came by and played us this song "Olympic Platinum" from a day when no one else showed up to the studio. Somebody said, "Why don't we do a joint thing? That way we each have to come up with one song." "Live for Today," I think, was a demo I did. If I'm not playing all the instruments, it's pretty close. Michael just pulled out some lyrics and recited them over the top. I think it was cool for our fans because it was something they would never have expected—to turn it over, and it's a free Pearl Jam song. We were expecting "Olympic Platinum" from Pearl Jam, but we got "Happy When I'm Crying," which is just as cool.

BEACON
THEATRE
NYC
NEW YEARS
w/ KEITH, WINOS

CHAPTER 1998

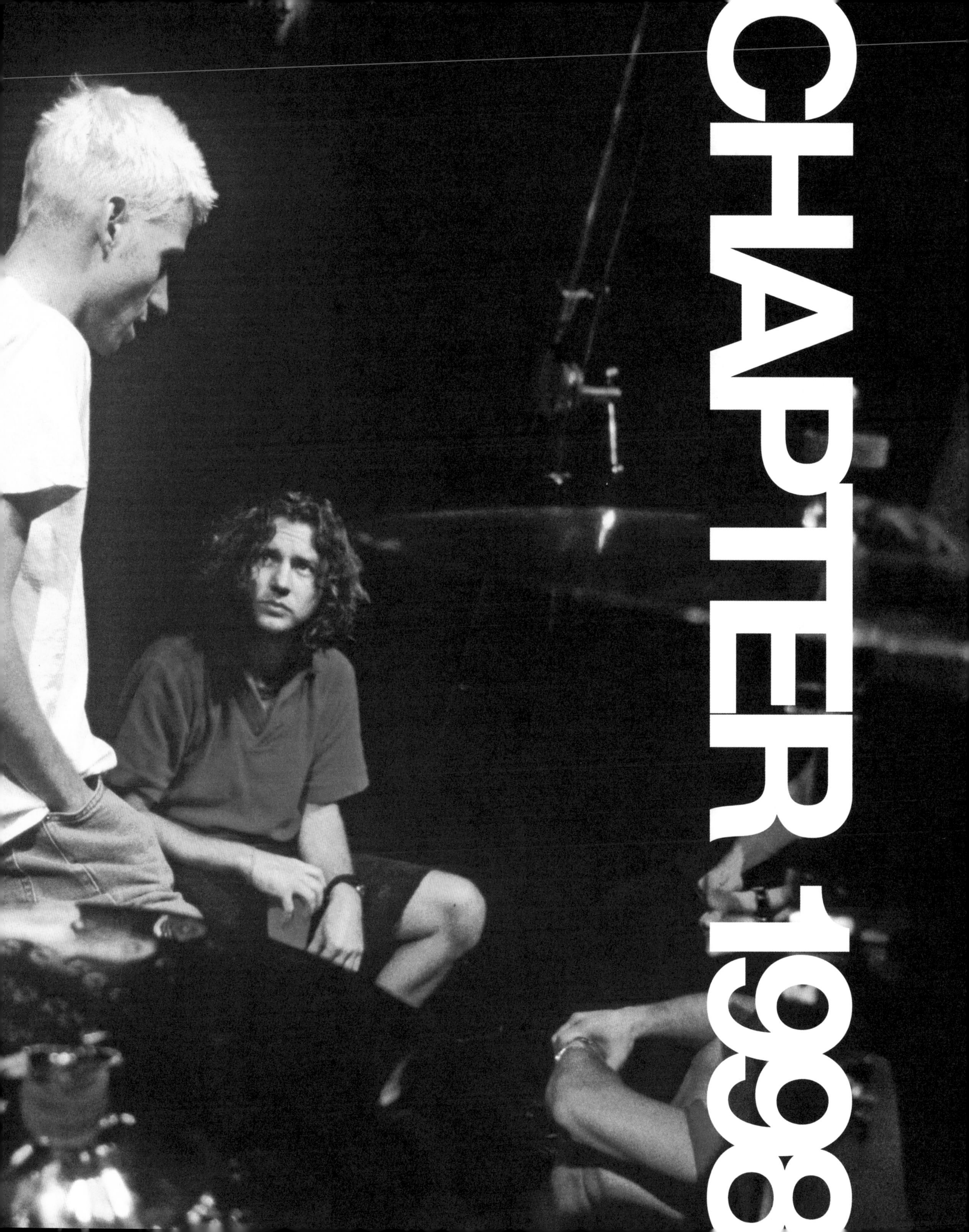

CHAPTER 198

1998

Pearl Jam hadn't been away long, but rock radio sure missed the band. Indeed, "Given to Fly," the first single from the quintet's fifth album, *Yield,* burned up the charts in early 1998, setting the stage for a big debut for the album in March. Pearl Jam then hit the road for its most extensive tour in five years, starting in Australia. But the stability the band had fought so hard to achieve was upended shortly afterward, when drummer Jack Irons announced that he was leaving Pearl Jam for personal health reasons. With hardly any time to find a replacement before another touring leg was about to begin, the band turned to a familiar face. And just like he'd done in 1990, when Pearl Jam was still in its embryonic stage, Matt Cameron would come to the rescue when his friends needed him the most.

January 7

Stone Gossard's side band Brad begins a tour of Australia and New Zealand as the opening act for Ben Harper.

January 31
225 Terry Avenue North, Seattle

From its Seattle warehouse, Pearl Jam hosts its second satellite broadcast. Titled *Monkeywrench Radio,* the show is offered free to radio stations across the United States. The three-and-a-half-hour program includes live performances of six songs ("Do the Evolution," "Given to Fly," "Pilate," "Wishlist," "Brain of J.," "In Hiding") from the soon-to-be-released *Yield* album, plus sets from Mudhoney, Brad, Tuatara, and the Washington hardcore punk group Zeke; a DJ segment featuring songs by Sonic Youth, the Ramones, and Stereolab; and Eddie Vedder taking on-air phone calls from Gloria Steinem and Mike Watt.

February 3

Pearl Jam's fifth studio album, *Yield,* is released by Epic. The following week, it debuts at no. 2 on the *Billboard* 200 with sales of 358,000 copies in the United States, according to Nielsen SoundScan.

February 20–21
Alexander M. Baldwin Amphitheatre, Maui, Hawaii

Pearl Jam kicks off a tour of the South Pacific in Hawaii. "Faithfull" and "MFC" from *Yield* are played live for the first time.

February 26
Queen's Wharf Events Center, Wellington, New Zealand

The first of thirteen shows in Australia and New Zealand with support from longtime Eddie Vedder favorites Shudder to Think. The last of three concerts in Melbourne on March 5 is broadcast live on the radio and the Internet by venerable Australian station JJJ. On March 9 in Sydney, the band plays Pink Floyd's "Interstellar Overdrive" as an intro to "Corduroy," which would become a common occurrence on future tours. The tour finale on March 20 in Perth is drummer Jack Irons's last show with Pearl Jam.

March 29
Shrine Auditorium, Los Angeles

Alongside Tom Waits, Steve Earle, and Ani DiFranco, Eddie Vedder and Jeff Ament perform at Not in Our Name— Dead Man Walking: The Concert, an anti–death penalty benefit for Murder Victims' Families for Reconciliation and Hope House. After performing Cat Stevens's "Trouble" solo, Vedder is joined by Ament for "Dead Man," which was cut from the film soundtrack in favor of Bruce Springsteen's title track. "It's a seniority thing," Vedder says with a smile during the show. The late Nusrat Fateh

Ali Khan's nephew Rahat Nusrat Fateh Ali Khan, percussionist Dildar Hussain, and Doors drummer John Densmore assist on "Long Road," while all the musicians lend a hand on a finale of Waits's "Innocent When You Dream." Highlights from the show are later released on a bonus DVD with the 2006 reissue of the original 1995 *Dead Man Walking* film soundtrack.

Jeff Ament: My main memory is working on the songs backstage with acoustics and hearing Steve Earle fingerpicking up a storm just down the hall—really shredding. I was honored to be included. I just loved Nusrat.

April

Pearl Jam announces that drummer Jack Irons will not join the band on its summer North American tour due to undisclosed health reasons. Unbeknown to anybody outside the band's inner circle, Irons, who had struggled with a bipolar condition since his midtwenties, had suffered through "a major manic episode" during the Australian tour.

Jack Irons: About eight months prior to that tour, I had kind of decided to stop taking medications. I kind of was done with that. I felt like they weren't doing me right. I made that decision and had to adapt my life. I had to take on spiritual practice and really become responsible for my behavior.

I sort of cruised. I was living for the first time in ten years without taking it. I was doing okay until the tour, but when the tour came, my nervous system went haywire. I just literally couldn't sleep. I stopped sleeping. I was just so overwhelmed that I had to go out and play every night. I thought I was having a heart attack and all kinds of things. It was like a panic attack that wouldn't come down. I completed the tour, but it was really hard for me.

I knew I was in the middle of something really big when I got to that point. It has only happened a few times, but it lasts a long time. I knew there was no way for me to tour, but I also knew there was no way I'd start taking medications again, because I'd already been off for seven months. I just fully believed there was a way to live without them. I stuck to my guns, but,

PEARL JAM

19 98
SOUTH PACIFIC
TOUR

unfortunately, that meant not being in Pearl Jam anymore. It wasn't that simple. I was really not well.

Irons is replaced on the tour by former Soundgarden drummer Matt Cameron, who is offered the job without warning during a phone call with Stone Gossard to discuss the possibility of Gossard's Loosegroove Records label releasing a new album from Cameron's side project, Wellwater Conspiracy. Eventually Gossard hands the receiver to Vedder to make the official ask.

Matt Cameron: I was talking to Stone on the phone about this Wellwater Conspiracy thing, and then Stone was like, "Oh, hold on, Eddie wants to say hi." So I was like, "Hey, Eddie, what's going on?" and he's like, "Hey, what are you doing this summer?" "Uh, nothing, no plans." And he was like, "Well, Jack Irons just decided he can't do a six-week tour of the US, but we need to leave in three weeks." When I first said, "Yeah," I felt like I did when I was doing the demos—like I was just going to help them out until they found their feet again and until I figured out what I was going to do, because I wasn't really sure I wanted to go back in the big rock world again.

Eddie Vedder: I was afraid to ask Matt to join, and I was elected to be the one to ask. I didn't want it to affect our friendship if the answer were to be no or if it were to be yes and it didn't work out. But at the risk of losing a great friendship, our friendship became much deeper, and our relationship to each other as bandmates. And what he's done for the group is, like, unfathomable—not just as a drummer but as a human, as a musician, as a songwriter. It's not just the songs that he brings in. It's the way we write songs because we know he's in our group. There was a definite period for a while where I would write songs that I knew he'd be enthused to play on and that had tricky changes and, you know, things to keep him excited and awake and enthralled with this venture that we were on together.

Mike McCready: So, as it came full circle with Jack, it came full circle even more with Matt. It's very Spinal Tap of us to have this many drummers, and it's just what happened. That's our career.

May 1
Ed Sullivan Theater, New York

Pearl Jam welcomes Matt Cameron into the fold with a performance of "Wishlist" on CBS's *Late Show with David Letterman.*

May 7
ARO.space, Seattle

Matt Cameron's first full show with Pearl Jam is a surprise gig at the venue formerly known as Moe's, with the band billed as Harvey Dent and the Caped Crusaders. A cover of the Wayne Cochran–written, J. Frank Wilson and the Cavaliers–popularized "Last Kiss" is played live for the first time, with Vedder explaining from the stage that earlier that day, he'd bought the vinyl single for ninety-nine cents while shopping at Seattle's Fremont Antique Mall and learned the tune immediately.

Matt Cameron: I spent a good three weeks in my basement with the CDs. They had a list of probably sixty or seventy songs. I would go like that [*pointing finger*]: "Okay, do I know that song? No!" So I'd have to find the record and play it. Because that's kind of how the set list felt to me; like it was just going to be different every night, and I really had to be prepared with all this music. We didn't have that much rehearsal time. I want to say, like, a week or a week and a half. It was crazy high pressure, but it turns out I need that pressure to get to that level of performance.

June

Tim Bierman becomes the head of Pearl Jam's Ten Club fan organization, and begins to oversee long-term improvements to its online ticketing and merchandise operation.

Tim Bierman: In the early days, the fan club was just trying to hold it together and ride this huge wave. Eddie was answering fan mail personally, and there'd be piles and piles of letters all over the place. When they came to me, they knew they had a huge base of fans that wanted to engage in the commerce part of things, especially merchandise.

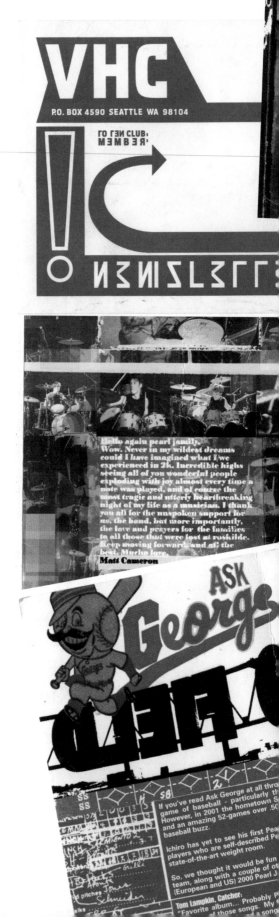

TAKES PICTURES LURKING ABOUT EXCITEDLY, AND WE INCLUDED A COUPLE OF THOSE PICTURES TO
HELP VISUALIZE THE MOMENT... SO WHILE THE WHO ARE A BAND WHO PIONEERED PLAYING ROCK
MUSIC IN GIANT SIZED ARENAS AND HAVE SUSTAINED THE ABILITY TO DO SO, I KNOW NOW THAT
THEY ARE ALSO ONE OF THE GREATEST GARAGE BANDS ON EARTH. THE NIGHT OF THE CONCERT WAS
MOVING TO SAY THE LEAST,... WHEN GREAT SONGS ARE PLAYED WITH A REASON OR CAUSE
ATTACHED TO THEM, THEY BECOME MORE POTENT. IT'S
JUST THE WAY IT WORKS,... IT HEIGHTENS THE MEANING OF
THE LYRICS AND EVEN THE GUITAR SOLOS!... AT THE
FINALE WHEN ROGER INVITED SOME OF THE KIDS WHO CAME
FROM THE HOSPITALS TO TAKE IN THE SHOW UP ONTO THE
STAGE TO SING "LISTENING TO YOU, SEE ME FEEL ME", IT
FELT LIKE THE ROOF WAS RAISED A FEW FEET OFF ITS
SUPPORTS. THERE WAS TALK OF RELEASING IT ON TAPE OR
DVD, SO MAYBE IT WILL BE ...BLE AT SOME POINT,...
...AVE ALL BEEN GREAT
...L TO BE WITH THEM AT
...HANT YEAR OF THE WHO
...OINT TOWARDS THE END,
...T MAY HAVE BEEN THE
...ERE PLAYING LIVE,...
...T I FELT OK ABOUT IT.
...MEN AND WOMEN I GOT
...WARD OF CANCER TREAT-
...LITTLE FRENZIED,...
...AKING PICTURES AND
...ERE SPECIAL PEOPLE
...SPEED BECAUSE OF
...OURS PASSED AND AS THE
...ULD STICK AROUND,...
...MUSICIAN SHOWING UP
...THE COUNSELORS THERE
...MSELVES WAS CRITICAL
...R STRUGGLE,... THE
...OW THEY HAD COME TO
...OVER A SHIT JOB AND
...IVIAL MATTERS SEEMED
...D GO ON AND ON... I
...NCLUDE SO YOU COULD
...NA... SHE WAS THERE
...ITH THE REALLY COOL
...H... WHEN HE FIRST
...JUST TO ACCEPT THE
...CH A PRECARIOUS TIME
...NTS AND BECAME MORE

1999
calender
newsletter 14

PEARL JAM

MIKE

maybe we could film a couple of the same son
always pretty much just been me and one cam
thought it would be nice to get a few camera
Liz had a camera-so our initial idea was to
LIZ- put up a full song on the web.
KEVIN- a song a night...a song a week.
progressing.
LIZ-The first one we all shot and tried to edit la
from Stockholm.
TIM- Right.
LIZ- That was the first one we actually talked a
the bootleg thing going.. with the way it loo
TIM- Everybody fell in love It wasn't like it was
LIZ- Yeah, we were out. I mean..I think that real
any of our other jobs.
KEVIN- definitely DIY factor.
LIZ-All the pieces were already in place.
KEVIN- Ed and I have talked before about
off tour and then when we go out, trying to g
access channel in that town. It's been talked
bootlegs...for years and years. Finally technol
could do it on the bus and not take up a lot
contained. Then it grew from three cameras to
the stationary cameras on stage left and right.
TIM- Liz, tell us about the version of GIVEN TO
everyone would like to hear about the woma...
the band know she was there...
LIZ- I think a couple of songs into the set, th
There were two women who were signing... the
would do a song, then the other would do a
right over by where I was shooting. I noticed
filming them because I'd never seen that bef
And I think they did notice her eventually and
Ed planned on bringing her up for GTF.
TIM- It works perfectly.
LIZ- It really fit the song. There are some w
that have an organization come in and sign
This was one of those venues so those people
all the shows there. We happened to have Kin
once she was brought up on stage, we knew
we were filming a truly magical moment. And
over, I went running over to Kevin and I sai
GTF...WE HAVE TO!" Steve was a little wa
coverage?..how was the performance? how th
KEVIN- That's the thing...we'd film most of
nights like Las Vegas or Seattle 2, we'd try to
the most part we would discuss our plans an
would concentrate on. Then we'd talk,
change tapes and maybe miss a song or two.
club issues and missed it - or Liz would ha
LIZ- yeah I'd usually miss the first couple of the
KEVIN- I was getting set lists and the other
so I usually missed the first song as well.
LIZ- But we knew...we knew right after the
...the sound wasn't so great.

KEVIN SHUSS

NEIL YOUNG - MIRRORBALL EUROPEAN TOUR 8-12...TOCKHOLM,SWEDEN8-13HEY DEY, COP...
...NAGEN8-14BERLIN, GERMANY8-16PRAGUE, CZECH REPUBLIC...
...26DUBLIN,IRELAND8-27READING FESTIVAL
...ISRAEL8-28CANAL...8-20BERLIN...PUKKELPOP, BELGIUM8...
...FESTIVAL,SWITZERLAND8-22JERUSALEM...

EVERYONE CAN TAKE DINNER AND TURN IT INTO ART,
THESE BOYS HAVE DONE IT. ED CASPER'S FILM TRILO-
...ED THEM BOTH THE GRAND PRIZE. YOUR CREATIVE
...RS HAVE EARNED YOU ONE OF MIKE'S MR. POTATO
...FROM HIS VERY OWN POTATO FARM, AS WELL AS A
...OTOGRAPHED BY THE ENTIRE BAND.
...HE TEN CLUB THANK EVERYON...
...ND TIM MCNAMARA'S SUPER-SIZED MR. POTATO HEAD
RUN...
CRAIG...
GWEN...
CHRIS...
BENNY...
CHRISTI...
BRITTAN...

201

They brought me on to bring a business sense to the Ten Club. Beyond the commerce part of it, we wanted to figure out a way to superserve the fans with tickets and live music.

June 7
United Center, Chicago

Eddie Vedder sings the national anthem at game three of the Chicago Bulls–Utah Jazz series for the NBA championship. The Bulls destroy the Jazz 96–54, with Utah setting a record for the fewest points scored in NBA finals history.

June 14
RFK Stadium, Washington, DC

After midafternoon lightning injures eleven concertgoers and forces several cancellations and abbreviated sets the day before, Pearl Jam plays eight songs during the second day of the third Tibetan Freedom Concert. Vedder dedicates "Better Man" to "the abusive relationship between us and our government . . . seems like no matter what we do, we're always getting shit on."

June 20
Washington-Grizzly Stadium, Missoula, Montana

Pearl Jam starts the first North American leg of the Yield tour, and its first extensive major-market tour in more than four years, in Jeff Ament's home state. The Missoula show draws twenty-two thousand people, the biggest concert audience in the state's history. The three-month trek, on which the majority of shows are ticketed by Ticketmaster, features support from Goodness, Frank Black, Murder City Devils, Spacehog, X, Zeke, Tenacious D, the Wallflowers, Sean Lennon, Iggy Pop, Cheap Trick, Mudhoney, Ben Harper, Hovercraft, and Rancid.

Eddie Vedder: I think we've made a point, and our point is that we're running the business side of what we do the way we think it should be done. No one can really question that; that's just what we do. But why take this stuff to your grave? In the big picture, it's just not that important.

Kelly Curtis: What we ultimately realized was that we weren't doing our fans any favors. We somehow had been cast as the people to save the world, but nobody was helping us or climbing on board. It wasn't our fight. It was a consumer fight. So we thought we should go back to just playing shows in venues that are convenient, comfortable, and have toilets. It just took us a while to figure that out. The funny thing is, still to this day when we tour, there's some article somewhere saying, "I can't believe they're playing Ticketmaster venues." It's unbelievable.

Mike McCready: I got Iggy Pop to sign an original copy of the Stooges album *Funhouse.* Iggy wrote, "To Mike, don't drop out." Great advice!

Matt Cameron: The first couple weeks of the tour, I knew how to play the whole set, but I didn't know the titles, so I'd always have Jeff stand right by my drum riser. I was like, "Okay, hum the first few notes of this song!" Once I got the first few notes or the first bar, I could do it. On that tour, Eddie and I hung out a lot. After the show, we'd go to either my room or his room, have a couple beers and maybe smoke a joint, and just talk about the show. He was always concerned with how I felt about it and how I feel like I'm fitting in with the music. That first tour, I think I was playing a little too bash-y. I probably wasn't fitting dynamically as well as I should have. But I think he kind of liked that. It brought a different sort of direction.

June 24
Rushmore Plaza Civic Center, Rapid City, South Dakota

Pearl Jam plays its "man" trilogy of "Leatherman," "Better Man," and "Nothingman" in a row for the first time. The three songs have since been played together as a group, although in different orders, fifteen times.

July 4
Wrigley Field, Chicago

Having enjoyed several beers in the bleachers beforehand, Eddie Vedder warbles "Take Me Out to the Ballgame" during the seventh-inning stretch of a Chicago Cubs home game against the Pittsburgh Pirates. He remains in the press box for the following half inning, providing commentary with announcer Steve Stone on Chicago TV station WGN.

July 5
Reunion Arena, Dallas

NBA star Dennis Rodman spends much of the show clowning around onstage with Pearl Jam, pouring wine into Vedder's mouth and then holding him in his lap during "Wishlist."

July 14
Great Western Forum, Inglewood, California

Johnny Ramone joins Pearl Jam to play the Ramones' "The KKK Took My Baby Away" as the closer at the second of two shows in Los Angeles. It's the last time Ramone ever performs live. The opening acts are X and, in one of its first major shows, Tenacious D.

July 21–22
Memorial Stadium, Seattle

In the biggest fund-raiser of its career, Pearl Jam raises approximately $500,000 for charities such as the Seattle Public Schools, Chicken Soup Brigade, and the National Association for American Indian Children and Elders during a two-night stand in its hometown.

August 4

Single Video Theory, a look behind the scenes at the making of *Yield* and rehearsals for the 1997 shows opening for the Rolling Stones, is released on home video by Epic. "Jeremy" video director Mark Pellington is also behind the camera for *Single Video Theory.*

Stone Gossard: We thought it might be interesting, and that people that like the band might be into seeing how we work together. We rehearse and hear some songs from the new record and try to let it hang out a little bit and be ourselves. I think we accomplished that, and I don't think it's too embarrassing.

August 18
Breslin Student Events Center, East Lansing, Michigan

At the second show of the East Coast leg of the Yield tour, Pearl Jam debuts its cover of Arthur Alexander's sixties soul song "Soldier of Love," which Vedder was turned onto by Billy Childish of the British group Thee Headcoats. Two nights later in Montreal, "Hard to Imagine" is played live for the first time in more than four years, while "No Way" debuts on August 25 in Pittsburgh, and "Push Me, Pull Me" premieres on August 29 in Camden, New Jersey.

August 25

Stone Gossard's Loosegroove Records releases the soundtrack to the film *Chicago Cab,* featuring the first official recording of "Hard to Imagine" plus Pearl Jam's "Who You Are" and Brad's "Secret Girl."

August 28

"Do the Evolution," Pearl Jam's first music video since "Jeremy" six years earlier, premieres on MTV's *120 Minutes.* The animated clip, which compresses the history of Earth into less than four minutes, was directed by artist Todd McFarlane, creator of the popular comic *Spawn.*

September 10–11
Madison Square Garden, New York

Pearl Jam plays its first concerts at the historic Manhattan arena. At the start of the encore during night one, fake security guards carry out several enormous file boxes as part of Vedder's joke that the band traded prosecutor Kenneth Starr passes in exchange for all the records pertaining to President Bill Clinton's affair with White House intern Monica Lewinsky. To start the encore during night two, fans hold up thousands of signs requesting "Breath," which hadn't been played in more than four years, as part of a campaign that had begun three shows earlier by fans Jessica Letkemann and Paris Montoya. It's the first such mass Pearl Jam fan mobilization to be spread largely through online discussion.

1998

Eddie Vedder from the stage before "Breath": "You fucking cocksuckers. You fucking dicks! You know, we come up here as a collective band, and we give and we give, and you just fucking want more. And you know what? You deserve it. This is like some kind of organized religion here. I've never seen anything like it. Do you see what's happening? The third night in a row, right? Well, fuck you. We're gonna play it!"

September 19
DAR Constitution Hall, Washington, DC

Pearl Jam and Hovercraft play a benefit for Voters for Choice, returning to the site of a similar event three and a half years earlier. That January 14, 1995, show featured the premiere of the Neil Young–Pearl Jam collaboration "Act of Love," which is reprised here for the first time since that era.

September 22–23
Coral Sky Amphitheatre, West Palm Beach, Florida

The Yield tour ends with two sweltering shows in Florida. The band holds an onstage Ping-Pong tournament during the encore of the second show, and hosts a legendary wrap party later that night, with everyone dressed in disco attire.

Matt Cameron: After that tour, I really knew that it would be a great fit and I meshed really well musically with the band live. I knew I could play with them musically in a recording or songwriting setting, but live it's sometimes a different sort of dynamic that you sort of need to feel with a group. But after that '98 summer tour, they offered me the job, and I was just like, "Let's do it."

October 10
Crocodile Cafe, Seattle

Pearl Jam materializes for a surprise ten-song set opening for Cheap Trick at the 350-capacity Seattle club, with Jeff Ament borrowing a twelve-string bass from Cheap Trick's Tom Petersson during "Corduroy."

Mike McCready: Another reason I loved rock 'n' roll as a young guitar player was Cheap Trick. Getting to play with them was a dream come true. I have been influenced by Rick Nielsen, who is superimportant. I throw too many picks out because of him.

November 6
Karma Club, Boston

Sporting a hand bandaged due to a recent surfing accident, Eddie Vedder makes an unannounced appearance at a Neil Finn show in Boston to perform songs from throughout Finn's catalog with Split Enz and Crowded House, including "Stuff and Nonsense," "World Where You Live," and "History Never Repeats." Finn and his son Liam also back Vedder on Pearl Jam's "Off He Goes."

November 24

Epic releases Pearl Jam's *Live on Two Legs,* the band's first concert album, culled from the just-concluded Yield tour.

Jack Irons: Pearl Jam recorded some Australia shows with the intention of releasing them, but realized after they listened to what they did with Matt in America that it was just a better choice for a live record. Matt just didn't have the issues I did. He was way more solid out there.

December 23

The Pearl Jam photo book *Place/Date,* shot by official Pearl Jam photographers Lance Mercer and Charles Peterson, is published in hardcover exclusively for Ten Club members. A softcover general release follows in spring 1999.

Christmas

"Last Kiss" b/w "Soldier of Love" is released as Pearl Jam's seventh seven-inch vinyl single for fan club members only. Both are live versions recorded during the second North American leg of the Yield tour. The cover art is an X-ray

of Vedder's injured hand making the Hawaiian shaka sign.

Jeff Ament: The Christmas singles are something that Tim Bierman mainly tells us around August to start thinking about. Usually it's superhard unless somebody just takes the bull by its horns and goes into the studio and lays something down. But it's a fun thing, and even in the years when we're not doing a whole lot of playing, it gets us back in a room together. All of those have been really important.

Breath

is is a sign to hold up to the band requesting the song "Breath". • It is a great song and one of the oldest Pearl Jam songs. • It was last played 4/11/94 in the Boston Garden. • On the nd's official web-site it was the #1 most requested song for this tour. • Please hold up this sign when the band returns for the first encore. • For the band to see/hear this message and rform the song would truly be special. • Thank You.

Yield

By 1998, Pearl Jam was the last of the Seattle big four that had included Nirvana, Soundgarden, and Alice in Chains still actively making music. The group had slowly come to terms with not only its celebrity but also the myriad external pressures and delicate interpersonal dynamics that had often made the simple act of creating music seem like a Herculean task.

"It's evolved," Eddie Vedder says of the band's collaborative acumen. "It was actually pretty good right from the beginning, but then there was probably a middle period where we didn't write so much. The middle records. Maybe the third record, I think I was just writing a bunch of songs on guitar myself. But now it's, like, a total collective. It's all five of us in there with our hammers and claws, banging it out."

Working together like that was no accident, according to Vedder. "I remember there being a stressful conversation, bordering on an argument, based on what was probably typical singer bullshit: 'If you thought about this stuff in lyrical terms, I think you would write differently. A riff is a riff, but a song is a song. And there's a big difference there,'" he says. "We had to turn a corner on people relating to whatever they wrote as being a song, and not just a riff. It had to have space. It had to have room to allow another part, which might be potentially an important part. I think for them to do that took a little while. But by *Yield,* we were doing that. The guys were coming in with a better understanding of space and lyrics. It was a turning point with getting everybody involved in the songwriting, meaning songs versus riffs. I think it was liberating for everybody, like, 'Oh! I can write songs in this group, too! Great!'"

When Pearl Jam first began assembling material for its fifth album in early 1997, the band members agreed they wanted the tunes to be more accessible than those on the prior album, *No Code.* But they also had an even more radical idea: to produce the recording sessions themselves, without longtime producer Brendan O'Brien's assistance.

"I remember getting on a conference call with Eddie, Stone, and Jeff," O'Brien says. "They said they were going to make the next record a little more listener friendly. But then they said, 'We want to try it on our own and maybe bring you in at the end to help us finish it and mix it.' And I said, 'What? Listen! I helped you on this last record. I went through all of that with you guys to get to *this.* And now you're telling me you want to make a more commercial-sounding record without my help? You're out of your mind!'

"I knew they were rehearsing in Seattle at the time," he continues. "I said, 'With your permission, I'm getting on a plane tomorrow morning, and you're going to tell me why I shouldn't be helping you make this record. And if that makes sense, I'll do whatever you want me to do. But you're going to have to explain to me why this is a good idea, because I don't think it is.'

"So I got on the plane, infuriated. My wife had to calm me down. I'd done my homework with all the demos. I sat with everybody in the kitchen, and we talked for a couple of hours. The long and short of it was, we just started working, right then and there. I didn't go home for another couple of weeks."

The resulting collection, *Yield,* is the sonic equivalent of the sun bursting through the clouds. Aside from being the group's most collaborative album to date, particularly with first-time lyrical contributions from Stone Gossard and Jeff Ament, it's also the most cohesive and listener-friendly piece of work Pearl Jam has produced to this point in its career.

Band members attribute that distinction to O'Brien, who was behind the board with Pearl Jam for its fifth album in a row (counting the Neil Young collaboration *Mirror Ball*). "Working with Brendan, his ear will gravitate toward certain things," Gossard says. "We've got commercial things in us, and we always like songs that are memorable, interesting, and cool."

"I'm very glad Brendan flew up. I'm glad we didn't produce *Yield* ourselves," observes McCready. "It wouldn't have sounded as good. It's always nice to have someone you respect that has equal or better ears than you. I don't know if we would have had that perspective at the time."

At the center of *Yield* are "Wishlist" and "Given to Fly," which would become two of Pearl Jam's most popular songs ever.

Set to a C chord with two simple melodic variations, the Vedder-penned "Wishlist" is a catalog of thirteen unfulfilled desires ranging from the universal ("I wish I was a messenger, and all the news was good") to the uniquely personal ("I wish I was the full moon shining off your Camaro's hood"). Ultimately, the narrator decides his greatest wish has already come true: "I wish I was as fortunate, as fortunate as me."

Vedder wrote "Wishlist" after McCready invited him to jam with a mutual friend. "It was just one of those things where he said, 'I have some studio time; do you want to come down?' And you know, it looked like a boring *Hard Copy* that night, so I decided to go in the studio, and that just popped out," says Vedder, who estimates that the original version was at least eight minutes long. "I listened to the tape and picked out the better wishes."

Powered by an undulating McCready guitar riff, "Given to Fly" in some ways embodies the band's topsy-turvy first decade. That it crests into a roof-raising, chill-inducing chorus authoritatively confirmed to listeners that Pearl Jam had made it through the nineties with its sense of purpose and commitment to rock 'n' roll intact.

"'Given to Fly' came out of a period of time when I was finally getting my life together after going through some dark stuff prior to that. Musically, it represents kind of an awakening for me, and it represents a period of renewal, a period of just kind of learning how to relive my life," McCready says. "I was more clear headed, and I was coming up with these ideas that were kind of celebratory. 'Given to Fly' musically was kind of that statement. That's why there's all the peaks and valleys in it. It starts off slow and then kind of builds."

McCready wrote "Given to Fly" and the fist-pumping midtempo rocker "Faithfull" on the same snowy day in Seattle when he couldn't get his Volvo out of his driveway and decided to play guitar to pass the time.

"The thing about 'Faithfull' is, to put that together, it took a phone call," McCready recalls. "I called up Stone, and I played the intro part to him, and I played the heavier part to him. I was like, 'How do you put these two things together? Can you help me?' I played it over the phone to him, and he hummed how to do the transition. That was the first time I had called him to ask him for songwriting help. Stone is the most integral in our band in putting things together. He and Jeff are very good at that. Stone is probably the master of it, and Jeff is right underneath that or right next to him."

Other highlights on *Yield* include the raging, punky opener "Brain of J.," which was performed live as early as November 1995 but wasn't recorded for *No Code;* the Stooges-y blast "Do the Evolution"; "MFC," another Vedder car song featuring a protagonist speeding away from a bad situation; and "In Hiding," which builds from quiet verses to a majestic chorus.

"I'd recorded that riff on my little microcassette recorder," Gossard says of the latter, which was initially titled "Morning Song." "That was probably the first one where I went, 'This is one I really want to concentrate on trying to get the band to fall in love with and keep playing every time there's a rehearsal.'"

Band members thought that *Yield* was complete, when at the last minute, Gossard and Vedder teamed up for "Do the Evolution," which became a minor rock radio hit despite never being released as a single. It even scored a Grammy nomination for best hard rock performance.

"It felt like there should be something on the record that was a little bit more rock," says Gossard. "We had 'Brain of J.,' which had been around for a while. I think it's a great album opener. But I just kind of concentrated for a couple days. I thought, I'm going to play every night this week, and if I come up with a riff, I'm just going to go in the studio and record it. I came up with a couple riffs that I liked and went in and demoed them."

Luckily for Gossard, Vedder again happened to be "sitting around for the weekend" without any plans, so he met his bandmate in the studio. "He gravitated toward that one right away," says Gossard of the proto–"Do the Evolution" riff. "And we ended up just using the demo version of the song, which is really exciting. I play some bass and a bunch of guitars on it. It's probably one of my favorite lyrics I've ever heard him sing, as far as the sarcasm and the angle he approached."

Inspired by Daniel Quinn's 1992 novel *Ishmael: An Adventure of the Mind and Spirit,* which deconstructs the concept that humanity is the peak of evolution, Vedder narrates "Do the Evolution" as someone convinced of the superiority of people and technology: "This land is mine, this land is free / I do what I want so irresponsibly."

Gossard and Ament each wrote lyrics for two songs apiece on *Yield.* Gossard's "No Way" reflects his ambivalence about Pearl Jam's superstardom ("I'll stop trying to make a difference / I'm not trying to make a difference"), while "All Those Yesterdays," with its loping groove reminiscent of tunes from the Beatles' "White Album," suggests "it's no crime to escape" from the self-imposed walls of everyday life.

Ament's contributions, "Pilate" and "Low Light," stemmed from a group of a half dozen songs he'd written with the motivation from "Ed saying he wanted help and more complete ideas. Everybody was around for most of the record, whereas a lot of the time previously, it would end up being Ed in there by himself. He was over that by then. It was such a creative time for the band, because everybody was really open to everybody's ideas."

Adds drummer Jack Irons, "I remember a lot more group involvement. For some reason in the band's evolution, there was a movement toward having everybody participate more. It just sort of naturally happened. From my point of view, it was always collaborative. In general, the nature of that album fit the openness for everyone's participation.

"For me, it was a transition in terms of my life," he continues. "I was probably feeling most comfortable in the band at that point. I had gotten over the whirlwind of changing my life and bringing my family north. I had settled into the idea of being in a band that goes onstage and plays to all those people. All those things were finally settled in for me, and it was becoming more ordinary, which always makes for more relaxed playing. That's why I think *Yield* sounds a little more focused, polished, and cohesive than *No Code.*"

The recognition that Pearl Jam and its members were in a very good place informed the choice of title. For Gossard, *Yield* was indicative of Pearl Jam taking charge of what made the quintet happy, as opposed to giving in to what the band members thought was expected of them.

"We kind of stopped doing all the things that we felt like we were obliged to do, in terms of press and in terms of feeling like we had to go tour," he says. "We started making decisions based on whether we wanted to do stuff. Ultimately, it kind of left us faced with ourselves. Any problems we were having within the band after that point, it was like, 'Okay, then, it's not just that stuff. It's us, too!'"

Ament says the album cover developed out of a band meeting when Gossard threw out the word *yield,* and the members "all started talking about what 'yield' meant to us. There was talk of, like, yielding to nature, and I kept thinking it would be cool if there was a yield sign but there was nothing to yield to, just in the middle of nowhere."

"My whole mind-set, or what's been processing constantly," reflects Vedder, "is this challenge of looking really close at the game that everyone's playing—this myth of an existence and seeing how you can eke out something that's a little different without becoming totally insane. Not necessarily stepping back in the evolutionary process, 'cause that seems impossible, but how do you help shape the future? Not just society, but my own or my family's or my immediate surroundings and the people in it. So I think *Yield* is kind of saying, 'Give way.' Now, to explain it, you'd have to say, 'Give way to what?' And it's really, give way to nature, is what I've been thinking, 'cause that's the one thing we have to yield to."

Before *Yield* was released but after it was finished, Pearl Jam accepted a rare gig as an opening act for the Rolling Stones at four November 1997 shows in Oakland. The following spring, the band began touring in support of the album with a run through Australia, which, unfortunately, wound up being the last outing with Pearl Jam for Irons, who was battling bipolar disorder.

"I never really had a chance to enjoy *Yield* from the point of view of playing it," the drummer says. "What was always one of the greatest things about Pearl Jam was that they could really rock you, but they could really bring it down and make it dynamic. For me, as a personal experience of playing, I hadn't had that before. At a long show, it's like working out or something. When you go real hard and then you relax for a second, your body starts to release and you start to sweat. Then you get warmed up. And then you can relax even more on the faster songs. If I have a regret, it's that I never really got a chance to fully participate in that as a well guy."

And although Irons was unable to join the rest of Pearl Jam on the continuing journey, his presence was crucial to Pearl Jam evolving during its most challenging period. "Jack made us be able to talk to each other a lot more and made the lines of communication open," says McCready. "He would usually say, 'Hey, this is weird, and this is how I feel about it.' So we'd sit down and talk about it. It feels like we're finally a band. We're all talking to each other."

"*Yield* was a fun record to make," Gossard says. "I didn't know that it was going to be, but it ended up being really one of our better records. We had a lot of important songs come off that record for our show. That's how you can kind of tell. We try to play a couple from every record every night, and that one has a lot that we can play from."

Adds Ament, "We made it through the storm, and we're sitting back in a room together as friends with all of these experiences behind us."

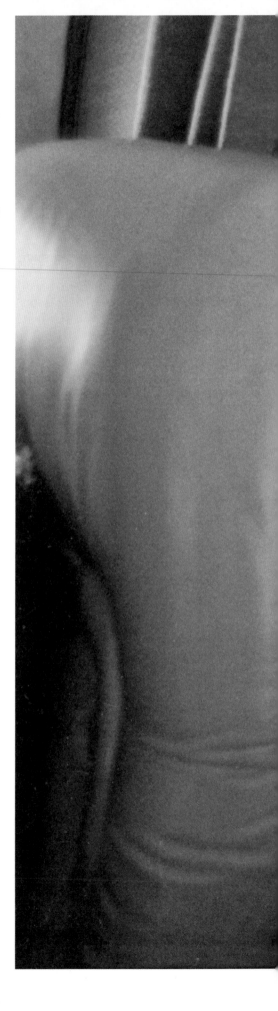

CHAPTER 199

1999

By the late 1990s, the notion that Pearl Jam would somehow score the biggest pop hit of its career via a song originally released as a fan club single seemed about as likely as Eddie Vedder dying his hair blond, forming a pickup band, and playing everything from giant benefit concerts to keg parties. Yet all those things happened in 1999, a year that found Pearl Jam loose, relaxed, and more successful than ever, seemingly without even trying.

March

Pearl Jam begins work on its sixth studio album at Stone Gossard's Studio Litho in Seattle, its first with drummer Matt Cameron.

March 16

Ten is bestowed with the Diamond Award by the Recording Industry Association of America (RIAA) for US shipments of ten million copies.

April

Pearl Jam's cover of "Last Kiss," available only on the 1998 Ten Club holiday single, begins receiving US radio airplay. By early summer, it is in heavy rotation at multiple formats, including modern and mainstream rock and Top 40, eventually appearing on thirteen different *Billboard* airplay charts.

May 29

"Last Kiss" enters the *Billboard* Hot 100 at no. 84 in its first of twenty-one weeks on the chart.

June 1

Jeff Ament's side band Three Fish releases its second Epic album, *The Quiet Table,* and begins a monthlong US club tour in Chicago on the heels of playing with musicians in Turkey and Egypt.

June 8

With airplay increasing exponentially and demand increasing for a more widely available commercial version, "Last Kiss" is finally released as a single, backed by "Soldier of Love," as on the 1998 holiday vinyl. Both songs appear on the Epic benefit compilation *No Boundaries: A Benefit For The Kosovar Refugees,* released a week later. By April 2000, nearly $7 million is raised from sales of *No Boundaries* and the "Last Kiss" single for international aid groups CARE, Oxfam, and Doctors Without Borders' efforts on behalf of Kosovo refugees.

Kelly Curtis: The song was becoming huge, and there was talk of putting it out as a single or on something. We said, If we put it out, we'll put it on a benefit album. From a business point of view, the label probably wasn't that into it, but they helped us put the record together, and I think it raised millions for refugees. We'd released it as a Christmas single for the fan club, so, really, it just happened naturally. That sure doesn't happen very often, though. Nobody was working it to radio or anything. It just started blowing up by itself. I guess that means a good song is a good song, right?

Michele Anthony: Suddenly, we have the biggest single of the band's career, which, of course, is not on an album. Talk about a classic Pearl Jam scenario. We put our heads together to figure out how we could make good use of this incredible airplay. We had been approached to do a record for Kosovo, providing funding for Doctors Without Borders. I called Kelly and suggested it to him, and he loved it. He took it to the band, and we made sure that the repertoire on there was something complementary to Pearl Jam.

June 12
Wrigleyville Tap, Chicago

In what amounted to a very intimate warm-up for their Tibetan Freedom Concert performance the next day, Eddie Vedder and C Average's Jon Merithew and Brad Balsley play a private party in front of approximately one hundred people at a Chicago dive bar down the street from Wrigley Field. The venue's back room is so small that the musicians set up on the floor, performing "Last Kiss," "Corduroy," Talking Heads' "Love → Building on Fire," Dead Moon's "Diamonds in the Rough," and a punked-up take on Steven Van Zandt's "I Am a Patriot." Vedder tells the lucky attendees, "It's so nice to just play for the sake of playing and drink some beers. I like the idea that people are walking by on the street and don't know what the fuck is going on in here."

June 13
Alpine Valley Music Theatre, East Troy, Wisconsin

At the fourth Tibetan Freedom Concert, Vedder arrives for an afternoon performance with nobody onstage to join him on bass and drums, and opens with a solo version of "Last Kiss." He then asks audience members if they want to come up and jam, before selecting two people from the crowd (who are actually C Average's Merithew and Balsley). They proceed to hack their way through "Better Man" before Vedder reveals the ruse, and the trio goes on

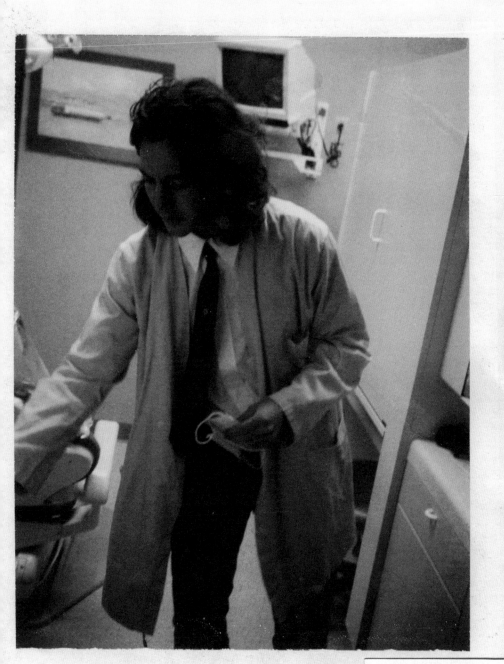

IN HIDING

I shut andlocked the front door,...
no way in or out,....
I turned and walked the hallway
pulled the curtains down,...
I knelt and emptied the mouths
of every plug around,...

a nothing sound,... |nothing sound.

I stayed where my last step left me,..
ignored all my rounds,...
soon I was seeing visions in cracks a

upside down,...

I followed a wish just to keep from
I followed a truth just to keep me t
I swallowed my breath and went deeps
I peeled back my brain and became en

Im in hiding,...   2 new

I followed a wish just just to keep
I traded a kiss just to keep from ly
I swallowed my breath andwent deep,..
I opened my being became enlightened
EYE OPEN_.

Im in hiding,....

hiding.

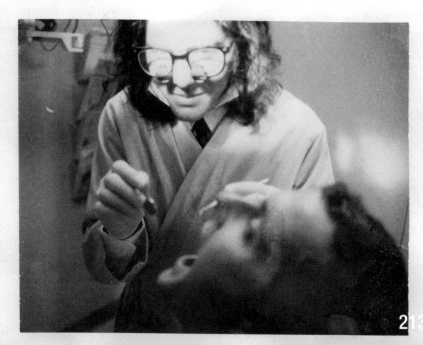

DON'T WANNA HAVE to LOSE
nt WANT to HAVE 2 TAK U BACK
KNOW ILL NEVER LOSE yw
            ABUSE
            USE

U NO I'LL ALWAYS HELP U
nt I JUST CAN'T DO THAT
KNOW I SAID I'D HELP yw BABY
that's my

to perform such songs as the Police's "Driven to Tears," the Mono Men's "Watch Outside," and the Dead Moon and Talking Heads selections from the night before.

June 25
Hollywood Palladium, Hollywood, California

Vedder and C Average make a surprise appearance at a benefit for the Musicians' Assistance Project featuring the Red Hot Chili Peppers, Mike Watt and the Black Gang Crew, and Perry Farrell. Vedder and Watt perform "Against the '70s," their contribution to Watt's 1995 album *Ball-Hog or Tugboat?,* before Watt's set. During Vedder's set, he continues the joke about his ties to C Average, telling the crowd that they'd never played together before the Tibetan Freedom Concert and that they thought they'd try it again tonight. The set list is nearly identical to the one played that day.

June 26

"Last Kiss" rockets from no. 49 all the way to no. 2 on the *Billboard* Hot 100, the greatest jump to that position in more than forty years, giving Pearl Jam the biggest hit of its career. The band's only other prior Top 10 single was "I Got Id" b/w "Long Road," which reached no. 7 just before Christmas 1995.

Eddie Vedder: I was on an island in Hawaii away from everything when Kelly Curtis called and asked if I'd heard what was happening with "Last Kiss." It seemed surreal to me. Even crazier was that I turned on the radio, and it was playing first thing. It's the biggest song we ever had on radio, and it wasn't even for sale. That's much more exciting and magical than accomplishing some successful marketing plan.

Mike McCready: It just blew up. We had no idea. It just proves over and over again, when people try to figure out what a hit is, whether they're in a band or they're an A&R guy, nobody has a clue. It was so out of left field. It was like, "Wow, it is being played a lot, and people are into it." It was, like, the most bizarre thing for us, singlewise.

June 26
La Paloma Theatre, Encinitas, California

Vedder and C Average play early (eight o'clock) and late (eleven o'clock) shows at this 390-capacity venue near San Diego, with $10 tickets going on sale that afternoon only at the theater's box office. Vedder plays the first three songs of each show solo, including Cat Stevens's "Trouble," Bruce Springsteen's "Bobby Jean," and Hunters & Collectors' "Throw Your Arms Around Me," before Merithew and Balsley join him to bash out Joe Jackson's "Got the Time," the Who's "Naked Eye," "The Good's Gone," and "I Can't Explain," and a frenetic, punk-influenced version of Pearl Jam's "Corduroy."

July 14
510 Columbia Street, Olympia, Washington

In one of his most intimate concert appearances ever, Vedder plays a forty-five-minute set of Who songs with C Average in front of fewer than one hundred people at a woodworking shop in Olympia during the city's Yo Yo a Go Go festival. Dressed in a white jacket and jeans and sporting a curly blond wig a la classic-period Roger Daltrey, Vedder stays in character throughout the show, even recycling bits of between-song banter from vintage Who bootlegs during song breaks. Among the songs performed: "Heaven and Hell," "I Can't Explain," "Young Man Blues," "Fortune Teller," "Tattoo," "A Quick One, While He's Away," "I'm a Boy," "My Generation," "See Me, Feel Me," and "Sparks." In true Who fashion, the musicians destroy the stage at the end of the show, which cost only $4 per ticket at the door.

July 28
Ed Sullivan Theater, New York

Vedder joins Pete Townshend to perform "Heart to Hang Onto," from Townshend's 1977 album with Ronnie Lane, *Rough Mix,* on CBS's *Late Show with David Letterman.* Backed by Paul Shaffer and Letterman's house band, Vedder and Townshend shift into the Who's

"Magic Bus" as the segment goes to a commercial break.

July 28
Supper Club, New York

A few blocks south of the Ed Sullivan Theater, Vedder is a poorly kept secret guest at a private show intended to promote Pete Townshend's upcoming album, *Pete Townshend Live: A Benefit for Maryville Academy.* After Townshend plays the first seven songs solo, he welcomes Vedder out to join him for "Heart to Hang Onto," "Let's See Action," "Better Man," "Till the Rivers All Run Dry," "Sheraton Gibson," "Magic Bus," and "I'm One."

July 29
House of Blues, Chicago

Another private show to promote Pete Townshend's upcoming live album. The set list is nearly identical to the night before in New York, but this time with a loud, talkative audience that clearly bothers the performers. Vedder says from the stage, "The last couple of days, spending time with Pete has taught me new things about music and new things as a human. One of those things is to say what you feel. And I feel like you people talking between songs are driving me nuts."

August 6

Ten is certified eleven times platinum by the Recording Industry Association of America (RIAA) for US shipments of eleven million copies.

August 17

Interscope releases the third edition of the benefit compilation *MOM: Music for Our Mother Ocean,* featuring the Jack Irons–written and sung Pearl Jam track "Whale Song." Proceeds benefit the Surfrider Foundation.

215

October 30–31

Shoreline Amphitheatre, Mountain View, California

Pearl Jam makes its fourth appearance at Neil Young's Bridge School Benefit concerts and premieres two brand-new songs pegged for the as-yet-unannounced *Binaural* album: the Stone Gossard–penned ballad "Thin Air" and Jeff Ament's psychedelic rock–leaning "Nothing As It Seems." Members of Pearl Jam also assist on a group sing-along during Bob Dylan's "I Shall Be Released"

and guest with Brian Wilson during the Beach Boys' "Surfin' U.S.A." From the stage, Vedder tells the crowd, "Neil had a little get-together at his place last night. We walked out into the woods, and he said, 'I've been meaning to tell you this, but it never seemed like the right time . . . but I'm your father.'" He then dedicates "Footsteps" to "Dad and all of my new brothers and sisters." During the long drive to Young's house the night before, Vedder writes a new song, "Driftin'," on the back of a plane ticket.

November 12–13

House of Blues, Chicago

Vedder and C Average regroup to open two $300-per-ticket benefit concerts for the Who in Chicago, playing much the same repertoire from their shows earlier in the summer ("Driven to Tears," "Love → Building on Fire," and Pearl Jam songs like "Wishlist" and "Last Kiss"). Near the end of both shows, Vedder and company give a nod to the Who by tearing into "Leaving Here," a song that the group originally performed in

the mid-1960s, when it was known as the High Numbers. At the second show, Vedder plays an acoustic guitar that Townshend used during the *Tommy* era that was purchased for him during an auction at the show the night before. "All my Christmases for the rest of my life are right here, and I'm fine with that," Vedder says of the guitar. He and C Average also join the Who for "Let's See Action" during both shows.

December 3

Pearl Jam launches TenClub.net, the official website for its fan club. Visitors are greeted by a hand-typed letter from Vedder, which lays out plans to eventually provide "live shows, radio broadcasts, demo songs, etc. Until then, there are a few goods for sale. Browse and be entertained by our lack of humility, offering T-shirts with our name on them." Discussing Pearl Jam's foray into the Internet world, he writes, "If you're reading this on a computer

screen, you have found yourself in a new communication world, as have we. It's an interesting place; none of us are quite sure of the end-all ramifications of this newfound technology, but as with anything, our approach will be to extract something positive."

Christmas

Pearl Jam releases its eighth fan club holiday single featuring two new songs: "Strangest Tribe" and "Driftin'."

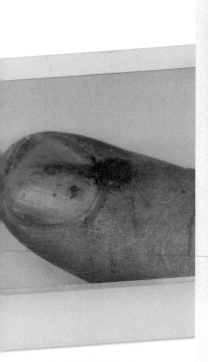

MINNE

APOLIS

BRONCO

L

HAMBURG

BYE POP '92

BOWL

DALLAS

BREMEN. Germany
w/ BAD RELIGION

PEARLJAM
SOLDOUT
8PM JAN17

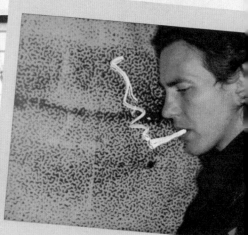

CHAPTER 200

2000

The new decade meant not only new music but also new ideas from the Pearl Jam camp. Foremost among them was a hitherto unheard-of plan to sell authorized recordings of the band's entire 2000 tour through traditional retail outlets. Pearl Jam had allowed fans to tape its shows since the fall of 1995, but high-cost, poor-sounding bootlegs persisted. The new endeavor thus beat the bootleggers at their own game by offering a product of infinitely higher audio fidelity at a substantially lower price. In support of its sixth album, *Binaural*, Pearl Jam hit the road in the spring for an international tour, with a tenth anniversary show planned for October 22 in Las Vegas. On June 30 the band arrived at Denmark's Roskilde Festival for what it thought would be just another gig. Within a few hours, nine lives would be lost, and Pearl Jam would be forever changed.

February 1

The self-titled album by the Rockfords is released on Epic Records. The band consists of Mike McCready, Danny Newcomb, Rick and Chris Friel, and Carrie Akre. McCready, Newcomb, and the Friel brothers were in the band Shadow when they were in high school in Seattle. Heart's Nancy Wilson writes the lyrics and sings on the song "Riverwide."

April 11

"Nothing As It Seems," the first single from Pearl Jam's sixth studio album, *Binaural*, debuts at worldwide radio. The track, which was first played the previous November at the Bridge School Benefit outside San Francisco, debuts the following week at no. 5 on *Billboard*'s Mainstream Rock Tracks chart and no. 11 on the Modern Rock tally. A commercial single, backed by the *Binaural* track "Insignificance," is released on April 25.

Jeff Ament: "Nothing As It Seems" was like a little folk song. When Stone got excited about it, I was like, "Wow, if it had drums on it, and if Mike was kind of featured . . ." All of a sudden, it became this whole other thing.

April 12
Ed Sullivan Theater, New York

Pearl Jam debuts another *Binaural* track, "Grievance," on CBS's *Late Show with David Letterman.* Mike McCready attempts to smash his guitar at the end of the performance, afterward presenting the instrument to Letterman.

May 10
Mount Baker Theatre, Bellingham, Washington

Pearl Jam debuts seven more *Binaural* songs ("Of the Girl," "Breakerfall," "God's Dice," "Light Years," "Evacuation," "Insignificance," "Soon Forget") at its first headlining, full-length concert since the end of the 1998 Yield tour. "What a fine dump. It's the nicest practice space I've ever had," Vedder tells the intimate audience of 1,100 fans.

May 11
Commodore Ballroom, Vancouver, Canada

Just over one thousand radio station contest winners are on hand for another live *Binaural* preview, featuring nine songs from the still unreleased album.

May 16

Pearl Jam's sixth studio album, *Binaural*, is released by Epic Records. It debuts the following week at no. 2 on the *Billboard* 200 with first-week sales of 226,000 copies in the United States, according to Nielsen SoundScan.

May 23
Restelo Stadium, Lisbon, Portugal

Pearl Jam begins a world tour in support of *Binaural* with six weeks of headlining shows and festival dates in Europe. Support acts include the Vandals, the Monkeywrench, and the Dismemberment Plan. At the Lisbon tour opener, pro basketball star Dennis Rodman appears onstage right before the closing song, "Yellow Ledbetter."

Travis Morrison, Dismemberment Plan front man: I remember admiring how Eddie knew how to talk to twelve thousand people who were staring at him. I am sure to a certain extent he learned on the job, but he clearly had a gift for it. Between songs, he was very intimate and really made these huge crowds feel really comfortable. Coming from a place where we had just played for four hundred fifty people in New York City and thought we were enormous, seeing someone handle that, especially after our own thirty-minute spazz-out, was the thing I remember most intensely.

June 1
The Point, Dublin, Ireland

"Garden" is played live for the first time since June 20, 1995.

June 4

In order for fans to have easy, affordable access to quality recordings of the band's concerts, Pearl Jam announces a groundbreaking plan to officially release authorized CD recordings of its complete 2000 European tour.

Kelly Curtis: I started buying every bootleg I could find, and the idea was, the really good-sounding ones, we'd put out. We thought it would be funny,

The Rockfords

because we couldn't very well be sued. I was looking for the best-quality ones, but most of them sounded like shit. But people were buying them. So we thought, What if we were to provide them with something officially from us at a cheaper price that sounded so much better? We never intended to market it. It was just for the fans who were buying them already. The thought wasn't to put bootleggers out of business but to give our consumer a better-quality, cheaper version.

June 9
Rock Am Ring Festival, Koln, Germany

Pearl Jam plays its first European festival date since June 27, 1993, in front of an estimated crowd of sixty thousand. Festival appearances follow on June 11 (Rock Im Park, Nuremberg, Germany) and June 12 (Pinkpop, Landgraaf, Netherlands).

June 16
Spodek, Katowice, Poland

After having sold out the eight-thousand-capacity venue the night before, Pearl Jam returns the following evening to find it barely a third full. As such, the band immediately deviates from the printed set list, opening with four slow songs in a row ("Release," "Of the Girl," "Sleight of Hand," "Thin Air"). From there, the quintet makes things up as it goes along, trotting out tour rarities like "In Hiding," "Dissident," "I Got Id," and "Smile," in what turns out to be one of its most unusual shows in years.

Jeff Ament: We came out with a set list, and the set list was definitely a lot different than anything we'd done on the tour. Pretty much right at the beginning, we just said, "Let's relax and do whatever comes to mind." That was a musical highlight for me live, just taking all the

pressure off of being an entertainer, and just going up and playing songs like you're in your living room.

Matt Cameron: Eddie just decided to call songs out. There was no set list or anything. It was kind of like playing a kegger.

June 28
Sjöhistoriska Museet, Stockholm, Sweden

Eddie Vedder surprises the crowd with a five-song solo performance ("Last Kiss," "Trouble," "Dead Man," "Parting Ways," "Throw Your Arms Around Me") prior to the Dismemberment Plan's set, reprising a mini-preset that he had done when Pearl Jam played this venue in 1992.

June 30
Roskilde Festival, Copenhagen, Denmark

Nine concertgoers between the ages of seventeen and twenty-six are killed and thirty more are injured during a crowd surge while Pearl Jam is playing "Daughter," the twelfth song of its set. The band immediately cancels the last two dates of the European tour.

Pearl Jam released a statement after the incident: "This is so painful. I think we are all waiting for someone to wake us and say it was just a horrible nightmare. And there are absolutely no words to express our anguish in regard to the parents and loved ones of these precious lives that were lost. We have not yet been told what actually occurred, but it seemed to be random and sickeningly quick. It doesn't make sense. When you agree to play at a festival of this size and reputation, it is impossible to imagine such a heart-wrenching scenario. Our lives will never be the same, but we know that is nothing compared to the grief of the families and friends of those involved. It is so tragic. There are no words. Devastated."

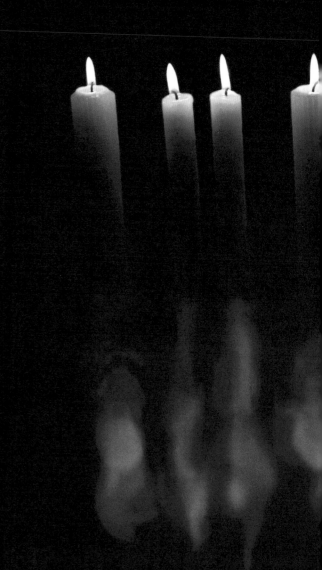

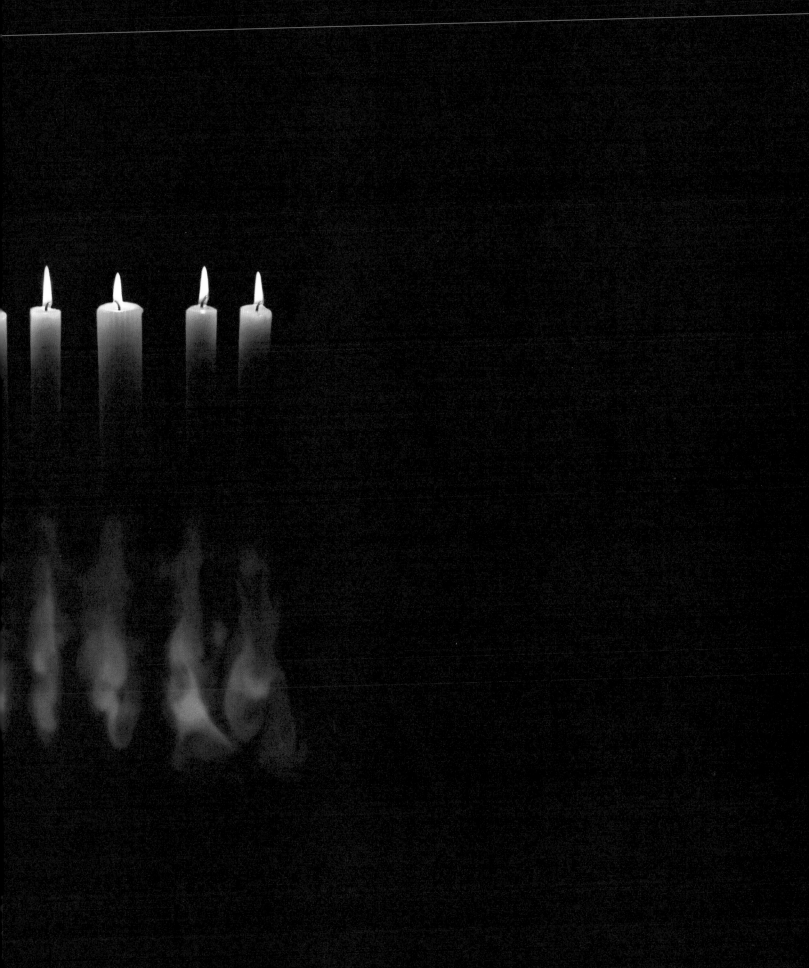

July 18

A commercial single for "Light Years" is released, backed by live versions of "Soon Forget" and "Grievance" from the May 10, 2000, show in Bellingham.

August 3
Virginia Beach Amphitheatre, Virginia Beach, Virginia

After an emotionally wrenching month off, Pearl Jam resumes its Binaural tour in Virginia Beach, the first of forty-seven more planned dates. Vedder modifies a handful of lyrics in the wake of Roskilde ("I have wished for so long, how I wish for them today," in the opener, "Long Road"; "Absolutely everything's changed," in "Corduroy").

Stone Gossard: Our first show after the tragedy of Roskilde. We all felt a deep sadness at our recent memories and shared in the relief of playing again as brothers.

Eddie Vedder: There was a pivotal moment watching Sonic Youth open the first show back in the States. All the questions, doubt, and despair were all laid to waste by the power of the sound and those who were making it.

September 5
Post-Gazette Pavilion, Burgettstown, Pennsylvania

The first leg of the Binaural North American tour concludes with a show featuring the first performance of "Wash" since September 24, 1996, played by request for a fan named Amy who'd been following the tour around the country. Before Sonic Youth's set, Vedder plays four songs, including "Parting Ways" and the Who's "Naked Eye" with help from Sonic Youth's Lee Ranaldo, Steve Shelley, and Jim O'Rourke.

September 12

The soundtrack to Cameron Crowe's *Almost Famous* is released by DreamWorks Studios. Mike McCready plays guitar on a Nancy Wilson–penned song, "Fever Dog," credited to the film's fictional band, Stillwater.

September 23
Key Arena, Seattle

In support of the Green Party for the 2000 US presidential election, Eddie Vedder makes the first of three performing appearances at candidate Ralph Nader's Super Rallies. From the stage, he tells the audience of several thousand, "I've never been to one of these. I think the reason why is I've never had anyone I could believe in before." Vedder actually donates a few thousand dollars of Pearl Jam money to the Nader campaign, without asking his bandmates first.

Eddie Vedder: Basically, I told them the next day, "Hey, we donated a few grand to Nader." I just assumed they'd agree with me. They said, "Okay. But we have a few questions. I think those questions are getting answered."

September 26

Following a three-week prerelease period for fan club members, an unprecedented twenty-five double-disc live Pearl Jam albums hit record stores nationwide. The series consists of uncut recordings of each full show of the 2000 European tour. The "official Pearl Jam bootlegs" are priced at $10.98 on the band's website for the first two weeks they are available. CDs are then available in retail stores for under $15 per concert. This is the first of three "legs" of official bootleg releases, which as a whole include seventy-two shows and chronicle Pearl Jam's entire 2000 world tour.

October 4

With five charting entries from the official bootleg series, Pearl Jam sets a new *Billboard* 200 record for most debut titles in one week. *Katowice 6/16* (no. 103), *Milan 6/22* (no. 125), *Verona 6/20* (no. 134), *London 5/30* (no. 137), and *Hamburg 6/26* (no. 175) post total sales in excess of fifty-four thousand copies, according to SoundScan. *Manchester 6/4* and *Cardiff 6/6* miss charting by fewer than one thousand copies.

Stone Gossard: It was another situation where our initial instinct was just to make these live records available on our website. Based on our deal with Sony, Sony was convinced we needed to put them out through their system, or else retail would be upset, and there would be all these sorts of political ramifications. We said, "Well, whatever, we can do it." When they sold as well as they did, everyone was pretty surprised. Our initial instinct was that there were maybe ten shows people are really talking about, but the rest of them are probably still sitting on people's shelves, gathering dust or being returned. I've certainly taken some teasing on that front, as to whether I was going to release another seventy mediocre live albums the following year [*laughs*]."

Kelly Curtis: The first time, we had Brett, our sound guy, mixing, like, forty-eight shows after the tour. How awful that must have been for him. We put everything out at retail, and talking the label into that was kind of a chore. The mistake we had there was, there'd be ten thousand copies of Madison Square Garden's show and ten thousand of Boise, Idaho. We learned from that. We were friends with the people from the Grateful Dead and talked to them a lot about how they did it. We just took it to the next level.

Michele Anthony: I think I said to Kelly, "You're killing me!" Retail was overwhelmed by it, but some of the accounts were really interested, because nobody had ever done it before. In those days, there were real record stores that carried deep inventory. So we put out all of the bootlegs. It was a wonderful experiment, and historic. Pearl Jam always had an instinct for picking things to do that were the most innovative. It didn't necessarily mean that we'd do it the same way the next time, but the bootlegs at retail was another great example of the band thinking outside the box and making the label better and more creative. In many ways, they influenced Epic more than Epic influenced them.

October 4
Molson Centre, Montreal

The Binaural tour resumes in Canada with opening act Supergrass.

PYRAMY—

BREAKERFALL
WHIPPING
SPIN THE BLACK
HAIL HAIL
CORDUROY
IN MY TREE
DISSIDENT
GIVEN TO FLY

NOTHING AS IT SEEMS
GRIEVANCE
LIGHT YEARS
DAUGHTER
LUKIN
MFC
WISHLIST

BETTER MAN
EVENFLOW
INSIGNIFICANCE
R.V.M.

EVOLUTION
ONCE
TIMELESS MELODY
SMALL TOWN
LEATHERMAN
NOTHINGMAN
PORCH

SOON FORGET
SAVIOUR OF LOVE
YELLOW LED

(SCHENECTADY)

EVENFLOW
HAIL HAIL
ANIMAL
CORDUROY
GRIEVANCE
IN MY TREE
NOTHING AS IT SEEMS
LIGHT YEARS
DAUGHTER
LEATHERMAN
BETTERMAN
SLEIGHT OF HAND
GIVEN TO FLY — LAST EXIT
REARVIEW MIRROR
I GOT SHIT
BLACK
PORCH

?

RELEASE   BOSTON
ANIMAL   #2
CORDUROY HAIL HAIL
IN MY TREE
GIVEN TO FLY
BREAKERFALL
GRIEVANCE
EVALUATION
BORN AGAIN (KINDLER IS HOLY) Footsteps
                              JEREMY CHRIST
EVENFLOW
DAUGHTER
NOT FOR YOU (I GOT ID)
LUKIN
BRAIN OF J
INSIGNIFICANCE
BLACK
DAVE GO RVM EVOLUTION/LAST EXIT

WISH SMALL TOWN GARDEN BREATH
BETTERMAN STATE LAST EXIT LAST KISS
EVENFLOW LIGHT YEARS SOON FORGET RVM
NOTHINGMAN ONCE IMMORTALITY C MONEY
LEATHERMAN IMMORTALITY HAIL HAIL

PEARL JAM
JONES BEACH NEW YORK
AUGUST 24 2000

SARATOGAA NEW YORK
UST 27 2000
BREAKERFALL WHIPPING SPIN THE BLACK CIRCLE HAIL HAIL CORDUF
IN MY TREE DISSIDENT GIVEN TO FLY NOTHING AS IT SEEMS GRIEVAN

October 8
Alpine Valley Music Theatre, East Troy, Wisconsin

Pearl Jam braves twenty-eight-degree temperatures to soldier through a twenty-six-song, 130-minute set in front of forty thousand fans outside Milwaukee, in what becomes known as the "Ice Bowl" show.

Jeff Ament: Jesus. That was one of the strangest shows I think we've ever played. We had little heaters onstage, so in between songs we could warm our hands up. But usually about a minute and a half into a song, your hands went completely numb, so . . . But the crowd was so into it, and it was kind of like, you know what? They're all here ready to make it happen, so we need to make it happen. It really did feel like a Packers game or something, or how you'd imagine a Packers game to be.

October 10
UIC Pavilion, Chicago

Eddie Vedder appears at a second Ralph Nader rally, performing solo acoustic renditions of "I Am a Patriot" and "The Times They Are A-Changin'."

October 10

Eddie Vedder's guest appearance with the Supersuckers on their song "Poor Girl" is released on *Free the West Memphis Three: A Benefit for Truth and Justice* (Aces & Eights Recordings). Vedder had become interested in the case of the West Memphis Three four years earlier, after seeing the acclaimed documentary *Paradise Lost,* which raises doubts about the 1993 murder convictions of the young men. In the years to come, he tirelessly raises funds for their ongoing legal defense.

October 11
Riverport Amphitheatre, Maryland Heights, Missouri

Pearl Jam performs the *Yield* B-side "U" for the first time, but, comically, has to resort to finding and downloading the song from the online file sharing service Napster in order to relearn how to play it.

October 13
Madison Square Garden, New York

Alongside Patti Smith, Ben Harper, and Ani DiFranco, Eddie Vedder turns up for a third time at a Ralph Nader rally, performing the same two songs as in Chicago three nights earlier. Vedder says, "I think the youth that aren't voting [are] just having a hard time getting excited about anything. And they have concerns. But the fact that they're not acting and not voting is leaving them out of the process. If that youth vote gets out there and proves they're a force, then their issues may soon be addressed. If Ralph was in these debates, there'd be a dozen extremely, extremely important issues that would be addressed that aren't going to be addressed with the other two [candidates]. Ralph can speak out about these because he is not for sale."

October 22
MGM Grand Arena, Las Vegas

Pearl Jam celebrates the tenth anniversary of its first performance (as Mookie Blaylock) on October 22, 1990, at Seattle's Off Ramp Cafe. The band is in a nostalgic mood, with Vedder telling the story of how Stone Gossard's tape of instrumentals made its way to him via Jack Irons. Later, Pearl Jam stuns the crowd with its debut performance of Mother Love Bone's signature song "Crown of Thorns," featuring longtime producer Brendan O'Brien on keyboards. Vedder had previously hinted in a 1993 *Rolling Stone* interview that he had a favorite Mother Love Bone song but that he wasn't planning on telling his bandmates what it was. O'Brien sticks around to assist on "Black" and Elvis Presley's "Can't Help Falling in Love With You."

Stone Gossard: I was just so thankful for Ed to say, "Let's do this. I want to do this. This song means something to me." And not really ever knowing that he had a favorite. I always felt like Mother Love Bone wasn't really his bag. It's not in his strike zone in terms of . . . Mother Love Bone isn't the kind of band that necessarily he would have thrown on. It wasn't his taste, which is what makes Pearl Jam so interesting. For him to sing it in the way that he sings it—which is absolutely reverential to the

way Andy sang it—all of a sudden, we get to acknowledge the past and say, "This is part of where we came from." Ed's got hundreds of songs and lots of his own stories from his own past that are worthy of celebration and worthy of remembrances, and for him to come in on that particular day and say, "We're going to do this one about you guys." If you don't have an agenda and you just let something happen, that's where people can give you something that you never could have expected.

Mike McCready: It was exhilarating. I wanted to do it right, you know? I wanted to not mess the song up. That was mainly what I was thinking. Ed wanted that to be a very special song for a special night. I think it was his thought process of, If Andy had still been alive, he may have been playing this song in this place. When we did it, it brought back memories of me seeing them at little clubs. Most of the crowd knew it; maybe not all of it. But they were receptive and excited about us doing it.

Jeff Ament: All of a sudden, playing "Crown of Thorns," it was the first time I properly reflected on what we'd gone through and what a journey it's been. And that moment was reflected in a purely positive way, feeling blessed, happy to still be playing music.

Eddie Vedder: I could see emotions coming out of the top of our heads like heat vapors off summer blacktop.

Chris Cornell: If Pearl Jam does a song by the Who, to me that actually makes more obvious sense than Pearl Jam

doing a Mother Love Bone song. I don't know why, because two of the guys were in Mother Love Bone. But "Crown of Thorns" became a Pearl Jam song when I heard Pearl Jam do it. They're not trying to be Mother Love Bone, and it conveys different emotions, but in a really natural way. It's pretty incredible.

October 31
Shoreline Amphitheatre, Mountain View, California

Pearl Jam gets in the Halloween spirit by playing the second encore dressed as the Village People: Vedder as the Indian, Gossard as the policeman, McCready as the biker, Ament as the construction worker, and Cameron as the soldier. Wearing chaps over underwear, McCready is depantsed by Ament while soloing, forcing him to hide behind a monitor to finish the song.

November 5–6
Key Arena, Seattle

Pearl Jam concludes the Binaural tour during two emotional hometown shows, with proceeds nearing a half million dollars donated to eighteen local and national charities. "Alive" is played at the second show for the first time since the Roskilde tragedy. That performance runs so long (160 minutes) that it requires three discs for its official bootleg, the only such instance in the 2000 series.

November 14

Matt Cameron guests on Rush singer-bassist Geddy Lee's solo debut album, *My Favorite Headache* (Atlantic).

November 27
Royal Albert Hall, London

Having flown in from vacation in Hawaii, Eddie Vedder performs a host of songs with the Who, including "I'm One," "Let's See Action," "Gettin' in Tune," and "My Generation," at a benefit for Teenage Cancer Trust.

Christmas

Pearl Jam releases its ninth fan-club-only seven-inch single: Mother Love Bone's "Crown of Thorns" backed by Elvis Presley's "Can't Help Falling in Love With You," recorded at the tenth-anniversary concert on October 22, 2000, in Las Vegas.

Binaural

As the century flipped from twentieth to twenty-first, the Internet had exploded into the dominant mode for communication of all types, including the naked theft of recorded music via programs like Napster, angry protesters were shattering the tranquility of Pearl Jam's Seattle hometown during a World Trade Organization summit, and the United States was on the verge of electing a president who would lead the country into a highly questionable war in the Middle East.

In the midst of the tumult, Pearl Jam was hitting the restart button as it recorded the album that would come to be called *Binaural.* Drummer Matt Cameron, who joined the band just before the start of its 1998 summer tour, was behind the kit in the studio with Pearl Jam for the first time. There was also a new face manning the mixing console: producer Tchad Blake, best known for his work with singer-songwriters like Suzanne Vega, Tracy Chapman, and Tom Waits, as well as his love of the recording technique from which the album eventually took its name.

Binaural recording aims to approximate the way human ears process sound and, when played back, offers a depth and nuance often lacking in modern rock 'n' roll production. "Tchad has a very distinctive way of recording the sound of the room, and we were interested in exploring that atmosphere," Eddie Vedder says. "A lot of the time on *Binaural,* it's almost like the listener is there in the room with us."

One of the first songs written for the album, and an ideal candidate to be recorded binaurally, was Jeff Ament's moody, atmospheric "Nothing As It Seems." The track was debuted in October 1999 during a performance at Neil Young's annual Bridge School Benefit outside San Francisco, where

Pearl Jam has often experimented with new songs and unusual arrangements, and wound up becoming the lead-off single from *Binaural.*

"I was out in Montana by myself, and I wrote two songs," Ament recalls. "I wrote 'Nothing As It Seems' and a song called 'Time to Pay,' based on witnessing this horrific domestic dispute going on down at the local gas station. I came back home, and I ended up writing these two songs that night, and that song in particular was just kind of a little sad, minor key drone that I took to the band with full lyrics.

"The idea was that at the beginning, it was going to have a real heavy Pink Floyd vibe. So I went to Mike McCready and said, 'I need you to make this song happen. It isn't going to be good enough unless you come up with something that's just unreal.'"

McCready did just that, employing a Fender pedal from the 1960s that combined wah-wah and phaser effects for a sound inspired by Pink Floyd epics such as "Comfortably Numb." The pedal has since crapped out, preventing McCready from replicating in concert how he played it on the album, but he still views the song's solo as "one of my favorite solos ever."

"That's my realization of Jeff writing really dark songs," McCready says. "I think his original lyric was 'One-way ticket tombstone.' And then Ed changed it to 'One-way ticket headstone.' I thought the tombstone is so appropriate because he's from Montana, and that's maybe what he was thinking."

That McCready was even contributing to *Binaural* on a creative level was something of a miracle, as the guitarist was struggling deeply with health and personal issues. "*Binaural* is a dark time for me, for sure. I was struggling with Crohn's disease and

struggling with addiction," he says. "I was taking pills to take care of that. And then that got out of hand, and it was dark."

Meanwhile, Vedder found himself faced with the worst case of writer's block he'd ever experienced in his life, which he humorously acknowledged by including thirty seconds of a typewriter chattering as a hidden track on the album's closer, "Parting Ways."

There were only a couple days left in the studio, and Vedder still hadn't finished the lyrics to two songs he'd written, "Insignificance" and "Grievance." According to the singer, he stayed up all night and even experimented with writing melodies on piano in an attempt to get his creative juices flowing. Then, a happy accident occurred in the form of the song "Soon Forget."

"I wasn't allowing myself to pick up a guitar and write something new, because I had all these other things I had to finish," he says. "But I looked over and saw this ukulele, and I said, 'Well, that's not a guitar.' [*Laughs*] So I didn't finish my assignment as prescribed, but I opened things up a bit. 'Soon Forget' probably took me twenty minutes, and it was done. And it has some merit to it. Then I went back to the other ones, and suddenly they were no problem to finish."

The minute-and-a-half-long "Soon Forget" is a sly dig at a Bill Gates–style gazillionaire who "counts his money every morning" because it's "the only thing that keeps him horny." It's also a cautionary tale, according to Vedder: "Make sure you don't turn out like that."

Besides on the voice-and-ukulele "Soon Forget," Blake's techniques are put to best use on songs like "Of the Girl," a bluesy strut written by Stone Gossard on which the thick bass and galloping drums give the impression of charging through twilight.

Ament's meditation on the rat race of humanity, "Sleight of Hand," features bass lines so deep and rich that they almost seem alive. The track is one of Pearl Jam's most successful experiments in how to express its artier side, its chorus sporting a wall of sound previously unheard on any of the band's albums.

For all the intricate textures heard on *Binaural,* the album begins with a trifecta of patented breakneck rockers, the surging, classic Who–style "Breakerfall," Ament's whiplash-inducing "God's Dice," and the jerky, punk-flavored "Evacuation," Cameron's first songwriting contribution in Pearl Jam.

"Evacuation" gave McCready fits in the studio in his attempts to figure out the abrupt time-signature changes, and it has often bewildered Pearl Jam fans, who find it simply too weird. Indeed, according to Gossard, Cameron always jokes about the song, "because on some Pearl Jam website, it was the most hated Pearl Jam song."

"It's a drummer tune! What do you want, man?" Cameron says with a laugh. "Drummer tunes don't make sense. They're rhythmically weird. There's no way a guitar player could come up with a drummer tune. I think Mike had trouble with 'Evacuation' in the studio, but they nail it live. It didn't take *that* long. Once again, never let your drummer write songs. I did not have a vocal melody for it; that was Eddie all the way. I normally write music first, listen to it for a while, and if I come up with something, great. If not, I'll hand it off to a real singer. I was really lucky that they wanted to do this song. I had no idea what to do with it."

"Personally," says Vedder, "I think I wrote and sang the shit out of that song. It's got three bridges, for God's sake! It's like Pittsburgh!"

Binaural downshifts beautifully on "Light Years," an uplifting tribute to someone very close to Vedder who'd passed away around that time. What began as a quiet-verse, full-throttle-chorus type of construction titled "Puzzles and Games" eventually gave way to a more measured, emotional piece of music.

"It sounded nothing like what it sounds like now," Ament says of the song. "Mike had a couple of riffs, and Ed really sat down and tried to write to it. He initially had some problems, and one day he came in on his own and had some lyrics that were really heartfelt. He ended up completely rearranging the song. It got played a million different tempos and a million different angles on the drums."

The unease in the world circa 2000 most definitely informed the song lyrics on *Binaural,* specifically on "Grievance" (about technology's impact on individuality), "Insignificance" (inspired by the protests against the World Trade Organization and whether such actions actually accomplish anything), and "Rival" (based on the 1999 massacre at Columbine High School in Colorado).

"You tend to get frustrated and say, 'Fuck it. I can't do anything about it,'" Vedder says. "But you can empower yourself, and you can make a difference. There's ways of doing it, whether it's just checking out the rally going on down the street. You don't even have to agree with what is going on. Just hear the arguments in public. Expand your pool of information beyond your major media."

After Columbine, Gossard was inspired to write the grinding "Rival," which begins with the sound of Tchad

Blake's dog snarling into the binaural microphone, as he mulled "what makes people kind of snap and how people are unpredictable. I tried to think about what those guys may have been thinking the night before."

For Cameron, Pearl Jam's preference for in-studio jamming was a welcome counterpoint to the exacting methods utilized by Soundgarden. He says, "We rehearsed our dicks off before we got in the studio, and we were completely like, 'This is how the song goes. This is how it's going to be recorded. End of story.' So it was kind of cool to work in that off-the-cuff manner in which Pearl Jam works, like, rehearse a song two times and record it."

Once recording for *Binaural* was complete, the band and Blake were faced with assembling a coherent track list from nearly twenty finished songs. A number of more straightforward cuts, including Cameron's grungy "In the Moonlight," Gossard's acoustic ballad "Fatal," and a "great pop song" at that time titled "Letter to the Dead" and later renamed "Sad," were left on the cutting

room floor but luckily were revived for the 2003 rarities album *Lost Dogs.* Three instrumentals ("Thunderclap," "Foldback," and "Harmony") from early in the recording sessions also appeared as bonus material on the *Touring Band 2000* DVD.

"There's certainly a few songs that Ed wrote, like 'Sad' and 'Education,' that could have been hits, or given the album a more commercial angle," Ament says. "I remember when we sequenced it, there were no huge fights about what should be on or not. Having made that record with Tchad and the way it sounded and the vibe it had, it was darker. It made sense to us at the time that we put the record out the way we did. But we look back and think we didn't put some of the best songs on it."

Near the end of the process, the band decided it wasn't happy with Blake's mix and turned to the collaborator with whom it had always been most comfortable: Brendan O'Brien, who'd produced the four prior Pearl Jam albums. Says McCready, "Tchad had some good ideas. He did a great job on the slow songs, like 'Nothing As It Seems.' But other songs were harder for him, so we called Brendan to remix, to make the songs heavier."

Looking back, band members concede that although *Binaural* has its moments, various distractions and missed opportunities contributed to make the album less powerful than it could have been.

"That's an album I need to listen to in another ten years," Gossard says. "We weren't as loose with one another or sharing as well as we usually did. It was our first record with Matt Cameron. He's a genius, and one of the heaviest drummers of all time. It feels like we should have gotten more out of him. It should have devastated in a way that Temple of the Dog

devastated. But I don't think we wrote the songs that really had Matt in mind in that way. We were still writing individual songs and trying to continue to be Pearl Jam, which was cool, but it just seems like we could have done more. I think there's some beautiful things that came out of it, but we're never going to remember that record as one of the greats."

That said, Vedder believes *Binaural* marked an important evolution in the way he approached singing, at a time when the front men for countless rock bands were obviously copying his vocal style all the way to the top of the charts.

"A lot of people told me about these singers who sound like they're doing an impersonation of me, but the thing is, I was not really in tune with my own voice on the first two or three records," he says. "I'd sing the angry songs one way and the quieter songs one way. That's different for me now, but it took some time. On *Binaural,* the songs felt like they really came from my voice."

Evacuation
In hiding
Daughter
GN FLOW → CORDUROY
~~GOD SAY~~
off he goes
Better Man
Animal
Once
RVM

OF THE GIRL
BLACK footsteps
Evolution

235

ROSKILDE

On June 30, 2000, while Pearl Jam played its headlining set at the Roskilde Festival in Copenhagen, the unthinkable happened: Nine people were killed and another thirty injured in a crowd surge during the twelfth song of the show, "Daughter." Near the beginning of the performance, front man Eddie Vedder pleaded with the audience of fifty thousand strong to stop pushing toward the stage and asked people to take "two steps back," but a number of fans lost their footing on the mud-soaked field and were trampled. The tragedy shook the band to its core.

"I didn't personally think anything was amiss, just because we got there and hit the stage and played," says Matt Cameron. "But those big festivals . . . it's just so hard to tell what's really going on. The whole vibe was a little dark. It was rainy. It was just another gig for us. But then we realized something was terribly wrong, and responded. From the onset, we couldn't tell that it would be anything different from a normal European festival."

"I just wanted to get out of there," says Eddie Vedder. "I just didn't want it to be true. It was happening right in front of us, but I just didn't want it to be true."

Within two weeks of the accident, Danish police concluded that the deaths were an accident and did not constitute a criminal case against festival organizers. But in a move that stunned observers, on July 20, 2000, Roskilde deputy chief constable Bent Rungstrom sent a report to the Danish parliament claiming that Pearl Jam was "morally responsible" for the tragedy. The report claimed to draw on interviews with nearly three hundred witnesses, many of whom allegedly told investigators "that Pearl Jam are well known for almost appealing for violent behavior."

In a statement, band manager Kelly Curtis immediately responded, "Pearl Jam are well known for their exciting live shows, but they have never, in their ten-year history of performing, 'appealed for violent behavior.' As the band's manager, I find it hard to believe that after all that has transpired, the band's devastation over the [tragedy] that occurred at the Roskilde Festival during their performance, and their long history of attention to fan safety, that anyone would assign 'moral responsibility' to them. That, I find 'appalling' and ludicrous."

In retrospect, Curtis points out, "The ironic thing is that it all went down during 'Daughter,' which is probably the least frenzied Pearl Jam song, you know? When we realized how it was set up and how the lines of communication were confused, it could have easily been prevented."

The members of Pearl Jam issued a separate statement:

It is our feeling that what happened at the Roskilde Festival cannot be written off entirely as a "freak accident" or "bad luck," as some have called it. When something this disastrous occurs, when this many lives are lost, it is essential that every aspect be examined thoroughly and from all angles. To date, we don't feel this has been done.

It is our understanding that at least 15 minutes passed between the time a member of the festival security team identified a potential problem and the time we were informed. We stopped the show immediately upon being informed that there might be a problem, even though we were asked to wait until the nature of the problem could be determined. It is our belief that if we had been informed of a potential problem at the moment that it was first identified by the festival security, we could have stopped the show earlier and lives could have been saved.

On August 3, 2000, in Virginia Beach, Virginia, Pearl Jam returned to live performance for the first time since Roskilde. Five days later, Roskilde police officers met with band members and other key individuals in the Pearl Jam organization in West Palm Beach, Florida, in an attempt to clear the air over claims of responsibility. Vedder was personally questioned for more than six hours in a small hotel room. The Danish investigators also attended the West Palm Beach show "in an effort to learn about security and safety measures that might be implemented at the Roskilde Festival next year."

Afterward, Roskilde police commissioner Uffe Kornerup said in a statement, "We are in agreement that we will all do everything possible in an effort to identify all factors that may have contributed to the tragedies at the Roskilde Festival with the hope that we might learn ways in which tragedies of this nature can be avoided in the future. We look forward to continuing to work together cooperatively in an effort to achieve this goal."

"I personally never felt like we should break up or that it was our fault," Stone Gossard says candidly. "We rethought everything from that point on. When we were in charge of our own security, when we were in charge of our own shows, they were wild, but we were very aware of what was going on on our sidelines. And that was the end of us trusting in any other event where we weren't contractually allowed to step in and oversee security in the way that we knew needed to be done, particularly dealing with crowds as big as that."

"We never reacted from a point of protecting ourselves," Curtis says. "From day one, we all wanted to know what happened and how. If it was our fault in any way, we certainly wanted to know that. I think that would have impacted if the band would have continued. There was some sort of poetic justice that this is the band it happened to, because they were not going to sweep it under the rug.

They were going to do everything in their power to make sure nothing like this ever happened again."

"You know, my years with Soundgarden were definitely up and down; a little more down toward the end. But that's not to say we all didn't feel just tragically lost after what happened in Denmark," Cameron adds. "I think the whole band kept going, and that was the best thing we could have done. It was definitely a very emotional thing for everyone involved."

Toward the end of 2000, the Danish Justice Ministry concluded that despite poor communication between the volunteer security force and a lack of clarity about the chain of command, the Roskilde Festival would not be held responsible for the nine deaths, which it said were caused by "a combination of unfortunate circumstances and violent audience behavior."

The festival returned to the same grounds the following summer. As a memorial to the lives lost, nine birch trees were planted in a circle, with stones in between them and a large stone in the middle. Organizers said "the nine trees carry life further, and the stones provide a place for people to sit and contemplate."

The emotions involved in coming to terms with Roskilde became a dominant theme in Pearl Jam's songwriting over the next two years, beginning with "I Am Mine." Because it wasn't released until 2002 on the *Riot Act* album, lines like "And the meaning, it gets left behind / All the innocents lost at one time" were interpreted by some to be about the September 11, 2001, terrorist attacks.

But Vedder had actually written the song in his Virginia Beach hotel room during a rainstorm the night before the band's first post-Roskilde concert, and lyrics such as "There's no need to hide / We're safe tonight" spoke to his conviction that something positive could come from the tragedy.

Another *Riot Act* song, "Love Boat Captain," addresses the situation much more directly: "It's an art to live with pain / Mix the light into gray / Lost nine friends we'll never know / Two years ago today." And on that album's "Arc," Vedder built nine loops of his wordless vocalizing in tribute to each person who died that day.

In 2003 Stone Gossard met face-to-face with the families of some of the Roskilde victims for the first time. "Nothing could be more powerful than their dignity and openness during that visit," he reflects. "I tried to convey our band's sadness and acknowledge and feel some of their loss. Maybe my visit was helpful in some small way." Since then, Pearl Jam's members have opened lines of communication with six of the nine families of the deceased, and Vedder has become particularly close with the family of Australian victim Anthony Hurley.

For the band, the healing process took another important step in late 2005 and summer 2006, when it returned to playing general admission headlining shows and multi-act festivals for the first time since Roskilde. Band members have also stayed in close contact with the families of some of the victims, several of whom were on hand for a Berlin show on June 30, 2010 — the tenth anniversary of the incident.

"First and foremost, the industry in general has changed since Roskilde," Gossard observes. "The circumstances have been addressed, particularly in the barricade situation and sight lines and the issues of crowd surge. We have a heightened awareness of what needs to happen every night so people are as safe as they can possibly be. Now we understand the lay of the land better than we did in 2000. In terms of letting somebody else be in charge, it's just never going to happen again. But we'll be very observant and attentive to those sorts of issues, for sure."

"It's really, really hard," Cameron says. "It took a while to just process how we were going to get back to feeling right playing festivals. I knew that our shows would be fine because they're our shows. We take care of security in a way that's completely unique and all-encompassing. We did a run of European festivals in 2010, and I think it was hard for Eddie especially to see all those people, but he did it. It was a big hump to get over, because we do really well in that setting. I'm glad that we all felt comfortable enough to bring it to the people in that environment."

Pearl Jam continues to mourn the lives lost in Denmark, but band members say the tragedy brought them closer together. "Roskilde was obviously the worst thing that could happen to a group or that you could be a part of as a human," Vedder says. "It's something that most people don't have to go through. Having to get through it and be there for each other and go through it together and get close to some of the families and live with it, that was a turning point. I think we got closer.

"In order to honor all the lives that were lost, you do something positive with it," he continues. "And I think that's what some of the families have done, and that's what we tried to do. It made you appreciate life more, made you appreciate your situation in life. It made you appreciate families who lose their kids as soldiers in war, because you felt it up close. You knew how it affected this immense multitude of people that were family and friends."

VEDDER/ED

~6445
~1559   TKT-0161503792625   PAGE 1 OF 1
248.15   TAX- 104.85   TTL AIR- 1353.00   22JUL99

TTLE   **8:00**AM NONSTOP SEAT:**05-B** (CLASS-F)
YORK/KENNEDY   **3:59**PM

88410   AMT: 15.00

YOU FOR YOUR BUSINESS

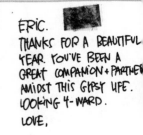

ERIC. ▮
THANKS FOR A BEAUTIFUL
YEAR. YOU'VE BEEN A
GREAT COMPANION + PARTNER
AMIDST THIS GYPSY LIFE.
LOOKING 4-WARD.
LOVE,

JEFF

PEARL JAM

SEXECUTIONER, OUR CREW BAND W/ ED ON DRUMS CIRCA '91

Erin —

this bill for all
the drinks I been
drinking.

E.

Hay Ed,
       we all want
the Ramones guy to
come to the next
place also.

Nickey   Kevin Shus
Buzz Mcd
Eric
Ramie
Bett

243

2001

In the wake of the Roskilde tragedy, Pearl Jam's very existence was in doubt. After a brief break, the group came back together to complete its 2000 North American tour, which included a tenth-anniversary show in Las Vegas in late October and a cathartic finale a few weeks later in Seattle. Exhausted, Pearl Jam's members spent nearly all of 2001 working on individual projects: Eddie Vedder with Crowded House's Neil Finn on a short tour and live album; Stone Gossard on *Bayleaf,* the first solo album by a member of Pearl Jam; and Matt Cameron with a new record from his side band, Wellwater Conspiracy. And although the band was already conceptualizing ways to turn the program into more of a digitally driven concept, CD copies of the live bootlegs from the 2000 tour continued to sell briskly.

After nearly a year away from the live stage, and directly on the heels of the September 11, 2001, terrorist attacks, Pearl Jam returned to performance at Neil Young's Bridge School Benefit, where it debuted two new songs. Despite playing in front of a hometown crowd, the band ceded headlining status to R.E.M. the next night at the finale of the Groundwork benefit concert series in Seattle. The studio beckoned, and Pearl Jam had plenty more to say.

March 7

Seven titles from Pearl Jam's live bootleg series on Epic debut simultaneously on the *Billboard* 200, breaking the band's own record of five set the previous October. The charting entries, which comprise the first leg of Pearl Jam's 2000 North American tour, are led by *Jones Beach 8/25/2000,* at no. 159, which sells more than 7,900 copies. Also charting are *Boston 8/29/2000,* at no. 163; *Indianapolis 8/18/2000,* at no. 174; *Pittsburgh 9/5/2000,* at no. 176; *Philadelphia 9/1/2000,* at no. 179; *Tampa 8/12/2000,* at no. 181; and *Memphis 8/15/2000,* at no. 191. All told, the albums shift more than fifty thousand copies combined. On April 4 *Seattle 11/6/2000* and *Las Vegas 10/22/2000* enter the charts at nos. 98 and 152, respectively.

April 2–6
St. James Theatre, Auckland, New Zealand

Eddie Vedder joins a star-studded list of musicians such as the Smiths' Johnny Marr and Radiohead's Ed O'Brien and Phil Selway for five Neil Finn shows in New Zealand, all of which were recorded for future release. The musicians collaborate closely with one another throughout the run on everything from Pearl Jam songs ("Better Man," "Parting Ways," "Around the Bend," "Not for You") to Crowded House and Split Enz classics ("I See Red," "History Never Repeats," "I Got You," "World Where You Live").

Neil Finn: It was kind of an amazing time. It was just a whimsical notion that came up with Radiohead guitarist Ed O'Brien one time when we were at the beach. We were talking about how often a conversation with another musician ends with, "It would be great to do something sometime!" And it almost never happens for one reason or another. We thought, "Let's just make some calls and do some shows with no other agenda." I rang Eddie up and said, "I've got this idea. Do you think you might be into it?" And he said, "Yeah! Sounds good." And I said, "Okay, well, you know, think about it and get back to me in a couple of weeks." And he said, "No, no, I'm in!" I was kind of shocked. I didn't think it would be that easy. He turned up with two days to spare. The very first night,

he was rehearsing three Split Enz songs with my son Liam and his band in this little shack out by the beach. We learned a couple of his songs, too. We did play "Better Man," which was relatively okay. That was within our realm. We also tried "Corduroy," which was just an absolute dog's breakfast. I remember looking at Phil Selway, Radiohead's drummer, and he was dying a thousand deaths. He loved the song and wanted to play it, but he was missing everything. It was pretty funny. I think Eddie loved the experience. He was having a difficult time on a personal level, and I think the friendship side of it was really valuable for him. Everyone left revitalized and invigorated.

May 1

Pearl Jam's first live DVD, *Touring Band 2000,* is released by Epic. Drawn from the previous year's North American tour in support of *Binaural,* the project features twenty-eight songs from nineteen different concerts. *Touring Band* is shot by Pearl Jam crew members Liz Burns, Steve Gordon, and Kevin Shuss, who "would finish their regular duties by showtime, then grab cameras, and become a documentary film team," Vedder says. Bonus features include European tour footage set to three previously unreleased instrumentals, Todd McFarlane's 1998 animated video for "Do the Evolution," the previously unreleased 1992 video for "Oceans," and three songs shot from Matt Cameron's vantage point. After debuting with sales of thirty-three thousand copies in the United States, according to Nielsen SoundScan, *Touring Band* finishes at no. 11 on *Billboard*'s 2001 year-end music video chart.

Liz Burns: We really wanted to make the fans feel like if they weren't there at a show that they knew what happened and what went on and that they were part of it.

May 22

Matt Cameron and guitarist John McBain's third album as Wellwater Conspiracy, *The Scroll and Its Combinations,* is released on TVT Records. Eddie Vedder sings lead vocals on "Felicity's Surprise," credited as Wes C. Addle.

Wellwater Conspiracy

Matt Cameron: I had no idea what he was going to do when he came in, but it fit perfectly. It was also the first time he'd ever double-tracked his vocals. I was happy that he chose our band to do that with.

June 12

A live Pearl Jam rendition of the Who's "The Kids Are Alright" taken from the 2000 tour is included on the Pete Townshend–sanctioned Who tribute album *Substitute: The Songs of the Who*, released on EAR Records.

July 9
Showbox, Seattle

Eddie Vedder joins Wellwater Conspiracy and Supersuckers at a benefit organized by ex–pitching star Jack McDowell for several Major League Baseball charities. Vedder sings "Red Light Green Light" and "Felicity's Surprise" with Wellwater Conspiracy and "Poor Girl" with Supersuckers. Mudhoney and Pete Droge also perform.

August 4
Rose Garden, Portland, Oregon

Eddie Vedder performs "Soon Forget," "Gimme Some Truth," "I Am a Patriot,"

and Patti Smith's "People Have the Power" at a political rally featuring Ralph Nader.

August 24
Casbah, San Diego

Eddie Vedder makes a surprise appearance with Wellwater Conspiracy to sing "Red Light Green Light" and "Felicity's Surprise."

September 1–3
The Breakroom, Seattle

Brad debuts new material during a three-show run in Seattle.

September 8
Street Scene Festival, San Diego

Mike McCready jams on Jimi Hendrix's "Machine Gun" with Band of Gypsys members Buddy Miles and Billy Cox.

September 11

Stone Gossard becomes the first Pearl Jam member to release a solo album under his own name with *Bayleaf* (Epic). While he's in New York to do press for the project, terrorists crash two hijacked

commercial airliners into the World Trade Center, killing thousands of people.

Stone Gossard: In the time off between Pearl Jam, I've always liked to get up and play guitar and write. In the process of doing that, I wrote a bunch of songs. I had been recording and trying to learn how to sing and attempting to finish something without it having to be a Pearl Jam song. I just happened to be the first guy to get them all together and make the final push of getting them out.

September 21

Eddie Vedder, Mike McCready, and Neil Young perform "Long Road" on a CBS soundstage in Los Angeles as part of the *America: A Tribute to Heroes* telethon, which raises money for victims of the September 11, 2001, terrorist attacks on the United States. The concert is released commercially on December 4, with proceeds to benefit the September 11th Fund. Vedder had originally wanted to cover John Lennon's "Gimme Some Truth" but opted for "something to participate in the grieving process instead."

September 25

The Who and Special Guests Live at the Royal Albert Hall is released on DVD and

FARSIDE (INST)
NIGHTMARES (MATT)
THE ENDING (MATT)
LUCY LEAVE (MATT)
HAL MCBLAINE (INST)
~~BROTHERHOOD~~ (INST)
RED LIGHT (ED)
FELICITY (ED)
TROWERCHORD (BEN)
SLEEVELESS (BEN)

2001

247

VHS by Image Entertainment. Taped November 27, 2000, in London at a benefit for Teenage Cancer Trust, the film features guest appearances by Eddie Vedder, Noel Gallagher, and Paul Weller.

October 20–21
Shoreline Amphitheatre, Mountain View, California

Pearl Jam makes its first live appearance since the September 11 terrorist attacks and its fifth at Neil Young's Bridge School Benefit. On the first night, the 1999 holiday single "Driftin'" is played live for the first time, as is a brand-new Mike McCready–penned song, "Last Soldier." During the second show, "Low Light" and another new song, "I Am Mine," premiere, with the lines "And the meanings that get left behind / All the innocents lost at one time" striking a post-9/11 chord. Ben Harper joins Pearl Jam for "Indifference" both nights.

Ben Harper: I started covering "Indifference" at least ten or twelve years ago. It always just felt natural. Ed got word of that, and we started doing it together. That song, I feel like it's a part of me. I feel it deeply, and I mean it more every time I sing it. I'm glad to be reinvited to sing it with them every so often.

October 22
Key Arena, Seattle

Pearl Jam, R.E.M., Alanis Morissette, Rahat Nusrat Fateh Ali Khan, and Maná cap off the Groundwork 2001 concert series. Proceeds from the weeklong event—estimated at $1 million by organizers—are used by the US Committee for Food and Agriculture Organization (FAO) to contribute to the global TeleFood fund, which channels money directly to small-scale food-producing projects around the world. Pearl Jam again plays the new "I Am Mine" and goes heavy on *Binaural* tracks such as "Insignificance," "Grievance," "Nothing As It Seems," and "Light Years." Pakistani vocalist Khan, who flew thirty-two hours from his home as a last-minute addition to the bill, joins the group for an extended version of "Long Road."

October 23
Crocodile Cafe, Seattle

Eddie Vedder guests frequently during a secret R.E.M. club show, at one point serving the band margaritas off of a tray. Michael Stipe butchers the lyrics to "Better Man" but amiably agrees to duet with Vedder later in the show on R.E.M.'s "Begin the Begin," despite claiming that he doesn't remember the words.

Peter Buck: We were all just having fun and taking requests. We even did "Better Man," which none of us had ever rehearsed. We got, like, ninety percent through it. Ed said, "Do 'Begin the Begin,'" and Michael said, "Okay, if you sing it!" Those chords don't go where you expect them to go. We were all looking at each other, like, "What the fuck? How does this go?" But Ed knew it.

November 26—December 2

Brad plays a five-date West Coast tour that finishes in Seattle, playing material set to appear on its third album, *Welcome to Discovery Park.*

Christmas

Pearl Jam's tenth fan-club-only seven-inch singles are a double release of "Last Soldier" backed with "Indifference," featuring Ben Harper (both from the recent Bridge School Benefit), and "Gimme Some Truth" (from the Groundwork concert) backed with Jeff Ament's solo cover of the Ramones' "I Just Want to Have Something to Do."

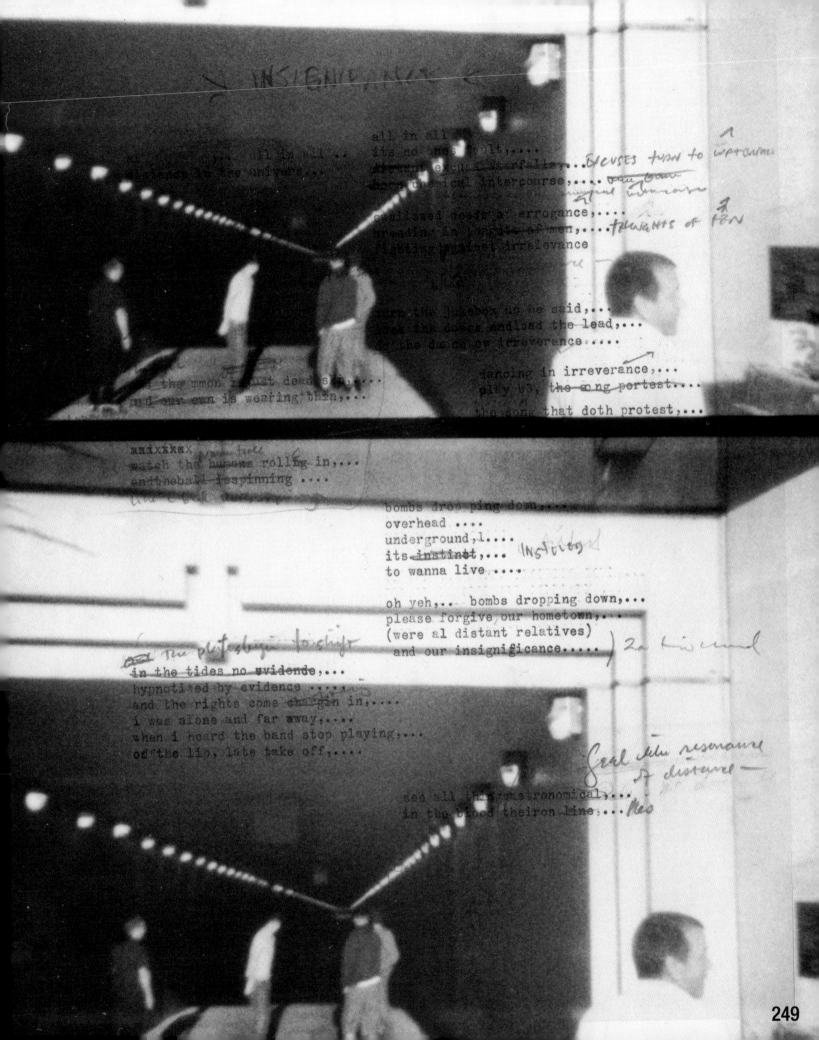

249

2002

Pearl Jam spent the first part of 2002 dealing with a challenge as difficult as any it had ever faced. Two major tragedies had occurred since the band last went into the studio: Roskilde—where nine fans were killed in a crowd surge during the band's set at the Danish festival in June 2000—and the September 11, 2001, terrorist attacks. Addressing these events in its new music in a way that was appropriately respectful and significant was something that Pearl Jam took very seriously. "Universal themes aren't easy to come up with when you're just a guy and a typewriter and a guitar," Eddie Vedder says. Indeed, Roskilde remained deeply heartbreaking for the band, and each member was still trying to come to terms with it in his own way. For Stone Gossard, it was by reaching out to the families of the victims. For Eddie Vedder, it was by journeying to remote parts of the globe and testing out new forms of creative expression via unfamiliar instruments and collaborators. The album that would arrive that fall would be Pearl Jam's last under contract for Epic Records, its home since before the "Seattle sound" exploded into a worldwide phenomenon more than a decade earlier.

January 8

Recorded in a day and featuring him playing all the instruments, Eddie Vedder's cover of the Beatles' "You've Got to Hide Your Love Away" is released on V2's *I Am Sam* soundtrack. The film stars longtime Vedder friend Sean Penn; Vedder's version of "Love" quickly becomes a staple of his pre–Pearl Jam show surprise solo sets.

January 26
Spin Alley Bowling Center, Shoreline, Washington

A newly mohawked Vedder plays two sets (solo acoustic and electric, backed by C Average) of covers and a few Pearl Jam originals at RealNetworks CEO Rob Glaser's fortieth birthday party. Glaser in turn donates $400,000 to the West Memphis Three's legal defense fund.

Eddie Vedder: I wasn't in support of bombing. That was how I was feeling, so I just made my own personal statement with the mohawk. There was an actual reason for it, as silly as it was to think

that I could make a statement with a haircut. Especially seeing that I'd kind of isolated myself on some crazy little island—a secret island in the South Pacific—so it wasn't like I was around anybody else. The haircut was done by a little old lady in an island gift shop. She had some sons that she'd given mohawks to, so she'd done it before.

February 26
Wiltern Theater, Los Angeles

Another unusual Vedder concert appearance, this time at a benefit for the Recording Artists' Coalition. He debuts several songs that would eventually appear on *Riot Act* later in the year, including "Can't Keep," on ukulele, and "Thumbing My Way," on acoustic guitar, plus two more that wouldn't see official release for nearly a decade ("You're True" and

"Broken Heart"). Throughout the show, Vedder also collaborates with Beck and Social Distortion's Mike Ness on covers of songs by Skip Spence (the creative spark plug of the little-known but much-beloved sixties band Moby Grape) and country star Lee Hazlewood. He also tells the crowd that he plans to keep the mohawk until "we stop killing people abroad."

March 15
Royce Hall, Los Angeles

Vedder performs at the first US installment of the popular UK-originated All Tomorrow's Parties festival, curated by Sonic Youth and held on the campus of UCLA. This time, he promises not to say "anything political" and instead focuses on a host of new ukulele songs (which he describes as falling under the genre "speed thrash ukulele"), including "You're True," "Longing to Belong," and "Satellite." The set closes with "Parting Ways," as Vedder stomps on the ukulele. At the end of the night, he joins J Mascis, Mike Watt, and the Stooges' Ron and Scott Asheton for that band's classic "No Fun."

Jim O'Rourke, Sonic Youth bassist-producer: When he played solo, I loved it. You could hear the parts of the songs. I like singer-songwriters, and these shows were much more in that vein. It was really magnetic. Eddie spent a lot of time with Kim, me, and Thurston. On days off, he'd go record shopping with us. The fact that he showed genuine examples of enthusiasm for learning about new stuff—if we played him Loren Mazzacane and he really liked it, he would go out and buy the records.

March 18
Waldorf Astoria Hotel, New York

With his punk mohawk looking more appropriate than ever, Vedder inducts his heroes the Ramones into the Rock and Roll Hall of Fame. His sixteen-minute speech, which was cut in half for the eventual television broadcast, emphasizes how the Ramones greatly influenced nascent rock 'n' rollers. "They obliterated the mystique of what it was to play in a band," he says. "You didn't have to know scales. With the knowledge of two barre chords, you could play along

with their records. That's what people did. They sat in front of their parents' hi-fis and played along with *Road to Ruin* or *It's Alive.* Within weeks, they were starting bands with other kids in town who were doing the same thing. The Ramones were a blueprint, a blueprint so necessary at the time." Bassist Dee Dee Ramone dies less than three months later; singer Joey Ramone had died of cancer the previous year.

July 9
Showbox, Seattle

Still riding high from the experience of performing in an all-star band with Neil Finn in Auckland in April 2001, captured on the *7 Worlds Collide* live album, Vedder joins the Split Enz–Crowded House star for the songs "The Kids Are Alright," "Watch Outside," and "History Never Repeats" at the latter's Seattle show.

July 11
Chop Suey, Seattle

Vedder sings with two hastily assembled Who tribute bands, the Low Numbers and the How, featuring members of the Fastbacks and C Average, in tribute to Who bassist John Entwistle, who died of a heart attack in Las Vegas on June 27.

August 13

Brad releases its third studio album, *Welcome to Discovery Park,* on the short-lived Redline label.

Stone Gossard: When you have a record through Epic and there's a relationship with Pearl Jam and all that, it's all sort of convoluted as far as why things are happening because of Pearl Jam and not because of Pearl Jam. We thought that if we're really a good band, we should be able to go out and get a deal. So let's just cut our ties with Epic and believe that we're a good band and that somebody's going to be excited about putting us out. So that's what we did.

September 6–7
Chop Suey, Seattle

Pearl Jam performs a host of material from its upcoming album during a promo video shoot directed by James Frost. Clips for "I Am Mine," "Save You," "Love Boat Captain," "Thumbing My Way," and "1/2 Full" are gradually released through various online partners.

September 23
House of Blues, Chicago

Pearl Jam plays live for the first time ever without one of its core members at this rare club show opening for the Who, as Stone Gossard is in New Guinea honoring a prior commitment to work on a project with Conservation International. A life-sized cardboard cutout of Gossard, dressed in a shiny gold suit, is brought onstage early on, with Vedder joking, "Stone is very one-dimensional tonight."

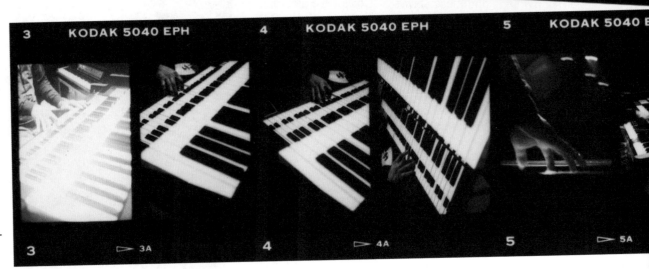

"It takes a lot of guts to come onstage when you know a guy named Pete Townshend is gonna come out later and wipe it with you," Vedder says. This is also keyboardist Boom Gaspar's first show with Pearl Jam, and the official live debut of the yet-to-be-released *Riot Act* songs "Love Boat Captain" and "Green Disease." In a nod to the late John Entwistle's outfit from the Who's famed 1970 performance at the Isle of Wight festival, Jeff Ament wears a human skeleton T-shirt. Proceeds from the event benefit Chicago-area youth charity Maryville Academy.

LOVE BOAT CAPTAIN

is this just another day,... this god forgotten place?
first comes love, then comes pain. let the games begin,...
questions rise and answers fall,... insurmountable.

love boat captain
take the reigns and steer us towards the clear,... here.
its already been sung, but it cant be said enough,
all you need is love

is this just another phase? earthquakes making waves,...
trying to shake the cancer off? stupid human beings,...
once you hold the hand of love,.. its all surmountable.

hold me, and make it the truth,...
that when all is lost there will be you,....
cause to the universe i dont mean a thing
and theres just one word i still believe
and its

its an art to live with pain,.. mix the light into grey,...
lost 9 friends well never know,.. 2 years ago today.
and if our lives became too long, would it add to our regret?

and the young, they can lose hope cause they cant see beyond
today,....
the wisdom that the old cant give away
hey,....
constant recoil,....
sometimes life
dont leave you alone.

hold me, and make it the truth,....
that when all is lost there will be you.
cause to the universe i dont mean a thing
and theres just one word that i still believe and its
love,... love. love. love. love.

love boat captain
take the reigns,.. steer us towards the clear.
i know its already been sung,... cant be said enough.
love is all you need,..... all you need is love, ...
love,... love,...

love

255

September 25
United Center, Chicago

Introduced as "a hometown boy," Vedder makes a surprise appearance to sing "My Hometown" at a Bruce Springsteen and the E Street Band concert.

Bruce Springsteen: I remember Eddie first stepping out onto our stage as being a lovely moment for me. We were early in the regrouping of the E Street Band, and hearing and seeing where some of our energy had gone was a sweet thing. Plus, he sounded really beautiful singing my song.

November 12

Pearl Jam releases its seventh studio album for Epic Records, *Riot Act.*

November 14–15

Pearl Jam appears two consecutive nights on the *Late Show with David Letterman* in New York, playing "I Am Mine" and "Save You."

November 19

Riot Act debuts at no. 5 on the *Billboard* 200 with first-week sales of 166,000 copies.

December 5–6
Showbox, Seattle

Pearl Jam plays its first full concert in more than a year with two hometown club gigs, at which the rest of the *Riot Act* songs premiere. At soundcheck on the first night, the band records a cover of the Sonics' "Don't Believe in Christmas" for release a few weeks later on the annual fan club holiday single. At the second show, which was later released on DVD as *Live at the Showbox,* Vedder for the first time dons a George W. Bush mask while performing "Bu$hleaguer." Previously on the Binaural tour, Vedder had often performed "Soon Forget" with a rubber Bill Gates mask on the microphone stand.

December 8–9
Key Arena, Seattle

Pearl Jam donates proceeds from these two concerts to a number of local charities. Both Vedder and McCready smash guitars during the run, while Vedder again wears the Bush mask for "Bu$hleaguer" and doesn't shy away from a lot of between-song political chatter.

2002

December 22

Former Clash vocalist-guitarist Joe Strummer dies of a heart attack in London. Strummer and his band the Mescaleros had confirmed just days earlier that they would open for Pearl Jam during the last leg of the 2003 Riot Act tour. The band had previously asked Strummer out on the road without success, but this time around he'd run the idea past Pete Townshend, who gave his support for the pairing.

Jeff Ament: A couple of months before Joe passed, Mike and I saw him play at the EMP Sky Church, possibly the worst venue ever built, and Joe and the Mescaleros delivered one of the better shows I've ever seen. Better than both times I saw the Clash. Joe said, midshow, "Can somebody turn off the fooking air-conditioning? James Brown couldn't get a sweat in here." Really sad he's gone.

2002

Joe Strummer R.I.P.

Christmas

Pearl Jam's eleventh fan-club-only seven-inch single includes a cover of the Sonics' "Don't Believe in Christmas," recorded during soundcheck at the recent Showbox show, with the B-side featuring Beck and Vedder's take on the Everly Brothers' "Sleepless Nights" from the Recording Artists' Coalition benefit.

Riot Act

Pearl Jam_378786_FMQB/ROCK 9/11/02 11:32 AM Page 1

PEARL JAM
I Am Mine
The first single
from their forthcoming album
Coming November 12, 2002

"Sony" and ⊗ Reg. U.S. Pat. & TM. Off. Marca Registrada /
© 2002 Sony Music Entertainment Inc.

SONY MUSIC GA: sara syms   Job #: 378786-001   Publ: FMQB/ROCK   Bleed: 9.75" x 12.75"   Trim: 9" x 12"   Safety: 8.5" x 11.5"

Ask Eddie Vedder why after more than a decade in Pearl Jam, the creative process continues to inspire him, and he's quick with a proud smile. "We have five songwriters," he says. "The band has really become a vehicle for everyone to offer up their songs, have very adept musicians play them, and have a very good communication with those players. That's why I can see us going on for a long while."

"No lead singer of his caliber has come anywhere near worrying about whether everybody in the band has written a song. Most of them could give one shit about that," Stone Gossard says. "And for him, it's important, and that's the difference. That's one of his weapons. He's very thoughtful, in that sense."

Indeed, *Riot Act* is an exceedingly collaborative affair, channeling that creative energy into a host of showcases for the band's signature rock power: the tense, psychedelic opener "Can't Keep"; the unhinged guitar assaults "Get Right" and "Save You"; and the propulsively melodic "Green Disease" and "Cropduster." Elsewhere, "Thumbing My Way" and the gorgeously bittersweet closer, "All or None," reveal the band's deft dynamic touch, trading power chords for acoustic strumming and Hammond B3 organ flourishes.

Produced by Adam Kasper, who had previously worked with Matt Cameron in both Soundgarden and the drummer's side band, Wellwater Conspiracy, the album also finds the group realizing its collective creativity to an often stunning degree, with myriad songs that find little basis in any prior Pearl Jam album. "You Are," penned by Cameron, is a monster of jagged guitar outbursts fed through a drum machine and welded to a gritty groove, while Jeff Ament's "Help Help"

T1B

careens from sweetly sung verses to maniacal choruses and an even more intense instrumental breakdown.

"When somebody has a clear idea what a song is going to be, inevitably the band will say, 'Well, I don't know. Let's try something else,'" Gossard says with a laugh. "Instead it will be some riff you've played three times. You just wrote it this morning and don't even care about it, but everyone will say, 'That's killer! Let's do that!' The process of letting go is constant in this band. Sometimes you have to."

The sessions got an extra boost of experimentation thanks to the presence of keyboardist Kenneth "Boom" Gaspar, whom Vedder met and quickly began collaborating with in 2001 in the midst of a yearlong sabbatical to a remote Hawaiian island. One of their songs, "Love Boat Captain," serves as the album's emotional centerpiece, as it reaches out to the families of the nine fans who were killed after a crowd surge during Pearl Jam's June 30, 2000, set at Denmark's Roskilde Festival.

"I started disappearing into surfing areas about five or six years ago, as a way to refuel whatever I'd lose being around a lot of people," Vedder says. "I'd just go where there was no people. This place where there's no stoplights. It's very small-town living. I met this big kahuna–type guy on the island. His friend was this other guy who was a musician. There was another guy on the island who was recording some of the locals there. He passed away; a young guy. He left a wife and kid. I would never go to functions or whatever, but I went to this wake on a big porch. Musicians were playing all night; the guys he had recorded. It was pretty intense and very sad. I noticed this guy playing B3, just world class! I bumped into him a couple other times, and then I threw it out there that we should play sometime. I had a little recording setup for when I wanted to get away and do some writing. He just showed up, and we started playing. That night we wrote what turned into 'Love Boat Captain.' Within an hour, we

had this thing we put on the stereo and played it loud. It was probably about an eleven-minute version at that point."

Prior to meeting Vedder, Gaspar had never heard of Pearl Jam, much less recorded with a multiplatinum rock band. Vedder says, "Without really any knowledge of our band dynamic—although I have to admit, since it's such a solid one, it's a little easier to fit in—he was able to find his place and was doing just what we were: adding things and not subtracting."

When it came time to write lyrics, focusing more on the bigger picture—love, loss, and the struggle to make a difference—eased Vedder into the prospect of commenting directly on such tragedies as Roskilde or the terrorist attacks of September 11, 2001. "You start feeling like, 'What do I have to say? What is my opinion?'" Vedder muses. "Then I realized I did have an opinion. Not only did I have one, but I felt like it was formed by processing a lot of information and having good influences.

"You'd think it'd be easy, with so much material out there and so much in the atmosphere to choose from and write about," he continues. "If you think about it, it's all very confusing and overwhelming to try to grasp it all and put it down."

The job ahead was made even more difficult thanks to a conversation with a familiar face at Neil Young's 2001 Bridge School Benefit. "I saw Michael Stipe. Of course, we drank a lot," Vedder recalls. "At the end of the night, he said, 'Write a great record.' And then all of a sudden I was like, 'Oh, fuck. That's going to be tough.'"

Cameron says "I Am Mine" was a key starting point. "It has all the elements this band is known for: strong lyrics, strong hook, and a good sense of melody." Mike McCready adds, "It's kind of a positive affirmation of what to do with one's life. I'm born and I die, but in between that, I can do whatever I want or have a strong opinion about something."

"Can't Keep" was debuted by Vedder on ukulele during two solo concerts in early 2002, but the slow-burning track is transformed here with layers of buzzing, treated guitars and a rumbling beat in the vein of Led Zeppelin's "Poor Tom," which would have fit nicely on the band's 1996 album No Code. Vedder's ukulele demo was the first song on a tape of

ideas he gave to the rest of the band and was quickly seized upon by Gossard as one that would be "killer" if it could be translated to the full band.

"This is the cool thing about letting yourself go and not trying to maintain control over your vision," Vedder says. "Sometimes you write a song, and you have a certain way you hear it in your head. The ukulele version of 'Can't Keep' is much faster. It's much more punk rock than what it ended up, for sure. And that's okay. You can almost feel the band feeling each other out and building together."

In contrast, Vedder's acoustic ballad "Thumbing My Way" was barely modified from its original demo and captured on tape during one of the band's first run-throughs. "We were out in the room playing the song and learning it," Ament recalls. "In the process, Adam went and remiked everything very covertly. So all of a sudden, when we were ready to play it, it was up, and he captured it. Nailed it. That to me was really critical and kind of how the record sounds. A lot of times, there's that cool thing when you don't quite know the song and everybody is really concentrating. It lasts for four or five takes, and then it's gone. After that, it's all cerebral."

The song also presaged Vedder's acoustic-driven work a few years later on the Into the Wild soundtrack. "'Thumbing My Way' is kind of a beginning in terms of Ed really getting more into an acoustic singer-songwriter thing in a way that you always knew that he could," Gossard says. "He was just finally getting comfortable with the idea that maybe he'd bring a little of that into Pearl Jam. The sentiment of the song is amazing."

Elsewhere, songs like "Save You" and "Green Disease" offer relentless, punk-leaning rock harking back to Pearl

Jam's second and third albums. "I came in with that riff, and we just kind of started jamming on it," McCready says of "Save You," the tale of a mutually detrimental love-hate relationship. "It was a blast to play. The track that actually ended up on there, halfway through the song, Matt lost his headphones. He was going off. That's my favorite part of that song—his crazy drum fills."

With a tinge of Split Enz's new wave–punk hybrid, "Green Disease" finds Vedder trying to make sense of a culture of greed: "I said there's nothing wrong with what you say / Believe me, just asking you to sway / No white or black, just gray / Can you feel this world with your heart and not your brain?"

"It's like, okay, I'm not saying capitalism is what's wrong about this," Vedder says of the song, for which his vision of a superthin and dry sound led him to record the basic track with just Cameron and Ament backing him. "It's more like corporate responsibility. You can't tell me there's not other ways of making it good for everybody."

There's no doubt about the subject of "Bu$hleaguer," a comic swipe at then president George W. Bush, on which Vedder utilizes a spoken word delivery for his pointed opinions in the verses: "A confidence man, but why so beleaguered? / He's not a leader, he's a Texas leaguer." Although it would become most closely associated with Vedder once he began performing it live while wearing a Bush mask, the song was actually written by Gossard.

"It's so satirical," he says. "The four-on-the-floor drum feel that Matt is playing—he's playing a kick drum pattern we don't have a lot of in our songs. The groovy, spooky outro is kind of a different thing." Adds Ament, "Everything Stone brought in was kind of dark. The one lyric he had was, 'Blackout weaves its way through the city.' That's a totally heavy line. The way Ed wrote lyrics around that, they were almost kind of humorous. It made the song even creepier to me."

On the other end of the spectrum is a song like "You Are," which remains one of the strangest-sounding Pearl Jam tracks ever. It features reverb-soaked guitar riffing

and a funky, strutting beat, while the middle break finds Vedder in multitracked falsetto, repeating the title phrase.

"I had gotten a new drum machine that allows you to make up patterns, and then they'll play through whatever audio instrument you plug in," Cameron says. "It was more of an experiment to use the parameters of this machine as well. It came out really cool, and the guys really liked it. I took my machine down to the studio, dumped it into the computer, and did an arrangement. Eddie finished up the small bit of lyrics I had written for it. It's just another example of having your band elevate your music to a level you've never envisioned."

Says Gossard, "It was a moment of inspiration, for sure."

Adds McCready, "Perspiration for me! I was blown away by it. It kind of reminded me a little of the Cure, maybe, or something that this band has never really experimented with before. I was real excited and proud to play that song to all my friends, you know, 'Check this one out! This is a way different kind of vibe.'"

GHOST

THE MIND IS GREY,.. LIKE THE CITY
PACKING IN AND OVERGROWN
LOVE IS DEEP,..   DIG IT OUT
STANDING IN A HOLE ALONE

WORKING FOR SOMETHING
THAT ONE CAN NEVER HOLD
A FACE IN THE CLOUDS
GOOD PLACE TO HIDE OH MY OH

SO IM FLYING   away away
      DRIVING   away away

FINDING HOPE IN WAYS I MISSED BEFORE

THE TV,..   SHE TALKS TO ME
BREAKING NEWS AND BUILDING WALLS
SELLING ME,..   WHAT I DONT NEED
I NEVER KNEW SOAP MADE YOU TALLER

SO IM WRITING   away away
      HIDING   away away

SO MUCH TALK IT MAKES NO SENSE AT ALL

MY SENSES GONE AWOL

SO IM RIDING   away away
      DRIVING   away away
PASSING NEW FRIENDS I WON'T KNOW AGAIN

IT DOESNT HURT,...   WHEN I BLEED
BUT MY MEMORIES THEY EAT ME
IVE SEEN IT ALL BEFORE
BRING IT ON CAUSE IM NO VICTIM

DIVING
 DYING

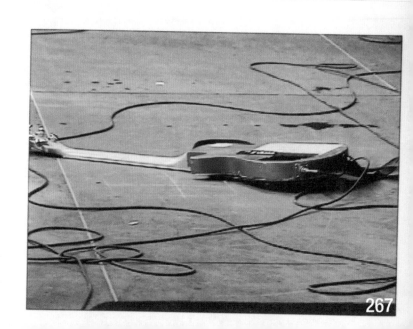

CHAPTER 2003

2003

For the first time in three years, Pearl Jam hit the road hard in 2003, delighting fans with marathon shows featuring ever-changing set lists packed with rare songs. Historic venues and milestones seemed to inspire the band, with tour highlights including a July run at New York's Madison Square Garden that yielded a live DVD, and an October benefit show at the Santa Barbara County Bowl that featured Chris Cornell's first performance of "Hunger Strike" with the full Temple of the Dog lineup in more than eleven years. But Pearl Jam's open criticism of President George W. Bush's policies, specifically the nascent Iraq War, didn't sit well with some listeners still grappling with the impact of the September 11, 2001, terrorist attacks. Keeping that dialogue going with its fans was foremost in the band's mind as the 2004 presidential election loomed, and Pearl Jam was committed to using its voice to make a difference.

February 8–9
Brisbane Entertainment Centre, Brisbane, Australia

Pearl Jam begins a world tour in support of *Riot Act* with ten shows in Australia and five in Japan, its first in this part of the world with Matt Cameron on drums. Former Smiths guitarist Johnny Marr opens the Australian portion with his new band the Healers, as does Betchadupa, featuring Neil Finn's son Liam. Covers debuted on this trek include the Clash's "Know Your Rights" and Creedence Clearwater Revival's "Fortunate Son." For the first time on this tour, the Ten Club expands the official bootleg program to include next-day access to unmastered MP3s from concerts as a perk for purchasing the CD versions.

Eddie Vedder: I can recall Johnny Marr's band going to the beach and swimming in the same outfits they played the shows in. And I'm not talking shorts and T-shirts.

February 11

Eddie Vedder's covers of the Ramones' "I Believe in Miracles" and "Daytime Dilemma," with backing by Zeke, are released on Columbia's *We're a Happy Family—A Tribute to Ramones.*

February 18

Chan Marshall's sixth album as Cat Power, *You Are Free,* featuring vocals by Eddie Vedder on the songs "Good Woman" and "Evolution," is released by Matador Records.

Chan Marshall: I think it's the disconnection between men and women with each other which is the reason for problem marriages, abused children, neglected love, mistrust, lies, and infidelity. That missed connection is why "Good Woman" was written. Having Eddie sing on the track really helped show the flip side of what's important about men and women in relationships.

February 23
Burswood Dome, Perth, Australia

Pearl Jam invites Mark Seymour of Australian band Hunters & Collectors onstage to perform that group's "Throw Your Arms Around Me," which Pearl Jam has been playing at shows since 1992.

April 1
Pepsi Center, Denver

The North American leg of the Riot Act tour begins and generates immediate national media attention after an unknown number of fans reportedly get up and leave when Vedder dons a George W. Bush mask and the band plays "Bu$hleaguer." The *Rocky Mountain News* also reports that Vedder "impaled" the mask on his microphone stand. The incident occurs less than a month after the Dixie Chicks told a

London concert audience that they were against the just-underway Iraq War and were "ashamed that the president of the United States is from Texas." Country radio stations promptly blacklist the group, previously one of the genre's most played artists.

Eddie Vedder: It was our first show since the war started. I come out with the mask on and do a dance, a little moonwalk, to let people see George Bush with rhythm, being free. But I can't sing through the mask. So I take the mask off, take the mike off the stand, and set the mask on there. I have to be gentle, because I want the mask facing forward. Then I sing to him. Somehow, this was interpreted as "impaling."

The review said something like, If you are a music fan on this planet, if there were anywhere on the Earth that you would have wanted to be, tonight at the McNichols Arena or whatever is the place you should have been. It was this glowing review. A day or two later, he wrote this other piece that said, "Fans Jam Exits in Response to Anti-Bush Song." Same guy. So, the thing about safety of the people in the crowd after going through Roskilde, that was a sensitive issue for us. And for him to suggest that there was any kind of danger involved was beyond insulting, but we took it very seriously. And then if you read the article, he said, "Dozens of fans went to the exit." Now, mind you, it was already, like, the second encore or something, but to say dozens of fans? I think there were 18,000 people there. The story could have been, "17,250 People Loved the Anti-Bush Song." But once it was written that way, I guess right-wing media took it as just another thing to jump on that we were anti-American and antipatriotic, and that became an issue.

Nicole Vandenberg: It was an interesting time in the country. We'd had 9/11 happen. We were at war. People were afraid and angry and uncertain. Music and artistic performances have always been a place where people grapple with, and question, the big issues of the day. And the band was doing that. But there was a local media report of the audience's response to the performance of "Bu$hleaguer" that seemed to me misleading even if it wasn't illegal. Suddenly you could see how these things happened: how a nonincident

could be made into one with a good headline. I was afraid that this would have a nonproportional quieting effect on musicians and citizens in general, which was not useful at a time when people needed to be asking tough questions and speaking out. I was very proud of the band's resistance to that. It would have been so much easier to shut up and do nothing.

April 3
Ford Center, Oklahoma City

"Deep" is played live for the first time since October 7, 1995, while "Driftin'" is played for the first time since its live debut at the 2001 Bridge School Benefit concert.

April 11
Sound Advice Amphitheatre, West Palm Beach, Florida

"Glorified G" returns to the set list for the first time since November 17, 1996.

April 12
House of Blues, Orlando, Florida

Pearl Jam plays a rare small club show, which is broadcast online two days later via RealNetworks. Vedder offers a solo ukulele rendition of the Who's "Blue Red and Grey."

April 19
Hi Fi Buys Amphitheatre, Atlanta

Longtime Pearl Jam collaborator Brendan O'Brien joins the band on organ for just the third-ever performance of Mother Love Bone's "Crown of Thorns."

April 23
Assembly Hall, Champaign, Illinois

The Police's "Driven to Tears" is played for the first time since June 25, 1992.

April 30
Nassau Coliseum, Uniondale, New York

Once again "Bu$hleaguer" meets with an adverse reaction from the audience

at the start of the second encore, with boos clearly heard throughout the venue. Vedder replies, "You didn't like that one. I don't understand. Maybe you like him 'cause he's gonna give you a tax cut. Maybe you like him because he is a real guy, that relates to you, because he is so down home." The audience begins chanting "USA, USA!," to which Vedder responds, "I'm with you. USA. I just think that all of us in this room should have a voice in how the USA is represented. And he didn't allow us our voice. That's all I'm saying. We love America. I am up on a stage in front of a big crowd. I worked in a goddamned drug store. I love America, right? This is good, this is open, honest debate, and that's what it should be. If we keep this back and forth, good things will happen. If you don't say anything, you don't know what will happen. 'Cause we are on the brink of forever. And if we don't participate in where this thing is going, when we are the number one superpower in the world, you want to have a part in it and make sure it is a good thing, yeah? Plus or minus, be active. This is a good thing." The band plays two more songs ("Know Your Rights" and "Rockin' in the Free World") before Vedder slams down the microphone in clear frustration and leaves the stage three songs early, according to the printed set list.

Matt Cameron: There was a hail of quarters being thrown at us, and that was the first time at a Pearl Jam show where, like, I felt the crowd was really mad, and they were trying to hurt us.

Mike McCready: I've been booed offstage a few times in my life. And once was in Shadow. Nassau Coliseum reminded me of that a little bit, but it was a little more scary because it was a bigger crowd. It was more passionate in that we were somehow being anti-American, anti–Bush values. Another thing I love about Ed is he'll write a song like that. And he'll back it up with logic and demeanor, and he means what he says. I remember there was one fireman in the front row, and he was, like, showing me his badge. He looked at us like, "You've betrayed us." I felt like as Americans, we should have the right to say what we have to say. And "Bu$hleaguer" was the example of that, we thought. People didn't agree with it, and they were bummed with us. And we probably lost a lot of fans that night. That was another one of our dark chapters.

Eddie Vedder: It felt like it was part of the conversation. I felt like we were communicating, and it really didn't bother me for a second. And it was only until other members of the band expressed discomfort that I had to take it into account and understand what other people were feeling, because I didn't feel it at all. We had done that song many, many times and had nothing but positive things, and then all of a sudden . . . I think that's what was shocking.

Jeff Ament: I've been in bands where we got booed. Green River would open up for the Dead Kennedys or Public Image, and people were there to see them and not you. Even in this band a little bit, on the first couple weeks of that Chili Peppers tour. But not like what happened at Nassau. I actually walked offstage and felt great. That was a brand-new experience. Killer. We got booed standing up for something we wholeheartedly believed in. At least from my end of it, and I know from Ed's end of it, I felt one hundred percent proud of that song and what we were saying, especially when we were saying it. At that time, the freedom of speech and all that stuff; people were afraid, including some people in our camp. And rightly so. I don't have kids. Within the band, there were a lot of different things going on, and I don't think everybody was that psyched about getting booed. But I was totally fine with it. I was ready to go out and open up with that fucking song every night. I was proud of it. I wasn't going to be a part of something and then take it back. We recorded the song and put it on a record, and that's how we felt.

May 3
Bryce-Jordan Center, State College, Pennsylvania

Pearl Jam wraps the first leg of the Riot Act North American tour with a thirty-six-song, three-hour-and-thirty-eight-minute show, the longest concert of its career to this point. The three encores alone encompass seventeen songs, including the first performance of "Satan's Bed" since October 7, 1996, and the first "Mankind" since October 22, 2000. The performance is released commercially on July 15.

273

May 7

Pearl Jam's website begins selling the DVD *Live at the Showbox,* filmed December 6, 2002, at the Seattle club. It is made available through traditional retail outlets on June 30.

May 13

Mike McCready goes public with his fifteen-year battle with the debilitating gastrointestinal disorder Crohn's disease during a speech at the Northwest Chapter of the Crohn's & Colitis Foundation of America's (CCFA) third annual Many Faces of Hope luncheon in Seattle. McCready says he finally summoned the courage to talk about Crohn's after meeting the previous fall with others who had the disorder at the Painted Turtle, a Los Angeles–area camp founded by actor Paul Newman and Page Adler for children with chronic diseases.

Mike McCready: The stories they told me were far worse than what I've experienced. One kid was fourteen and had had six surgeries and still wasn't cured. I wanted to put myself out there and say, "I've had a career in spite of Crohn's disease." I learned from these kids, and that gives me a lot of strength and hope.

May 28
Adams Field House, Missoula, Montana

The second North American leg of the Riot Act tour gets under way in Jeff Ament's home state.

May 30
General Motors Place, Vancouver, Canada

Despite earlier claims that it would be retired, "Bu$hleaguer" returns to Pearl Jam's live set list without incident.

Stone Gossard: We still pull the song out at some of our shows. We don't like to restrict ourselves about what we can and cannot play. Ed hasn't been doing it with the animation of the Bush mask and the theatrics that were associated with it before. Now he allows people to focus more on the song and less on the controversy surrounding it. That's been the right choice at this time for us.

June 3
Verizon Wireless Amphitheatre, Irvine, California

Former Pearl Jam drummer Jack Irons makes his first appearance with his ex-bandmates since exiting in 1998 when he mans the kit for "Rockin' in the Free World."

Jack Irons: There was a five-year period where I had at most three or four conversations with the guys in Pearl Jam. At most. When I left, it wasn't totally understood what I was going through. On another level, all of those guys were going through things in their own lives. So it was hard for them to get involved in my journey. I sort of just left it. I started thinking, Man, are they ever going to call me? But I thought, This is stupid. I have to just go down there and say hi. If I go down there and show them how much better I'm feeling and doing, and where I was at that time is really not who I am . . . those guys mean a lot to me. That's what happened. I ended up going down there, and they were really happy to see me.

June 5
San Diego Sports Arena, San Diego

Back in the city where he began playing music professionally, Vedder reminisces fondly about seeing Ted Nugent, Kiss, the Who, David Bowie, and Cheap Trick in this venue. To start the third encore, Vedder utilizes a loop pedal to build the nine individual wordless vocal parts of the *Riot Act* track "Arc," a tribute to the victims of the Roskilde tragedy that had never been played live. This performance, and the eight others that followed (one for each person killed at Roskilde), are omitted from the official bootlegs of the 2003 shows.

Eddie Vedder: There's no words because there's no words for what that situation was. It's kind of like a prayer.

June 20
Wrigley Field, Chicago

Eddie Vedder makes his second appearance in the press box at a Chicago Cubs game to sing "Take Me Out to the Ballgame." The crosstown Chicago White Sox defeat the Cubs 12–3.

July 1
Nissan Pavilion Stone Ridge, Bristow, Virginia

Sandwiched between "Blood" and the Clash's "Know Your Rights," "Why Go" reappears in the set list for the first time since November 7, 1995.

July 2–3, 11
Tweeter Center, Mansfield, Massachusetts

Pearl Jam begins the first of three shows outside of Boston by challenging itself to play each of the one-hundred-plus songs in its current repertoire without repeating any during the run. The first two concerts have no songs in common but feature only fifty total tracks, due to the area noise curfew. To make up for lost ground, Pearl Jam plays two sets during the third show: a twelve-song mostly acoustic set prior to opening act Sleater-Kinney packed with rarities like "All Those Yesterdays," "Driftin'," and "Off He Goes," and thirty-three more songs during its regular set later in the night.

Eddie Vedder: It would be a lot easier to play a similar set every night. It would be so much easier on all of us. And yet we can't find it in ourselves to do that. We just can't. And whether I'm the driving force behind that feeling of not repeating ourselves, even if we hadn't played in the place for ten years, I don't want to play the same songs we played ten years ago, except for maybe some of the ones that they like to hear, you know? Johnny Ramone had a thing about letting people hear the songs they've come to know and love. And that was one of the things I kind of acquiesced to over the years; putting in hit songs. I mean, I guess if you've got them, you should play them. But not all on one night [*laughs*].

When you get to the size of the places that we're playing, you want to make it enjoyable for all so they can rock out to the songs that they fell in love to, and songs that got them through things, just like songs did for me. And so you play those. It becomes a real Rubik's Cube kind of thing. A set list back in 1991 or '92 was ten songs long. And in '94, they were twenty songs long. And that was still all the songs we knew how to play. Now there's more

† DON'T GO - 72 G / D

- ANIMAL - 53 G

Θ E. FLO - 72 G 🎯

- R. VIEW - 53 G / Ed

- WHIP'N - 53 G / Ed

- SMALL TN. - 53 G / Ed

- DIS'DENT - 53 G

ONCE - 53 G

- Y. GO - 53 G

- JEREMY - 53 G

STATE - 53 G

- GLOR G. - STRAT / DG

- DAUGHT - AC / GG

- BLOOD - 69 B / GG

- DEEP - 72 G / E SLIDE

? ⒶLIVE - 53 G

- RATS - 53 G

LEASH - 72 G / D

HARD TO I. - 53 G

- INDIF - 53 G

- BLACK - 53 G

OCEANS - 72 G / D

GARDEN - 69 B / DROP D

- FOOTSTEPS - 53 G

W. M. A. - 69 B / EADGAE / Ed / Ebo

BREATH - 53 G

- RELEASE - 53 G

speed WASH - 53 G

- NOT 4 U - 53 G / Ed

- CORD - 53 G / Ed

~~BLACK - Θ - 53 G~~

- ALREADY IN LUV - 53 G

- T. CHRIST - 53 G

- B. MAN - 53 G / Ed

- IMMORT. - 53 G / Ed

- LUKIN - 53 G / Ed

- I GOT SHIT - 53 G / Ed

- LAST EXIT - 53 G

NOTH'N' MAN - EADGCD w/ kpaw 5th ADGCFG work w/stone

YELLOW LED

- LONG ROAD

LEANING HERE

F. UP - 72 G / DROP D

SONIC - 53 G

ROCK'N - 53 G

THE KIDS - Ed

- BABA - 53 G

I GOT U - 53 G / Ed

THR. YR ARMS - Ed

ACT OF LOVE - 53 G

CATH. BOY - 53 G

MY LOVE - 53 G / Ed

LONG ROAD

CEREMONY

~~LAST X~~ SPIN

THUMBER

ANIMAL

~~DEEP~~ WHY GO

JEREMY

Better Man

~~NOTHING~~

~~GLORIFIED~~

LUKIN

NOT 4 U

WHIPPIN'

GLORIFIED

DAUGHTER

Don't Go > ALIVE

IMMORT

BLOOD

_____

BLACK

I GOT SHIT
(porch)

275

than one hundred. So the puzzle gets more detailed. The strokes are finer, and there's an art to it. It would be great to just think of the audience as your blank canvas, and that you can paint whatever you want on it. But they deserve more than just scribble.

Jeff Ament: Boston '03 was an exercise in challenging ourselves. It was a shitload of work, but really fun—even when something ended up as a trainwreck.

July 8–9
Madison Square Garden, New York

Pearl Jam makes its first visit to "the world's most famous arena" in nearly five years, and the crowd responds so loudly that the stage literally shakes during the first show, which is filmed for future release. "I was just told that it's only bounced like that for a few other people, and they were Grateful Dead, Iron Maiden, and Bruce Springsteen," Vedder says. "We're really proud to be part of that group, but I've gotta tell you—it scared the fuck out of us!" Surprise guest Ben Harper joins the band for "Daughter" and "Indifference" during night one, which also features "Crown of Thorns" and a furious run through the Who's "Baba O'Riley" with all of the arena lights turned on. The July 8 show runs so long that the band is fined $14,000 for breaking curfew, although the fee is waived by the venue and promoter. Earlier that night, Vedder, Ament, and McCready sing with opening act the Buzzcocks on their song "Why Can't I Touch It?"

Eddie Vedder: The Buzzcocks were a big influence. I had met them ages ago when I was a stagehand, and they remembered. I begged them to play the song "Why Can't I Touch It?" Apparently the singer Pete Shelley thought I was going to sing it. The song started, and he looked at me on the side of the stage. I shook my head no. I have a recording of it as he yells out, "You bastard!"

Ben Harper: I've never before or since seen or felt anything like the stage shaking. I was sitting on the stage, and it went from a shake to a bounce. I get chills thinking about it. Heavy road cases started jumping. It was intensity and excitement and all of a sudden, for a second, it felt downright dangerous.

The turbulence on the airplane was getting just a little bit too heavy. I looked around, and everyone is just jumping and throwing their fists. It was like, you know what? If this is how I have to go, I'm cool with that. It was a moment.

Tim Bierman: It's incredible to be in the Garden on a Pearl Jam night and go out among the fans and hang out with them. I'm just a fan like they are. I'm not looking at how much money the merch stand is taking in. I'm there for the music. I love knowing that I'm involved with each one of those people. I feel like I'm spreading the joy.

July 14
PNC Bank Arts Center, Holmdel, New Jersey

The final North American show on the Riot Act tour sports one of the most unusual Pearl Jam set lists ever. The concert begins with the first performance of the *Ten*-era B-side "Wash" since September 5, 2000, and goes on to feature two songs from each Pearl Jam studio album in chronological order ("Once" and "Even Flow" from *Ten,* followed by "Go" and "Dissident" from 1993's *Vs.,* and so on). Even "I Got Id" from the Pearl Jam–Neil Young album *Mirror Ball* is wedged into its proper place between "Corduroy" and "Nothingman" from 1994's *Vitalogy,* and "In My Tree" and "Present Tense" from 1996's *No Code.* During the second encore, the band dusts off Temple of the Dog's "Hunger Strike" for its first complete performance since Lollapalooza 1992, with Sleater-Kinney's Corin Tucker handling Chris Cornell's vocal parts as the crowd screams with delight.

Corin Tucker, Sleater-Kinney guitarist/vocalist: It was wild. It was like a crazy dream I was having. I think it was Matt Cameron's idea for me to sing that song, and at first I was like, "Really?" And that's what's so fun about all of those guys. They're so game. They're up for anything.

July 17–19
Palacio De Los Deportes, Mexico City, Mexico

Pearl Jam completes its Riot Act tour in Mexico. The band holds a rare press

conference with Latin American media before the first show, discussing its first-ever visit to Mexico, US politics and patriotism, as well as the band's history and experiences. Afterward, everybody celebrates with a karaoke party.

Mike McCready: The crowd was fantastic. I recall many lighters being flicked in unison. First time I ever saw that.

Corin Tucker: There was all this crazy, illegal Pearl Jam merchandise down there. They have no rules there for that kind of thing, basically. We bought these insane, illegal Pearl Jam T-shirts with condoms glued onto them. We decided to wear those for the encore. The guys had all bought those Mexican wrestling masks and came out wearing them while we were doing our set. It was all hijinks and loopy craziness.

August 19

The song "Powerless," featuring Mike McCready on vocals and guitar, Stone Gossard on guitar, Chris Friel of the Rockfords on drums, and Cole Peterson of the Seattle band Sweet Water on bass, appears on the benefit compilation album *Live from Nowhere Near You.* Proceeds benefit homeless and street youth aid initiatives through the charity Outside In. On August 29 the Rockfords perform at Seattle's annual Bumbershoot festival.

September 7
Street Scene Festival, San Diego

Eddie Vedder makes a surprise appearance with R.E.M. to sing "It's the End of the World As We Know It (And I Feel Fine)."

September 9

Matt Cameron and John McBain's Wellwater Conspiracy release a self-titled album through Transdreamer-Megaforce Records.

Matt Cameron: I never would have thought we'd be on our fourth record. It's still a lot of fun, and we enjoy doing it together. There's never been any reason to write a radio single or try to compete in any way. It's just the chance to try to work on your songwriting or just try to

2003

put together some stuff that works as music and can also be fun.

September 16

Official bootlegs from the July 8–9 Madison Square Garden shows and the July 11 Mansfield, Massachusetts, show are released to retail.

October 22
Benaroya Hall, Seattle

Pearl Jam performs a special acoustic concert to benefit the Seattle-based YouthCare Orion Center. The band debuts two new songs: "Man of the Hour," which is set to appear on the soundtrack to the upcoming Tim Burton film *Big Fish,* and "Fatal," a previously unreleased track tipped for inclusion on the upcoming rarities album, *Lost Dogs.* Also on the set list are rarely performed tracks such as "Low Light," "Thin Air," "Around the Bend," "All or None," "Dead Man," and "Parting Ways," plus a cover of a Shel Silverstein song popularized by Johnny Cash, "25 Minutes to Go." The performance is later released on CD in late July 2004 as *Live at Benaroya Hall.*

Jeff Ament: I figure it's only a matter of time before we go out and at least do a few shows that way. It's really fun to play loud, but it's great to play quiet, too.

October 25–26
Shoreline Amphitheatre, Mountain View, California

Pearl Jam makes its sixth appearance at Neil Young's Bridge School Benefit concert, playing mostly covers such as "Last Kiss," Victoria Williams's "Crazy Mary," Bob Dylan's "Masters of War," and the Ramones' "I Believe in Miracles," along with the brand-new "Man of the Hour" and "Long Road," the latter with Young on pump organ.

October 28
Santa Barbara County Bowl, Santa Barbara, California

Pearl Jam welcomes a host of famous friends at a benefit for the Louis Warschaw Prostate Cancer Center at Cedars-Sinai Medical Center. The group is joined by former drummer Jack Irons, Jack Johnson, guitarist Lyle Workman, Red Hot Chili Peppers guitarist John Frusciante,

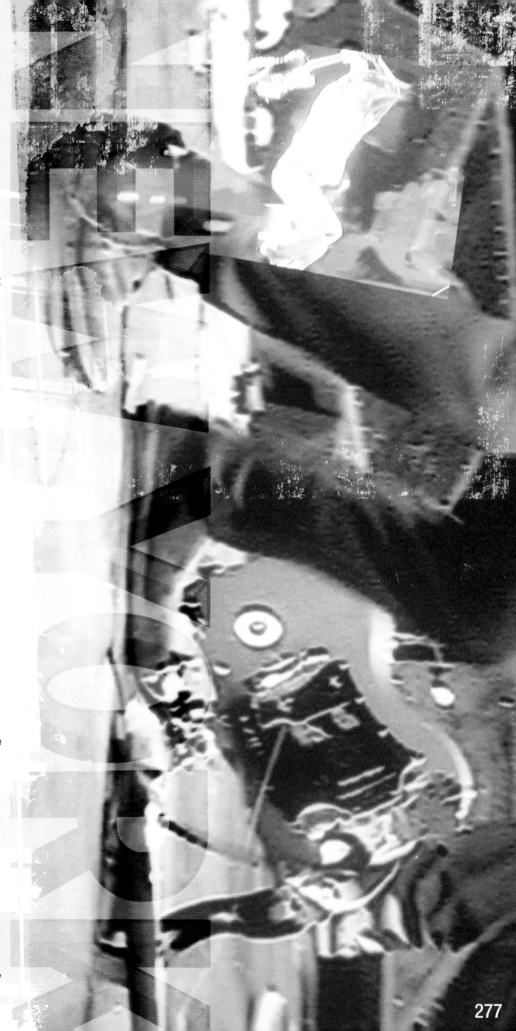

and Soundgarden/Audioslave front man Chris Cornell for a rare Temple of the Dog reunion. ("We didn't invite any of the shitty friends," quips Vedder.) Irons drums on "In My Tree" and "Hail, Hail," two *No Code* songs clearly influenced by his style, while Johnson joins Vedder for "Soon Forget" and "Better Man." After a two-song solo acoustic set, Cornell reprises his duet with Vedder on Temple of the Dog's "Hunger Strike" for the first time since the 1992 Lollapalooza tour, followed by a nearly ten-minute version of the group's "Reach Down." All the guests return for a show-closing collaboration on the Byrds' "So You Want to Be a Rock 'n' Roll Star."

Eddie Vedder: We organized this show to raise funds combating prostate cancer at the request of Johnny Ramone. He was dying, and his friends were doing whatever we could do not just to keep him alive but to make him happy. John Frusciante flew in from thousands of miles away after the end of a Peppers tour. Cornell came up. It was also the day I told loved ones we were expecting a child. It wasn't just a life-or-death gig . . . it was life and death—emotional. Turned out to be the last time Johnny saw myself or the band play live. He was happy, I was proud. I'm thankful he stuck around so my daughter could meet her Uncle John.

November 10

"Man of the Hour," Pearl Jam's contribution to the Tim Burton film *Big Fish,* is released on a CD single backed with Eddie Vedder's home demo of the track, exclusively through the band's website. Amazon.com becomes the exclusive distributor of the single on December 17, although "Man of the Hour" also appears on Sony's *Big Fish* soundtrack, which comes out December 23. The song runs over the end credits of the film, which arrives in US theaters on December 10.

November 11

Pearl Jam unveils two eagerly awaited releases through Epic: the career-spanning rarities collection *Lost Dogs* and the DVD *Live at the Garden,* taped July 8, 2003, at the New York venue.

Jeff Ament: Every record has a group of a dozen songs or so that are works in

progress. Some of them get finished and end up as B-sides or Christmas singles, and some of them never see the light of day. *Lost Dogs* was a great way to get those songs out there.

November 24

Eddie Vedder is one of the judges for MoveOn.org Voter Fund's "Bush in 30 Seconds," a contest to find the most creative and memorable ideas for TV ads telling the truth about President George W. Bush's policies.

December 17
Ed Sullivan Theater, New York

Wellwater Conspiracy performs "Wimple Witch" from its self-titled album on CBS's *Late Show with David Letterman.*

Eddie Vedder: We were all nervous at home watching, and Matt went out and killed it. We were real excited for him.

Christmas

Pearl Jam releases its twelfth fan-club-only seven-inch single, featuring the live version of "Reach Down" with Chris Cornell from the October 28, 2003, show in Santa Barbara as the A-side and a cover of the Ramones' "I Believe in Miracles" on the B-side.

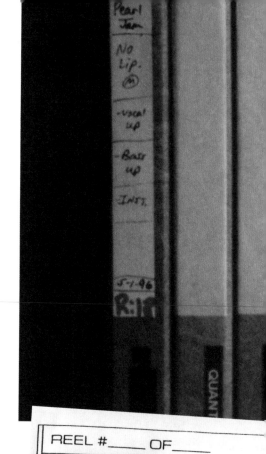

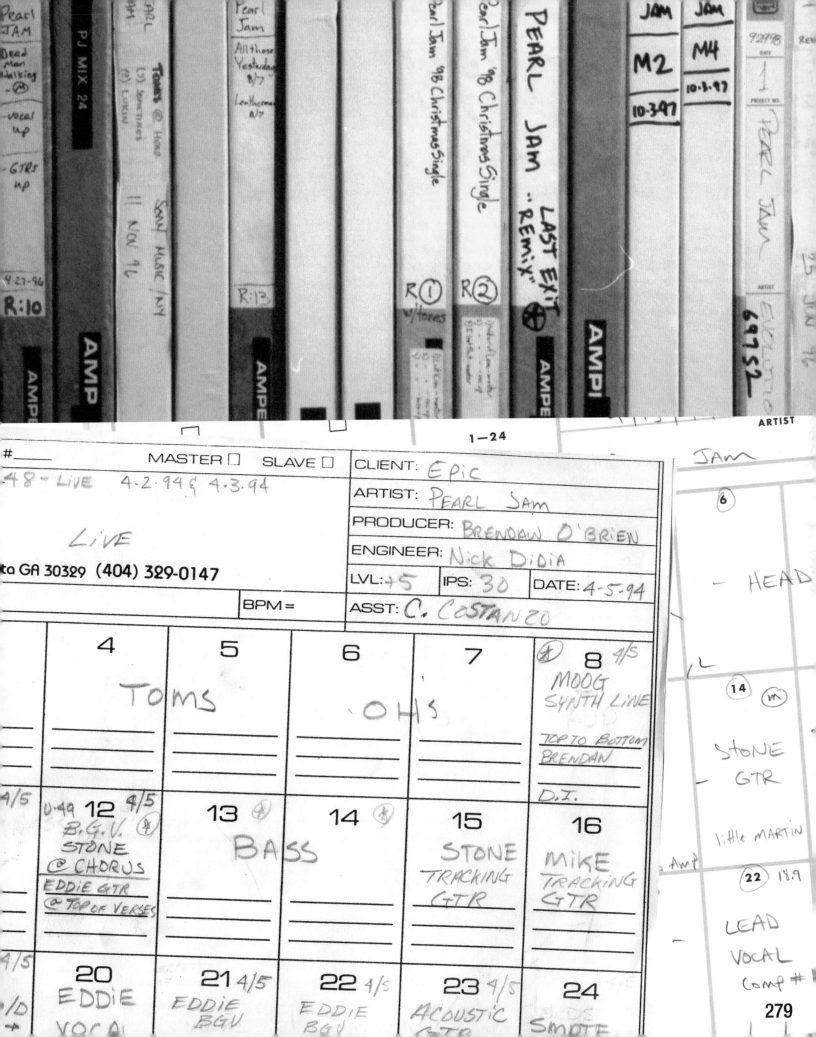

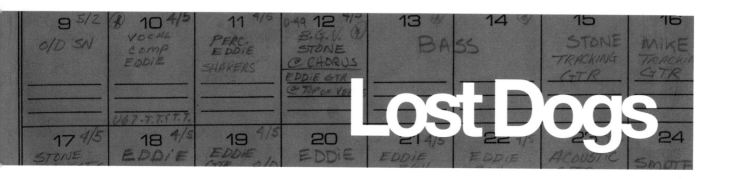

Lost Dogs

In November 2003 Pearl Jam closed out its decade-plus association with Sony Music's Epic Records with a bang, releasing the double-disc, three-and-a-half-hour DVD *Live at the Garden,* as well as a long-in-the-works double-disc rarities set, *Lost Dogs.*

With thirty-one tracks, *Lost Dogs* features eleven songs that had never been released in any form, encompassing outtakes from throughout the band's career. Among them are potent doses of Pearl Jam's harder-hitting side such as the Matt Cameron–penned "In the Moonlight," the *No Code*–era outtake "All Night," the *Ten* reject "Hold On," the anthemic "Sad," and the slow-burning, acoustic-driven "Fatal," the latter two of which were both cut from *Binaural.*

Also included are perennial fan favorites such as "Yellow Ledbetter," "Last Kiss," "Wash," "Footsteps," and "Hard to Imagine," which was recorded for potential inclusion on several Pearl Jam albums but was previously available only on the 1998 *Chicago Cab* soundtrack. The band's frequent benefit album contributions are represented by "Leaving Here," "Gremmie Out of Control," and "Whale Song," while cuts like "Let Me Sleep (It's Christmas Time)," "Driftin'," and "Strangest Tribe" are drawn from the annual holiday singles for members of its Ten Club fan organization. Below, the stories behind some of these overlooked cuts:

"Yellow Ledbetter"—One of Pearl Jam's most popular songs despite being released only on the import "Jeremy" single and never being worked to radio, it still reached seven different *Billboard* charts in the mid-1990s. The slow, bluesy track features borderline indecipherable lyrics from Eddie Vedder and is a frequent closer at the band's live shows.

Mike McCready: It's crazy. In Seattle, KISW had a special featuring Pearl Jam's ninety-nine top songs, and "Ledbetter" was number five. I was just like, "Wow!" That was written around the time of *Ten.* I think that was the second thing Ed and I wrote together. It came out of a jam in the studio, and Ed didn't really have any lyrics. He came up with some ideas right there on the spot, and that's what we recorded. For some reason, it didn't make it on *Ten.* I was kind of bummed at the time. I really wanted it to be on our first record. But at the time, I was really young and just happy to be around this situation, so I did whatever.

Back when we recorded it, we were playing short sets on Lollapalooza and stuff. We wanted to hit them with the really heavy, hard stuff—you know, bam and get off. At club shows, we'd do the record and something like a cover of the Beatles' "I've Got a Feeling." It just kind of got put on the back burner. We in the band forgot about it. But when it came back up, it began to seem like a bookend at the end of the show.

Over the years, it has just gotten immense support, live specifically. People are just into it, and they're singing it. *I* don't even know what the lyrics are! Depending on whatever is going through Ed's head that day, he will change them. It does happen all the time, where he throws in a different verse. I watch people singing it, and they're passionate, and that makes me totally excited and humble. It turned into something without us even trying.

Eddie Vedder: The lyrics to "Yellow Ledbetter" do constantly evolve. I admit that, at times, I have sung total nonsense. The song was originally written about the first Gulf War, and I'd created this image of a young guy with long hair and grunge-wear clothes who had just got a yellow telegram telling him that his brother has been killed in action.

He's walking by these conservative-looking, older folks on a porch, flying an American flag, and he waves to them in a show of solidarity, and they brush him off and give him the finger. So, you know, what did his brother die for?

Jeff Ament: Mike had this killer riff, and I said, "Man, let's work on that thing." It was really Hendrix-y and sort of what we loved about Mike. When we started playing with him, he came over to my apartment, and we worked up a couple other parts to it and maybe played it twice in the studio. Ed just ran all over the top of it, and then the song never got finished. We ended up focusing on these other eleven or twelve songs that ended up on the record. And then six months down the road—I think it was for the "Jeremy" single—we needed a B-side. We weren't recording songs live at that point, so we didn't have anything for a B-side. I had a tape of our takes of the instrumental songs, and that was one of the songs on there. Instead of ending up being the B-side of "Jeremy," which was the last single that we'd released, radio stations grabbed on to that song, and it ended up being huge. I think at the time it was the highest-charting non-album track to chart at rock radio. So it was obvious that we should have worked on that song a little bit more. It probably should have been on the first record. We probably did it a disservice by not putting it on the first record, but that happens every record.

"Last Kiss"—A cover of a J. Frank Wilson and the Cavaliers song from 1964, originally released on the 1998 fan club single and later on the *No Boundaries* benefit album. Improbably, the track reached no. 2 on the *Billboard* Hot 100, making it the biggest hit of Pearl Jam's career.

Mike McCready: It originated from Eddie buying two singles, "Last Kiss" and "Soldier of Love," at the Fremont Antique Mall up here. He brought it in, and we thought it was cool. It has a very fifties/early-sixties vibe to it. Ed also had learned the song "Soldier of Love." We decided to record them at a soundcheck, and I think we did both songs only twice. We did it again that night at a show, but the version we did at soundcheck was better. I wanted to put, like, a Keith Richards thing on the end of it. We decided to keep that and then release it for the Kosovo relief fund. It just blew up. We had no idea.

"Dirty Frank"—A humorous ditty penned on Pearl Jam's 1991 tour with the Red Hot Chili Peppers and Smashing Pumpkins, and clearly inspired by the Peppers' elastic brand of funk rock. It was released on a handful of early import singles and even played live as a lark at a handful of shows.

Mike McCready: We had a bus driver at the time, this guy Frank, who we called "Dirty Frank" because we were scared of him. We thought he may have been a serial killer and he was going to eat *me*. They were just picking on me. And at that time, I was the skinniest guy in the band, so there wasn't a lot of meat on me. We stole that middle part from the Peppers when we were opening up for them, which was one of the most fun tours we've ever done. It was so rad.

"Dirty Frank" reminds me of the whole world opening up in a new way I'd never experienced: going on tour, riding in a bus, and opening for the Peppers. Sometimes Anthony Kiedis would wear a Pearl Jam hat onstage, and it was like, "Oh my God. That's the height of how big we're going to get." I couldn't fucking believe that. I was so psyched. They were supercool to us. It was an amazing time. We just wanted to go out and slay it every night. Getting to go out on that tour was a total dream. It set a lot of our

standards early on for how we wanted to treat bands that opened up for us. I have nothing but love for the memories of that time.

Eddie Vedder: Anthony, Flea, and the Peppers gave us unfathomable amounts of support back in the day. I've never properly expressed my gratitude, though I've tried. It's almost impossible to put into words what that meant to us, and me personally.

"Brother" (instrumental)—An early candidate for *Ten,* having made it as far as the rough mix of the album sent to Epic executives, the song disappeared from the Pearl Jam canon shortly thereafter and is presented here as an instrumental. Six years later, Eddie Vedder finally recorded new vocals for a version that appeared in the spring of 2009 on the deluxe reissue of *Ten.* In this form, "Brother" improbably reached no. 1 on *Billboard*'s Modern Rock chart and, at an August 8, 2009, show in Calgary, Alberta, was played live for the first time in more than eighteen years.

Mike McCready: "Brother" was a big point of contention between Stone and Jeff. I remember Jeff really loving it and Stone either not liking it or being indifferent about it. Jeff and Stone were arguing a lot about this song and were kind of mad at each other. Jeff got so pissed, he went off and started dunking basketballs. It was like, "What's up, dude?" He got really pissed.

It was the typical Stone goes one way, Jeff goes the other way. That is just how they work. They have been together forever, and the dynamic between the two of them makes things work. There was a big, heated argument. But I thought it was a cool song with a cool vibe. It may have been another example of midtempo-itis. I recall the big argument between the two. Jeff said it was almost like he was going to quit. It was serious shit. When it came back up, they didn't argue, but it was kind of being relived in a way smaller way. Stone was still not into it. Ed didn't really like the original lyrics. He was like, "Hey, man, if you want, go in and put some guitar stuff on it." I didn't have really any idea what to do, but I went down and listened to it and thought I'd do some

layered guitars on it, like Brian May of Queen. I guess this is a final chapter and a lyrical burial.

"Let Me Sleep (It's Christmas Time)"— A holiday-themed track released in 1991 on Pearl Jam's first-ever holiday single for members of its Ten Club fan organization.

Mike McCready: I think it was the first thing Ed and I ever worked on. I had just started messing around with open tunings. I had this little part, the main riff, which I'd had for a couple years even before the band started. We just started messing around with it in the studio, and it sounded kind of neat. It's one of those things that just happened. It's just a stream-of-consciousness kind of thing. It was really cold out, around Christmastime. It was my first insight into Eddie's socially conscious type of behavior and thought process. It was just when I was first beginning to get to know him. He was living in our rehearsal space in downtown Seattle. His lyrics were very dark, poetic, and deep and touching. That was my first experience really listening to him on that kind of level.

Eddie Vedder: I was staying at Jeff's apartment that night, but when I got there, I didn't have a key. I sat on the stoop in the cold and wrote the song, thinking of all the other homeless folks in Seattle freezing just like me.

"Down"—A track McCready penned for Pearl Jam's 2002 album *Riot Act,* featuring a strummy, major-key melody in the vein of the Replacements or Wilco. It was released as a B-side on the "I Am Mine" single.

Mike McCready: That's a song I wrote in the studio. In between takes, I just started hitting this riff, which Matt thought was cool. It's a cool song, kind of Social Distortion-y to me. In the end, it didn't seem to fit. I had to let go of wanting to have it on the record. It didn't seem to fit musically with the other songs. I don't know why. I'm still proud of the song, but it didn't seem to work.

Matt Cameron: To me, it sounded like Hüsker Dü or a really nice Bob Mould song. I actually really like that song and was hoping it would make the cut.

Jeff Ament: It really is a different kind of song. That was part of the thing I was having a hard time with, was how it fit in. It's funny you say Hüsker Dü, because I was thinking more like the Replacements or Social Distortion.

Eddie Vedder: It suffered from the "one thing here is not like the others" syndrome. Inspired by the writings of, and friendship with, historian-activist Howard Zinn. For a while, it was my favorite number we recorded for *Riot Act*. I'm not sure how it got cut. It should have been the single.

"Alone"—A midtempo rocker written by Stone Gossard that dates back to the earliest instrumental demos recorded before Eddie Vedder joined the band. It was attempted in the studio during sessions for both *Ten* and *Vs.* but released only as a B-side on the 1993 "Go" single.

Mike McCready: Eddie did sing new lyrics on that. The guitar solo, I think, is a slide with a bottle. It just never really worked, but I don't know why it didn't. I have a videotape of us from years ago, at, like, our third show, playing "Alone." It was actually sounding pretty cool, but we just stopped playing it after a while. I think it's a really good song. For the first record, it may have been too midtempo, along with "Alive" and other songs that were of that same vein.

"Fatal"—An outtake from the 2000 album *Binaural,* marked by a melancholy acoustic melody. The song was played live for the first time during Pearl Jam's October 22, 2003, benefit concert at Seattle's Benaroya Hall.

Mike McCready: Stone wrote that. He sang on the original demo. It sounds very Bowie-ish when he sings, I think. It's just kind of a dark tune. I think he writes a lot of songs that are like that now. I know he writes a ton of stuff on acoustic, and he experiments with different tunings. It's just kind of where his mind-set is. In recent years, he'll bring in those songs as opposed to the heavy riffs like "Animal." Stone has always been pretty dark, but he's also superfunny. There's a mixture of those two kinds of things.

"Gremmie Out of Control"—An endearingly off-the-cuff cover of a Silly Surfers song from 1964, released on the 1996 *MOM: Music for Our Mother Ocean* benefit album.

Mike McCready: I'm not even on that. Brendan O'Brien, our producer, is playing the lead guitar lick. I could not claim to play that great. That's Brendan just making it happen. When I heard it, I was like, "We *have* to have this on here." It's Brendan kicking ass on the guitar.

Eddie Vedder: Stone couldn't play the surprisingly complex guitar part, but he more than made up for it with his wacked-out and fully committed background vocal.

"Sad"—Originally titled "Letter to the Dead," this high-energy, Vedder-written song was dropped from *Binaural* late in the selection process.

Jeff Ament: Just a great pop song. Pretty much every record, Ed will write a great pop song. And a lot of times, those songs end up not fitting the record as much, because we haven't really written very many pop records [*laughs*].

"Sweet Lew"—Basketball obsessive Jeff Ament wrote and sang this groovy number about the life and times of Lew Alcindor, who went on to NBA superstardom as Kareem Abdul-Jabbar. The song started appearing on set lists in 2009, with Vedder dribbling a basketball into a microphone for added oomph.

Jeff Ament: That was a complete song that actually the whole band worked up. It really didn't fit on *Binaural*. I never expected it to be on a record, but I thought it might have been a B-side. I believe it is known as the worst Pearl Jam song of all time!

Eddie Vedder: There's an undeniably wicked-cool chordal bass line by Jeff.

"4/20/02"—Vedder wrote this on guitar using a ukulele tuning the night it was learned that Alice in Chains front man Layne Staley had died after a long battle with drug addiction. The band was in the studio recording *Riot Act* at the time. The cut is a hidden track at the end of "Bee Girl" on some editions of *Lost Dogs.*

Mike McCready: That's Ed by himself. I got a call from Kelly Curtis that Layne died. We were in the studio at probably eleven at night. I wasn't surprised, but I was. It was sad. I hadn't seen him for, like, three or four years. Ed has this guitar kind of tuned like a banjo. He recorded it at, like, two or three in the morning, just with producer Adam Kasper. I think he was just so angry, and he wanted to get it out. I think the reason it's hidden is because he wouldn't want it to be exploitative. I think he wants it to be hidden so you have to find it and think about it.

Stone Gossard: *Riot Act* overall has such a universal feel to it, much more so than some of our other records. Most of the songs are about bigger kinds of things. The energy was feeling so positive, and there was something about the song that felt like it maybe wasn't right for this particular record.

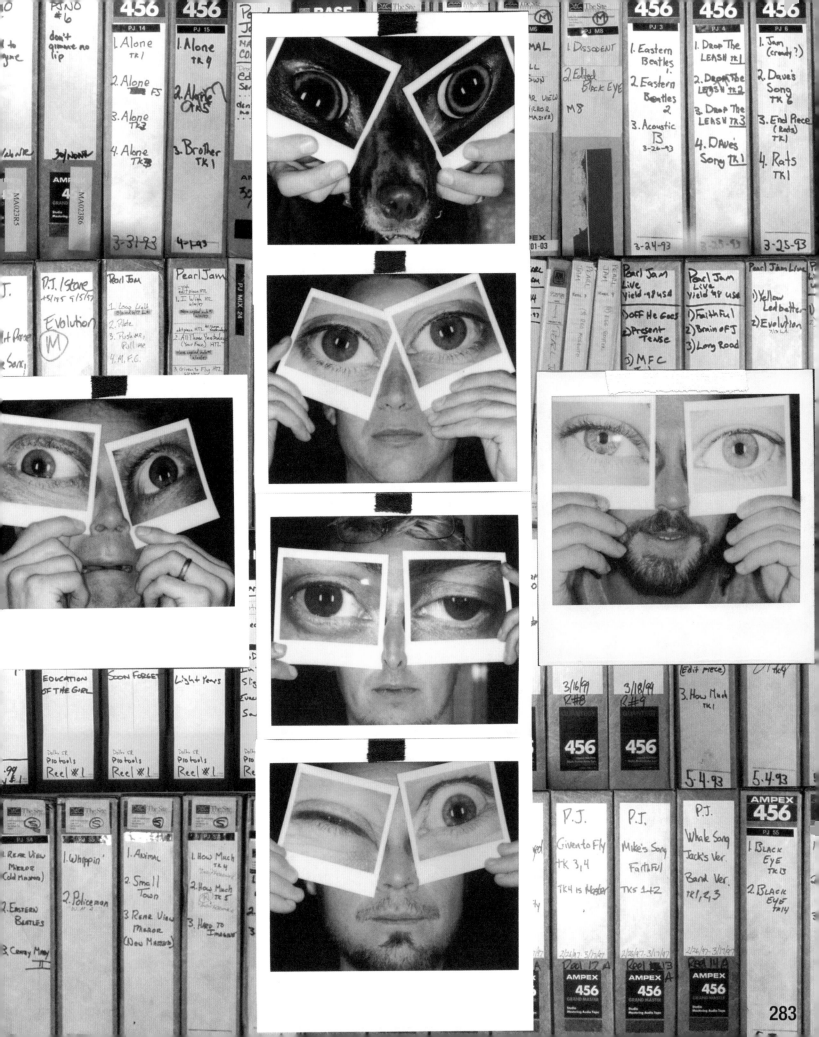

2004

Emboldened by standing up for what it thought was right, even if it meant being booed at shows or pilloried in the press, Pearl Jam was front and center on the Vote for Change Tour in 2004, joining some of the most popular artists in rock 'n' roll for a get-out-the-vote trek through key swing states. "This is the fourth presidential election which Pearl Jam has engaged in as a band, and we feel it's the most important one of our lifetime," Eddie Vedder said at the time. Ultimately, Democrat John Kerry fell just short of winning over incumbent George W. Bush. For the members of Pearl Jam, it was a disappointing defeat. But the process inspired the band both personally and musically, laying the groundwork for new songs that were more powerful than ever.

January 20

Pearl Jam contributes the version of "Bu$hleaguer" from the April 1, 2003, show in Denver that prompted a miniwalkout to *Peter Gammons Presents: Hot Stove Cool Music.* Proceeds from the album benefit the Jimmy Fund, which supports cancer research at Boston's Dana-Farber Cancer Institute.

February 22
Paramount Theatre, Seattle

Mike McCready plays guitar on "Killing Floor" at the opening date of the Experience Hendrix tour, which also features such artists as bluesman Buddy Guy, Jerry Cantrell, Heart vocalist Ann Wilson, Paul Rodgers (Free, Bad Company), and former Hendrix bandmates Mitch Mitchell and Billy Cox.

March 6
Key Arena, Seattle

Mike McCready plays the national anthem in the style of Jimi Hendrix's Woodstock performance before a Seattle Thunderbirds game. A portion of the proceeds from ticket sales benefit the Crohn's & Colitis Foundation of America.

April 9
Westin Seattle hotel, Seattle

Pearl Jam performs in public for the first time in 2004 after receiving an IMPACT award from the Pacific Northwest Chapter of the Recording Academy, in recognition of its significant philanthropic contributions to the area's music scene. The band plays "Last Soldier" for only the second time ever, as well as "Down" and "1/2 Full."

May 6

"Yellow Ledbetter" plays in the background as Jennifer Aniston's character Rachel is about to board a

plane to Paris in the final episode of *Friends,* marking the first time Pearl Jam has ever licensed its music for a television show. The show's producers simply asked permission, which the band granted.

May 14
Showbox, Seattle

Eddie Vedder and Stone Gossard (with his side band Brad) make surprise appearances at Mike McCready's annual benefit concert for the Crohn's & Colitis Foundation of America. After opener Vast Capital, Vedder plays "Parting Ways," "Man of the Hour," the Who's "The Seeker," "Porch," and, with help from Gossard and McCready, "Yellow Ledbetter." On the latter, Vedder plays drums and sings, kicking over the drum kit at the song's end—a drum kit that didn't belong to him.

June

Pearl Jam contributes music to two documentaries. "Go" is featured in Stacy Peralta's *Riding Giants,* a historical documentary of big-wave surfing culture in America. "Down" appears in *Howard Zinn: You Can't Be Neutral on a Moving Train,* produced by Deb Ellis and Denis Mueller, about the life and times of the historian-activist-author.

July 27

Pearl Jam releases *Live at Benaroya Hall,* taped October 22, 2003, in Seattle, via a one-off distribution deal between its own Monkeywrench imprint and BMG Distribution. The following week, *Benaroya* debuts at no. 18 on the *Billboard* 200 with first-week US sales of fifty-two thousand copies, according to Nielsen SoundScan.

August 2
Splashlight studios, New York

The artists involved in the Vote for Change Tour, including Pearl Jam, Bruce Springsteen and the E Street Band, R.E.M., John Fogerty, John Mellencamp, Ben Harper, the Dixie Chicks, Death Cab for Cutie, and the Dave Matthews Band convene for a photo shoot in New York. Unveiled two days later, the tour includes nearly forty shows in nine presidential election battleground states. Although most acts do not explicitly support Democratic nominee Senator John Kerry over President George W. Bush, there is little doubt that this is the intent of the tour. Participating artists also team with the Portland, Oregon–based Bonneville Environmental Foundation to fund several new small-scale solar energy and wind power plants.

Vedder stated at the time, "We believe in the power of the First Amendment and have always exercised our right to free speech in every aspect of our lives and music. This year there is no more powerful way for all Americans to exercise that right than by voting. Given the extreme political climate of a country at war, we are proud to stand among the many artists involved in this tour and to encourage Americans not only to vote for a president, but to vote for the change they wish to see in the world."

Kelly Curtis: We were getting bombarded with requests to play around the election, and I thought I would seek out some advice. So I called Bruce Springsteen's manager Jon Landau to see how they were dealing with all the stuff coming in. The more we talked, the more we thought it would be a good idea to get a bunch of managers together and try to get educated. What came out of there was five managers connecting and deciding that we should try to pull off some kind of swing-state tour. Then it became a logistical nightmare.

August 17

Former Pearl Jam drummer Jack Irons releases his first solo album, *Attention Dimension,* via his own Breaching Whale imprint with distribution assistance from the Pearl Jam organization. Eddie Vedder sings on a cover of Pink Floyd's "Shine On You Crazy Diamond," Stone Gossard plays guitar on "Water Song," and Jeff Ament plays bass on "Dunes."

Jack Irons: I used to think, years ago, it would be really great if I could do something and get my friends to donate parts, because it would make the record way more musically diverse. It just would be interesting for the people, too, to hear it. I got the music to the point where it was like, "Okay, if they say yes or no, this is going to be done." That took, you know, four and a half years! Most of the guests came in at that point where I could say, "What do you think? Can you do something on that?"

September 10
Vera Project, Seattle

Eddie Vedder performs such songs as "Better Man," "Long Road," and "Love Boat Captain" with ten members of the Walmer High School Choir from Port Elizabeth, South Africa.

Eddie Vedder: They were a pure embodiment of the power of music. This music got them through apartheid, and it empowered them to travel abroad and share it. These kids respect the music for the opportunities it has given them. When they sang, it inspired everyone who came into contact with them. The transcendent melodies they invented for "Better Man" and the like was a mind-blow.

September 12
Avalon Hollywood theater, Los Angeles

Eddie Vedder joins the Red Hot Chili Peppers, X, Rancid's Tim Armstrong, Henry Rollins, and the Dickies, among others, at a concert celebrating the Ramones' thirtieth anniversary. Proceeds are donated to the Lymphoma Research Foundation (lymphoma being the form of cancer that Joey Ramone succumbed to in 2001) and the Cedars-Sinai prostate cancer research center in Los Angeles. Vedder is among a group of close friends and family present when Johnny Ramone dies three days later at his L.A. home after a five-year struggle with prostate cancer.

Eddie Vedder: The day he died, he and I watched the Cat Stevens concert DVD *Majikat* and did baseball trivia together. We were very different people, but he really made a tremendous impact on my life.

September 24
Showbox, Seattle

Introduced by Washington congressman Jim McDermott, Pearl Jam plays its first full show since October 28, 2003, in support of No Vote Left Behind, a Seattle-based political action committee raising funds and awareness for the upcoming presidential election. The *Yield*-era B-side "U" is played for just the ninth time, while the band debuts covers of the Avengers' "The American in Me" and X's "The New World," the latter with X's John Doe guesting.

September 28–29
Fleet Center, Boston

Pearl Jam plays two Boston shows before an audience heavy with fan club members, with proceeds benefiting the legal defense fund for the West Memphis Three. The group debuts covers of the Dead Kennedys' "Bleed for Me" and the Germs' "Lion's Share," and also dusts off "Alone" and the Beatles' "I've Got a Feeling" for the first time in more than a decade. During the first show, Howard Zinn appears onstage before "Down," telling the crowd, "Stop the war."

September 30
Ed Sullivan Theater, New York

Pearl Jam plays a gripping rendition of Bob Dylan's antiwar song "Masters of War" on CBS's *Late Show with David Letterman.*

October 1
Sovereign Center, Reading, Pennsylvania

Pearl Jam's stint on the Vote for Change Tour begins, with support from Death Cab for Cutie. The *Lost Dogs* track "Sad" is played live for the first time as part of a set list featuring a wide range of Pearl Jam originals and covers ("Masters of War," "Bleed for Me," John Lennon's "Gimme Some Truth"). The first encore is an acoustic set, beginning a tradition for the rest of the trek. And as he would do for the rest of the shows, Vedder opens the evening playing solo acoustic or electric, this time offering Cat Stevens's "Don't Be Shy" and Bruce Springsteen's "Growin' Up." At one point, he tells the audience, "Johnny Ramone was a hardcore Republican, and we were able to be friends. It's not about hatred or direct opposition, it's about finding the best way through for all of us. And when I say all of us, I mean the whole globe. But if you're going to participate in voting as well as you do in singing along, we don't have to talk about politics at all."

October 2
Sports Arena, Toledo

Neil and Pegi Young, plus Peter Frampton, make surprise appearances on the second Vote for Change show, performing such songs as "Harvest Moon," "All Along the Watchtower," "Act of Love," "Cortez the Killer," and "Rockin' in the Free World" with Pearl Jam. Vedder reads from a newspaper at the start of the show: "Four percent of the whole US population is in Ohio. You account for twenty-five percent of the jobs that have been lost in the last four years. That's staggering. And this is a swing state?"

October 3

DeltaPlex, Grand Rapids, Michigan

Pearl Jam debuts two new covers: James Taylor's "Millworker" and the MC5's "Kick Out the Jams." Holding an American flag thrown onstage by an audience member, Vedder rails from the stage, "I want to be proud of this again. I want to own it—not hollow-bodied patriots putting cheap plastic ninety-eight-cent versions on their SUVs."

October 5

Prior to Pearl Jam's Vote for Change concert at the Fox Theatre in Saint Louis, fans organize a grassroots campaign to meet up and donate supplies for the St. Louis Area Food Bank. The movement becomes known as the Wishlist Foundation and has since raised $400,000 for charitable causes supported by the members of Pearl Jam.

Tim Bierman: Now, at every show, there's some kind of Wishlist get-together. Someone locally hosts a fund-raiser, fans bring Pearl Jam stuff, and they auction it off for charity. The band is such a powerful presence in the philanthropic world, and they have inspired fans to not only gather around the music but to try and make a difference.

October 11

MCI Center, Washington, DC

The Vote for Change Tour wraps with a superstar-packed show only a few blocks from the White House that is broadcast live on the Sundance Channel. Pearl Jam plays a quick five-song set, with John Mellencamp, Kenneth "Babyface" Edmonds, Bonnie Raitt, Jackson Browne, Keb' Mo', Jurassic 5, R.E.M., the Dixie Chicks, James Taylor, Dave Matthews Band, John Fogerty, and Bruce Springsteen and the E Street Band also performing throughout the evening. Vedder joins R.E.M. for "Begin the Begin," and the full company hits the stage for a finale of "(What's So Funny 'Bout) Peace Love and Understanding?" popularized by Elvis Costello, and Patti Smith's "People Have the Power," backed by the E Street Band. The trek raises $15 million for America Coming Together's efforts to raise voter awareness for the upcoming election.

October 13

Continental Airlines Arena, East Rutherford, New Jersey

Eddie Vedder makes a surprise appearance at a Bruce Springsteen and the E Street Band show tacked onto the end of Vote for Change, performing "No Surrender" and "Darkness on the Edge of Town" with the band. He also plays Pearl Jam's "Better Man" backed by Springsteen and company, replete with a Clarence Clemons saxophone solo. "Hello, New Jersey!" Vedder says before "Better Man." "Bruce asked me to do this song, and since he's the boss and I'm the employee, here it is." The crowd responds with a thunderous "Ed-*die*!" chant, which brings a smile to Springsteen's face.

Bruce Springsteen: Eddie joining us was a small revelation. As we broke into "Better Man," it became obvious, as the audience sang loudly along, that they were as familiar with Pearl Jam's music as they were with mine. Our audience had just begun to creep younger, with a lot of kids hearing us for the first time, and realizing there was someplace where two bands crossed over—some common home place—was a nice surprise.

October 14

Eddie Vedder joins twenty-five other artists to write essays for the October 14 issue of *Rolling Stone* about the importance of the upcoming presidential election:

"A year ago it seemed impossible to criticize Bush, because of September 11th. The Dixie Chicks and Michael Moore were attacked for speaking out.

October 5

Pearl Jam's cover of Bob Dylan's "Masters of War" from the 2003 Bridge School Benefit appears on *Songs and Artists That Inspired "Fahrenheit 9/11,"* a companion piece to Michael Moore's film about the Bush administration's response to the September 11, 2001, terrorist attacks. Sony BMG Music Entertainment donates half the net profits from US sales to the Fallen Patriot Fund.

October 8

Silver Spurs Arena, Kissimmee, Florida

Pearl Jam plays its second-to-last gig on Vote for Change and dusts off a cover of the La's' "Timeless Melody" with help from Death Cab for Cutie front man Ben Gibbard.

Now you've got books full of facts that show how Bush has failed. Those people dissenting a year ago were right. We have to stop treating the rest of the world like our subjects. What is the only institution more powerful than the United States government—one that can move things in a different direction? It's the American people. It's the voters. That's what I feel most strongly about: encouraging people who don't normally vote to understand their responsibility."

October 19
Key Arena, Seattle

Eddie Vedder and Mike McCready show up unannounced during the Seattle stop of Michael Moore's Slacker Uprising tour. Vedder plays the Beatles' "You've Got to Hide Your Love Away" and Cat Stevens's "Don't Be Shy," and is joined by McCready for "Masters of War."

October 23–24
Shoreline Amphitheatre, Mountain View, California

Eddie Vedder plays solo at the eighteenth annual Bridge School Benefit concert, joining Neil and Pegi Young both nights for "Harvest Moon" and offering stripped-down versions of "Masters of War,"

"Better Man," "I Am Mine," and even kid music legend Raffi's "Baby Beluga," by request of one of the Bridge School students.

October 26

Pearl Jam contributes a live version of "Better Man" recorded at the Bridge School Benefit to Rhino Records's double-CD benefit album *For the Lady.* The project aims to raise awareness of Nobel Peace Prize winner Aung San Suu Kyi, who had been under house arrest by the government of Myanmar (formerly Burma) since 1989. She was eventually released in November 2010.

November 16

Pearl Jam fulfills its contract with Epic Records via the release of the career-spanning retrospective *Rearviewmirror (Greatest Hits 1991–2003),* which includes three songs from *Ten* ("Once," "Alive," and "Black") remixed by producer Brendan O'Brien. The double-disc, thirty-three-track set sports sixteen Top 10 hits on *Billboard*'s Mainstream Rock Tracks chart, including the number ones "Daughter," "Better Man," and "Given to Fly," as well as twelve Top 10 entries on the Modern Rock Tracks survey.

Jeff Ament: I think those songs changed so much the first couple months we were out touring. That's what was hardest about listening to the record. Not only were the songs slower on *Ten,* they had a really soft sound to them. We felt like it didn't represent us, so here they are, represented via O'Brien's remix.

December 5

Pearl Jam announces that its next studio album will be released "on the BMG label." The deal is actually a one-off joint venture between BMG's J Records and the band's own Monkeywrench label for a studio album, allowing Pearl Jam to experiment with aspects of a self-release in the wake of fulfilling its contract with Sony Music.

December 15

Pearl Jam self-releases *The Molo Sessions,* an album featuring Eddie Vedder's collaborations with the Walmer High School Choir from South Africa. Proceeds benefit Molo Care, a Seattle nonprofit that raises money for schools in Port Elizabeth, South Africa. The album version of "Better Man" is used as the B-side for the 2005 Ten Club holiday single, with a new recording of the classic Motown holiday song "Someday at Christmas" as the A-side.

m-tour-album-tour cycle can be the bane of a rock band's
, but it's a cycle that's often hard to break. For Pearl Jam, that
ity finally came in 2005, when it hit the road for a robust series
without any new music to promote. Work was continuing on its
udio album, but the group opted to let the material simmer rather
the process. In doing so, Pearl Jam realized that simply playing
ithout an album to promote could be a whole lot more fun.
d of the year, the band traveled to South America for its first-ever
the continent. Several of the performances were in stadiums with
rs, the first time that Pearl Jam had played in such places since
lde tragedy. "It was time for us to test those waters again, to make
d feel comfortable," Stone Gossard says. "Everything went smoothly,
crowds were amazing. It gave us a huge jolt of confidence."

y 14

lder joins friends and fans for the
ceremony of Johnny Ramone's
he Hollywood Forever Cemetery
geles. Ramone passed away
er 15, 2004.

y 17
heater, Los Angeles

lder plays a five-song solo
side Tenacious D, Beck, Dave
sh Homme, Chris Rock, and
ll at an American Red Cross
r victims of the recent tsunami
ast Asia. The set includes "I
and four covers: "Last Kiss,"
ens's "Trouble," the Who's "The
and the Beatles' "You've Got
our Love Away," the latter with
Tenacious D's Kyle Gass on
er, all the performers tackle the
s Brothers' "Time Has Come
he Byrds' "So You Want to Be
' Roll Star," and Led Zeppelin's
nes Bad Times."

18
nt Theatre, Seattle

n plays its first show in nearly
ns as part of a benefit for the
st anniversary of the Northwest
which Stone Gossard attended
n. This is the first performance

of a song provisionally called "Crapshoot
Rapture," which would appear in a slightly
different form as "Comatose" on Pearl
Jam's self-titled eighth studio album.

April 8
Showbox, Seattle

Mike McCready's UFO tribute band
Flight to Mars headlines a benefit for the
Northwest Chapter of the Crohn's and
Colitis Foundation of America (CCFA),
raising $18,000.

April 25
Key Arena, Seattle

Eddie Vedder joins new friends Kings of
Leon, who are on tour in support of U2,
on vocals and tambourine for the song
"Slow Night, So Long."

April 29
Easy Street Records, Seattle

In front of a stunned crowd of about
two hundred people, Pearl Jam crams
into this beloved Seattle record store to
play an unannounced show to celebrate
the tenth anniversary of the Coalition
of Independent Music Stores (CIMS).
X's John Doe joins Pearl Jam to cover
his band's "The New World," while
"Crapshoot Rapture" reappears in its
early form. Highlights from the show are

released on an EP, *Live at Easy Street*,
the following year.

Jeff Ament: That room sounded great. We
talked about rebuilding it as a stage set.

May 25
Neumo's, Seattle

Following the Seattle International Film
Festival's screening of the documentary
Rock School, Eddie Vedder and Heart's
Ann Wilson perform songs like the
Ramones' "I Wanna Be Sedated," Pearl
Jam's "Corduroy," and the B-52's' "Rock
Lobster" with students featured in the film.

August 24

Pearl Jam reveals plans to release
high-quality digital downloads of
upcoming US and Canadian shows
on PearlJam.com hours after their
completion. The concerts are made
available without DRM (Digital Rights
Management), so fans can burn them to
CD or transfer them to MP3 players.

August 29
Adams Field House, Missoula, Montana

Pearl Jam performs a benefit concert
in the town where Jeff Ament went to
college, in support of Montana politician
Jon Tester's election bid for the US
Senate. The set list features two of the
rarest songs in the band's catalog: "Bee
Girl," which hadn't been played since
October 20, 1994; and the *No Code*–era
B-side "Black Red Yellow," which had
been played only twice before, and not
since November 24, 1996. Vedder tells
the audience, "It's been a while since we
played live, so while we spend time living
normal lives, we have no idea that there's
this kind of energy out there waiting for
us. So thanks again."

September 1
*Gorge Amphitheatre, George,
Washington*

In preparation for an extensive Canadian
tour, Pearl Jam visits the Gorge for the
first time since September 5, 1993,
playing both acoustic and electric over the
course of a thirty-six-song set. "Hard to

"Imagine" closes the acoustic set, its first performance since September 6, 1998. The *Riot Act* B-side "Undone" is also played for the first time ever later in the show.

Mike McCready: I think it's one of my top three favorite places to play in the world. The drive's a little bit of a pain in the butt, but you get to see the Columbia River Gorge behind you as you're standing onstage, and then you look up and see all these screaming fans looking the other way. There's nothing quite like it. It's quite spiritual, and it's quite fun and rocking.

September 2
General Motors Place, Vancouver, Canada

Pearl Jam begins a three-week Canadian tour with a hits-filled twenty-nine-song set. Vedder joins opening act the Supersuckers to sing X's "Poor Girl" while dressed in a silver suit and white Mexican wrestling mask—a costume he'd trot out throughout the trek. Other highlights of the run include a cover of the Guess Who's "Runnin' Back to Saskatoon" during a September 7 show in the titular city, the debut of the Stone Gossard–sung *Lost Dogs* track "Don't Gimme No Lip" on September 16 in Ottawa, and a Vedder preshow solo song nearly every night. The band's performance of "Given to Fly" from the Saskatoon show aired on the multinetwork *ReAct Now: Music & Relief* special for Hurricane Katrina victims on September 10.

September 19
Air Canada Centre, Toronto

With U2 still in town following a four-night run the previous week, Bono joins Pearl Jam to perform "Rockin' in the Free World" in the second encore. The vocalist emerges to deafening cheers just before the second verse and proceeds to improvise lyrics while the band jams. "It would be difficult to work harder than that man," Vedder says of Bono during an instrumental break. The intense performance ends with Bono chanting "Rock! Rock!" as Mike McCready solos wildly.

Eddie Vedder: Two nights earlier at the same venue, I was asked impromptu to

sing "Ol' Man River" with U2. Then Bono did "Rockin' in the Free World" with us. Who do you think got the better song?

September 28
PNC Park, Pittsburgh

Pearl Jam plays a fourteen-song set opening for the Rolling Stones, whom they'd last supported during a short California run in 1997. Later, Vedder sings "Wild Horses" with the Stones during their own set.

September 30, October 1
Borgata Events Center, Atlantic City

Pearl Jam squeezes into the 2,400-capacity Borgata for two shows, during which band members join opening act Sleater-Kinney for such covers as Bruce Springsteen's "The Promised Land" and Danzig's "Mother." Vedder also covers Springsteen's "No Surrender" and "Atlantic City" during preshow solo performances. At the second show, Vedder debuts the as yet unreleased "Gone," which he'd written in his hotel room the night before; a demo version is released as the B-side on the next Ten Club holiday single. Kiss guitarist Ace Frehley joins the band for "Rockin' in the Free World" to close the October 1 gig.

Eddie Vedder: I was actually sitting down to just learn another song for the next night. I went to learn it, and it didn't come right away, so I started playing something else, and it was "Gone."

October 5
House of Blues, Chicago

Pearl Jam and Robert Plant headline a $1,000-per-ticket benefit for Hurricane Katrina victims, with proceeds benefiting Habitat for Humanity, the American Red Cross, the Jazz Foundation of America, and the New Orleans Musicians' Clinic. During Pearl Jam's second encore, Plant and his Strange Sensation bandmates take over the stage to perform Led Zeppelin's "Going to California" and remain afterward for Elvis Presley's "Little Sister," Barrett Strong's Motown classic "Money (That's What I Want)," Zeppelin's "Fool in the Rain" and "Thank You," and, to close the show, "Rockin' in the Free World," with Plant playing Vedder's Fender Telecaster guitar. "Little Sister" later appears as the A-side of the next Ten Club holiday single.

Mike McCready: It was just one of those moments in my career that you never dream will happen, and that happens and you go, "Wow. I'm very lucky and grateful to be here." "Fool in the Rain" was a hard one to do because that's certainly a well-orchestrated song. And the solo on that, I kind of hacked through it.

November 22–23
Estadio San Carlos de Apoquindo, Santiago, Chile

Pearl Jam starts a twelve-show stadium tour of South America, its first-ever concerts on the continent, with support from longtime friends Mudhoney. In Buenos Aires, Argentina, the audience actually sings key guitar parts from songs like "Even Flow," "Rearviewmirror," and "Do the Evolution," prompting Vedder to say, "We should be paying you for coming here." On November 28 in Porto Alegre, Brazil, the Ramones' Marky Ramone drums on a cover of his former band's "I Believe in Miracles."

Mark Arm: The shows were in soccer stadiums, and they were the first ones that the guys had done since Roskilde, where there weren't assigned seats. In Chile, I remember them being freaked out about what could potentially happen but then feeling relieved afterward that everything went okay.

Christmas

Pearl Jam prepares its fourteenth fan club holiday single featuring a cover of Elvis Presley's "Little Sister" performed with Robert Plant at the Hurricane Katrina benefit in Chicago and a demo of the then unreleased Eddie Vedder composition "Gone."

TESTER
SENATE 2006

PEARL JAM
AUGUST 29, 2005
MISSOULA, MONTANA

KODAK SUPRA 800

CHAPTER 2006

2006

No record label, no contract, no obligations: Pearl Jam was finally free to go its own way with its self-titled eighth album, on which it had worked longer than any other in its history. In the two years since parting ways with longtime home Epic Records, the band experimented with self-releasing music through its Ten Club fan organization. But it didn't yet have the resources at its disposal to put out a proper Pearl Jam album without the help of a traditional label. Enter Sony BMG's J Records, established by legendary music mogul Clive Davis. The band agreed to a short-term, joint-venture deal with J for its own Monkeywrench label, a fresh start that offered a bridge toward even greater independence in the future. After two musically challenging albums, Pearl Jam was revitalized creatively as well, scoring a number one rock hit with its new single, "World Wide Suicide," after just two weeks of airplay.

February 24

A fifteen-second snippet of "World Wide Suicide," the first single from Pearl Jam's upcoming self-titled album, is released to US radio outlets. Within a few hours, the full song leaks on Seattle station KNDD-FM, which spins it nearly thirty times over the weekend.

March 6

"World Wide Suicide" is released as a free digital download from Pearl Jam's website, a rare move for a superstar band at that time. The track is available free for four days and garners more than 150,000 downloads. Fans who do so get a special surprise in the form of a November 30, 1993, show from Las Vegas, the first authorized download in a long-discussed series of special performances from the Pearl Jam vault.

March 13

"World Wide Suicide" lands at no. 3 on *Billboard*'s Modern Rock chart, the band's highest debut ever and its thirty-first career appearance on the tally. On March 23 the song jumps to no. 1 on the chart.

Stone Gossard: We've had lots of records where if it wasn't happening, we were like, "Oh, everything's fine." We're all pretty jaded. We try not to get too hyped up about what somebody's telling us, as far as the numbers. But I just think that song has got something that means "right now" in it.

April 15

Pearl Jam performs "World Wide Suicide" and the still unreleased "Severed Hand" on NBC's *Saturday Night Live,* its third appearance on the show and first since 1994.

Jeff Ament: A lot of people have come up to us and said, "I didn't even know you guys put any records out in the last five or six years." Some people only pay attention to bands on the covers of magazines and whatever. Being outside of that has been fine for us. But at the same time, I think we feel like we could still compete in that arena.

April 20
The Astoria, London

Pearl Jam plays its first London show since 2000 at the two-thousand-capacity Astoria and premieres seven songs from its upcoming album: "World Wide Suicide," "Life Wasted," "Severed Hand," "Unemployable," "Gone," "Army Reserve," and "Marker in the Sand." "Comatose" is played for the first time in its album version, differing slightly from the rendition debuted in March 2005.

May 1

Hundreds of fans line up at Tower Records in New York for a chance at tickets to a secret Pearl Jam concert, the location and date (Irving Plaza, May 5) of which would only be revealed on the ticket. Just before midnight, J Records head Clive Davis arrives to pass out a thousand donuts to the throngs. A few minutes later, Pearl Jam's eighth studio album, represented only by a sliced-open avocado on the album cover, is officially released in the United States.

May 4
Ed Sullivan Theater, New York

Pearl Jam plays "Life Wasted" during its seventh appearance on CBS's *Late Show with David Letterman.* Afterward, lucky Ten Club members are ushered into the studio for a special Pearl Jam concert that is streamed live on CBS's website. The set list includes six new songs plus "Present Tense," "Do the Evolution," "Why Go," and "Porch," which was teased with the Beatles' "I Want to Hold Your Hand" in a nod to that band's historic 1964 US television appearance in the theater. To close out the evening, Eddie Vedder joins the Strokes to sing their song "Juicebox" at Hammerstein Ballroom as part of a party to celebrate *Rolling Stone*'s one thousandth issue.

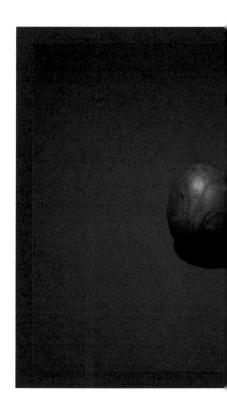

EARLY "AVOCADO"
AUDITION
SHOTS BY ED

May 15, 2006

Dear Eddie, Stone, Jeff, Matt and Mike:

On behalf of the California Avocado Commission, please accept this gift of fresh California avocados. We are thrilled that the band chose to feature the avocado as the quintessential minimal pop art image on the cover of the new release, "Pearl Jam." It is a great honor to have one of the most influential rock bands of our time using the avocado as part of its newest artistic venture. The buzz swirling around our industry right now is amazing!

Best regards,

Scott McIntyre
Chairman Of The Board
California Avocado Commission

LIFE WASTED
WORLD WIDE SUICIDE
COMATOSE
SEVERED HAND
MARKER IN THE SAND
PARACHUTES

UNEMPLOYABLE
BIG WAVE
GONE
WASTED REPRISE
ARMY RESERVE
COME BACK
INSIDE JOB

PEARL JAM

Julian Casablancas, Strokes front man: When I first met Eddie, I feel like I sensed genuine surprise when he learned how much we were influenced by Pearl Jam. People have never understood that about us. They'd always say the Ramones and the Stooges. But my favorite band was always Pearl Jam. People would be like, "Huh? I don't get it." When we met him and knew every detail about the songs, I think he was a little taken aback. He might have had a bad taste from the wave of Pearl Jam copies that got more and more diluted.

May 5

Pearl Jam's six-song set for America Online's "Sessions@AOL" and its three-song set on the UK show *Later with Jools Holland* (taped the previous month) hit the Internet and the airwaves, respectively.

May 5
Irving Plaza, New York

Pearl Jam plays another intimate warm-up show at the 1,200-capacity Irving Plaza, populated mainly by the fans that had waited for tickets four days earlier at Tower Records. The twenty-one-song set is notable for being completely free of covers and including the then rarely played *Ten* songs "Garden" and "Why Go."

May 9–10
Air Canada Centre, Toronto

Pearl Jam begins a world tour in support of its new album, now being dubbed "Avocado" by fans. My Morning Jacket supports on the North American leg, and are joined several times during their set by Vedder for a cover of the Band's "It Makes No Difference."

Jim James, My Morning Jacket front man: The first couple of nights we played with them, Ed would do a really sweet thing and come out and play a couple of songs acoustically to get people back in the arena from buying their beer. Then he'd introduce us. I thought that was so above and beyond the call of duty. We started talking about maybe collaborating on something. He heard us playing "It Makes No Difference" at soundcheck and

told us he really liked it, so we thought we'd try and do it. *Ten* was definitely a pivotal album for me, as it was for much of our generation. I will never forget seeing the video for "Alive" on MTV when I was in seventh grade. So to be lucky enough to find myself onstage playing with them was a shit-your-pants moment.

May 10

Pearl Jam debuts at no. 2 on the *Billboard* 200 with first-week sales of 279,000 US copies, according to Nielsen SoundScan. The figure is the band's best sales week since *Yield* debuted at no. 2 with 358,000 copies in 1998.

May 14
Wrigley Field, Chicago

Eddie Vedder sings "Take Me Out to the Ballgame" for the third time at a Chicago Cubs home game against the San Diego Padres.

May 19

Pearl Jam unveils its first music video since the 1998 clip for "Do the Evolution" in the form of "Life Wasted," the first video directed by visual artist Fernando Apodaca. After premiering on VH1, the clip is available from various sites as a free download under the Creative Commons Attribution—Noncommercial—No Derivatives license, allowing for legal copying and distribution. The video utilizes lifelike casts of Pearl Jam's members as well as bronze, wax, and leather sculptures; the imagery also appears in the liner notes of "Avocado." In July the clip is nominated for best special effects at the MTV Video Music Awards.

May 31
Avalon, New York

A few hundred lucky fans pack into what is normally a dance club to witness Pearl Jam tape an episode of the VH1 series *Storytellers,* which airs on July 1. The band had actually played the same venue in 1992 when it was called Limelight. Vedder is in a political mood throughout the ten-song set, noting that

although "truth seems to be a vanishing commodity" under President George W. Bush's leadership, the band was keeping in mind the old saying "Don't let the truth get in the way of a good story."

Filling in background and inspiration for songs old and new, Vedder riffs on the abusive relationship at the heart of "Better Man" ("It's much more tricky to end them than I would have thought," he says) and explains how the audience response to "Alive" forever altered the song's meaning for him.

"In the original story, a teenager is being made aware of a shocking truth that leaves him plenty confused," he says of the tale, based on his own teenage discovery that the man he believed to be his biological father actually was not. "It was a curse—'I'm still alive.'" But as fans quickly turned the title phrase into a self-empowering anthem, particularly at Pearl Jam concerts, Vedder says, "they lifted the curse. The audience changed the meaning for me."

June 13

Columbia/Legacy reissues the 1996 *Dead Man Walking* soundtrack, which included two Eddie Vedder duets with Pakistani vocalist Nusrat Fateh Ali Khan. The new edition sports a previously unreleased studio version of "Dead Man" recorded in 2005 by Vedder; the song was written for the original soundtrack but wound up instead as the B-side to the Pearl Jam single "Off He Goes." Also appended is a DVD of *Not in Our Name—Dead Man Walking: The Concert,* which was held March 29, 1998, at Los Angeles's Shrine Auditorium and included Vedder and Jeff Ament, Ani DiFranco, Lyle Lovett, Tom Waits, and Steve Earle.

June 20

A seven-song EP drawn from Pearl Jam's April 29, 2005, show at Seattle's Easy Street Records is released to celebrate the tenth anniversary of the Coalition of Independent Music Stores (CIMS). In addition to PJ originals "1/2 Full," "Lukin," "Save You," and "Porch," the EP features covers of the Avengers' "The American in Me," the Dead Kennedys' "Bleed for Me," and X's "The New World," with that band's John Doe on vocals.

June 26
Xcel Energy Center, St. Paul

Pearl Jam plays the first of six shows opening for Tom Petty and the Heartbreakers, with Vedder joining that band on most nights to sing "American Girl" and "The Waiting." During the July 2–3 shows in Denver, the Heartbreakers' Benmont Tench fills in for regular Pearl Jam keyboardist Boom Gaspar, who is in Hawaii following the death of his mother. "It's been great being around a band that's been doing it for thirty years and sounding as good as ever, if not better," Vedder says of the Heartbreakers. "And a little bit of wisdom in the late-night hours: I think that's gonna keep us going for the next fifteen years."

July 7
Viejas Arena, San Diego

During the first encore, Vedder gives a speech about his former high school drama teacher, the late Clayton Liggett, for whom he wrote the song "Long Road." Some of the show's proceeds go toward a theater named after Liggett. Surfer Kelly Slater plays guitar on the show-closing "Rockin' in the Free World."

July 9–10
The Forum, Inglewood, California

Pearl Jam dusts off its cover of Daniel Johnston's "Walking the Cow" for the first time since a fall 1994 appearance at Neil Young's Bridge School Benefit, and also debuts a rendition of X's "I Must Not Think Bad Thoughts" featuring actor Tim Robbins on vocals.

July 10

Pearl Jam announces its 2006 carbon portfolio strategy, with a goal of 0 percent net emissions for touring and business operations. The band reveals it will use pure biodiesel for its production trucks on the second leg of the summer tour, and pledges a $100,000 donation to nine organizations doing innovative work around climate change, renewable energy, and the environment.

2006

July 13

Santa Barbara County Bowl, Santa Barbara, California

Returning to the site of one of its most memorable shows (October 28, 2003), Pearl Jam starts off with a ten-song acoustic set including the Rolling Stones' "Waiting on a Friend," plus "Hard to Imagine," "Oceans," "Daughter," and "Black."

July 20

Arlene Schnitzer Concert Hall, Portland, Oregon

Pearl Jam performs a benefit concert for the Northwest Chapter of the Crohn's and Colitis Foundation of America (CCFA). Special guests include comedian David Cross and Sleater-Kinney, with the latter joining in for the Neil Young covers "Harvest Moon" and "Rockin' in the Free World." Guitarist Johnny Marr (Smiths, Modest Mouse) guests on "All Along the Watchtower." On August 12 at Portland's Crystal Ballroom, Vedder returns the favor by playing a three-song set prior to Sleater-Kinney's farewell performance before an indefinite hiatus.

July 22–23

Gorge Amphitheatre, George, Washington

The *Ten*-era B-side "Dirty Frank" is played live for the first time in more than twelve years at the first of two sweltering shows at the Gorge.

July 24

Eddie Vedder lends his voice to a cover of Marvin Gaye's "Mercy Mercy Me (The Ecology)," which serves as the B-side to "You Only Live Once," the first single from the Strokes' third album, *First Impressions of Earth*. The single, which also features Queens of the Stone Age's Josh Homme on drums, is released first internationally and then on September 26 in North America.

August 23

The Point, Dublin, Ireland

Pearl Jam kicks off a European tour with the first-ever performances of the *Binaural* outtake "Education" and Thin Lizzy's rock radio classic "The Boys Are Back in Town." Along the way, the band returns to the Netherlands for the first time since the Roskilde tragedy and also plays in Belgium for the first time in its career. Wolfmother's Andrew Stockdale joins Pearl Jam on two occasions to handle Chris Cornell's vocal part for "Hunger Strike." During the latter portion of the trek, Danny Clinch films five shows in Italy, highlights from which are released in 2007 on the DVD *Immagine in Cornice*.

September 12

Mike McCready and Matt Cameron guest on the original "Blowin' Smoke" and a cover of Soundgarden's "Black Hole Sun" as part of guitar legend Peter Frampton's instrumental album *Fingerprints*.

October 11

Longtime Pearl Jam photographer Lance Mercer releases a book of images of the band, *5X1: Pearl Jam Through the Eye of Lance Mercer*. The volume focuses on the first half of Pearl Jam's career and follows Mercer's 1998 Pearl Jam photo book *Place/Date*, which was compiled in tandem with fellow photographer Charles Peterson.

October 13

Pearl Jam is honored with the Marleen Alhadeff Volunteer of the Year Award for its contributions and commitment to helping YouthCare raise money for homeless youth in the Seattle area.

October 21–22

Shoreline Amphitheatre, Mountain View, California

Pearl Jam makes its eighth appearance at Neil Young's annual Bridge School Benefit. The band strikes a balance between sing-along hits ("Elderly Woman Behind the Counter in a Small Town," "Daughter," "Better Man") and songs perfectly suited to the day's acoustic approach ("Parachutes," "Man of the Hour"). The band also covers Tom Waits's "Picture in a Frame" as well as the traditional drinking song "I Used to Work in Chicago."

Eddie Vedder: I talked to Neil a number of years ago right after something he'd gone through with his health that was a little bit scary, and I took the opportunity to tell him a few things that I needed to say while I had the chance. I told him how grateful we were for everything that he had imparted to us and how much we had learned from him, and he said, "Well, if you ever figure out what it is, make sure to tell me [*laughs*]."

October 26

Eddie Vedder and surfer Laird Hamilton are featured in an episode of the Sundance Channel show *Iconoclasts*, interviewing each other about their achievements and creative processes.

November 7

Acer Arena, Sydney, Australia

Pearl Jam begins a three-week Australian tour, its first shows in the country in more than three years, with support from Kings of Leon.

November 14

Jack Johnson's Brushfire Records releases the soundtrack to the surfing documentary *A Brokedown Melody*, featuring the previously unreleased Eddie Vedder ukulele song "Goodbye."

November 17

Myer Music Bowl, Melbourne, Australia

Pearl Jam makes a surprise appearance with U2's Bono and the Edge during the Make Poverty History benefit concert, singing "Rockin' in the Free World" with lyrics modified specifically for the occasion. Sings Bono: "You can write it on your T-shirt or write it on your heart / It's a long, long way, but tonight we're gonna start / You gotta adjust vision or your visibility / if you want to make poverty history!" Vedder tells the audience, "We've just seen a lot of activism here, and you should be proud of yourselves to have so much hope and keep it going. We're rooting for you."

November 30
Waimea Valley Audubon Center, Waimea, Hawaii

Pearl Jam gives an unannounced performance to celebrate the opening of the Quiksilver Big Wave Invitational surfing competition in front of approximately 250 lucky fans. Surfer Kelly Slater joins the band again on "Rockin' in the Free World" and "Indifference." Earlier in the day, Vedder and Slater participate in a paddle-out at Waimea Bay as part of the opening ceremonies for the Eddie Aikau Big Wave Invitational surfing contest.

December 2
Neal S. Blaisdell Center, Honolulu

Boom Gaspar plays his first show with Pearl Jam in his home state. Proceeds benefit Hui Malama o ke Kai, an after-school, ocean-based program for Waimanalo youths.

Boom Gaspar: My father built a shack for us when we were kids to play music and to have a place to hang that wasn't in the streets. We didn't have youth programs or after-school programs, so a lot of my friends got lost in the shuffle.

Eddie Vedder: One of the better shows. Played an Israel Kamakawiwo'ole song, to the appreciation of the locals. Matt Cameron's birthday. Threw a rather large cake into a rather large audience. It landed on exactly one person: a girl. She was rescued and went home wearing Mike McCready's clothes. Next day, gave surf lessons to the Kings of Leon. Successfully, I might add.

December 9
Aloha Stadium, Honolulu

Pearl Jam ends its 2006 world tour before a crowd of nearly fifty thousand while opening the last date of U2's Vertigo trek, which eventually becomes the third highest-grossing tour of all time at $389 million. Pearl Jam's thirteen-song support slot is heavy on hits and sing-alongs, including native son Israel Kamakawiwo'ole's classic "Hawaii '78." Vedder and Mike McCready join U2 later on to reprise their new version of "Rockin' in the Free World."

Eddie Vedder: Finishing off the tour with a big wave. Many of the greatest surfers of all time were at that show, including Laird Hamilton, the one depicted on the show poster. He charged his way to the front of forty-seven thousand people, spreading love and hurting a few of them.

Christmas

Pearl Jam and the Ten Club prepare their fifteenth fan club vinyl holiday single, which features a pair of classic rock covers: the Who's "Love, Reign O'er Me" and Neil Young's "Rockin' in the Free World." The latter was recorded at the Make Poverty History benefit in Melbourne in November, with U2's Bono and the Edge guesting. The Who cover appears the following March in the Adam Sandler–Don Cheadle film *Reign Over Me*. The song is produced by Brendan O'Brien, his first work with the group since he remixed three songs from *Ten* for the 2004 compilation *Rearviewmirror*.

Mike McCready: Eddie asked Stone and me what the guitar players thought, and I told him, "I know you can nail this."

I've heard him messing around in the studio, singing Who songs by himself in the vocal room in between takes, and he's nailing it there. I knew he'd put everything into it, because he'd know Pete Townshend might someday listen to it. It's funny: Stone says he has this natural fuzz box on his voice, and he's definitely using it here.

1st night playing with Boom
2001

Pearl Jam

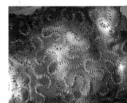

Eddie Vedder couldn't face the day, and he wasn't alone. Millions of Americans woke up on November 3, 2004, faced with the realization that President George W. Bush had narrowly defeated Senator John Kerry and been reelected to a second term in office. For Vedder and his bandmates, the news was especially crushing, considering that they had devoted the past two years of their lives to helping prevent this very thing from happening.

Earlier that fall, the band had made plans to go into the studio in Seattle on November 1, even though there wasn't really any material to work on yet. But the next forty-eight hours were lost in a haze of disappointment and frustration—a state of mind that in this case was not conducive to creative expression.

"I didn't get out of bed," Vedder remembers. "However, while I couldn't get myself out of bed, I heard that Springsteen on that day was making a call to someone he makes records with, saying, 'I have to make a record.' Two different approaches there." He speculates about what would have happened if Pearl Jam had indeed gone back to the studio the day after Bush beat Kerry: "I would have imagined some angry music would have come out of that. The only problem was, we didn't have any music to emote to at that point. Again, just being a couple of days into it, things were still forming. I was cocked and loaded, for sure. It took a while for the music to provide a target."

Once it did a few weeks later, Pearl Jam came out blazing. Among the first songs to take shape for what would become the band's eighth studio album were "Life Wasted," Stone Gossard's hardest-rocking track in ages; the speed-punk "Comatose," then called "Crapshoot Rapture"; an oddly funky

Vedder rocker called "Severed Hand," which he'd actually started writing in 2003; and the tune that would wind up becoming the album's first single, "World Wide Suicide."

"Those were the ones that came out initially," Ament says. "There were probably ten ideas, of which maybe five or six had vocal melodies and some lyrical ideas. Every song that came out of that first session was pretty up-tempo, which was the benefit of actually coming right off the road, going into the studio, and having our chops. And, having lost an election we felt more involved in than ever benefited the record, energywise, for sure."

In early 2005, the plan was to try finishing the new album in time to release it by the end of the year. But by late spring, Pearl Jam uncharacteristically put the brakes on that timetable and decided to give the process more time to breathe.

"We started it like any other record," Vedder says. "But it was only as we were making it that we realized it was going to be a different kind of process. After our second session of three weeks or so, we realized we were going to need more than just an additional session to finish up. In the end, there were probably another four sessions on top of that. I think that came from the guys affording me the extra time to write, and my needing more time to write, simply because I was going to be writing more songs than on the last few records, where everybody brought in some complete ideas."

"I think the expectation was that we'd probably go in three times and knock it out," Ament says. "There was a point in the summer where we met in the studio and said, 'So, is this really going to be ready?' There'd be ten songs

ready that would be pretty great. But we just kept thinking, there are five or six of these other ones that we think are going to be as good or better than the top five of this ten. It was almost like we had a double record, and half the double record wasn't quite finished."

Says Gossard, "There were probably demos for twenty-five or thirty things, including jams. But thank God we came back to it. At the end, there's this consensus that if you're in love with a song and two or three of your other bandmates are in love with it, chances are it's a song that will be important for the record. It's hard to let go of songs sometimes. You can have a personal need for a particular song to develop or come out. But whatever the process was that happened on this one, it was a great collaboration between a band process and Ed really taking the best from the band and really getting the best out of us."

When it became clear the album was not going to be ready by the end of 2005, for the first time ever, Pearl Jam opted to dispense with the album-tour-album-tour cycle and hit the road without any new music to promote. After a fund-raising concert for Montana politician Jon Tester's US Senate election bid in Missoula, Montana, and two local area shows at the Gorge, the band trekked north for sixteen shows in Canada.

For Pearl Jam, it was a pressure-free environment in which the members could just be themselves, whether it meant jamming with Bono on "Rockin' in the Free World" in Toronto or playing before a few thousand devotees in such out-of-the-way locales as Thunder Bay, Ontario, and Halifax, Nova Scotia. "It was important for us to break patterns," Gossard says. "We were separating the touring aspect of the band from the recording process. We could go out, be Pearl Jam, and tour."

After Canada, Pearl Jam tacked on a one-off gig opening for the Rolling Stones in Pittsburgh, a handful of US headlining shows, and, to wrap 2005, its first concerts ever in South America. In Atlantic City, Vedder debuted a new song called "Gone," which he had written the night before in his hotel room.

"I've got a tape player that has become a real friend to me," he says. "After the show, you like to hang out with friends, and that night, the friend was the tape machine. It came quick. What's nice about it was that it was done in an hour or so, with backgrounds.

"The idea was that this guy was leaving Atlantic City and needing to find a new life without his past, without his possessions, and not really looking for more possessions," Vedder continues. "Because it takes place in a car, it's probably very similar to 'Rearviewmirror,' in a way. But I think this car is a hybrid, because I think he's got only one tank of gas, so I want him to go far."

For "Gone," Vedder borrowed a line from Pete Townshend—"Nothing is everything"—which he'd sung often with the Who guitarist when they played together in the late 1990s. "It stems from the Meher Baba teachings that Pete has followed over the years: Desire nothing but desirelessness," he explains.

Two songs that fought their way onto the new album came at the tail end of the year, Ament's chunky rocker "Big Wave," and "Inside Job," one of the only Pearl Jam album tracks featuring music completely by Mike McCready, who also penned the lyrics.

Aside from its epic, cathartic rock, in the vein of "Present Tense" from *No Code,* "Inside Job" is particularly notable for its sentiment. McCready seems to be addressing not only the struggle of an individual to make a difference in modern society but also his personal battle with Crohn's disease.

"He certainly didn't cop out and make it about somebody else, like another writer I know," Vedder says. One way to deal with negative energy and frustration is "to kind of look within. If nothing else, effect some change in yourself. If you're in a position of feeling pretty together at that point, then you feel like you can make a contribution to society, as opposed to being a fucking wreck and just adding to the pile of

destructive forces you can find yourself surrounded by. And that's exactly, verbatim, what's in the song, really. Like 'shining a human light.' That's all from Mike.

"He came up in South America, and we recorded it on my little machine, his demo. The other thing, too, he knew we were coming down to the end. The songs that had words were going to make it, and the songs that didn't weren't. He really wanted that one to make it, and he was motivated to make something really poignant, and he did."

As Vedder was writing lyrics, he found himself channeling his profound disgust for the policies of the Bush White House into more personal stories: the family of the fallen soldier staring at his photo in the newspaper ("World Wide Suicide"), the army reservist on the other side of the world from his loved ones ("Army Reserve"), the rank-and-file infantryman getting wacked out of his mind on drugs just to make it through another day in the Iraqi desert ("Severed Hand"), and the pink-slipped blue-collar worker who has nothing but "thirty bills unpaid" and a dented gold ring that says "Jesus Saves" to show for his efforts ("Unemployable").

Other songs, like the R&B-drenched ballad "Come Back," the bittersweet acoustic love song "Parachutes," and "Life Wasted," while about specific people and events, explore a more general sense of longing and loss. This was the kind of Vedder storytelling that had been so vivid and captivating on Pearl Jam's earliest material.

"Through telling stories," he reflects, "you may be able to transmit an emotion or a feeling or an observation of modern reality rather than editorializing, which we've seen plenty of these days." In addition, writing from perspectives other than his own was "a right that I'd forgotten that I had."

Once all the material was finished, Vedder began to realize that Pearl Jam may have inadvertently assembled one of the most divisive, argument-starting pieces of work in the rock 'n' roll canon: a concept album. Of course, Vedder was intimately familiar with the art form thanks to his love of the Who's *Tommy* and *Quadrophenia,* but it still came as something of a surprise that Pearl Jam had found itself in a similar position.

"It wasn't a conscious approach. It just started to happen," Vedder

observes. "Because there was so much music and because the other guys hadn't brought in finished lyrics, there was a big, giant obelisk of clay ready to be molded, which was the music. It seemed like, wow, you could really make a sculpture out of this, where one song would be the leg, the arm, the heart, and the head. Basically, this has potential to be a concept record.

"The worst part about that process was that I didn't feel like I could listen to the Green Day record *American Idiot,* which I was hearing so much about. I felt like I was prohibited from listening to it because I heard that theirs was a concept record. So while I was following their success with pride, I wasn't allowed to hear any of their music, just because I was in my own mad-scientist bubble."

What ultimately led to a less structured theme guiding the album's flow was a first pass at sequencing. "We tried one, and it just absolutely didn't work," Vedder says. "That was almost the one that told a story. By just shifting a few things around, all of a sudden it just worked, and that was it."

Still, "even toward the end, it almost seemed like it came close to winding up concept driven," Vedder says. "You could have tied it all in with a bit of narration or even just some liner notes. It was interesting to think, 'Severed Hand'—is that the same kid who ends up being the army reservist? Really, 'Army Reserve' is about his wife and kid. So, in some ways, they do kind of all tie in. The other thing we said is that if this does come out like a concept record, we can't *tell* anybody it's a concept record, you know what I mean? Maybe years later we'll admit to it. So the fact that it isn't a concept record, I can admit to it now that it's not, but it could have been."

Released on J Records, *Pearl Jam* was the band's first studio album since leaving Epic Records after fourteen years.

"In general, it's a fresh start more than anything," Gossard says. "We had a long road with Sony. Some of it was fantastic. Sony, for the most part, did everything they could to try and make us happy. Toward the end of the relationship, it was difficult to gauge what was really happening, because there was so much water under the bridge and so many people had come and gone. We just needed a change. By having that, it freed us up to get a little hungrier and challenge ourselves a little more. It also gave some fresh people the chance to touch the record."

"I don't know if any label could have kept up with us because of the way things evolved," Vedder admits. "If right at the outset we were selling ten million records, and years down the road we were selling one million, and we were fine with it, I can understand why they'd feel a little crazy when they wanted to achieve past successes. For us, the most successful times were when we found it difficult to stay healthy and to keep grounded. You get growing pains when you get taller, but we got them when we were trying to shrink [laughs]."

Overall, the songs on the album—officially known as *Pearl Jam*—are more direct musically and less obtuse lyrically than on its two predecessors, *Binaural* and *Riot Act.* That listeners took this to heart was evident from the immediate positive reaction to "World Wide Suicide," which debuted at a career-best no. 3 on the *Billboard* Modern Rock chart, and Pearl Jam's willingness to promote the new music with major appearances like *Saturday Night Live.*

"The melody is really strong," Gossard says of "World Wide Suicide." "It sounds like AC/DC. Fuck, kick ass! I like it. It's blowing up. It doesn't sound slick or that we polished it for too long. That's the main thing, really, politics aside. The song just has some energy in it. It has the intangibles."

Specifically on songs like "Marker in the Sand," Vedder made a concerted effort to find the best melody he could to convey the meaning of the lyrics. Extra ammunition came from the late Johnny Ramone, who not only inspired the lyrics to "Life Wasted" but challenged Vedder to study the building blocks of rock 'n' roll.

"There's this funeral energy, when you literally sit there with the loss of your friend and you realize how precious life is," Vedder says of Ramone's death. "Funerals and weddings are good for that. You have this renewed sense of living life to the fullest, when you see how quickly it evaporates. You take it for granted. At one point, someone is living, breathing, thinking, and talking, and a week later, it's a memory and a spirit. 'Life Wasted' came from that: 'I've faced it, a life wasted, I'm never going back

again.' Live life to the fullest. I wasn't going to let this deep loss go without recognition."

"You weren't just a friend, you were kind of a student," he adds of Ramone. "He played me rock music over the years, from Bill Haley and Jerry Lee Lewis to the Smith Brothers, the Everly Brothers. Just great songs. We'd just sit around and listen to great songs. Then we'd listen to songs that weren't great and figure out why they weren't great. Maybe he was sitting on my shoulder on this record, and we were listening to those songs and saying, Is that great? Because they were still being written, you could choose options or try to create or keep hammering it out until you felt like it was something that was great. Now—now it sounds great to me. And I will imagine in years it will, too."

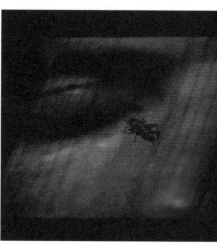

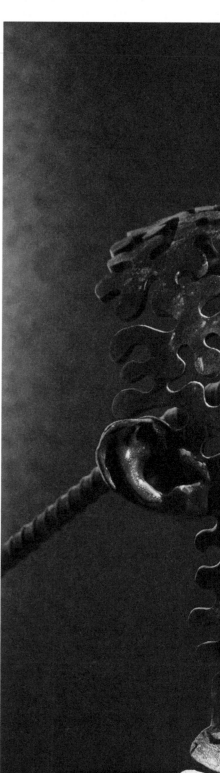

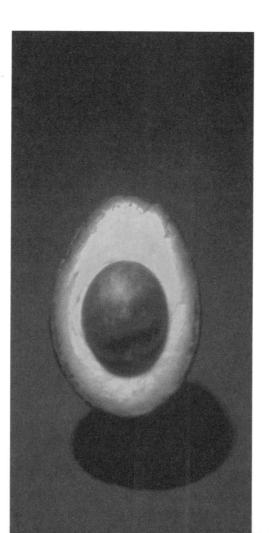

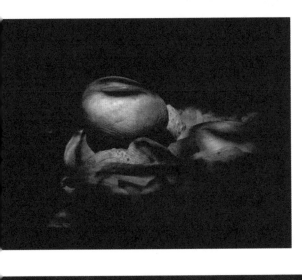

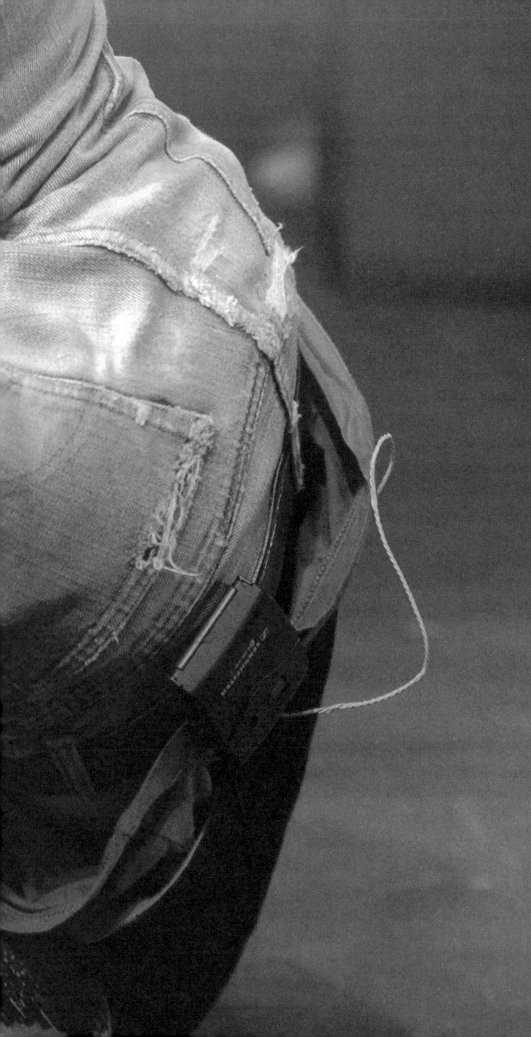

CHAPTER 2007

2007

The adventuresome spirit that marked Pearl Jam's activities in 2006—the band even made its first music video in eight years—continued the following year. Satisfied that it had taken the necessary steps to insure that something like Roskilde would never happen again, Pearl Jam played its first American festival in fifteen years in front of nearly sixty thousand fans at Lollapalooza in Chicago. And, inspired by close friend Sean Penn, Eddie Vedder not only crafted his first solo album, in the form of the soundtrack to the film *Into the Wild,* but also wrote several original songs for the documentary *Body of War,* about a young soldier injured in Iraq. After more than fifteen years together, Pearl Jam was still expanding its creative palette, and reaching a new generation of fans in the process.

March 12
Waldorf Astoria Hotel, New York

Eddie Vedder inducts R.E.M. into the Rock and Roll Hall of Fame, having previously inducted the Doors and the Ramones. Vedder says he listened to R.E.M.'s seminal debut album *Murmur* more than 1,200 times in the summer of 1984 after seeing the group live, and he salutes the band for taking Pearl Jam under its wing, saying, "They became like big brothers." Afterward, Vedder joins R.E.M.'s original lineup of Michael Stipe, Peter Buck, Mike Mills, and drummer Bill Berry for a performance of "Man on the Moon."

Peter Buck: To have someone induct us who was influenced by us to a certain degree was great. He's a real fan. He's always telling me about a great new band or a great old record he discovered. I'm kind of that same way, too. I spend all my time going to record stores. He's always talking about what he's listening to. A lot of people in our position stop listening to music besides their own.

April 7
Showbox, Seattle

Mike McCready's side band Flight to Mars headlines the fifth annual CCFA benefit concert, with proceeds going to the Northwest Chapter of the Crohn's & Colitis Foundation of America.

April 21–22
Waikiki Shell, Honolulu

Eddie Vedder and Boom Gaspar join Jack Johnson at the fourth annual Kokua Festival on Earth Day weekend in Honolulu. Throughout the weekend, Vedder and Johnson play on each other's songs, with Johnson at one point flubbing a verse on "Elderly Woman Behind the Counter in a Small Town." Vedder also debuts the song "No More" from the forthcoming documentary *Body of War.*

May 5
Henry Fonda Theater, Los Angeles

Eddie Vedder plays a solo acoustic set featuring "Driftin'," "I Am Mine," and "No More" at a Flea-organized benefit for the Silverlake Conservatory of Music. Flea and former Pearl Jam drummer Jack Irons join him for "Corduroy" and "Better Man," while Sex Pistols guitarist Steve Jones gets in on the fun during a cover of the Who's "The Kids Are Alright."

May 15

Pearl Jam is awarded a Conservation Creativity Award for the carbon portfolio strategy on its 2006 world tour, including band donations totaling $100,000 to organizations doing innovative work around climate change, renewable energy, and the environment.

June 9
Festimad, Madrid, Spain

Actor Javier Bardem, a Pearl Jam devotee, introduces "Black" at the start of the second encore during the second show of the group's summer tour.

Eddie Vedder: In the early 2000s, we had an idea to make a film with the band, kind of like the Beatles' *Help!,* with other characters interacting with us. We talked to Mudhoney, Laurie Anderson, and Tim Robbins about being in it. Like, everybody was on a train while the band was on tour. Tim said, "The filmmaker should be the instigator. He'd get the band to break up." We wanted Javier to be the filmmaker. That really should have happened.

June 15
Parco San Giuliano, Heineken Jammin' Festival, Venice, Italy

Pearl Jam is unable to perform at this Italian festival, which is cancelled after high winds topple lighting and speaker towers, injuring twenty fans before the band even arrives at the site.

June 18
Wembley Arena, London

At its first proper London headlining show in seven years, Pearl Jam gets political in the second encore by playing the new song "No More" plus "Bu$hleaguer" and "World Wide Suicide" back to back to back.

Eddie Vedder: The Who were in Hamburg, Germany, but Pete Townshend's brother Paul, nephew Ben, and a slew of Townshends came to the gig. In what is almost becoming a custom, we went back to their flat and talked round the kitchen table 'til morning about the power of music.

June 26

Pearl Jam's Monkeywrench label releases the seven-disc boxed set *Live at the Gorge 05/06,* rounding up three shows recorded at the famous Washington State outdoor venue.

August 2
Vic Theatre, Chicago

A fan-club-only crowd is treated to this intimate warm-up for Lollapalooza three days later. Vedder opens the show solo with covers of Cat Stevens's "Trouble"

FLIGHT TO MARS

319

and Tom Waits's "Picture in a Frame," plus Pearl Jam's "Dead Man" and "All the Way," a made-up ditty about the Chicago Cubs. The twenty-song set is loaded with obscurities such as "All or None," "Education," "Undone," "Low Light," and "I'm Open." "Forgive us," Vedder says. "But most of these songs we decided to play about four thirty this afternoon." Matt Cameron sings on a cover of Kiss's "Black Diamond" in the second encore.

August 3

Eddie Vedder sings "Take Me Out to the Ballgame" for the fourth time at a Chicago Cubs game at Wrigley Field. Earlier, Vedder warms up with pitcher Kerry Wood in the Cubs bullpen and throws out the ceremonial first pitch while wearing one of Wood's jerseys.

August 5
Grant Park, Chicago

Fifteen years after performing on the second installment of the traveling festival, Pearl Jam plays its most-watched US show in a decade by headlining the third night of Lollapalooza, now an annual event in Chicago. Vedder, who grew up in nearby Evanston, Illinois, makes clear the band's appreciation for the occasion, telling the audience, "There's a deep amount of meaning that comes with playing on this stage tonight."

While performing "Daughter," the band segues into a portion of Pink Floyd's "Another Brick in the Wall, Part II," during which Vedder sings, "George! Bush! Leave this world alone" and "George Bush, find yourself another home." In a move that causes widespread outrage, those lyrics are censored by AT&T during its cybercast of the performance, which the company later attributes to "a mistake by a Webcast vendor" that is "contrary to our policy." Pearl Jam later posts the unedited clip on its website. The band's set ends with a stageful of friends (including Ben Harper and ex–NBA star Dennis Rodman) and fans flanking Pearl Jam for "Rockin' in the Free World."

Afterward the band releases a statement on its website regarding the song's censoring: "This, of course, troubles us as artists but also as citizens concerned with the issue of censorship and the increasingly consolidated control of the media. What happened to us this weekend was a wake-up call, and it's about something much bigger than the censorship of a rock band."

September 1
Memorial Stadium, Seattle

Eddie Vedder joins Neil Finn and the reunited Crowded House during its performance at the annual Bumbershoot festival for "Something So Strong" and "World Where You Live."

Neil Finn: We have jammed quite a bit at his house and at my house. The first time we took them out to Kerikeri in New Zealand, in 1995, we had a jam that is on a tape somewhere. Who knows if it adds up to anything. We had a great night one night at Eddie's place with producer Adam Kasper. We were in the middle of this mad, amped-up, punky kind of jam. All of a sudden, my guitar went dead, and I looked over to see Eddie's dog Hank there, wagging his tail and feeling really happy with himself because he'd just chewed through my guitar cable.

September 11

Body of War, codirected by talk show legend Phil Donahue and Ellen Spiro, premieres at the Toronto International Film Festival. The movie chronicles the travails of Tomas Young, who was paralyzed by a bullet during his first week of military service in Iraq on April 4, 2004. Vedder was inspired to write material for the film after meeting Young. Following the screening, the Pearl Jam singer performs.

Eddie Vedder: Tomas Young went over there to fight the good fight—he thought he was going to Afghanistan, and he ended up in Iraq. Now he lives and will live the rest of his life with incredible challenges.

September 18

Eddie Vedder's first solo album, the soundtrack to *Into the Wild,* is released by J Records.

September 25

The Danny Clinch–directed concert DVD *Immagine in Cornice* (Italian for "Picture in a Frame") is released by Monkeywrench/Rhino. Shot during five Italian shows on the 2006 tour, *Cornice* also features bonus footage of Vedder performing the Who's "A Quick One, While He's Away," with opening act My Morning Jacket.

Jim James: He just heard us running through it at soundcheck. It had always been one of our favorites, but it seemed pretty tough to pull off. He came running in and was like, "Oh my God! Let's do this!"

Eddie Vedder: I think the best part of the film is the people of Italy. They were a great representation of the people that come see us in general, wherever it is. To me they're like a character in the film, and incredibly well cast.

October 30

Backed by the Million Dollar Bashers (Sonic Youth guitarist Lee Ranaldo and drummer Steve Shelley, Television guitarist Tom Verlaine, Wilco guitarist Nels Cline, guitarist Smokey Hormel, keyboardist John Medeski, and Dylan bassist Tony Garnier), Eddie Vedder covers Bob Dylan's "All Along the Watchtower" on the Columbia soundtrack to Todd Haynes's Dylan-themed film *I'm Not There.*

November 1
Beverly Hilton, Beverly Hills, California

Eddie Vedder, Sean Penn, and *Into the Wild* score writer Michael Brook discuss their collaboration on the film's music during a panel at the *Hollywood Reporter/Billboard* Film & TV Music Conference. As Vedder explained, "Sean had found the perfect wave by the time he talked to me about it. It was just a pleasure to surf this perfect wave. All I had to do was get back on the boat and sing for my supper. In our group, or the way we're used to doing it, we have five guys, and we're all kind of the boss. This felt more like, these people I felt responsible to were the boss. I felt really comfortable in that position."

December

The book *Pearl Jam vs. Ames Bros: 13 Years of Tour Posters* is published through the Ten Club. It features more than two hundred poster art images from renowned artists such as Ames Bros and Brad Klausen.

December 6

Eddie Vedder's song "Guaranteed" from the *Into the Wild* soundtrack receives a Grammy nomination for best song written for motion picture, television, or other visual media. Five days later, the song is nominated in the best song category for the Broadcast Film Critics Association's Critics' Choice Movie Awards.

December 13

Eddie Vedder is nominated for two Golden Globe Awards for *Into the Wild*: he shares a nod with Michael Brook and Kaki King for best original score, motion picture, while "Guaranteed" is nominated for best original song, motion picture.

Christmas

Pearl Jam and the Ten Club release the sixteenth fan club vinyl holiday single, with the songs "Santa God," written by Eddie Vedder, and "Jingle Bells," performed entirely by Mike McCready.

'N MY TREE   CARRY DIAMOND

UP HERE IN MY TREE   yeh
NOTHING MATTERS MUCH TOO ME   no
NO MORE CROWBARS TO MY HEAD —   yeh
                                              il
I GOT WHISPERS OF THE LEAVES INSTEAD,
                                              yeh—.

A WAVE TO ALL MY FRIENDS yeh—.
they don't seem to NOTICE me —..no
AN EYES ARE ON the STREET —...
IN contradiction w/ THEIR DREAMS yeh—.

I REMEMBER WHEN ——. yeh—.
THOUGHT I KNEW EVERYTHIN yeh

FOR IF KNOWLEDGE IS A TREE, yeh—.

Is GROWING up just like me yeh—.

Into the Wild

When Eddie Vedder is off the grid at his Hawaii home, often for weeks at a time, the phone will ring, but odds are it won't be answered. Such was the case in early 2007, when Sean Penn tried to get through to Vedder to tell him about the film adaptation he was making of Jon Krakauer's 1996 book *Into the Wild*.

Vedder and Penn became friends during the filming of *Dead Man Walking* in 1995 via an introduction by Tim Robbins. "I had written a script that I wanted him to act in," Penn says. "We got to talking for some time about that. He's got a real good story about how the end came to that process, because it came with a song, which I have the only copy of. That was his explanation of why he didn't feel he should do it."

"I came to my senses and said, 'I don't think I can do it,'" Vedder says. "But he would write me. Every time, I'd say, 'I hate to do this but I just can't. Somebody will do it better.' He'd say, 'You can, and you will, and I'll get you through the big waves.' The reason why there was a song is that he just wouldn't take no for an answer. It was an aggressive song—kind of L.A. punk scene aggressive—called 'I Can't.'"

A segue into acting wasn't in the cards for Vedder, but he and Penn crossed paths again during the making of the 2002 film *I Am Sam,* the soundtrack of which features exclusively Beatles covers. "My favorite Beatles song was 'You've Got to Hide Your Love Away,' and about the only person I could imagine covering it was him," says Penn, who plays a mentally challenged Beatles devotee in the movie. Vedder accepted the invitation to record the song, which quickly became a fan favorite during his preshow surprise solo sets.

That spring day in 2007, Penn was immersed in *Into the Wild,* the true story of Christopher McCandless, a recent college graduate who in 1990 cut ties

with his family and embarked on a two-year odyssey that ended tragically with the twenty-four-year-old man starving to death in the Alaskan wilderness.

Penn had used songs like Neil Young's "Hey Hey, My My (Into the Black)," Cat Stevens's "Miles from Nowhere," Joe Henry's "King's Highway," Lynyrd Skynyrd's "Simple Man," and Philip Glass's "Cloudscape" as models for how he eventually wanted music to work as a transitional device in *Into the Wild.* But he had a suspicion that Vedder might be the right man to augment or even replace those songs with original ones of his own.

"I think I called him back within an hour or a half hour," Vedder remembers of Penn's reaching out. "You never know what it's about with Sean." Having been brought up to speed on the project, Vedder got ahold of Krakauer's book and tore through it. And within days, Penn was at Vedder's Seattle home showing him a three-hour-and-fifteen-minute rough cut of the movie.

"I could see the landscapes, and I could hear music in my head," Vedder says. "The film ended, and we shared a moment of silence, because it was heavy. I think I just asked Sean, as I'm reaching over to light a cigarette, 'What do you want?' And he said, 'Whatever you feel. It could be a song, it could be two, it could be the whole thing.' So I went in for three days, starting the next day, and gave him a palette of stuff to work with. And then he started choosing. Immediately he had a few things he put in. I wasn't expecting that. After that, then it was really on."

Although making a solo album may seem a lonely proposition, Vedder surrounded himself at Seattle's Studio X with familiar faces like longtime Pearl Jam producer-engineer Adam Kasper. "You're playing the music by yourself, but you end up in a band with the guys

pushing the buttons and sorting out the guitars and amps," he says. "Also, Sean is in the band, and Chris McCandless is in the band. The film becomes the record. In a way, I wasn't in the band. It was like being a songwriter for a band—serving the voice of Chris McCandless. Not my voice, or something I wanted to say. In almost every aspect of this process, it simplified things. There were fewer choices. The story was there, and the scenes were there."

On a typical day, "We'd go in knowing we had a few duties to fulfill. Something would start coming together and I'd realize, That's not what we want here. But I'd just go ahead and finish it and make something out of it," says Vedder, who played nearly all the instruments on what became the *Into the Wild* soundtrack. "It's a song. Why force that song into being something else? Since it was just happening, just go with that. We were moving so quick. If at noon you sit down, and there's just silence or blank tape, in an hour if you have a song, that didn't exist an hour ago. Now it exists and it might exist for a long time."

Far from the roaring rock 'n' roll for which Pearl Jam is known, the music Vedder wrote is for the most part gentle, contemplative, and often acoustic based. Jaunty, confident songs like "Rise," "Setting Forth," and "No Ceiling" embody the utter freedom McCandless must have felt as he began his solo journey, while "The Wolf," the fingerpicked "Long Nights," and the instrumental "Tuolumne" take more serious turns, soundtracking the pure isolation and life-or-death consequences inherent in McCandless's wilderness experience.

Two of the songs are collaborations: "Society" was written by Irish-born, Bay Area–based singer/songwriter Jerry Hannan, who also plays on the *Into the Wild* version, while the driving "Hard Sun"—originally recorded by a Canadian singer-songwriter called Indio (real name, Gordon Peterson) on his one and only album, 1989's *Big Harvest*—features backing vocals by Sleater-Kinney's Corin Tucker.

But the musical centerpiece is "Guaranteed," a rumination on McCandless's worldview and his motivations for experiencing life on terms that were difficult for others to comprehend. Accompanied only by an acoustic guitar, Vedder sings, "Everyone I come across, in cages they bought / They think of me and my wandering, but I'm never what they thought / I've got my indignation, but I'm pure in all my thoughts / I'm alive."

"When he sent 'Guaranteed,' I was still holding out for 'Miles from Nowhere,'" says Penn. "But 'Guaranteed,' just in its origin coming from this movie and not being an easy play of something to hit you outside the context of the movie, it wasn't borrowing somebody's else's baggage to make it appealing. It had grown out of this movie. It was such a great song. I thought for the purposes of the movie that I'd never be able to beat 'Miles from Nowhere,' but 'Guaranteed' seemed so much more a part of this movie organically, and not like it was cheating."

Vedder admits he found it "startling how easy it was for me to get into McCandless's head. I found it to be uncomfortable how easy it was, because I thought I'd grown up. I think all this stuff was right under the surface for me, barely."

In retrospect, Vedder describes writing the *Into the Wild* songs almost like a dream. Indeed, it took watching the interview he and Penn did about the film and soundtrack on *The Charlie Rose Show* to cement the experience in his memory.

"It came on, and I was sitting on the floor with a beer and a smoke, and it was late," he recalls. "I thought I'd catch it. I'm sitting there watching it, and I realized it was the exact place I was sitting on the floor with Sean when we watched the movie. It really didn't feel like much time had passed. It was interesting to go from sitting on the floor with an ashtray and a six-pack a few months ago to watching us talk about a finished product on the TV. It bookended the whole odyssey. It made it real, in a way. I had to see it on a screen to make it real. I don't remember much of the process because it went real quick and

it was real unconscious. I almost don't remember anything of the time of making it. It was a weird way to be notified that it had actually taken place."

Released September 18, 2007, by J Records, which had put out the self-titled *Pearl Jam* album the year before, *Into the Wild* was a quick hit, debuting at no. 11 on the *Billboard* 200 and becoming an immediate contender for a number of prestigious awards. Vedder eventually won the 2008 best original song Golden Globe for "Guaranteed," which was also nominated for a Grammy for best song written for a motion picture, television or other visual media. In addition, "Rise" was nominated for a best solo rock vocal performance Grammy.

"Lucky for me, there was a writers strike at the time, so they didn't have an awards show I had to worry about attending," Vedder says with a laugh. "I had surfed some big waves that day and was working on another batch of songs on my eight-track. When I got the call that bestowed me with the honor of winning, I remember looking down, and my shorts were dripping down onto the tile. Still wet from the surf and working on new songs—that's a nice way to win an award. It will be the most favorite award I will ever win because it came at a great time."

And while some critics took issue with McCandless's refusal to contact his heartbroken family during his travels or to properly equip himself for survival in the brutal, unforgiving Alaskan wilderness, Vedder and Penn both say these decisions were what most inspired them to help tell his story.

"Some of his actions were really bold," Vedder says. "To do what he did without money to fund his trip and make it comfortable, without taking classes or waiting for permits to go down rivers or to hike trails, or the fact that he didn't take a map, were choices he made in order to get to the truth of the matter, whatever that matter was to him. The truth of his existence, or a human's existence on this planet. A lot of people aren't going to understand that, and that's their prerogative. I actually respect those decisions. I'm going to respect anyone's choices if they want to live this life to get ultimate value out of it. I think one of the reasons a lot of people are uncomfortable with this idea is that maybe they haven't done it themselves."

To be sure, working on *Into the Wild* had unintended positive consequences

for Vedder in his own life, both musically and personally. "The combination of Sean and the story—meaning McCandless himself and the work Jon Krakauer did, and also the performances in the film—the amount of respect I had for those entities was so huge that it offered an opportunity to get deeper into writing than maybe I had in a while," he says. "It was just the most welcome set of demands I've come across in a long time. It ended up to be a great exercise in writing. Our band is going to be better for it and from it, which I'm pretty excited about."

Asked if it was difficult for him to turn off the creative energy that fueled his songwriting for the project, he replies, "Well, no, because then we started living it. We went down to the Grand Canyon, and I almost made it to Alaska. I started making choices in my own life. I started living outdoors this summer. It was using that inspiration to do things in my life. When I was working, I was inspired to make the music. That's what I was requested to do. After that, I took the inspiration and put it into my real life and my family life. We spent the summer outdoors. We did some camping. I felt like a real human being."

*Such is the way of the world
you can never know—.
Just where to put all your faith
and how will it grow?*

*Gonna rise up
Burning black holes in dark memories
Gonna rise up
Turning mistakes into gold*

*Such is the passage of time
too fast to fold
Suddenly swallowed by signs
lo & behold*

*Gonna rise up
find my direction magnetically
Gonna rise up
Throw down my ace in the hole*

2008 was a year when the members of Pearl Jam enjoyed the best of both worlds: high-profile festival and arena gigs with their main band, and personally fulfilling musical projects on their own. While reaping acclaim for his *Into the Wild* soundtrack, Eddie Vedder embarked on his first solo tour ever. Stone Gossard recast rock favorites with his small combo Hank Khoir, while Matt Cameron went jazzy with Harrybu McCage, Mike McCready jammed on Jimi Hendrix with some of the greatest guitarists alive, and Jeff Ament unveiled his solo debut. Gossard and Ament even reunited with their Green River bandmates for the first time in twenty years. But there was something even greater on the horizon that promised the kind of creative and business independence the band had dreamed about for years.

January

Eddie Vedder's July 8, 1995, performance of "Forever in Blue Jeans" with the Neil Diamond tribute band Lightning & Thunder is featured in *Song Sung Blue*, a documentary by Greg Kohs. The film chronicles the career of husband-and-wife singing duo Mike and Claire Sardina.

January 7

The music video for Eddie Vedder's song "Guaranteed" from the *Into the Wild* soundtrack debuts on VH1 and VH1.com. It's his first music video as a solo artist.

January 14

Eddie Vedder wins a Golden Globe for best original song, motion picture, for "Guaranteed."

January 29

Monkeywrench and Vinyl Films Records release a vinyl edition of the *Into the Wild* soundtrack, which features an extended version of album track "The Wolf," a bonus seven-inch single with both studio and live versions of "No More," and liner notes from director Sean Penn.

February 5

In a show of support for Democratic presidential candidate Senator Barack Obama, Jeff Ament, Matt Cameron, Stone Gossard, and Mike McCready, augmented by Boom Gaspar on keyboards and Barrett Jones on background vocals, record a new rendition of Bill Haley's classic "Rock Around the Clock" with the title phrase changed to "Rock Around Barack."

Stone Gossard: This is a track I've been thinking about for a while. "Rock Around the Clock" was the first mainstream rock and roll hit in 1955, and it had a transforming effect on American music. At that time, rock and rhythm and blues music was traditionally only played on black radio. I am, by no means, an expert on the history of rock and roll, but this was a big deal. The rhythm of rock music and its energy were so overwhelming that traditional barriers of race and culture broke down with an enormous crash. So here's to new energy, rock, and the breaking down of cultural barriers.

March 4

Into the Wild is released on DVD. Interviews with Eddie Vedder and Sean Penn are included on a two-disc special edition.

March 18

Sire Records releases *Body of War: Songs That Inspired an Iraq War Veteran* as a companion to the documentary *Body of War*. The subject of that film, paralyzed Iraq War veteran Tomas Young, personally selects the track list, which includes live versions of Eddie Vedder and Ben Harper performing "No More" (from Lollapalooza 2007) and Pearl Jam covering Bob Dylan's "Masters of War" (from the 2003 concert at Seattle's Benaroya Hall).

March 24–25
Kenyon Hall, Seattle

Eddie Vedder stuns fans who'd bought tickets for an *Into the Wild* screening by instead performing full solo sets in advance of the April 2 launch in Vancouver of his first solo tour. Tickets to the gigs were sold for $5 by Easy Street Records, with fewer than 150 people on hand each night. A number of fans who lined up outside the venue but were initially unable to get inside are treated to coffee by the Easy Street staff, before being ushered in gratis after the shows have started. The set lists mix Pearl Jam tracks ("Around the Bend," "I Am Mine," "Dead Man") with songs from *Into the Wild* ("Guaranteed," "No Ceiling," "Society") and a bevy of covers (Bruce Springsteen's "Growin' Up," Tom Petty's "I Won't Back Down," Bob Dylan's "Forever Young," Tom Waits's "Picture in a Frame").

March 25

The guitar Eddie Vedder used to write "Love Boat Captain" sells for $8,000 at a West Memphis Three fund-raising auction held at the New York home of Peter, Paul and Mary's Peter Yarrow.

April 2
Centre in Vancouver for Performing Arts, Vancouver, Canada

At the kickoff of his first solo tour, Eddie Vedder unearths the vintage Butthole Surfers T-shirt he wore at Pearl Jam's first concert on October 22, 1990.

April 13
Wiltern Theater, Los Angeles

Ben Harper and former Pearl Jam drummer Jack Irons make surprise appearances at Eddie Vedder's solo show. Harper duets with Vedder on "No More" and joins opening act Liam Finn and Eliza-Jane Barnes for "Hard

Be it no concern
Point of no return —
Go forward in reverse —

This I will recall — ...
Every time I fall — .

aaahh — . oooh — .
Setting for a in the universe
aaah — . oooh — .
Setting for a in the universe

Out here, realising
A planet out of sight
Nature drank & high — -

aaaah — . ooh

331

Sun." Irons drums on "Last Kiss" and, in tandem with Harper on slide guitar, helps Vedder power through a show-closing cover of "All Along the Watchtower."

Ben Harper: What blows me away about Ed's acoustic shows is that it's hard to have a unique sound with a voice and a guitar. He has such a unique touch and feel, and his own unique acoustic sound is unlike anyone else. It's folk, blues, rock, Middle Eastern. Through his experiences of playing with other people and his constant open-mindedness to hearing new music, this unique solo sound has formed around him. How great to have both as an outlet? What he brings solo is only going to enhance Pearl Jam, and every step Pearl Jam grows will circle back and support Ed's solo stuff.

April 22

Pearl Jam is featured in the documentary *Wetlands Preserved: The Story of an Activist Rock Club,* released on DVD today. The film tells the story of defunct New York venue Wetlands Preserve, which hosted Pearl Jam's second-ever Manhattan show on July 17, 1991.

June 10

Pearl Jam's official bootleg program hits the mobile space for the first time through a partnership with Verizon Wireless, which makes available three live tracks per show from the band's summer tour through its V CAST service.

June 11
Cruzan Amphitheatre, West Palm Beach, Florida

Without new music to promote, Pearl Jam begins a short North American trek, roughly coinciding with the ten-year anniversary of Matt Cameron's first tour with the band.

Matt Cameron: One of the fascinating aspects of Pearl Jam is how they finally came to terms with how big the band was. I love the transition records like *No Code* and *Yield.* They were very experimental. And the music went to a place that a band at their level probably shouldn't have gone to, because I don't

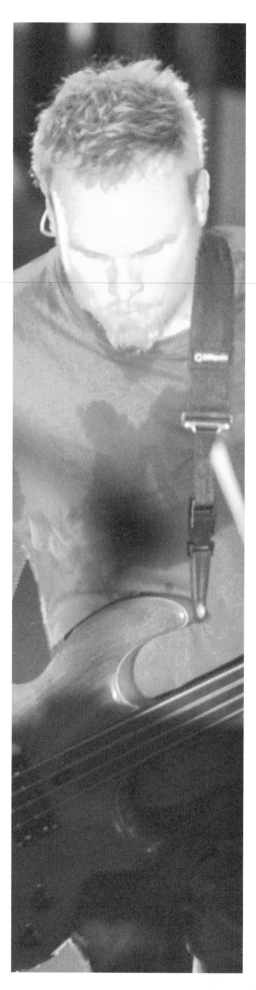

think they were trying to piss off their crowd, but they were really trying to find things within the group that they still wanted to do and were inspired to do. I felt like through that experimental music they were doing, they found a way to make the successful part of their career better somehow. They didn't change managers. They didn't become drug addicts. They just really focused on what was important to them, which was music.

June 14
Manchester, Tennessee

Pearl Jam headlines the second night of the annual Bonnaroo festival, just its second festival appearance in the United States since the Roskilde tragedy in 2000. "There was a time when we thought we'd never play a show like this again—and for good reason," Vedder tells the crowd. "This makes you realize how it could actually work. And on top of that, it's a great fuckin' night." The twenty-six-song set begins with the unusual opener "Hard to Imagine" and also includes the live debut of the *No Code*–era outtake "All Night," as well as the first complete live performance of "W.M.A." from *Vs.* in thirteen years.

Weeks earlier, rapper Kanye West insists on not performing before or during Pearl Jam's set, and only on the main stage. As such, when Pearl Jam finishes, it takes nearly two hours to set up West's elaborate stage design, and he finally starts performing at four thirty in the morning. The rapper later goes ballistic in a blog post, blaming both Bonnaroo organizers and Pearl Jam for his time slot.

June 18
Mann Center for the Performing Arts, Philadelphia

Eddie Vedder joins R.E.M. onstage to sing "Begin the Begin."

June 24–25
Madison Square Garden, New York

Pearl Jam gives a nod to its classic rock influences during a memorable two-night run at Madison Square Garden. C. J. Ramone plays bass both nights on a cover of the Ramones' "I Believe in Miracles," while Kiss's Ace Frehley plays on his former band's "Black Diamond" during the second show.

June 26

Harrybu McCage, Matt Cameron's jazz trio with keyboardist Ryan Burns and bassist Geoff Harper, releases its self-titled debut exclusively through Pearl Jam.com.

July 1
Beacon Theater, New York

Pearl Jam packs arena-sized power into the 2,800-capacity Beacon Theater during a private show that raises $3 million for the Robin Hood Foundation's poverty-fighting initiatives. Having played a two-and-a-half-hour set the night before in Boston, the band eases into the show, playing the first five songs seated. An under-the-weather Vedder tells the crowd, some of whom had paid $2,250 for floor-level seats, that he required a steroid shot in his posterior to get him stage ready for the evening.

July 12
UCLA Pauley Pavilion, Los Angeles

Pearl Jam performs "Love, Reign O'er Me" and "The Real Me" as part of VH1's *Rock Honors* tribute to the Who, backed by Brendan O'Brien on keyboards as well as string and horn players. The evening also features performances from Foo Fighters, the Flaming Lips, Incubus, Tenacious D, and the Who themselves. The event raises more than $1 million for charities such as VH1's Save the Music Foundation and Teenage Cancer Trust.

Jeff Ament: It's always cool to learn a song like "The Real Me," which is so different than our own style. We've also never played with horns and a string section before. In Pearl Jam, the Who was a really big connection early on. Ed talked a lot about how *Quadrophenia* was his reference point for living his life. It made me kind of go back and pay a little bit more attention to the lyrics, because when I was a kid, I was more interested in the emotive qualities of the song.

Green River

July 13
Marymoor Park, Redmond, Washington

Jeff Ament and Stone Gossard reunite with their Green River bandmates Mark Arm, Steve Turner, Alex Vincent, and Bruce Fairweather as part of Sub Pop Records's twentieth anniversary celebration. The group had played a secret show, its first in nearly twenty-one years, at Seattle's Sunset Tavern three days earlier. The shows feature two unreleased songs from Green River's earliest demo, "Baby, Help Me Forget" and "Leech."

Jeff Ament: In a weird way, those are probably some of the best songs we have. It's funny how it works. At the time, we thought they were way too simple or not challenging enough. But in retrospect, they're really great pop songs. We relearned those two, but there are five or six songs that never got released.

Stone Gossard: Green River was much more an amalgam of different influences that didn't necessarily make perfect sense together but created something that sounded sort of original in its intent.

August 1

Eddie Vedder begins the second leg of his maiden solo tour at the Boston Opera House.

August 21
Youngstown Cultural Arts Center, Seattle

Performing as Bison, Mike McCready teams with the Presidents of the United States of America's Dave Dederer, Guns N' Roses/Velvet Revolver's Duff McKagan, and others at an all-day fund-raiser for the All-Access After School Arts Program.

August 27
Tractor Tavern, Seattle

Mike McCready's pre–Pearl Jam band Shadow '86 reunites to play a Jimi Hendrix tribute at a benefit for Soulumination, which provides professional photos free of charge for families of children with life-threatening illnesses.

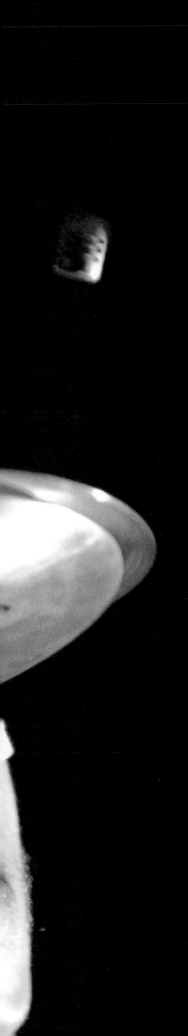

September

Pearl Jam contributes "Long Road" to the documentary film *Witch Hunt.* Directed by longtime Pearl Jam fans Don Hardy Jr. and Dana Nachman, and narrated by Sean Penn, the film tells the story of several Bakersfield, California, residents whose lives were destroyed by accusations of child molestation. After screening at film festivals in late 2008, *Witch Hunt* airs April 12, 2009, on MSNBC.

September 16

Jeff Ament's debut solo album, *Tone,* is released. The material represents an accumulation of ten years' worth of songs Ament never solicited for potential inclusion on a Pearl Jam album. Richard Stuverud, Ament's collaborator in his prior solo project Three Fish, plays drums on seven tracks, while King's X front man Doug Pinnick sings lead on "Doubting Thomasina." The song "The Forest" was actually recorded by Pearl Jam but never with vocals.

Jeff Ament: It just got to a point where I had to clean off the shelf a little bit. I broke this group of thirty-five songs into three groups and decided to finish one of them.

September 18

Pearl Jam's website begins selling a digital download of "All the Way," a Chicago Cubs–themed song written by lifelong fan Eddie Vedder at the request of Cubs legend Ernie Banks. The track, with lines like "Our heroes wear pinstripes / our heroes in blue / give us a chance to feel like heroes do," was recorded in August during Vedder's solo show at Chicago's Auditorium Theatre. During the Cubs' 2008 playoff run, a number of national radio stations begin spinning "All the Way," which is later made available on CD.

September 22

Eddie Vedder is nominated for mtvU's Good Woodie Award for humanitarian efforts involving veterans' issues, the Bridge School Benefit, People for the Ethical Treatment of Animals (PETA), and children's music programs.

October 1
Wilbur Theatre, Boston

Stone Gossard and the Hank Khoir kick off a four-show tour as part of Timberland's Dig It campaign, which promotes environmental activism through music. Tickets to the shows are primarily distributed to people who volunteer for daytime "regreening" events in each city. In tandem with the shows, Pearl Jam's website launches new solo music from Stone over the next several weeks, including "Your Flames," "Little One," and a cover of Prince's "1999."

October 28

Body of War is released on DVD. Among the bonus features is a music video for Eddie Vedder's original song "No More." A quarter of the proceeds from DVD sales on Pearl Jam's website go directly to Tomas Young, the paralyzed Iraq War veteran at the center of the film.

October 28

Peter Bogdanovich's film *Runnin' Down a Dream: Tom Petty and the Heartbreakers* is released as a two-DVD set, pared down from the four-DVD original. New to this edition is Eddie Vedder's duet with Petty on "The Waiting," recorded July 3, 2006, at the Pepsi Center in Denver.

November 3
Showbox, Seattle

Mike McCready and Stone Gossard join Rage Against the Machine/Audioslave guitarist Tom Morello and the Coup rapper Boots Riley for a Get Out the Vote rally and concert in Seattle.

November 4

Too Tough to Die: A Tribute to Johnny Ramone, a concert film/documentary directed by Mandy Stein, is released on DVD through Cactus Three Films. Shot on September 12, 2004, at the Ramones' thirtieth anniversary tribute concert and benefit for cancer research at the Avalon in Los Angeles, *Tough* includes Eddie Vedder covering "I Believe in Miracles" and "Sheena Is a Punk Rocker."

November 6
Paramount Theatre, Seattle

Mike McCready performs with Buddy
Guy, Eric Johnson, and former Jimi
Hendrix bandmates Billy Cox and Mitch
Mitchell during the Seattle stop of the
Experience Hendrix tour. Six days later,
drummer Mitchell dies of natural causes
in his hotel room in Portland, Oregon.

November 12

Yep Roc Records releases an EP with
five versions of John Doe's song "The
Golden State," including a cover by
Eddie Vedder and former Sleater-Kinney
member Corin Tucker.

December 3

Eddie Vedder is nominated for a best
solo rock vocal performance Grammy
for "Rise" from the *Into the Wild*
soundtrack.

THIS IS WHAT ED LOOKS LIKE AFTER
FEELING THE RELIEF OF FINISHING
AN INTRODUCTION TO A FAN CLUB LETTER—
THANKS FOR YOUR PATIENCE — — (OVER)

2009

Conventional music business wisdom said that a band as big as Pearl Jam couldn't possibly self-release an album. After all, it would take a staff of hundreds to handle marketing and distribution, not to mention coordinate the launch internationally. But Pearl Jam did exactly that with its ninth album, *Backspacer,* partnering with everyone from Target to iTunes to Verizon to bring the record to fans without the assistance of a traditional record label. The deals, including one with Universal to handle international distribution, ensured Pearl Jam's music was accessible at the biggest consumer chain and the tiniest independent store, all while embracing digital and mobile platforms like never before. While Pearl Jam was in complete control of its business, its music was resonating just as loudly: *Backspacer* debuted at number one on the *Billboard* 200, giving the band its first chart topper in thirteen years.

January 20
Tractor Tavern, Seattle

Eddie Vedder joins X's John Doe and Exene Cervenka to perform that band's "The New World" at a show by their side project the Knitters. The song was chosen as a nod to President Barack Obama's inauguration earlier in the day.

January 29

Mike McCready testifies before the House Judiciary Committee in Olympia, Washington, in support of House Bill 1138, which will allow persons with certain medical conditions (including Crohn's disease and colitis) access to private and "employee" restrooms at retail establishments across Washington State. Governor Chris Gregoire signs the bill into law on May 11, 2009.

March 16

Pearl Jam joins a select group of artists, including the Beatles and Elvis Presley, to reach no. 1 on a *Billboard* chart with a song recorded decades earlier, as "Brother" rises to the top of *Billboard*'s Modern Rock chart. The song was tracked during sessions for *Ten* but not officially released until the 2003 compilation *Lost Dogs,* albeit in instrumental form. The chart-topping version, this time with vocals, is the lead track from a deluxe boxed set reissue of *Ten* released on March 24. The set

features the remastered original album, a new remix of *Ten* by Brendan O'Brien, a DVD of Pearl Jam's 1992 appearance on *MTV Unplugged,* and a vinyl pressing of the September 20, 1992, show at Warren G. Magnuson Park in Seattle. On April 3 the reissue debuts at no. 1 on *Billboard*'s Top Pop Catalog, Top Hard Rock Albums, and Top Internet Albums charts.

Jeff Ament: I was really, really into "Brother." Stone wrote that song musically. There was a point during the recording of *Ten* that he was like, "Eh, I'm over it." And I was like, "No! Let's work on it." We actually got in a big fight about it in the studio. It didn't end up getting worked on anymore. I think maybe to some degree Ed probably wasn't totally happy with where it was at, so it never came out. I think there's great guitar on that song.

Ament is the driving force in getting O'Brien to agree to remix *Ten* in full, having initially convinced him to overhaul three songs from the album for the 2004 hits package *Rearviewmirror.*

Jeff Ament: Somewhere in the late nineties, I found a rough mix tape of *Ten.* I played it on cassette, and that's when I started saying, "We have to remix *Ten.*" It would usually happen after we'd been in a club or something, and we'd hear a song from it. It was like, "Ugh! This is killing me!" At one point, I told Brendan that I'd pay him to just do a version for me, just so if I had to listen to a song to relearn it or whatever, I'd hear the proper version.

He was always like, "It's a classic, and I don't want to touch it." He was very respectful. That's the reason the original is still part of this package, because it's the version that ten million or however many people bought. When you hear his version, though, it's just twice as powerful to me. It's so much more distinctive.

Brendan O'Brien: Jeff had been trying to get me to do it forever. I was like, "Jeff, for better or for worse, that record, like few others of that time, is part of people's psyches. They did crazy and amazing things while that record was playing. They don't want to hear it differently!" But Jeff was superadamant about it. I came up with what I thought was a good compromise: As long as you can get the remixes along with the original, and not separately, then I'm fine with it. They said, "Great. That makes sense." I felt like at that point I could do it with a clear conscience, and that I wasn't trying to permanently replace anything. Luckily, because it was done that way, I didn't hear a lot of vehement objections to it. If it had been offered by itself, I think people would have lost their minds, like, "What are you doing, you fools?"

March 31

Ten is certified thirteen times platinum for US shipments of thirteen million copies by the Recording Industry Association of America.

April 4
Radio City Music Hall, New York

Eddie Vedder, Paul McCartney, Ringo Starr, Donovan, Ben Harper, and Sheryl Crow are among the performers at the Change Begins Within benefit, proceeds from which go toward the David Lynch Foundation for Consciousness-Based Education and World Peace's effort to teach one million at-risk children the techniques of Transcendental Meditation. Vedder and Harper perform Queen and David Bowie's "Under Pressure," and Vedder also pitches in on backup vocals during Starr's "Yellow Submarine." The concert raises an estimated $3 million.

Ben Harper: Maybe seven years ago, I get a call out of the blue from Ed saying, "We've got to do 'Under Pressure.' You

2009

take the high, I'll take the low. We'll find the harmony spots. We should just record it. I don't know what we'll do with it." I was like, "Great idea. I'd love to. I'm a little intimidated by the scatting part, but I'm game." So in 2008, the guitar player in my band Relentless7 asked me if I'd ever consider doing "Under Pressure." I didn't say anything about Ed to him at the time; I just agreed. We learned it and got it down, but Ed called me and said, "Oh, man! You're doing it

without me? You didn't tell me the train is leaving the station." So I said, "Come on out, and let's do it." It turned out we were doing the David Lynch thing together and the stars finally aligned.

April 15

Stone Gossard, NBC announcer Rowdy Gaines, Olympic swimming champions Jason Lezak and Eric Shanteau,

Conservation International and Canadian Sea Turtle Network scientists, and representatives from National Geographic kick off "The Great Turtle Race" in a telephone news conference. The race follows eleven leatherback sea turtles tagged with state-of-the-art satellite tracking devices on a 3,700-mile journey from feeding grounds in the frigid waters of Nova Scotia to nesting beaches throughout the Caribbean. The event aims to raise awareness and support for

protection of the species and the world's oceans. Pearl Jam sponsors a lady sea turtle named Backspacer, who wins the competition eight days later when she crosses the finish line near Saint Lucia.

April 16

Pearl Jam attends the opening night of the Atlanta Film Festival for the world premiere of the documentary film *The People Speak,* based on Howard Zinn's acclaimed book *A People's History of the United States.* In the film, Vedder performs Bob Dylan's "Masters of War," as well as "Here's to the State of Mississippi" (Tim Robbins's 2006 rewrite of a Phil Ochs song), and "No More."

May 2
Showbox, Seattle

Mike McCready's UFO cover band Flight to Mars headlines a benefit concert for the Crohn's & Colitis Foundation of America's Camp Oasis and Advocacy for Patients. McCready's Shadow '86 also performs a tribute to Jimi Hendrix at the show.

May 3 and 10

Sixteen songs from Pearl Jam's catalog are used as the soundtrack for the two-part season finale of CBS's *Cold Case.* Of the ten artists who've had their music featured exclusively on the television series, Pearl Jam is the only one to be used for more than one episode. Songs played over the two episodes are "Corduroy," "Come Back," "Who You Are," "Why Go," "Rearviewmirror," "In Hiding," "Indifference," "Yellow Ledbetter," "Once," "Alive," "Man of the Hour," "Nothingman," "Given to Fly," "Release," "Immortality," and "Black."

May 6

Jeff Ament reunites with his old friends and former bandmates from Deranged Diction to release a double-disc set that includes the rerelease of the band's original cassette-only 1983 debut *No Art, No Cowboys, No Rules* and a second disc titled *Life Support,* featuring ten songs originally written twenty-five years ago but rerecorded in November 2008.

In celebration, the band performs live in Seattle at the Crocodile Cafe (May 15) and in Missoula, Montana, at the Palace (May 16).

May 19

Mike McCready performs the national anthem at the Seattle Mariners–Los Angeles Angels of Anaheim baseball game as part of CCFA Night at Safeco Field in Seattle. Proceeds from ticket sales that evening are donated to the Northwest Chapter of the Crohn's and Colitis Foundation of America.

May 28
Showbox, Seattle

Pearl Jam once again takes over the Showbox club to tape a Cameron Crowe–directed commercial for Target. This is the first hint of the deal, announced a few days later, that the forthcoming album *Backspacer* will be a Target exclusive for big-box retail in the United States and self-released through the Ten Club to indie stores. In front of an audience of approximately three hundred paid extras, some of whom had been recently laid off from jobs in the Seattle area, Pearl Jam premieres "The Fixer," the first single from *Backspacer,* and also runs through the Dead Boys' "Sonic Reducer."

June 1

Pearl Jam is the musical guest on the first episode of *The Tonight Show with Conan O'Brien* in Los Angeles. With a poor-quality bootleg of "The Fixer" from the Showbox taping having already hit the Web, the band opts to perform a different new song, "Got Some." That same day, manager Kelly Curtis reveals the specifics of the Target deal to *Billboard* magazine, including that *Backspacer* will be Pearl Jam's first self-released album after eighteen years under the Sony Music umbrella.

June 8

Eddie Vedder embarks on a fourteen-date solo tour in Albany, New York, with support from Liam Finn.

July 20

At the stroke of midnight, the first *Backspacer* single, "The Fixer," is premiered on the Ten Club's MySpace page and released globally to broadcast and satellite radio.

July 29

The artwork for *Backspacer* goes viral as part of an online treasure hunt to find nine panels from the album cover designed by political cartoonist Tom Tomorrow. Fans who complete the puzzle receive a demo of the *Backspacer* track "Speed of Sound."

Eddie Vedder: What Tom did was phenomenal. He put so much thought into it, to the point where we had so many conversations about each drawing, that I said, "Look, I just need a week to write lyrics." At the same time, it was invigorating. Certain ideas came from him as far as the overall scope: the randomness, but also the detail. It's really a cool piece of art.

August 8
Canada Olympic Park, Calgary, Canada

Pearl Jam plays its first show in more than a year at the Virgin Festival. "The Fixer" and "Got Some" make their concert debuts. The same day, "The Fixer" debuts at no. 2 on *Billboard*'s Rock Songs chart.

August 11
Shepherd's Bush Empire, London

Pearl Jam plays to an intimate audience of two thousand people, made up almost exclusively of Ten Club members and fans who had preordered *Backspacer* from hmv.com. Rolling Stones guitarist Ron Wood joins the band for an early-set cover of "All Along the Watchtower," while "Brother" is played live for the first time since February 7, 1991, its only prior airing. In addition, "Soldier of Love" is performed for the first time since July 3, 2003, and is dedicated to Thee Headcoats' Billy Childish.

2009

August 28
Golden Gate Park, San Francisco

Pearl Jam headlines the first day of the
Outside Lands Music and Arts Festival
in San Francisco's Golden Gate Park.
Vedder references the infamous 1995
show at the same venue where he had
to leave midset due to food poisoning.
"Luckily, we had a guy called Uncle
Neil Young to come help us out, and I
just want to thank him publicly again
for putting himself in harm's way," he
says.

September 20

Pearl Jam's ninth studio album,
Backspacer, is released in the United States
through its own Monkeywrench label.

September 21–22
Key Arena, Seattle

As is common around an album release,
Pearl Jam plays two hometown shows
to premiere new material. "Gonna See
My Friend," "Amongst the Waves,"
"Johnny Guitar," "Unthought Known,"

and "Just Breathe" are performed live for the first time on night one, while on night two, "No Way" makes its first concert appearance since September 7, 1998.

September 30

Backspacer debuts at no. 1 on the *Billboard* 200 with US sales of 189,000 copies, marking the band's first chart topper since *No Code* in 1996. In addition to being the only independent release to reach no. 1 on the album chart in 2009, *Backspacer* also gives Pearl Jam its longest run on the chart since *Yield* in 1998.

October 3
KLRU-TV Studios, Austin, Texas

Pearl Jam tapes a nineteen-song set for PBS's *Austin City Limits* program for broadcast on November 21. In front of an intimate crowd of about 350 people, the group alternates new *Backspacer* songs with old favorites, and Vedder jokes about how Mike McCready used to wear spandex in his band Shadow '86. To begin the show, Vedder and Jeff Ament play Austin native Daniel Johnston's "Walking the Cow" for just the third time ever.

October 4
Zilker Park, Austin, Texas

Pearl Jam headlines the Austin City Limits festival. Jane's Addiction front man Perry Farrell guests during the encore for a cover of his band's "Mountain Song."

October 6
Gibson Amphitheatre, Universal City, California

Chris Cornell joins Pearl Jam to perform Temple of the Dog's "Hunger Strike" during the third of four shows at this venue. He hadn't played the song live with the band since October 28, 2003. Additionally, Alice in Chains guitarist Jerry Cantrell handles the solo on "Alive." Cantrell returns the following evening to play on the MC5's "Kick Out the Jams."

Chris Cornell: There's obviously nerves involved, because we didn't do a soundcheck. I just came out and sang. We've done that or any Temple of the Dog song literally, like, two or three times, and it's been almost twenty years. Because Matt is now in Pearl Jam, there's the realization that this is actually Temple of the Dog. Not an extra person, not minus a guy. That's it.

October 9
Wallis Annenberg Building, Los Angeles

The Surfrider Foundation honors Pearl Jam with a Keepers of the Coast award for its contributions toward helping the Foundation preserve the world's oceans, coastline, and waves.

October 22

Pearl Jam joins a coalition of musicians in the National Campaign to Close Guantanamo. In addition, the musicians launch a formal protest of the use of music in conjunction with torture and seek the declassification of all secret government records pertaining to how music was used as an interrogation device.

October 27–28, 30–31
Wachovia Spectrum, Philadelphia

Pearl Jam plays 103 different songs across the final concerts ever at the fabled Philadelphia venue, including first-ever performances of "Bugs" from *Vitalogy* (with Vedder on accordion), the Ament-sung Kareem Abdul-Jabbar homage "Sweet Lew" from *Lost Dogs,* and the *Ten*-era outtake "Hold On," which fans didn't even know existed until 2004. On the final night, which coincides with Halloween, the band dresses in full Devo costumes and performs that band's classic "Whip It."

Jeff Ament: There were seven or eight songs that either we had never played or had only been played once. We had to sit in the hotel room before soundcheck and do homework and make notes and

write out arrangement things. You get to rehearsal and play it and then everybody would have their interpretation of [*laughs*] what the arrangement was, and you'd have to figure that out. A lot of times at those shows, we were going, "Shit, man, I hope this works!"

We'd been talking to people at the Spectrum for the last three years about the possibility of playing the last show there. We also played the last musical show at Chicago Stadium and one of the last at Boston Garden. Growing up being basketball fans and also just thinking about those buildings and how much happened in those buildings and how killer those old buildings sounded, it's pretty cool. I think there's five great arenas in the country. The Spectrum is number three, and four and five is the L.A. Forum and Madison Square Garden. So if they ever decide to tear those buildings down, we're going to be the first ones in line to say, "Dude, we closed out these other three, so we're veterans; nobody else has done that. You've got to let us close out these last two!"

November 25
QSAC Stadium, Brisbane, Australia

Pearl Jam covers AC/DC's "If You Want Blood (You've Got It)" for the first time, in front of a capacity crowd of thirty-five thousand.

November 27, 29
Mt. Smart Super Top, Auckland, New Zealand; AMI Stadium, Christchurch, New Zealand

Pearl Jam winds down its 2009 tour by welcoming Liam and Neil Finn to help the band cover Chris Knox's "Not Given Lightly" (November 27), Crowded House's "Better Be Home Soon" (November 29), and Split Enz's "I Got You" (November 29).

December 6
John F. Kennedy Center for the Performing Arts, Washington, DC

Eddie Vedder performs Bruce Springsteen's "My City of Ruins" during the annual Kennedy Center Honors, at which Springsteen is one of the honorees. On January 25, 2010, the

recording is made available on iTunes, with proceeds to benefit the poverty- and social justice–focused organization Artists for Peace and Justice Haiti Relief.

Bruce Springsteen: To keep your band alive for a long period of time requires the questions you're writing and dealing with to remain open. That can be uncomfortable and difficult if not impossible to sustain for a lot of artists, but it constantly pumps fresh blood into your group. That sense of continuing adventure, along with the ability to physically and emotionally hold it together, thwarts most artists aspiring to long careers. The Seattle groups carried with them a lot of hardwired dynamite that both made that music exciting and yet threatened its sustainability. Rising out of an "alternative" scene itself meant collision with the "mainstream" would be an enormous challenge that a lot of good musicians and music lost. You have to constantly be questioning how to hold on to the core of who you are while simultaneously forging a new identity. That's not easy. Pearl Jam was one of the few groups with both the physical durability and the self-analytical—and critical—qualities needed to push through that moment and to continue to serve an audience in search of essential music, and itself.

347

Backspacer

March 2009, Ed Vedder's house, Seattle. There were a bunch of empty beer bottles on the table and some scribbled notes. The kids were asleep upstairs. It was really late. Too late to call New Zealand, even.

Vedder was wrestling with a new Pearl Jam song written by Matt Cameron, whose love of tricky time signatures had bedeviled many prior attempts to take apart and reassemble the demos he submitted for the band's albums. Earlier that day, the rest of the group had put a version of the instrumental then called "Need to Know" on tape, and Vedder had then spent hours more on his own shaping it into something quite different.

"This is great," he thought. "But is it too poppy?" It was too late to ask anyone for advice—even Neil Finn, on the other side of the world, in Auckland. So Vedder kept playing his new version over and over in his headphones while his family slumbered; ten, twenty, thirty times before he lost count.

Realizing that the answer wouldn't come to him before dawn, Vedder finally went to bed. He could seek opinions from his bandmates the next day. After just one listen, it was unanimous: just poppy enough. And so Pearl Jam's ninth album, already with the provisional title *Backspacer,* had a rip-roaring rocker to anchor it. Now dubbed "The Fixer," the song went on to reach no. 2 on the *Billboard* Rock chart and spark a number of "Wait, this is Pearl Jam?"–type of reactions from blogs and critics.

The reason? Pearl Jam had arguably not written a song so catchy in the past decade, and certainly not one with lyrics so direct and upbeat: "If something's old / I want to put a little shine on it / When something's gone / I want to fight to get it back again."

"I brought it in as a two-part demo,

the verse and the intro part," Cameron recalls. "I had a vocal over those two parts. My demo version was a little bit darker sounding than what the song turned into. I did it on the fly in a pretty short amount of time, and I think [the finished song] turned out a lot better than my original version."

"When you don't have a vocal, you just put it all in there and hope for the best in terms of your arranging skills," Gossard says. "Literally, we went away and left Ed with it the night after we recorded it, and he came back with this three-minute pop song. He probably cut half the parts out and rearranged it."

"Ed's job is sort of to make sense of all the unfinished material we bring in," Cameron continues. "Sometimes we'll write lyrics to songs, but sometimes it's more of just getting a melody idea across to get to him. We know he's such a gifted lyricist, that we feel fine handing him over songs that aren't quite finished."

The band members had logged three brainstorming sessions without Vedder present before he joined in the process, yielding the jittery, Devo/Police-esque "Got Some" and the foundations for the songs "Speed of Sound" and "Force of Nature." But nearly everything else wound up scrapped.

"Immediately, everyone had five or six things on tape that they threw into the pot," Gossard admits. "But most of that stuff didn't make it. Most of the songs that did were from the second stage of the writing. I think I wrote five or six things, and none of them stuck right away." Things turned around with the second batch of material, during which Gossard finished the surging, anthemic "Amongst the Waves" and knocked the New York punk homage "Supersonic" into fighting shape.

"We ended up with a pretty concise

bunch of material and a pretty good variety," Gossard says. "There's that *Into the Wild*–sort of style that Ed does so well, and lots of high energy stuff, too."

Vedder actually found himself thinking ahead about set lists while the band was deciding which songs to pursue or which to leave behind. "When we're talking about how many times to play the bridge or how many bars to add, I'm thinking, If we double the bridge, this might end up being a song we play once a month, as opposed to three times a week," he says. "So, what do you think? How many times do you want to play this song? Is this song going to put wind in our sails, or will it be one we have to row through?"

At eleven songs and thirty-seven minutes, the finished product wound up as the most lean, mean Pearl Jam album to date. "We made this faster than we've made any record," Gossard says. "We were thirty days in the studio total, including mix. I think we had ninety percent of the record cut in the first nine days."

Even on a song like "The Fixer," with its slightly odd 6/4 time signature, the parts "break back down to something very three-chord and fun," Gossard says. "We need that. If Pearl Jam is thinking too much, we're not very good."

The person charged with making sure the band kept that idea top of mind in the studio was Brendan O'Brien, who hadn't produced a Pearl Jam album since *Yield.* His work with the band on its 2007 cover of the Who's "Love, Reign O'er Me" and his remix of *Ten* for the 2009 deluxe reissue had put him firmly back in the Pearl Jam orbit. Band members quickly realized what they'd been missing, as O'Brien provided crucial input on arrangements; played piano, keyboard, and percussion; and put together orchestrations for delicate Vedder songs like the acoustic guitar–powered "Just Breathe" and the gut-punch finale "The End."

Vedder describes the evolution of "Just Breathe" as the perfect example of O'Brien's contribution to the process. The song shares the same opening chord with the instrumental "Tuolumne" from *Into the Wild,* and after Vedder added some lyrics, he then wrote a bridge while the other band members were working on something else.

"It was like our own little Brill Building at the warehouse. I ran in and wrote the bridge, which became the chorus, because Brendan heard it that way," he says. "We were letting Brendan hear things objectively and following him whatever way he wanted to take it. We weren't that malleable ten years ago and all the years previous. You'd write something and say, 'Well, no, this is how I want it done.' One of the things as you get older is that you welcome others' input. You don't feel like you have to prove yourself."

"Brendan does those melodic things from his musician brain first, and then he's able to layer them within the music with his producer brain," Cameron adds. "He uses both sets of skills in a way that most producers aren't able to do.

"He was completely tuned in to the vocal, and that was one of the overriding themes for his production style on this record," he continues. "The arrangements really add to the vocal parts of 'The End' and 'Just Breathe,' in a real beautiful, classic, almost Phil Spector pop way. When Eddie brought those songs in, they were just nylon string acoustic guitar and voice. Brendan played a lot of percussion on those songs, too."

"Ed came in one afternoon with a demo of 'Just Breathe' that had one verse and one little half chorus," O'Brien says. "He said he wanted it to come at the end of the record, with him just playing acoustic guitar. I was blown away. I said, first of all, That's incredible. But that's not a little half song. That may be the centerpiece of our record. We're going to turn it into a real song. We're not going to be afraid of it. We may even do an arrangement. It will be the most beautiful Pearl Jam song ever, and people are going to love you for it. To their credit, they went, 'Okay!'"

And although O'Brien was certainly not shy about helping the band tinker with ideas, he also encouraged the members not to fuss over the fundamentals.

"A lot of the songs on this record were ones I just tried to get out of the way of, without self-editing," Vedder says. "It made it easier. That was the one thing I realized while putting together the *Ten* boxed set. It was interesting to hear that when we were just starting out, I just didn't edit that much. Whatever I wrote or the way I sang it the first time was the way it ended up being. Over the years, you get the luxury of taking more time and really refining and going through many different versions. Early on, we didn't have as many options. You made a record and made it quick. We kind of went back to that. Even if we have the luxury, why indulge if it's just going to create confusion?"

In the time since *Riot Act* and the politically charged tours that followed, Pearl Jam had deliberately toned down its lyrical rhetoric and begun to look inward. Continuing in the vein of the intensely personal story songs found on the "Avocado" album, Vedder didn't shy away from writing directly to those closest to him on songs like "Just Breathe" and "The End." But at the same time, the new songs had an optimism that hadn't been heard from Pearl Jam very frequently during the George W. Bush era.

"Overall with the record, because the last two were pretty political, Ed may have been five thousand feet above the ground looking at America," Gossard says. "This one feels like he's two hundred thousand feet above the planet looking down with a little more optimism."

"I guess we end up being conduits for whatever's around us," Vedder says. "You don't really think about it while it's happening, but then you look back on this group of songs, and that seems to come out. You write a song, you look to the sky, and it somehow comes out. It's no surprise that it's representative of the atmosphere. I do think there are things in there that are universal."

Among them are the radical changes that people go through after they have families. As he sat down to pen lyrics for the new songs, Vedder—now with two small children and a longtime partner at home in Seattle—found himself crafting some of the most unvarnished love songs of Pearl Jam's career.

On "Just Breathe" and "The End," he seeks penance for all the time spent away from his family: "Did I say that I need you? / Did I say that I want you? / Oh, if I didn't, I'm a fool you see / No one knows this more than me," goes the chorus on the former. The Vedder-only "The End" is especially gripping, thanks to Eddie Horst's string arrangement and the eye-opening line that brings the album to a dead stop: "My dear / the end comes near / I'm here / but not much longer."

"You know, I'll admit that even I felt some impact myself listening to it back the first time, and not even really knowing where it came from," Vedder says of the song, which he played publicly for the first time during his 2008 solo tour.

"There are some strings and French horns, and it became kind of emotional when we laid the strings down," he continues. "When I was a kid, I was really moved by this song called 'Street in the City' off of *Rough Mix* by Pete Townshend. It was such a powerful juxtaposition of strings and acoustic guitar. His was a full-on orchestral arrangement that I believe his father-in-law did. The visual was of one guy playing with an orchestra behind him. To get a chance to explore a little bit of that sound . . . it turned into something very cinematic."

Says Gossard, "I think that song is going to stand out as being one of his greatest songs ever. To have a song that is so simple in terms of the vocal melody and delivery, and for the words to have that much impact and to flow without a complex rhyme strategy. The words rhyme, but that's the last thing you think about. I just think it is a stunning example of Eddie on his own. It's just ridiculously good. He just about breaks his voice. It's so vulnerable."

"I remember clearly the first words spoken after I played the song for the guys, and they came from Stone," Vedder says. "He said, 'Wow. Now, that's a complete thought.' I still smile about that."

"The Fixer" also suggested a variety of meanings, with Gossard favoring one in which the title references Vedder's role within Pearl Jam. "My personal interpretation is that it's about how he makes our songs work," he says. "When someone inspires him, he's an incredible collaborator. If you know him as a friend, you know he has this enormous capacity to give. You don't get it every day, but when he works on your behalf, he really does something special. He puts a lot into it."

Vedder views the song a bit more broadly. "Stone might be right to a certain extent. If it were to be about the band, then it would actually be more about each different song. But that's not fixing; that's just directing it somewhere. I'm thinking more on a worldview or a community view," he says.

"On the other hand, it's a classic kind of man-woman thing, and this is where it's not necessarily a positive trait to always try to be fixing things. A partner will tell you what's going on with some issues, and then you say, 'Well, okay, we'll fix it! We'll do this and we'll do that.' Then they'll say, 'But there's something else.' 'Okay, we'll do this and we'll do *that*.' For some folks, it's just the desire to express their emotions of frustration. Certain kinds of knucklehead male counterparts that I can relate to will simply say, 'Don't get upset. We'll fix it.' It's not about the fixing. It's about the listening. That'll be the next one: 'The Listener' [*laughs hard*].

"Of course, I can't say anything in the song. It's going to be an instrumental, because I'll just be listening."

The album opens with "Gonna See My Friend," where a garage-rock boogie verse careens in less than thirty seconds into a passionate chorus, with Vedder's vocal deftly split between the high and low extremes of his register. It's a drug song with a twist: Rather than paying the titular friend a visit so as to score, the narrator is instead desperate to reach a friend who can help him stay clean.

Rock 'n' roll is the drug of choice on "Got Some" and "Supersonic," which revel in the simple, life-affirming pleasures of music. These songs are Pearl Jam distilled to its bare essence, bashing away on guitar, bass, and drums with anything-goes fervor.

Although it took a few years to bubble its way into Pearl Jam's sound, new wave was a formative stylistic touchstone for several band members, particularly Vedder, who worshipped Split Enz and early Talking Heads. On *Backspacer,* this influence is more apparent than ever, from the pounding

downstroke riffs of "Johnny Guitar," which wouldn't sound out of place on the Knack's first album, the galloping, dark power pop of "Got Some," and the robotic, half-time breakdown in "Supersonic."

Vedder sings from the perspective of the last guy in the bar on "Speed of Sound," which counters its somewhat morose lyrics with a slow-building music bed that eventually reaches arena size. The song was originally written by Vedder as a contribution to a solo album from Rolling Stones guitarist Ron Wood, who opted not to use it. Although the song "Unthought Known" has equally ambiguous words ("Dream the dreams of other men / You'll be no one's rival"), it turns more quickly into a fist pumper, almost like a turbo-charged "Wishlist."

And while old friend O'Brien was key in helping the band realize the *Backspacer* songs, for the first time, a new and outside collaborator was charged with developing a visual accompaniment to the music. Vedder had met politically minded cartoonist Dan Perkins, better known as Tom Tomorrow, at the Ralph Nader rally in New York in 2000. They stayed in touch in the ensuing years but didn't begin to ponder working together until the spring of 2009, just after Perkins's *This Modern World* strip had been axed from twelve alternative newsweeklies in a cost-cutting measure.

"Previous to meeting him, I wasn't sure that even our politics were up to par for his biting take on things," Vedder says. "I wasn't sure that as a popular band if we were underground enough for him. We just happened to be talking about the album cover at the time this came around, and we thought, We'll give it a shot, and we'll remain friends if it doesn't work."

As designed by Perkins, the front cover of *Backspacer* is a nine-panel board, in the style of tic-tac-toe. Both whimsical and thought provoking, the images include fish swimming around a Seattle submerged underwater, a flaming freight train bearing down on an unfortunate bystander, an astronaut free-floating through outer space while playing drums, and a beautiful woman literally lying "amongst the waves."

Vedder titled the album as an homage to an oddly named typewriter key that fell out of fashion fifty years ago. Vedder, who prefers typewriters for lyric

writing and personal correspondence, says he got upset when he saw vintage typewriter keys being used as jewelry: "For me it was like shark fin soup: 'You're killing typewriters for a bracelet!'"

Gossard sees additional meaning by parsing the words a bit further. "There's some retrospective moods on this record, where Ed is looking at both his past and his future," he says.

2010

The year 2010 was a cause for both celebration and reflection for Pearl Jam, which marked the twentieth anniversary of its first show on October 22. And while it had spent two decades honing its fans-first mind-set and commitment to using its fame and resources to help better the world, the band wasn't ready to rest. "It still feels like we're growing to this day," Eddie Vedder says. "I saw a review not too long ago about how it's a rarity to see a band that's been together so long still playing as hard as we do. And really, that shouldn't be a surprise. We've been doing it now for twenty years. You *should* be better. You *should* be able to work harder. But it's a numbers game, too, because rock 'n' roll and rebellion and all that stuff is kind of a young man's game. But that fire doesn't have to go out. In fact, it doesn't go out unless you let it. There's five people still wanting to keep throwing big logs on the fire."

January 28

Pearl Jam scores its first no. 1 on *Billboard*'s Adult Alternative Airplay (Triple A) chart as "Just Breathe" jumps from no. 2 to the top spot. "I Am Mine" was the band's previous highest single on the tally, having reached no. 3 in 2002.

March 13

Pearl Jam makes its fourth appearance on NBC's *Saturday Night Live,* performing "Just Breathe" with a string section made up of local players as well as "Unthought Known." Band members also appear briefly in a sketch parodying the famous *Twilight Zone* episode "Nightmare at 20,000 Feet," about a man having hallucinations during an airplane flight.

March 15

Mike McCready sits in with *Late Night with Jimmy Fallon* house band the Roots, jamming on Jimi Hendrix covers and improvisations made up earlier that day.

March 30
Royal Albert Hall, London

Eddie Vedder guests with the Who during a complete performance of the band's 1973 rock opera *Quadrophenia* during a benefit for Teenage Cancer Trust. Vedder appears as the character "The Godfather" on "The Punk Meets the Godfather," "I've Had Enough," and "Sea and Sand."

April 14
Showbox, Seattle

A who's who of Seattle musicians, including Stone Gossard and Shawn Smith, gather at the Showbox to celebrate the music of Pigeonhed, Brad, Satchel, and Malfunkshun. Smith also sings with the surviving members of Mother Love Bone, who perform together for the first time since the band broke up in 1990.

Stone Gossard: A big part of it was thinking about Andy Wood and how much his history has sort of touched on all of us. Andy's influence is definitely something I think about all the time. That show coming together grew out of the feeling of trying to bring together, just for one event, what everyone's been working on. It was a little bit of Hank Khoir, which is folks I've been playing with. It was a chance for Jeff Ament and I and Mother Love Bone's Bruce Fairweather and Greg Gilmore to play together with Shawn singing Andy's words, which was just beautiful.

April 16
Showbox, Seattle

With Matt Cameron on drums, Soundgarden plays its first live show since 1997 in front of a select audience of friends and fans.

April 19
McCaw Hall, Seattle

Eddie Vedder and Mike McCready make surprise appearances at Conan O'Brien's Legally Prohibited From Being Funny on Television tour stop in Seattle. Vedder plays "Rise" from *Into the Wild,* and also modifies the John Lennon song "Oh Yoko!" as "Oh CoCo!" Later, McCready joins Vedder to rock through "Baba O'Riley" with O'Brien's house band.

May 1
Fair Grounds Race Course, New Orleans

Pearl Jam begins its 2010 North American tour with its first appearance at the New Orleans Jazz & Heritage Festival. The show opens with the bizarre one-two punch of the Byrds' "So You Want to Be a Rock 'n' Roll Star" followed by "Lukin." Vedder reminisces about spending a night in jail in New Orleans in 1993 following a bar fight, and later speaks to US troops stationed in Iraq and Afghanistan via live satellite feed. Inspired by the visit, Pearl Jam pledges $100,000 to the Gulf Restoration Network in the aftermath of the massive BP oil spill, which had occurred less than two weeks earlier.

May 6
Nationwide Arena, Columbus, Ohio

Mike McCready opens the show with a solo set of the Rolling Stones' "Dead Flowers" and an untitled song about his infant son.

May 10
HSBC Arena, Buffalo

The *Binaural*-era outtake "Fatal" is played live for the first time since September 9, 2006.

May 15
XL Center, Hartford

Pearl Jam plays what Vedder calls a "one time, and one time only" cover of Van Halen's "Ain't Talkin' 'Bout Love."

Jeff Ament: Actually, it was Ed's idea, but Mike has been training for that moment his whole life.

May 20–21
Madison Square Garden, New York

Pearl Jam visits one of its favorite venues to end the North American portion of its 2010 tour. The second of two shows is packed with rarities, including a drastically slowed-down version of "Lukin" backed by a string section, the first live appearance of "Black Red Yellow" since September 12, 2005, the second-ever version of "Sweet Lew," and a roof-raising take on "Hunger Strike," with Ben Bridwell from opening act Band of Horses handling Chris Cornell's vocal part.

Jeff Ament: Usually Ed is the one who decides to play the super-rare songs, but we all throw those out there, especially toward the end of a long tour. How else would they talk me into doing "Sweet Lew"?

Ben Bridwell: I went to the side stage to watch the four or five songs before I was due to join them, and my nerves and emotions kicked into full gear. When the time came for me to hop up onstage, I could barely hold myself together. At the end of "my" first verse, the crowd gave me a great cheer of support, and I finally exhaled for what seemed like the first time in a half hour. I was on the verge of bawling right there and again had to compose myself. After that, it was pretty smooth sailing, even though I still had the difficult task of attempting Cornell's register on the choruses. Next thing I know, it's over. I must have sprinted off the stage and back to the dressing room. There's few moments I've found myself saying, "I can die a happy man." That certainly was one of those moments.

June 22
The 02, Dublin, Ireland

Pearl Jam begins a short European tour with a show featuring first plays of Joe Strummer and the Mescaleros' "Arms Aloft" and "Of the Earth," a song recorded during sessions for the "Avocado" album but not discussed publicly by the band in years.

Jeff Ament: We sort of barely got into that song on "Avocado," and we properly arranged the whole middle section of it when we made *Backspacer.* That was one of those four or five songs from "Avocado" that we needed to spend a lot more time with to make right, but it was the end of the process, and we didn't have the energy. We did it for *Backspacer,* but it ended up in the same spot. It just wasn't one of Brendan's favorites, partially because it's so long and has so many twists and turns. That's an Ed song, and he had it pretty mapped out. We jammed on it a few times during "Avocado," then we rearranged it. It's still morphing.

June 22

A new Eddie Vedder song, "Better Days," is released to iTunes in advance of the July 20 release of the soundtrack to the film *Eat Pray Love,* starring Julia Roberts and Javier Bardem. The album is released by Pearl Jam's Monkeywrench label in conjunction with Sony Pictures.

June 30
Wuhlheide, Berlin

Pearl Jam marks the tenth anniversary of the Roskilde tragedy by holding a minute of silence before playing "Come Back" in the second encore.

Stone Gossard: Those families still ache deeply for the loss of their children. I hope to acknowledge the past and honor those who died and those who lost them. As a band, we still feel that loss profoundly, and we hope and pray that in time it will lessen or transform.

The band also debuts a cover of Public Image Ltd.'s "Public Image" and is

joined by R.E.M.'s Peter Buck and Scott McCaughey, in town to work on their band's next album, for a cover of the MC5's "Kick Out the Jams."

Peter Buck: I was just standing back there, and Eddie goes, "Hey, are you going to play tonight?" I hadn't thought about it. I was just there for the show. We had a choice of three or four songs. It shocked me that they did "Public Image," and thankfully they didn't invite me up, because I didn't know it!

While in Berlin, Eddie Vedder drops by an R.E.M. studio session and winds up contributing to the band's in-progress album, *Collapse Into Now,* marking his first recorded collaboration with the legendary group.

Peter Buck: There's this great song called "It Happened Today." It's an elegy, but it's real up-tempo. There are a bunch

of vocals at the end; Mike Mills sings, Michael Stipe sings, and Eddie co-sings lead for the last half of the song. It's really a great song. He came by the studio, we played some stuff for him, and Michael must have said, "Do you want to sing on this?" I was actually out to dinner when it happened.

Eddie Vedder: Actually, maybe Peter was at breakfast. Michael Stipe called me in the morning as we were about to leave for a show in France. I skipped shaving and my other grooming habits in order to get to Hansa Studios and belt it out for a half hour instead.

June 30

Pearl Jam premieres a music video for "Amongst the Waves," combining live footage shot by Brendan Canty and Ryan Thomas in Philadelphia in October

2009 with ocean cinematography by Daren Crawford. Proceeds from sales of the video on iTunes go to benefit Conservation International's It's Our Ocean Campaign.

July 4
Werchter Festival, Werchter, Belgium

Pearl Jam shares a bill with reconstituted Seattle band Alice in Chains for the first time since August 1992. Adding to the familial vibe, Foo Fighters front man Dave Grohl joins Pearl Jam on tambourine during the encore for a cover of the MC5's "Kick Out the Jams."

Dave Grohl: When Pearl Jam released their last record, there was an article in a UK magazine that talked about how Kurt didn't like them, like it still mattered. Like, who fucking cares whether Kurt

liked Pearl Jam or not? It made me really upset, because Kurt's not around to defend himself, but also because that was considered a stamp of approval; that one person's opinion would matter that much. The next interview I did, I really stuck up for Pearl Jam. If there's one thing at the end of the day that will destroy music, it's guilt. That guilt that some musicians feel that keeps them from making music, any kind of music—that you could let something so petty get in the way of making something beautiful. It really affected me, because the last time I watched Pearl Jam, I sat on the side of the stage and cried, because I thought, Wow, man. These guys survived. They fucking survived! Out of everybody else, they're still fucking going. It made me really happy. I texted Eddie later on to tell him that it was an emotional moment for me. They survived, and they survived without the guilt and the shame. They survived on music.

Jerry Cantrell: Stone came into the dressing room and said, "Man, way to go. Way to not give up." They didn't give up, those guys. I'm really proud of them, and I'm proud to be part of the history of what happened in our town. It's amazing that they are still the force that they are, considering the cost they paid to get to that point. They set a great example for all of us to follow.

July 20

Pearl Jam unveils a live video for "Unthought Known," shot on a Mac laptop from onstage during the band's June 30 show in Berlin. Eddie Vedder, under his Wes C. Addle pseudonym, is listed as director, while Neil Young, as his pseudonym Bernard Shakey, is credited with the concept.

August 8
Grant Park, Chicago

Having warmed up with an intimate show three nights earlier at the Vic Theatre, Matt Cameron and Soundgarden headline the final night of the Lollapalooza festival.

August 10

Brad releases its fourth album, *Best Friends?*, for which recording began in 2003 but wasn't completed until recently. Distributed through Pearl Jam's Monkeywrench label, the project is supported by a fall North American tour featuring headline dates and a host of shows opening for Band of Horses, as well as an October 11 appearance on NBC's *Late Night with Jimmy Fallon.*

Stone Gossard: For whatever reason, it just fell by the wayside after we recorded it. I think our drummer, Regan Hagar, and I started picking it back up maybe a couple of years later. I started going back in and editing and adding some guitars, falling in love with it again. But still the process rolled on and singer Shawn Smith was really focused on some stuff that he was doing, and Regan was focused on stuff that he was doing. I was totally focused on Pearl Jam, and recording my own music. And then it comes around again, and all of a sudden you realize it's been seven years, and you still do have this record. You listen to it and go, "Wow, this is pretty good."

August 28
Robinson Center Music Hall, Little Rock, Arkansas

Eddie Vedder joins the Dixie Chicks' Natalie Maines, Patti Smith, actor Johnny Depp, and Ben Harper's new band Fistful of Mercy at a concert to raise awareness for the West Memphis Three. Playing solo and in collaboration with the other artists, Vedder performs covers of Tom Waits's "Rains on Me," Bob Dylan's "The Times They Are A-Changin'," Bruce Springsteen's "Open All Night," John Doe's "The Golden State," and James Taylor's "You Can Close Your Eyes." Vedder and Depp perform "Society" from the *Into the Wild* soundtrack and also back Smith during her miniset. All the artists team for a finale of Smith's "People Have the Power." The event is pegged to a September 30 hearing to consider new evidence in the controversial murder convictions in the case. On September 1 Vedder and Maines appear on CNN's *Larry King Live* to discuss their support for the cause.

Eddie Vedder: We weren't interested in doing anything publicly before. I think

Natalie and I are both in pretty well-respected bands, but I didn't think they needed a rock band on their side. That wasn't going to help their case at all. So, we've been kind of silent partners in this. We knew there was going to be a time that was the right time to reawaken this case in people's consciousness.

October 23–24
Shoreline Amphitheatre, Mountain View, California

At its eighth appearance at Neil Young's annual Bridge School Benefit, Pearl Jam offers up the live debuts of the *Riot Act*–era B-side "Other Side" and the 2008 Ten Club holiday single track "Santa Cruz," plus covers of Patti Smith's "Dancing Barefoot" and Young's "Walk with Me," from his new album *Le Noise.* Vedder tells the audience that Pearl Jam "wouldn't have made it past the first five or six" years of its existence without the friendship of "Uncle Neil."

December 1

Backspacer receives a Grammy nomination for rock album of the year, the fourteenth Grammy nomination of Pearl Jam's career.

Eddie Vedder: We set out to make music to satisfy ourselves. I think that was originally the plan. Something we would have never imagined is that people have made friendships, shared ideas, and shared their humanity with each other through the music. And they've become husbands and wives and best friends. That's all outside of us. All we did was play music, you know? The fact that it's happened is semioverwhelming and humbling, but it's great to know it's there. It's a big thing.

Stone Gossard: I think right now we're in a bit of a renaissance for the band. There really is a collective understanding of how lucky and how fortunate we are to still be playing music with the same group of people.

Jeff Ament: Every once in a while, we'll just say to one another, "Can you believe it? Can you believe we're still doing this?" And it's still real. It's fun and, in a lot of ways, it's more communicative and more healthy than it's ever been.

Eddie Vedder: So many people don't make it this far, and I would think they have the same appreciation for music and a drive to make music and create music and record music and share music. But somehow their bands weren't able to stay together. I think the one thing that could be missing for them is communication and understanding of each other. At some point, some of that stuff becomes unspoken. There's a communication which is unspoken, and that's the good stuff which enables you to keep going farther with it. I think the main thrust of this whole deal for us has

been to continue recording, continue writing, continue on this journey. When you get married, you don't want to get married after two dates or three dates or whatever, especially to four other people. But we got in that relationship pretty quick. And we appreciate that these relationships are what keep the music going and the songs coming. That's more important than anything.

If there's a record that sells millions and commands that much attention, then there's a theory that it's probably not that good. There's probably a large dose of mediocrity involved; that's why it

appealed to so many people. I always felt conscious of that with the hype and the amount of attention we received early on. It was tricky. It was difficult. In regards to that period, I'll always say, and Jeff will say the same thing, it was always our goal to make the next records, always our goal to get through this and survive in order to get to where we wanted to be creatively. Like, where could it go? What are the possibilities? I still think that's why we're making music together, because we're still wondering where it might go.

INDEX

ACKNOWLEDGMENTS

Jonathan Cohen thanks: All the members of Pearl Jam past and present; Kelly Curtis, Nicole Vandenberg, Michele Anthony, Christian Fresco, Tim Bierman, Sarah Seiler, Regan Hagar, Jason Mueller, Noelle Broom, Virginia Piper and everyone at Curtis Management and Vandenberg Public Relations; Cameron Crowe, Andy Fischer, Morgan Neville, Nicola Marsh and everyone at Vinyl Films and Tremolo Productions; Mark Wilkerson; Jofie Ferrari-Adler at Simon & Schuster; Jessica Letkemann, John Reynolds and Kathy Davis at Two Feet Thick; Dana Erickson, Kate Jackson, Matt Shay, Lianna Wingfield; Keith Caulfield at Billboard; and my loving family, especially my wife Kelly.

Mark Wilkerson would like to thank Eddie V., Kelly Curtis, Tim Bierman, Christian Fresco, Nicole Vandenberg, Virginia Piper and the PJ/Monkeywrench/Vandenberg Communications family, Darrin Funk, Jason Mueller, Jonathan Cohen, Alex Wilkerson, my wife Melissa and my children Alex, Nick & Sam.

Foreword and Additional Interviews by

Cameron Crowe

Words by

Jonathan Cohen

with

Mark Wilkerson

Creative Designer / Photo Editor

Regan Hagar

Research

Jonathan Cohen

Mark Wilkerson

Photo Research/Archive

Anna Knowlden

Jason Mueller

Susan Ricketts

Band Management

Curtis Management

Kelly Curtis

Michele Anthony

Andrea Dramer

Gary Westlake

Band Publicity

Vandenberg Communications

Nicole Vandenberg

Sarah Seiler

Allie O'Brien

Monkeywrench Records

Michele Anthony

Christian Fresco

Tim Bierman

John Burton

Jessica Curtis

Ten Club

Tim Bierman

Anna Knowlden

Regan Hagar

Karen Loria

Rob Skinner

Pete Crosby

Ryan Maxwell

Anna Nunn

Will Broad

Adrien Wilhite

Erik Sundahl

Kathy Salva

Marina Semel

Pearl Jam Touring

Mark Smith

Liz Burns

George A. Webb III

Josh Evans

Kevin Shuss

Simon & Schuster

Jonathan Karp

Jofie Ferrari-Adler

Michele Bové

Jonathan Evans

Nancy Singer

Larry Pekarek

Alexis Welby

Nina Pajak

Legal

Carroll, Guido, & Groffman, LLP

Elliot Groffman

Paul Gutman

Karen Pals

Additional Legal

Donaldson & Callif

Dean Cheley

Stokes Lawrence, P.S.

Accounting

Flood, Bumstead, McCready, McCarthy, Inc.

Jamie Cheek

Jeff Jones

Betsy Lee

Jason Anderson

Special Thanks

Eric Johnson

Andy Fischer

Lance Mercer

Jay Krugman

Morgan Neville

Jenny Mohr

Noelle Broom

Kerensa Wight

Mark Arm

Rob Bleetstein

Virginia Piper

Julie Ann Marsibilio

Julie Schroeder

Vinyl Films

Tremolo Productions

Sony Music

Universal Music Group

Epic Records

J Records

Sub Pop Records

Interns

Courtney Lightfoot

Stephanie Rasmusson

Christine Geronimo

Hannah Spencer

TEXT CREDITS

THE EARLY YEARS:

Alternative Press, May 1998: "I was wearing this pink . . ."

KIRO-TV, April 17, 2007: "There were ten-thousand-plus bands down there, and the odds of a band making it were very small . . ."

Just Rock Magazine, October 1991: "I worked in the middle of the night and that's how I made my living . . ."

1990:

Guitar World, July 2000: "At the time, I was so depressed about life . . ."

All That's Sacred podcast / TheSkyIScrape. com, July 7, 2010: "Stone had some songs that he'd demoed . . ."

All That's Sacred podcast / TheSkyIScrape. com, July 7, 2010: "The very first show, I remember being really nervous mostly because the songs had been worked up so fast that I was worried I was going to miss a part . . ."

Pollstar, Sept. 23, 1991: "It was really intense. It was really introverted because everything was so new, and we wanted to make sure we were playing our parts right . . ."

1991:

Spin, September 1992: "I was trying out the camp counselor thing: 'Let's all go to this club and check out these bands.' It really was the hell version of John Hughes . . ."

All That's Sacred podcast / TheSkyIScrape. com, July 7, 2010: "I've been a recovering alcoholic now for years. But then, I was a really bad alcoholic . . ."

The Island Ear, Dec. 23, 1991: "Green River played there in 1985 in front of, like, ten people, all workers . . ."

Seattle Post-Intelligencer, Jan. 3, 1992: "He was walking down the corridor at the end of the game, and I, like, reached over and yelled his name and handed him a shirt. He looked at me really puzzled . . ."

San Diego Union, Dec. 27, 1991: "I saw these girders . . ."

Ten:

Rockline, May 11, 1992: "It all just fell together. No one really compromised toward each other at all. It was kind of a phenomenon, in a way. We'd all played music for at least six, seven, eight years and been in different bands, and we were feeling something that we'd never really felt before, with the honesty and the way it was all coming out."

All That's Sacred podcast / TheSkyIScrape. com, July 7, 2010: "As fast as we were working on those first songs, new songs were cropping up . . ."

Rockline, May 11, 1992: "The one night Jeff stayed back with me, we made a bunch of noise and got into this ambient groove. That song is actually titled 'Master/Slave.' That's a good thing to go to sleep with. After you've listened to the record, it kind of lulls you . . ."

Rockline, May 11, 1992: "I think about why people need those other things in their lives to keep them happy or keep them going . . ."

All That's Sacred podcast / TheSkyIScrape. com, July 7, 2010: "They had to edit the middle because I was speeding up at the end. It was just a nightmare . . ."

All That's Sacred podcast / TheSkyIScrape. com, July 7, 2010: "We'd captured that song at that moment, and it was really good . . ."

1992:

East Coast Rocker, Aug. 26, 1992: "A lot of young people expressed thanks that I made a statement . . ."

Hit Parader, November 1992: "We're not concerned with how many people buy our albums—but we are concerned with how closely people listen to our music . . ."

KLOL-FM / Houston, Texas, radio interview, Dec. 17, 1991: "It means you kill yourself, and you make a big old sacrifice and try to get your revenge, and all you're gonna end up with is a paragraph in a newspaper . . ."

Melody Maker, May 21, 1994: "There was a lot of stuff that got said, but none of it really matters. There was a person we both knew, who told me that Kurt asked about me a lot . . ."

1993:

Guitar Player, January 1994: "Just being able to see Neil Young with Booker T. & the MG's every night from the front of the stage was amazing . . ."

Rockline, Oct. 18, 1993: "Our mind is on music, which is probably a really good thing for everybody. We'd love to do things on MTV and just have it kind of be a different form of public access . . ."

1995:

Guitar World, April 1995: "We did all the Mad Season music in about seven days. It took Layne just a few more days to finish his vocals, which was intense, since we only rehearsed twice and did four shows . . ."

Guitar World, April 1998: "We haven't lost anything, because we've learned from the experience . . ."

Mirror Ball:

USA Today, June 26, 1995: "In some ways, Pearl Jam seems older than I am . . ."

1996:

Spin, February 1997: "Singing with Nusrat was pretty heavy. There was definitely a spiritual element . . ."

Addicted To Noise, February 1998: "When it got to be a double-digit platinum-selling record, there's serious guilt involved there.."

No Code:

Musician, May 1995: "You'll still hear more of Eddie's songwriting, but there will also be elements that'll enable everybody's personality to shine through . . ."

1998:

New York Times, Feb. 8, 1998: "I think we've made a point, and our point is that we're running the business side of what we do the way we think it should be done . . ."

Toronto Sun, Aug. 16, 1998: "We thought it might be interesting, and that people that like the band might be into seeing how we work together. We rehearse and hear some songs from the new record and try to let it hang out a little bit and be ourselves. I think we accomplished that, and I don't think it's too embarrassing . . ."

1999:

USA Today, Dec. 5, 2002: "I was on an island in Hawaii away from everything when Kelly Curtis called and asked if I'd heard what was happening with 'Last Kiss' . . ."

2000:

Associated Press, Sept. 25, 2000: "Basically, I told them the next day . . ."

Pre-show press conference at Madison Square Garden, New York: "I think the youth that aren't voting [are] just having a hard time getting excited about anything . . ."

Spin, August 2001: "All of a sudden, playing "Crown of Thorns," it was the first time I properly reflected on what we'd gone through and what a journey it's been . . ."

Binaural:

MTV, April 19, 2000, ". . . what makes people kind of snap and how people are unpredictable. I tried to think about what those guys may have been thinking the night before . . ."

2002:

Pulse, December 2002: "I wasn't in support of bombing . . ."

2003:

Rolling Stone, May 29, 2003: "It was our first show since the war started. I come out with the mask on and do a dance, a little moonwalk, to let people see George Bush with rhythm, being free . . ."

Boston Globe, June 27, 2003: "We still pull the song out at some of our shows. We don't like to restrict ourselves about what we can and cannot play . . ."

Guardian, (Monroe, Mich.), Sept. 4, 2003: "I never would have thought we'd be on our fourth record . . ."

Lost Dogs:

Uncut, September 2009: "The lyrics to 'Yellow Ledbetter' do constantly evolve. I admit that, at times, I have sung total nonsense . . ."

2006:

Seattle Post-Intelligencer, May 5, 2006: "I think it's one of my top three favorite places to play in the world . . ."

Rolling Stone, April 20, 2006: "A lot of people have come up to us and said, 'I didn't even know you guys put any records out in the last five or six years . . .'"

Honolulu Advertiser, Dec. 1, 2006: "My father built a shack for us when we were kids to play music and to have a place to hang that wasn't in the streets . . ."

2010:

Billboard, Aug. 23, 2010: "A big part of it was thinking about Andy Wood and that how much his history has sort of touched on all of us . . ."

Billboard, Aug. 23, 2010, "For whatever reason, it just fell by the wayside after we recorded it . . ."

PHOTOGRAPHY CREDITS

Additional material by Barack Obama Campaign Fundraiser: 11 bottom right

Additional material by C/Z Records/*Deep Six* 1986: 27 top right

Additional material by C/Z Records/*Another Pyrrhic Victory* 1989: 27 top middle left

Additional material by Deranged Diction: 27 top middle

Additional material by Eddie Vedder (PHOTOS): 8 top right, 9 top left, 14 right, 19 full photo, 23 top right, middle left, bottom right, 29 all bottom Polaroids, 67 top right, 83 top left and bottom right, 87 all photos, 102 top right, 141, 145, 162–163, 171 bottom middle, 199 bottom left, 204 bottom right, 210–211, 215, 220 top left and bottom two Polaroids, 221 bottom right, 246, 278, 287 top left, 308 Polaroid

Additional material by Eddie Vedder (IMAGES): 27 bottom right, bottom middle, bottom left posters and middle, 28 bottom right, 29 bottom pay stubs, 54, 59, 79, 85 top, 95 bottom right, 100, 194 lyrics bottom, 212–213 lyrics, 229 set lists, 234 set list, 235 note, 243 bottom middle, 274–275, 303 middle, 327, 331 top

Additional material by Eddie Vedder/Epic Records/Sony Music/*Lost Dogs* 2003: 283 Polaroids

Additional material by Eddie Vedder/Epic Records/Sony Music/*No Code* 1996: 188–189 Polaroids

Additional material by Eduardo Apodaca: 312 lattice in sidebar

Additional material by Eric Johnson (PHOTOS): 240 middle right, 243 top right

Additional material by Eric Johnson (IMAGES): 47, 62 top and middle, 76, 77 bottom images, 78 middle images, 79 all images except note, 82 top right, 83 top letters, 85 bottom right, 112–113 background, 142, 149 all except news clipping, 166–167 all images, 176 top middle and top right, 177 top right and bottom left, 183 ticket, 189 ticket, 194 top right, 199 bottom right, 241 plane ticket, 242 middle right, 243 bottom left and bottom right images

Additional material by Eric Johnson from *Rolling Stone* magazine: 195 top

Additional material by Eric Johnson/photo Mark Seliger: 78–79 all access passes

Additional material by Fernando Apodaca/ Ananda Moorman/*Pearl Jam*/J Records/2006: 315 top left and top right

Additional material by Fernando Apodaca/ Eduardo Apodaca/*Pearl Jam*/J Records/2006: 315 top right CD art

Additional material by Fernando Apodaca/ Jason Mueller/*Pearl Jam*/J Records/2006: 312 top right

Additional material by Fernando Apodaca/ Margaret Lindsley/*Pearl Jam*/J Records/2006: 314–315 middle, 312 top right middle

Additional material by Fernando Apodaca/ Jesse MacDonald/*Pearl Jam*/J Records/2006: 314 top right, 315 right

Additional material by Green River: 27 bottom left

Additional material by Green River/Homestead Records/*Come on Down* 1985: 27 top right

Additional material by Green River/Sub Pop/ *Rehab Doll* 1988: 27 bottom middle

Additional material by Green River/Sub Pop/ *Dry As a Bone* 1987: 27 left middle

Additional material by Harrybu McCage/ Monkeywrench, Inc. 2008: 336 middle left

Additional material by Jeff Ament (PHOTOS): 11 top and middle, 23 bottom left, 83 middle, 253 filmstrip

Additional material by Jeff Ament (IMAGES): 27 middle, 76 middle left, 83 top middle image, 95 bottom left, 298 middle left

Additional material by Jeff Ament/Epic Records/ Sony Music/*Binaural* 2000: 234 bottom left

Additional material by Jeff Ament/Epic Records/*Riot Act* 2002: 264–256 all images except top right

Additional material by Jeff Ament/Epic Records/Sony Music/*Lost Dogs* 2003: 282 background

Additional material by Jeff Ament/ Monkeywrench/*Tone* 2008: 336 top left

Additional material by Ananda Moorman/Jesse MacDonald: 233, 322 all photos, 323 bottom and top right and middle

Additional material by Kevin Shuss (PHOTOS): 130 top right

Additional material by Kevin Shuss (IMAGES): 205 top, 243 bottom right, 288 left

Additional material by Malfunkshun/ Loosegroove Records/*Return to Olympus* 1995: 27 bottom right

Additional material by Matt Cameron (PHOTOS): 12 all photos, 247 top

Additional material by Matt Cameron (IMAGES): 247 bottom right

Additional material by Mike McCready: 17 bottom middle

Simon & Schuster
1230 Avenue of the Americas
New York, NY 10020

First Simon & Schuster hardcover edition September 2011

SIMON & SCHUSTER and colophon are registered
trademarks of Simon & Schuster, Inc.

For information about special discounts for bulk purchases,
please contact Simon & Schuster Special Sales at
1-866-506-1949 or business@simonandschuster.com.

The Simon & Schuster Speakers Bureau can bring authors to
your live event. For more information or to book an event,
contact the Simon & Schuster Speakers Bureau at
1-866-248-3049 or visit our website at www.simonspeakers.com.

Designed by Regan Hagar

Manufactured in the United States of America

10 9 8 7 6 5 4 3 2 1

Library of Congress Cataloging-in-Publication Data
Pearl Jam (Musical group)
    Pearl Jam twenty.
        p. cm.
    1. Pearl Jam (Musical group) 2. Rock musicians—United States—
Biography. 3. Pearl Jam (Musical group)—Pictorial works. I. Title.
II. Title: Pearl Jam 20.
ML421.P43P43 2011
782.42166092—dc22
[B]
                        2011010783

ISBN 978-1-4391-6921-6
ISBN 978-1-4391-6940-7 (ebook)